Lecture Notes in Computer Science　　10382

Commenced Publication in 1973
Founding and Former Series Editors:
Gerhard Goos, Juris Hartmanis, and Jan van Leeuwen

More information about this series at http://www.springer.com/series/7411

José Ángel Bañares · Konstantinos Tserpes
Jörn Altmann (Eds.)

Economics of Grids, Clouds, Systems, and Services

13th International Conference, GECON 2016
Athens, Greece, September 20–22, 2016
Revised Selected Papers

 Springer

Editors
José Ángel Bañares
Department of Computer Science
University of Zaragoza
Zaragoza
Spain

Jörn Altmann
Seoul National University
Seoul
Korea (Republic of)

Konstantinos Tserpes
Harokopio University of Athens
Tavros
Greece

ISSN 0302-9743   ISSN 1611-3349   (electronic)
Lecture Notes in Computer Science
ISBN 978-3-319-61919-4   ISBN 978-3-319-61920-0   (eBook)
DOI 10.1007/978-3-319-61920-0

Library of Congress Control Number: 2017945281

LNCS Sublibrary: SL5 – Computer Communication Networks and Telecommunications

Printed on acid-free paper

This Springer imprint is published by Springer Nature
The registered company is Springer International Publishing AG
The registered company address is: Gewerbestrasse 11, 6330 Cham, Switzerland

Preface

The 13th edition of GECON, the International Conference on the Economics of Grids, Clouds, Systems, and Services, took place in Athens, Greece, the cradle of Western civilization and the birthplace of democracy. The term economics comes from the Ancient Greek words *oikos* (house) and *nomos* (custom, law). Several ancient Greek thinkers made various economic observations, especially Aristotle, Xenophon, and Plato. We emulated ancient Greek thinkers on the main campus of Harokopio University of Athens, which is located close to many important cultural sites of interest such as the Acropolis Museum, Thissio, Panathenaic Stadium (Kallimarmaron), Keramikos, and the Benaki Museum.

The aim of the GECON conference is to bring together distributed systems expertise (e.g., in resource allocation, quality of service management and energy consumption) with economics expertise (focusing on both micro- and macro-economic modelling and analysis), in order to create effective solutions in this space. Thirteen years later, GECON continues to focus on the marriage of these two types of expertise, reinforced by the increasing intertwinement of economy and technology. The world of production is becoming more and more networked, until everything is interlinked with everything else with unexpected consequences. Today distributed systems include a network of physical devices, vehicles, buildings, wearables, and cyber-physical systems with capacity to act on the environment. In the connected world, we cannot separate the physical world from business processes. Economy and IT technologies cannot be considered as separate disciplines. In this context, we return to the ancient point of view of Greek thinkers and consider economics and IT technologies as a factor of ethics, politics, and laws.

For this year's edition, we received 38 submissions. Each submission was assessed by three to five reviewers of the international Program Committee. Of these 38 submissions, 11 were selected as full papers with an acceptance rate of 29%. Additionally, shorter work-in-progress papers were integrated in the volume. This combination of full and work-in-progress papers fulfills the twofold aim of gathering original work to build a strong multidisciplinary community in this increasingly important area of a future information and knowledge economy, and enabling a more open and informed dialogue between the presenters and the audience. Our intention in increasing the number of accepted work-in-progress papers is underpinned by the conviction that the GECON conference is the best framework for the presenters to better position their work for future events and to get an improved understanding of the impact their work is likely to have on the research community. The schedule for the conference this year was structure to encourage discussions and debates, with enough discussion time included in each paper presentation session, led by the session chair.

This volume is structured following the seven sessions that comprised the conference program (three of which are work-in-progress sessions):

Session 1: Business Models
Session 2: Work in Progress on Quality of Services and Service Level Agreements
Session 3: Work in Progress on Cloud Economics
Session 4: Energy Consumption
Session 5: Resource Allocation
Session 6: Work in Progress on Resource Allocation
Session 7: Cloud Applications

Session 1 started with two papers about brokers and application composers. The first paper by Zherui Yang, Slinger Jansen, Xuesong Gao, and Dong Zhang is a vision paper entitled "On the Future of Solution Composition in Software Ecosystems" that introduces the need for solution composers as an evolution or replacement of application stores. The authors sketch a solution composer framework, which illustrates how they believe software in the future will be shaped by end-users, consultants, and developers. The vision is evaluated through expert reviews at several leading platform providers. The next paper, "The Rise of Cloud Brokerage: Business Model, Profit Making and Cost Savings" by Evangelia Filiopoulou, Persefoni Mitropoulou, Christos Michalakelis and Mara Nikolaidou, focuses on the search for the best provider or the best bundle through a broker. The paper highlights the pros that arise from the use of the broker's services and the cons from the intermediation. The authors also review the contemporary literature on the pricing methods that can be adopted by a cloud broker in order to achieve cost savings; they also describe different pricing models for cloud brokers by summarizing the main characteristic and evaluation results.

Session 2 was a work-in-progress session on quality of service (QoS) and service-level agreement (SLA) management. The first contribution is the paper by Nikoletta Mavrogeorgi, Athanasios Voulodimos, Vassilios Alexandrou, Spyridon Gogouvitis, and Theodora Varvarigou entitled "Robust Content-Centric SLA Enforcement in Federated Cloud Environments." This paper presents an SLA management framework for declaring, enforcing, and negotiating SLAs in cloud environments, where commitments for using cloud services are defined. In this framework developed within the EU project VISION cloud, the SLA schema is enriched with content terms, and sections for storlets and federation. Dynamic SLAs are supported, since the SLA templates are generated according to the current supplies, and a renegotiation possibility is offered. Finally, dynamic rules are created and updated, in order to detect and handle proactively SLA violations. Along the same lines, the second contribution by Waheed Aslam Ghumman and Alexander Schill entitled "Structural Specification for the SLAs in Cloud Computing (S3LACC)" proposes a structural specification for the SLAs in cloud computing for the automation of a complete SLA life cycle, i.e., negotiation, monitoring, management, and recycling. The specification targets complex dependencies among different metrics and the composition of different metrics in one service-level objective. The proposed SLA structure can be used to implement almost all types of negotiation strategies and monitoring policies for an automated SLA life cycle. The third paper by Antonios Makris, Konstantinos Tserpes, and Dimosthenis Anagnostopoulos – "Load Balancing in In-Memory Key-Value

Stores for Response Time Minimization" – investigates key/data distribution within in-memory key-value stores and how this affects query response time. The paper focuses on an evaluation of the core factors influencing the performance of Redis. Experimental results show that key distribution and key length are contributing factors to the load balancing problem and impact the cluster's response times. Finally, in "Fault-Tree-Based Service Availability Models in Cloud Environments: A Failure Trace Archive Approach," Alexandru Butoi and Gheorghe Cosmin Silaghi present a probabilistic model for evaluating the service reliability in cloud systems. The authors provide a method for extracting failure events and then show how to use replication or migration to provide service reliability.

Session 3, which comprised work-in-progress papers on cloud economics related to security, recommender systems, and market models, started with the contribution of Mathias Slawik, Begüm Ilke Zilci, Axel Küpper, Yuri Demchenko, Fatih Turkmen, Christophe Blanchet, and Jean-Franois Gibrat, entitled "An Economical Security Architecture for Multi-Cloud Application Deployments in Federated Environments." The authors propose an architecture for security in federated environments, which fulfills the requirements of various stakeholders. They provide a design rationale, evaluate the resulting architecture, and offer readily instantiable components in their public code repository. The second contribution in this session is "Efficient Context Management and Personalized User Recommendations in a Smart Social TV Environment" by Fotis Aisopos, Angelos Valsamis, Alexandros Psychas, Andreas Menychtas, and Theodora Varvarigou. It focuses on smart TV recommendations. The authors present a new efficient context management approach, to provide personalized multi-level recommendations via a hybrid method combining graph analysis and collaborative filtering. The last paper in this session, entitled "When Culture Trumps Economic Laws: Persistent Segmentation of the Mobile Instant Messaging Market" by Maria C. Borges, Max-R. Ulbricht, and Frank Pallas, discusses the general characteristics of the mobile instant messaging market from a competition point of view. It highlights the fact that no single player has achieved domination of the global market, in contrast to what has happened in digital social networks. The authors point out that the distinct communication style of different cultures is one of the reasons the market has not tipped yet.

Session 4 consisted of four papers on energy consumption and cost in cloud systems, which is a consolidated research area within cloud computing and present in the last GECON conferences. The paper by Karim Djemame, Richard Kavanagh, Django Armstrong, Francesc Lordan, Jorge Ejarque, Mario Macias, Raül Sirvent, Jordi Guitart, and Rosa M. Badia entitled "Energy Efficiency Support Through Intra-Layer Cloud Stack Adaptation" focuses on the embedding of energy efficiency support in each of the typical cloud abstraction layers: SaaS, PaaS, and IaaS. The authors describe a properly conceived system architecture using an intra-layer self-adaptation methodology tailored for SaaS, PaaS, and IaaS to achieve an intra-layer support to energy efficiency. The second paper by Alexandros Kostopoulos, Eleni Agiatzidou, and Antonis Dimakis entitled "Energy-Aware Pricing Within Cloud Environments" presents pricing schemes used by a set of current infrastructure and platform-as-a-service (IaaS/PaaS) providers and then proposes a set of four different pricing schemes that take into account the energy consumption of virtual machines in an IaaS environment. In "Energy Prediction for Cloud Workload Patterns," Ibrahim Alzamil and Karim Djemame propose the necessity of having proactive and reactive management tools with energy-awareness at a virtual machine (VM) level in order to enhance decision-making. In this paper, the authors introduce an energy-aware profiling model that enables the attribution of a physical machine's energy consumption to homogeneous and heterogeneous VMs based on their utilization and size. The fourth contribution by Muhammad Zakarya and Lee Gillam entitled "An Energy-Aware Cost-Recovery Approach for Virtual Machine Migration" investigates how migration decisions can be made such that the energy costs involved with the migration are recovered.

Session 5 focused on resource allocation, one of the classic research areas in cloud computing and in previous GECON conferences. The contribution of Patrick Poullie and Burkhard Stiller entitled "The Design and Evaluation of a Heaviness Metric for Cloud Fairness and Correct Virtual Machine Configurations" presents a runtime prioritization mechanism for a fair assignment of resources to virtual machines according to their respective utility function and greediness. The paper "A History-Based Model for Provisioning EC2 Spot Instances with Cost Constraints" by Javier Fabra, Sergio Hernádez, Pedro Álvarez, Joaquín Ezpeleta, Álvaro Recuenco, and Ana Martínez presents and evaluates a framework for the analysis of the EC2 spot instances as a cheap public infrastructure. It uses the price history of such resources to generate a provisioning plan by means of a simulation algorithm considering cost constraints. The authors achieved savings of up to 88% using their framework to generate a provisioning plan for the deployment of a specific instance in regions of the EC2 cloud with different price variations observed.

Session 6 consisted of four work-in-progress papers focusing on resource allocation problems. Azamat Uzbekov and Jörn Altmann in their paper entitled "Enabling Business-Preference-Based Scheduling of Cloud Computing Resources" explicitly try to link economic and technical issues by presenting an architecture that connects the technical layer of resource allocation with the business strategy layer of a cloud service provider. The contribution of Benedikt Pittl, Werner Mach, and Erich Schikuta entitled "Bazaar-Score: A Key Figure Measuring Market Efficiency in IaaS-Markets" presents a novel genetic algorithm-based multi-round negotiation strategy between providers and consumers of services enabling the creation of approximately Pareto-optimal offers. The authors define the Bazaar Score, a key figure based on economic utility theory enabling the comparison of different resource allocations. The third paper in this session "Understanding Resource Selection Requirements for Computationally Intensive Tasks on Heterogeneous Computing Infrastructure" by Jeremy Cohen, Thierry Rayna, and John Darlington presents a decision support system to identify the most suitable computing platform and configuration for a computational task based on a user's financial and temporal constraints. The system builds on approaches presented in the extant economics literature, to help identify a user's risk aversion and the opportunity cost of different platform choices. The last paper in this session, entitled "Towards Usage-Based Dynamic Overbooking in IaaS Clouds" by Athanasios Tsitsipas, Christopher B. Hauser, Jörg Domaschka, and Stefan Wesner, looks into the issue of overbooking physical machines in a cloud data center. The authors investigate preconditions that have to be enabled in a data center to support dynamic overbooking, and they describe a prototype implementation with OpenStack.

The final session consisted of three papers on the economic implications of three different cloud applications. The session began with the paper by Hyeong-Il Kim, Hyeong-Jin Kim, and Jae-Woo Chang entitled "A Privacy Preserving Top-k Query Processing Algorithm in Cloud Computing." The paper deals with privacy concerns and databases that need to be encrypted before being outsourced to the cloud. The authors focus on preserving the privacy of a user query and propose a query-processing algorithm that guarantees the confidentiality of data and hides data access patterns. The second paper by Salman Taherizadeh, Ian Taylor, Andrew Jones, Zhiming Zhao, and Vlado Stankovski entitled "A Network Edge Monitoring Approach for Real-Time Data Streaming Applications" deals with the problem of enforcing service quality in streaming systems that must consider real-time variations in the network quality. The authors show how edge services for time-critical applications could be used to automatically optimize the process of allocating and choosing the best infrastructure, and they investigate network-level metrics that are particularly important for the development and adaptation of time-critical applications. The final paper in this session by Victor Medel, Unai Arronategui, José Ángel Bañares, and José Manuel Colom entitled "Distributed Simulation of Complex and Scalable Systems: From Models to the Cloud" deals with the problem of translating a simulation to the cloud, providing users with appropriate tools to hide the modeler low-level details of this migration process considering cost and performance requirements. The authors give a central focus to Petri net models, describing the behavior of the system including timing and cost information. They propose a way to automatically translate high-level specifications to an executable model suited to be partitioned on the cloud.

Finally, we would like to wholeheartedly thank the reviewers and Program Committee members for completing their reviews on time, and giving insightful and valuable feedback to the authors. Furthermore, we would like to thank Alfred Hofmann of Springer for his support in publishing the proceedings of GECON 2016. The collaboration with Alfred Hofmann and his team has been, as in the past, efficient and effective.

September 2016

José Ángel Bañares
Konstantinos Tserpes
Jörn Altmann

Organization

GECON2016 was organized by the Department of Informatics and Telematics of the Harokopio University of Athens (http://www.dit.hua.gr).

Executive Committee

Chairs

Konstantinos Tserpes	Harokopio University of Athens, Greece
Dimosthenis Anagnostopoulos	Harokopio University of Athens, Greece
Jörn Altmann	Seoul National University, South Korea
José Ángel Bañares	University of Zaragoza, Spain
Maria Nikolaidou	Harokopio University of Athens, Greece

Program Committee

Rainer Alt	University of Leipzig, Germany
Alvaro Arenas	IE University, Spain
Marcos Assuncao	Inria, LIP, ENS Lyon, France
Ashraf Bany Mohammed	The University of Jordan, Jordan
Jeremy Cohen	Imperial College London, UK
Costas Courcoubetis	SUTD, Singapore
Tom Crick	Cardiff Metropolitan University, UK
Patrizio Dazzi	ISTI-CNR, Italy
Alex Delis	National and Kapodistrian University of Athens, Greece
Javier Diaz-Montes	Rutgers University, USA
Patricio Domingues	Polytechnic Institute of Leiria, Portugal
Bogdan Franczyk	University of Leipzig, Germany
Felix Freitag	Universitat Politècnica de Catalunya, Spain
Marc Frincu	University of Southern California, USA
Wolfgang Gentzsch	The UberCloud, USA
Netsanet Haile	Seoul National University, South Korea
Chun-Hsi Huang	University of Connecticut, USA
Bahman Javadi	Western Sydney University, Australia
Odej Kao	Technische Universität Berlin, Germany
Daniel Katz	University of Chicago and Argonne National Laboratory, USA
Stefan Kirn	University of Hohenheim, Germany
Tobias Aurelius Knoch	Erasmus University Rotterdam, The Netherlands
Bastian Koller	HLRS, University of Stuttgart, Germany

Somayeh Koohborfardhaghighi	Dongguk University, South Korea
George Kousiouris	National Technical University of Athens, Greece
Dieter Kranzlmüller	Ludwig-Maximilians-Universität München, Germany
Dimosthenis Kyriazis	National Technical University of Athens, Greece
Hing Yan Lee	IDA, Singapore
Jysoo Lee	KISTI, South Korea
Dan Ma	Singapore Management University, Singapore
Richard Ma	National University of Singapore, Singapore
Roc Meseguer	Universitat Politècnica de Catalunya, Spain
Christos Michalakelis	Harokopio University of Athens, Greece
Mircea Moca	Babes-Bolyai University of Cluj-Napoca, Romania
Maurizio Naldi	Università di Roma Tor Vergata, Italy
Leandro Navarro	Universitat Politècnica de Catalunya, Spain
Marco Netto	IBM Research, Brazil
Frank Pallas	Technische Universität Berlin, Germany
George Pallis	University of Cyprus, Cyprus
Rubem Pereira	Liverpool John Moores University, UK
Dana Petcu	West University of Timisoara, Romania
Radu Prodan	University of Innsbruck, Austria
Peter Reichl	Telecommunications Research Center Vienna, Austria
Lutz Schubert	OMI, University of Ulm, Germany
Gheorghe Cosmin Silaghi	Babes-Bolyai University, Romania
Mathias Slawik	Technische Universität Berlin, Germany
Burkhard Stiller	University of Zurich, Switzerland
Stefan Tai	Technische Universität Berlin, Germany
Rafael Tolosana-Calasanz	University of Zaragoza, Spain
Johan Tordsson	Umeå University, Sweden
Dimitrios Tsoumakos	Ionian University, Greece
Bruno Tuffin	Inria Rennes Bretagne Atlantique, France
Iraklis Varlamis	Harokopio University of Athens, Greece
Dora Varvarigou	National Technical University of Athens, Greece
Luís Veiga	Universidade de Lisboa / INESC-ID Lisboa, Portugal
Claudiu Vinte	Bucharest University of Economic Studies, Romania
Stefan Wesner	University of Ulm, Germany
Phillip Wieder	Dortmund University of Technology, Germany
Ramin Yahyapour	GWDG, University of Göttingen, Germany
Ruediger Zarnekow	Technische Universität Berlin, Germany
Dimitrios Zissis	University of the Aegean, Greece

Steering Committee

Jörn Altmann	Seoul National University, South Korea
José Ángel Bañares	University of Zaragoza, Spain
Steven Miller	Singapore Management University, Singapore
Omer F. Rana	Cardiff University, UK

Gheorghe Cosmin Silaghi   Babes-Bolyai University, Romania
Kurt Vanmechelen   University of Antwerp, Belgium

Sponsoring Institutions and Companies

Seoul National University, Seoul, South Korea
University of Zaragoza, Spain
Harokopio University of Athens, Greece
Springer LNCS, Heidelberg, Germany
Future Generation Computer Systems Journal
Electronic Markets Journal

Contents

Cloud Applications

Business Models

On the Future of Solution Composition in Software Ecosystems

Zherui Yang[1]([✉]), Slinger Jansen[1]([✉]), Xuesong Gao[2], and Dong Zhang[2]

[1] Utrecht University, Utrecht, The Netherlands
y.z_ryan@hotmail.com, slinger.Jansen@uu.nl
[2] Huawei Technologies Co., Ltd., Beijing, China
{james.gaoxuesong,zhang.dong}@huawei.com

Abstract. The trend of application stores is currently at a peak. However, the lack of dynamic composition for complex solutions is the largest downside of the app store model, since solutions are increasingly created as compositions of multiple solutions, APIs, and applications. Therefore, in this vision paper, a superior model, *solution composers*, is proposed to the app store model. A conceptual framework is established to illustrate the inner workings of solution composers in software ecosystems. In order to outline that solution composers are significant for the future of software development, several industry cases are presented and compared to support this concept, further indicating that a standard for solution composition should be considered. In addition, the vision is evaluated through expert reviews at several leading platform providers and challenges for practice and implementation are identified.

Keywords: Software ecosystems · AppStores · Solution composers

1 Introduction

Software ecosystems are complex networks of organizations, that collaboratively serve a market [12]. Long value chains are formed in these ecosystems. The actors in these networks are Software Producing Organizations (SPOs), such as open source consortia and Independent Software Vendors (ISVs), and end-users, such as software consumers of mobile apps, or employees at large companies that require advanced business applications.

Whereas in the past end-users would accept pre-configured monolithic solution bundles in the form of, for example, large Enterprise Resource Planning applications or complicated mobile apps, increasingly there is a demand for flexible compositions of solutions from end-users that can be changed rapidly and dynamically. In many cases, even non-technical end-users want to compose such solutions. Therefore, in order to meet this demand, in this paper, the concept of a *solution composer* is proposed and a conceptual framework is presented.

Research and studies from previous period have gained promising and valuable results, but have mostly focused on specific aspects of solution composition

© Springer International Publishing AG 2017
J.Á. Bañares et al. (Eds.): GECON 2016, LNCS 10382, pp. 3–18, 2017.
DOI: 10.1007/978-3-319-61920-0_1

or service integration [8,17], which are fragmented and lack of a holistic view of the concept or the problem [4,6,14]. Therefore, a more holistic and consolidated framework is needed that attributes to the fundamental understanding of solution composers in terms of concepts, industry practices, innovation and development direction. This framework is useful and necessary to enhance the efficiency and effectiveness of solution composer establishment.

There is an emerging need for customization and composition of solutions. Firstly, there is an increase in interfaces and devices that provide access to valuable features. Secondly, platforms are increasingly the gateway to large collections of these features, such as Internet of Things (IoTs) platforms [2]. Pre-composed and configured feature bundles, such as apps in the current AppSotres, are rapidly losing their value, as these monoliths cannot easily be adapted to create new solution compositions. One illustration of this development is the Android Instant Apps platform [19], where apps can be downloaded and activated based on a set of predefined events, without having to use the Play Store. This paper focuses on the following research questions:

1. *Is there a need for solution composers?*
2. *Is the proposed solution composer framework valid?*
3. *What will the industry implications be of the introduction of solution composers?*

This paper continues with the research method, i.e., a number of industry case studies and evaluation interviews. In Sect. 3, a critical discussion is given on the current software industry. In Sect. 4, the solution composer concept is introduced and the proposed framework is described in detail. Moreover, the implementations of the framework in industry are discussed. Experts were invited to evaluate the framework in forms of interviews in Sect. 5. Final discussion is in Sect. 6 and we provided conclusions and an outlook in Sect. 7.

2   Research Method

This research can be seen as a light mixed study based on case study and interviews, using design science [24]. First, several industry cases were studied and compared to establish a conceptual framework for solution composer. Second, expert interviews were conducted to evaluate both the theoretical and practical aspects of solution composers.

The design research paradigm focuses on creating and evaluating innovative IT artifacts that enable organizations to address important information-related tasks [24]. This paper aims to determine the nature of solution composers. The research method is deemed appropriate when there is little evidence about a phenomenon and the researcher seeks answers to research questions [20]. The authors looked for experts who have a great deal to share about service composition and software ecosystems.

The cases were selected as representative service composition tools from the industry. And the interviews were conducted in a semi-structured way.

This method has been used to explore the framework, allowing new ideas to be brought up during the interview as a result of interviewees' answers [26]. All the authors contributed to the interview questions and the interviews were conducted by one of the authors. All the evidence including audio tape, transcripts and notes from the interview have been kept and these information was used to compose this report [26].

3   The Limits of AppStores

Jansen and Bloemendal [11] define an AppStore as an online curated marketplace that allows developers to sell and distribute their products to actors within one or more multi-sided software platform ecosystems. AppStores have striking advantages for the software business. They have changed the application industry significantly [11], introducing new business and deployment models to partners, and offering end-users the maximum freedom of choosing applications. Also they provide app developers with a wealth of opportunities to approach new niche markets with domain specific applications [10].

Despite the advantages AppStores have, the AppStore model is increasingly inflexible. Software applications in AppStores are monolithic collections of features that aim to solve problems for end users, whether it is to book a train ticket or to provide fun through a game. The downside of functionally composing such features into a collection is that end-users do not have the flexibility to break down those features and compose them into novel solutions. End-users are burdened with the job of carrying over content from one application to the next manually and are tired of the lack of dynamic composition for complex solutions. It appears AppStores have reached their peak. It is time for the "mini-monoliths" in the AppStore to be decomposed and offered as separate features to solution composers.

4   Solution Composers

The state of the practice introduces four types of software composition framework: developer platforms, API composers, SOA composers and orchestrators, and end-user service composers. After learning from and comparing with these frameworks, a conceptual framework of solution composers is proposed, highlighting necessary elements in any successful solution composer. Subsequently, several cases are presented and analyzed as the implementations of the proposed framework in industry.

4.1   State of the Practice

The following four types of software composition frameworks are identified that contain elements of solution composers.

Developer Platforms. Developer platforms [23] are platforms that enable developers to create complex solutions on top of existing platforms, typically with a rich set of developer tools to enable quick adoption of the platform. In the context of solution composers, they enable developers to integrate services from the ecosystem into their solutions, however, the facilitation of such composition is typically through regular programming.

Example: Force.com is Salesforce's developer platform, that enables developers to create domain specific solutions on top of Salesforce.com. In Force.com we find that developers integrate services from the platform and other APIs manually. It has an AppStore for end customers, but this does not enable automatic or supported composition of services and developers simply address the APIs of the apps.

API Composers. API composers help to manage APIs to fast, affordably and scalably communicate between all the values that have already been built down and the new projects that are building for today, analyzing API data and handle the IoT. In the context of solution composer, they allow separate functions to communicate with each other but they do not provide internal or external services for solutions composition.

Example: Apigee is an API composer, which allows end-users to secure, manage, analyze and connect all APIs. Although it enables end-users to manipulate APIs and provides API management to store all compositions, there is no service index in Apigee for end-users to choose available services from.

SOA Composers and Orchestrators. At a very high level, a crucial aspect of Service Oriented Architecture (SOA) is service orchestration. Enterprise systems and integration projects designed according to SOA principles depend on successful service orchestration. In the context of solution composer, SOA composer is a web-based application that helps to build new applications with granular and reusable software components, but it lacks the flexibility and agility to dynamically compose and integrate smaller units of services.

Example: Oracle SOA Composer allows users to work with Oracle Business Rules dictionaries and tasks for deployed applications. Moreover, Oracle SOA Composer provides a platform with enhanced service orchestration capabilities to ease the integration challenges, but still not flexible enough for dynamic complex solution composition.

End-User Service Composers. End-user service composers are platforms or web services that aggregates many other web services or applications into one place and can then perform actions given a certain set of criteria. End-users may therefore create customized criteria and perform the action as desired. Because of the customization character, end-user service composers might be the most similar one to solution composers, nevertheless, they are too user-friendly for developers to integrate and compose more complex solutions.

Example: IFTTT.com is a free web-based service that allows users to create chains of simple conditional statements, called "recipes", which are triggered based on changes to other web services such as Gmail, Facebook and Instagram. It has the necessary elements for solution composer, but it is way too immature for higher level of solution composition to be performed on.

4.2 The Solution Composer Framework

By learning from and combining with the software composition frameworks, a conceptual framework of a solution composer platform is proposed in Fig. 1, in order to create a better understanding of how solution composer performs.

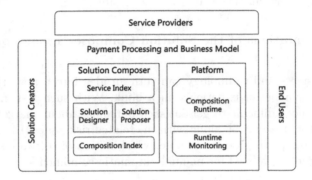

Fig. 1. The solution composer framework.

From the top, left and right sides of the figure, the different actors within the framework are modeled, respectively the service providers, the solution creators that might be end-users or consultants in the companies, and the end-users.

The communication between actors and the core of solution composer in Fig. 1 is payment processing and business model. When solution composer is carried into practice, the business model will therefore connect the theoretical framework to the industry.

In the center of this framework, solution composer represents how it works in detail with features as service index, solution designer, solution proposer and composition index. Service index stores all available services and presents to end-users in a certain form such as *Library* or *Service Catalog*. End-users can select a range of services or applications for the need of integrating and composing services according to their specific need. Solution designer is where end-users can get their selected services and applications designed in some pattern which is suitable for the final solution while Solution proposer is an entity providing solution propositions. The composition index is created to store compositions and benchmarks of solutions. The compositions are required to provide a list of solutions that have been created in the past and can now be reused. The solution benchmarks are especially useful for larger solution compositions where some knowledge is required about how the solution is going to perform in the future. In the field of Software Defined Networking, for instance, bringing together different parts of a solution is challenging, as little may be known about the performance of (a combination of) services. Having a set of benchmarks can remedy this situation to bring some predictability in the process of solution composition.

We separate solution composer and platform because solution composition is the phase where service composition is designed and proposed while composition run-time is the phase where the service composition is installed in the run-time environment and executed. When the service composition platform enables the selection process of individual services at deployment time, usually the composition from composition index can be re-configured. Moreover, the run-time monitoring will monitor and analyze how the service composition is executed and get as much performance evaluation as possible.

4.3   Implementations of the Solution Composer Framework in Industry

Nowadays, business and technology can turn an idea into a potential product, a new service or a better experience in a blink. With such fast growing, customers find it more difficult to get satisfied outcomes about market placement and development strategy [5], along with the related risk issues [13]. Also, as different SPOs attempt to produce complex combination of software systems and hardware [9], there is a need for manual-automatic-combined solution composition.

Different from applications from AppStores, where apps work as individually separate collections of features, the process of the solution composition and integration will require communications and interactions between features. Enterprise application integration has traditionally relied on software-based middleware, such as Service Oriented Architecture (SOA) middleware solutions [16]. Disadvantages of SOA middleware, such as the lack of standards, high cost and the inflexibility [3], make solution composers more appealing. Based on the ideals of middleware, solution composers provide an open, standards-based approach to integration. Unlike its predecessor, the Application Programming Interfaces (APIs) used in solution composers is not a piece of software. Instead, it is a fully functioning integration point. An API is much more flexible and agile than any existing set of routines, protocols, and tools for the purpose of connection [7].

As the possibilities to create service compositions become more complex, more technically oriented resources are required to create new solutions. Furthermore, as third parties will probably also provide basic APIs that are compatible with the platform, advanced mechanisms are required such as service indexes and semi-automatic service composition. Both of these lead to intricate value chains and software ecosystems with many participants in them.

For solution composers to present solutions to customers, four different ways are observed as manually through code (Manually), through a composition studio (Composition Studio), through a composition proposer (Composition Proposer), and hybrid (Hybrid) combinations of these three.

These four ways may be in different combinations to support end-users and composers optimally. In the first way, developers compose solutions with code, for instance by programming against APIs from third parties and combining them to create innovative solutions. In the second way, a complete composition studio is offered that enables developers, technical consultants, and even end-users to create new service configurations to create the best fitting solution. The third way does not actually lead to a configuration, but proposes a solution beforehand, which for instance enables benchmarking and comparison of different service configurations. The fourth way is a combination of the first two, where simple configurations can be created, but more advanced solutions still have to be coded traditionally.

In Table 1, several tools are introduced for comparative analysis. The tools evaluated were selected using a Google search for service composition tools. The tools needed to satisfy the following criteria: (1) Enable the composition of services to create a solution, (2) have a service index for the creation of solutions, (3) be exemplary in the industry, and (4) be commercially available. We grouped the API aggregation platforms, as there are many new entrants to the market.

Table 1. Implementations of the service providers, the Solution Composer, and End-users in Industry. ISV stands for Independent Software Vendor, IoT stands for Internet of Things.

Company	Party		
	Online service providers	Solution composers	End users
Android	API providers	APP and API provider	End users
APIGEE	API provider	Developers	Everyone
Azure	Cloud service provider	Cloud solution provider/developers	Companies
HP SDN	ISVs/HP open source	HP consultants	Companies
IFTTT.com	IoT/API providers	End-users	End-users
Pipemonk	ISVs	Developers/End-users	Companies
Salesforce.com	ISVs	Consultants	Companies
We-wired web	IoT/Web apps	End-users	End-users
X-formation connect	IoT/API providers	Developers	End-users
Zapier	IoT/API providers	End-users	End-users

In Table 2, cases are further compared based on the four different features in solution composers: service indexes, solution designers, solution proposers,

Table 2. Solution composer features observed in industry.

Case	Party			
	Service index	Solution designer	Solution proposer	Composition index
Mashup [15]	UDDI service catalog	Mashup environment	None	None
FEATUREHOUSE [1]	Tree index	None	None	None
Android	APP Store	None	None	None
APIGEE	None	Customer's own IDE	None	API management
Azure	Runbook gallery	Microsoft powershell	End-users/None	None
HP SDN	SDN APP Store	None	None	None
IFTTT.com	IFTTT.com channels	IFTTT interface	End-users/None	Recipes
Pipemonk	Shopify App-Store/Amazon sellers	Pipemonk interface	End-users/None	QuickBooks
Salesforce.com	AppExchange	App developer IDE	None	None
We-wired web	Service catalog	Visual wiring diagrams	End-users/None	None
X-formation connect	Application drop-list	Connect interface	End-users/None	None
Zapier	Library	Zapier interface	End-users/None	Zaps

and composition indexes. These four features define the character of a solution composer. Service and composition indexes indicate where users can find all services and composition available on the platform. The main features of solution composers are solution designer and proposer.

As for an example, IFTTT allows end-users to create, integrate and combine services into solutions and store these chains of simple conditional statements as recipes, or as we call it here composition index. Thus, IFTTT consists of service index (channels), solution designer (interface), solution proposer (end-users themselves) and composition index (recipes), which makes it actually one of the first to fully implement a solution composer. Also, Zapier shares the same construction with full implementation of a solution composer. However, with a more extensive service index and more flexible solution design patterns, Zapier, to an extent, is even one step closer to the ideal implementation of a solution composer.

For some tools, such as Pipemonk, We-Wired Web and X-formation Connect are more or less like IFTTT or Zapier. They share the idea of service integration automation and solution composition. What is different is that these tools do not have a handy composition index for end-users.

For the rest of the cases, they all miss some essential elements, but each of them contains significant part(s) of a solution composer. APIGEE is a API management platform, focusing more on the designer and composition index part. Microsoft Azure is a growing collection of integrated cloud services. It provides cloud services for the need of end-users but it does not have a composition index. HP SDN allows end-users to select from a range of SDN Applications that allow to program network to align with business needs. But HP SDN only has an AppStore for the selection, and arranging consultants to help with all the solution. There is no reference solution or relevant database for composed solutions. Salesforce.com is a developer platform. It only provides service index and solution designer.

After an extensive literature study, a couple of scientific frameworks were selected by conducting snowballing procedure [25]. Snowballing refers to using the reference list of a paper or the citations to the paper to identify additional papers. The FEATUREHOUSE framework [1] provides a method for software composition using superimposition. The framework, however, only concerns the composition of systems from different languages and does not provide tooling for suggestion of fitting solutions, nor does it provide an index of composed solutions. Another framework that was added is the Mashup framework [15], which is a mechanism for enabling end-users to create mashups from a UDDI registry of services, using drag and drop tools.

5   Evaluation

Based on learning and results from the industry cases, an interview question protocol was drawn. In the second phase of this study, semi-structured interviews were conducted. During interviews, experts were asked to provide insight on the concept of solution composers and to evaluate the proposed framework. The interviews were recorded, after which all the records were transcribed.

Table 3. The background of interviewees.

Background and occupations	Interviewee
CEO of the company	A
CTO and scientist innovator	B
Product manager ecosystem	C
Cooperation manager	D
Senior developer	E

Interviewees' Backgrounds - Interviewee A owns a company and is the CEO of the company for three years. The projects he has been working on based mostly on the idea of service composition. Interviewee B works as scientist innovator in a project based national company for almost 4 years and he may join a new project regarding service composition. And interviewee C works as a product manager ecosystem in a software company for nearly two years. While interviewee D works in a mobile company and is handling a project closely related to solution composers. And interviewee E is an developer in a e-commerce company with experience in the filed of web service. All backgrounds are indicated in Table 3.

Interview Analysis - Due to the wide range selection of questions, not all of the interviewees were able to answer 100% of the questions listed. However, the authors were able to combine and compare the information among all the interviews and draw conclusions about the validity of the proposed framework and the two-sides of solution composers. In this section, a thorough discussion and analysis is provided.

The Need of Solution Composers. During interviews, interviewees indicated that there indeed is a need for solution composer in the software industry that will fulfill the need of end-users. Solution composer has further affected the software ecosystem by providing standards and creating a new market. Currently, some significant big shots in the software industry have started developing similar services, such as Android Instant Apps platform.

Solution composers will offer standards and protocols to support the communication among component services. However, current service composition environments barely have productivity support tools which is similar to what modern Integrated Development Environments (IDEs) provided, such as code searching or debugging [14]. Solution composer could therefore benefit from environments with productivity techniques, for example, services index discovery and services integration. As interviewee B also confirmed in the interview, "*there is a lack of standards*". Thus, solution composer that provides standards is needed for services integration and composition.

Moreover, there is a market need for solution composer. With regards to the effect of solution composer, interviewee A, when asked about the impact on software ecosystem, replied: "*It's going to create a whole new way of apps (services) and not only apps*". He also suggested that some of the big companies with their own ecosystem have got hands on this field already, "*Google, for example, is already creating this alternative AppStore*", "*it's just about the first party who gets in the market as fast as possible*". In the meanwhile, interviewee B agreed on this point (Table 4).

Solution composer is more like a trend, rather than a tool needed to be developed or introduced to the industry. We foresee that the trend of composing software from small units of functionality will continue.

The Advantages of Solution Composers. Solution composer focuses on single applications no more. To some extent, solution composer represents a higher

Table 4. The need, advantage, challenge and validity of solution composers: Quotes from the Evaluation Interviews.

On the need for solution composers	Interviewee
"Change the industry"; "Offer completely new market place"	A
"It will create a profitable market for whoever is in part of this revolution"	B
"Obviously, there is a need for end-users"; "it's really getting there already"	C
"It can reach out to many fields and can be used in many ways. The ICT area will be affected"	D
"Bring in new concept"; "a big innovation"; "will actually build healthier software ecosystems"	E
On the advantage of solution composers	**Interviewee**
"Don't think of Apps anymore"; "make it easier for the users to get functions they need"	A
"Making it easier for the end-users"	B
"Allow end-users to customize"; "can make business around it"	C
"First, it includes a service consultancy. Secondly, it provides end-users with an experiential environment"; "attainability"	D
"The standardization and the attempt of customization"; "divide two phases of the design and the run-time"	E
On the challenges of solution composers	**Interviewee**
"Privacy is maybe still an issue. "Do you want it?"	A
"Practical problems"; "need well-defined APIs and standardized"	B
"Standardization"; "even without standardization, you will need to build an ecosystem"; "90% of what you need is person (manual work)"	C
"The technique support"; "how to simulate the environment"	D
"How you can persuade people to use"	E
On the validity of the framework	**Interviewee**
"Could work for the business"; "(will need to) customize their daily operations and the new technical infrastructure"	A
"Architecture for a framework that has not been implemented"; "A lot of manual work to get everything to work on their platform"	B
"It sounds technical and detailed"; "can already be valuable now"	C
"This is a good idea"; "will add value"	D
"Quite clever"; "will make things easier and smoother"	E

level of functionality and service composition. The idea of service composition indicates the future of software industry, which is to meet the need of end-users. This is also the most important aspect of software development. Thus, thinking of the end-users is the main advantage of solution composer, as interviewees all agreed.

Moreover, regarding the aspect of solution composer operation, interviewee D pointed out that solution composer can provide end-users with an experiential environment, allowing end-users to sense the final product they are going to purchase. In this way, a solution is proposed in advance before it is carried out into practice. Therefore, benchmarking and comparison of different service configuration are enabled. *"If the end-users could have the access to a trial product with consultant and specialist's advice, they may feel they've reached closely to their goal"*. This approach to present composed solution can soon meet end-users' requirement and satisfy end-users' expectation. For end-users, the actual outcome helps to make their finally decision.

The Challenge of Solution Composers. Nevertheless, challenges of the solution composer exist. The main concern addressed from interviewees is whether solution composer can successfully attract customers in the current market. As a matter of fact, with such a strong idea colliding with the AppStore nowadays, it is reasonable to have concerns over the result of solution composer reshaping the industry.

The interviewees reflected that standardization, which was also implied as predefined manual work, would cost a lot of time and labor. In addition, interviewee C brought up that implementing solution composer within an ecosystem is also something needed to be concerned. Nevertheless, solution composers need to be built on top of an existing ecosystem.

The Validity of the Proposed Framework. In the framework, we defined solution composer and platform as separated phases because they have different focuses. During the interview, Interviewee E agreed on this separation.

Furthermore, the proposed framework provides a standard for service composition that the current industry is lack of. *"I would say there is a lack of standards"*, said interviewee B, *"While some are very similar services but they just have different APIs and there are some much work to implement that specific API"*. The problem interviewee B brought up is what the solution composer is about to fix. We proposed service index in order to form a standardized interface for end-users, gathering all the services together rather than a whole bunch of scattered APIs. In addition, the composition index brings convenience as well. It allows end-users to easily look up composed solutions. Interviewee E said that the composition index could be very interesting.

In the framework, besides the technical side, we also included payment processing and business model in order to make it valid for business that will be the work in the future.

Moreover, interviewee B suggested how we should make the framework more valid or more advanced. *"If you have well-defined services"*, he gave suggestions on how the solution composer could support semi-automatic composition, *"if you have some precondition and some post condition, output and input then you could create an engine to do this"*.

However, interviewee B also addressed his concerns as the payment processing and business model being in the center of the framework. He said: *"If you are saying business models and payment processing, then you are talking about something in companies or back-ends."* In the meanwhile, interviewee A also had the same concerns about whether there is an appropriate ecosystem or a business background to support such framework, to bring it into practice and to make it profitable in the market.

6 Discussion

Implications for the Industry. In order to validate the framework for practical implementations in software industry, protocols and standards are needed for services to communicate. Within an environment for solution composer, different requirements in terms of component models are needed [14]. Since every service works differently, it will be quite a burden if there is no protocol for communications among services and consequently, it will increase the difficulty in the solution composition process. For a simple example, booking tickets for flight, every website is different. If there is standardized interface for travel information, it will make things much easier. Nowadays, some very similar services have different APIs and there will be abundant of manual work to implement specific APIs if there is no unified protocol.

Moreover, software services should be simplified to only focus on core features. With clear and distinguishable core features and without unnecessary communications among redundant functions, it is easier for services to follow the standardized protocol and for solution composer to perform concisely. Interviewees B also expressed the urge for the industry to simplify software services

In the meanwhile, automation is also needed. Nowadays, enterprises are increasingly looking for new chances to cooperate with other enterprises by offering and performing integrated services and solutions [21]. However, the development pace of solution composer that requires a considerable effort of low-level programming has not kept up with the rapid growth of available opportunities. Besides, the number of services to be integrated and composed may be huge, so even with a standard protocol for component communication, involving significant amount of manually coding work is inadequate considering the scale of solution composition. Therefore, solution composers call for automation.

In addition, when automation is included and manual work is reduced, more time and effort could be devoted into the main useful functional part of solution composer, which is solution composition and service integration. Also with a standardized protocol and simplified core service features, it will therefore make consultancy easier and consequently will enable rapid system integration.

Last but not least, in order to facilitate the development of solution composer, a healthy existing ecosystem is significant, either basing solution composer on an ecosystem, or building an ecosystem around solution composer. Only within an ecosystem, solution composer can be made the best use of, nourishing the health of the ecosystem.

Research Validity. This paper brings up with a new concept of solution composer. In order to further investigate the nature of it, we used exploratory research based on case studies from the industry [22] and interviews from experts [18].

With regards to internal validity, evaluating the framework with interviews was a pragmatic decision, since the implementation and testing of the framework in practice requires years of research. We do plan to implement the framework, however, over the course of the next years at several industry research partners.

Regarding external validity (generalizability), it refers to the extent to which the framework of this study can be generalized in industry. As observed in the interviews, this framework has been evaluated in a variety perspectives and the model can be applied to different parts of the software industry, such as the services business or the Internet of Things business, as platforms like IFTTT.com illustrate. Moreover, to minimize the external validity, we also analyzed practical cases from industry in order to show the general practice of the proposed framework.

In terms of construct validity, the interviews were prepared with an extensive interview protocol, consisting of a structure for the interview, but also definitions for the solution composer and its parts. Using this definition list, interviewees were sure to understand the concepts in the same way as other interviewees. The semi-structured interviews were conducted as part of the case study. An interview protocol was defined with questions including status quo in enterprise AppStore and service composition, the impact of solution composer on software ecosystem, and the future of service composition and software ecosystems. The interviews were recorded, and transcribed. The results were analyzed to extract observations, improvement suggestions, and conclusions.

7   Conclusion

From the industry cases and expert interviews suggested in the previous sections, it is clear that solution composers can be a major game changer in shaping and reshaping the complete software ecosystem. One of the main observations drawn from this study is that there is an undoubted need for the development of solution composers, which provide end-users with more relevant and satisfactory solutions. Furthermore, the proposed framework was considered useful for industry practice, according to the experts from related fields.

This paper functions as an exploratory study into solution composers and as a call for practitioners and researchers to further investigate solution composers in practice. The industry cases illustrate that current SPOs are working towards solution composers. According to the proposed framework, most of the participants of this evolution movement for service composition have not yet developed into maturity. Only a few have made the first baby steps towards solution composers, yet still need abundant guidance and instructions to fully grow into the real ones. Also the cases demonstrate, by performing solution composition, SPOs are actually benefiting and gaining market. In the meanwhile, the scientific frameworks from previous works indicate the implementability of solution composers.

In addition, expert interviews provide insight and evaluation from practical side and help to evaluate the research results. Interviewees expressed that there is a need for solution composers and the main advantages focus on customization for end-users and the new way to discover and connect software in the wider software ecosystem. However, most of the challenges brought up were from technical and practical side, which present directions for future research.

First, both industry cases and interviews suggest that in order to establish a robust solution composer, predefined standard will be needed, for instance, the standard protocol for component services to communicate with each other while composing solutions. Secondly, despite the need from market, solution composers will suffer pressures from other existing big shots in the industry. Whether thrive or not, depends largely on how solution composer will be unveiled by whom. Thirdly, persuading end-users to join this software evolution will encounter obstacles and barriers, because end-users may not realize how eager they need the existence of solution composer. However, we will leave these to future research and studies.

References

1. Apel, S., Kastner, C., Lengauer, C.: Language-independent and automated software composition: the featurehouse experience. IEEE Trans. Softw. Eng. **39**(1), 63–79 (2013)
2. Atzori, L., Iera, A., Morabito, G.: The internet of things: a survey. Comput. Netw. **54**(15), 2787–2805 (2010)
3. Azeez, A., Perera, S., Gamage, D., Linton, R., Siriwardana, P., Leelaratne, D., Weerawarana, S., Fremantle, P.: Multi-tenant soa middleware for cloud computing. In: 2010 IEEE 3rd International Conference on Cloud Computing, pp. 458–465. IEEE (2010)
4. Brønsted, J., Hansen, K.M., Ingstrup, M.: A survey of service composition mechanisms in ubiquitous computing. In: Workshop on Requirements and Solutions for Pervasive Software Infrastructures, vol. 2007, pp. 87–92 (2007)
5. Colville, R., Adams, P., Curtis, D.: It service dependency mapping tools provide configuration view. Gartner Research News Analysis, Gartner (2005)
6. Eid, M., Alamri, A., El Saddik, A.: A reference model for dynamic web service composition systems. Int. J. Web Grid Serv. **4**(2), 149–168 (2008)
7. Garber, L.: The lowly api is ready to step front and center. Computer **46**(8), 14–17 (2013)
8. Garofalakis, J., Panagis, Y., Sakkopoulos, E., Tsakalidis, A.: Web service discovery mechanisms: looking for a needle in a haystack. In: International Workshop on Web Engineering, vol. 38 (2004)
9. Ghezzi, C., Jazayeri, M., Mandrioli, D.: Fundamentals of Software Engineering. Prentice Hall PTR, Upper Saddle River (2002)
10. Hyrynsalmi, S., Mäkilä, T., Järvi, A., Suominen, A., Seppänen, M., Knuutila, T., Jansen, S.: App store, marketplace, play! an analysis of multi-homing in mobile software ecosystems, pp. 59–72 (2012)

11. Jansen, S., Bloemendal, E.: Defining app stores: the role of curated market-places in software ecosystems. In: Herzwurm, G., Margaria, T. (eds.) ICSOB 2013. LNBIP, vol. 150, pp. 195–206. Springer, Heidelberg (2013). doi:10.1007/978-3-642-39336-5_19

12. Jansen, S., Cusumano, M.A., Brinkkemper, S.: Software Ecosystems: Analyzing and Managing Business Networks in the Software Industry. Edward Elgar Publishing, Cheltenham (2013)

13. Jansen, S., Rijsemus, W.: Balancing total cost of ownership and cost of maintenance within a software supply network. In: Proceedings of the IEEE International Conference on Software Maintenance (ICSM 2006, Industrial track), Philadelphia, PA, USA (2006)

14. Lemos, A.L., Daniel, F., Benatallah, B.: Web service composition: a survey of techniques and tools. ACM Comput. Surv. (CSUR) **48**(3), 33 (2015)

15. Liu, X., Hui, Y., Sun, W., Liang, H.: Towards service composition based on mashup. In: 2007 IEEE Congress on Services, pp. 332–339. IEEE (2007)

16. Mahmoud, Q.H.: Service-oriented architecture (SOA) and web services: the road to enterprise application integration (EAI), 16 November 2005

17. Mani, A., Nagarajan, A.: Understanding quality of service for web services. IBM developerworks, 1 (2002)

18. Midgley, N., Parkinson, S., Holmes, J., Stapley, E., Eatough, V., Target, M.: Did i bring it on myself? an exploratory study of the beliefs that adolescents referred to mental health services have about the causes of their depression. Eur. Child Adolesc. Psychiatry, 1–10 (2016)

19. Protalinski, E.: Google unveils android instant apps that launch immediately, no installation required. http://venturebeat.com/2016/05/18/google-unveils-android-instant-apps-that-launch-immediately-no-installation-required/. Accessed 18 May 2016

20. Runeson, P., Höst, M.: Guidelines for conducting and reporting case study research in software engineering. Empirical Softw. Eng. **14**(2), 131–164 (2009)

21. Sheng, Q.Z., Benatallah, B., Dumas, M., Mak, E.O.-Y.: Self-serv: a platform for rapid composition of web services in a peer-to-peer environment. In: Proceedings of the 28th International Conference on Very Large Data Bases, pp. 1051–1054. VLDB Endowment (2002)

22. Stebbins, R.A.: Exploratory Research in the Social Sciences, vol. 48. Sage, London (2001)

23. van Angeren, J., Alves, C., Jansen, S.: Can we ask you to collaborate? analyzing app developer relationships in commercial platform ecosystems. J. Syst. Softw. **113**, 430–445 (2016)

24. von Alan, R.H., March, S.T., Park, J., Ram, S.: Design science in information systems research. MIS Q. **28**(1), 75–105 (2004)

25. Wohlin, C.: Guidelines for snowballing in systematic literature studies and a replication in software engineering. In: Proceedings of the 18th International Conference on Evaluation and Assessment in Software Engineering, p. 38. ACM (2014)

26. Yin, R.K.: Case Study Research: Design and Methods, vol. 5. Sage Publications, Incorporated, London (2008)

The Rise of Cloud Brokerage: Business Model, Profit Making and Cost Savings

Evangelia Filiopoulou$^{(\boxtimes)}$, Persefoni Mitropoulou,
Christos Michalakelis, and Mara Nikolaidou

Department of Informatics and Telematics, Harokopio University of Athens,
9 Omirou Street, Tavros, Athens, Greece
{Evangelf, Persam, Michalak, mara}@hua.gr

Abstract. Cloud computing has succeeded in transforming the ICT industry, making computing services more accessible to businesses. Nowadays, many cost effective solutions are available to users. However, searching for the best provider or the best bundle is not always an easy decision for the client. The cloud broker is a widely known business model derived from this necessity. It is a third-party business which assists clients to make the best decision in choosing the most suitable cloud provider and the most effective service bundle for their needs, in terms of performance and price. Into that context, this paper describes the cloud broker business model and its promising future. It highlights the broker's vital role and the benefits that arise from the use of its services, explores on the same time the drawbacks that derive from the intermediation of cloud broker. The economic context of the cloud broker model is also examined by reviewing the contemporary literature for the pricing methods that can be adopted by a cloud broker in order to achieve cost savings.

Keywords: Cloud broker · Cloud computing · Brokering models · Intermediary · Pricing models

1 Introduction

The cloud has succeeded in transforming the ICT industry, making software and hardware services even more accessible to businesses and offering no upfront capital investments for clients, leading to a faster market to market time in many businesses [1]. From a provider's standpoint, it offers a plethora of different features to adopt, while on the demand side, users benefit by choosing the appropriate services or combinations of them according to their needs. The task of finding the best service and best pricing at the same time, raises new challenges on how to make this selection.

As a consequence, the necessity of cloud brokerage was realized and the business model of cloud broker was developed. The broker acts as an intermediary between users and providers, assisting the former to choose the services that meet their requirements and the latter to schedule resources and apply effective pricing schemes. The broker's role is very important for reaching a point where both the demand and the supply side agree with a price set, settling the best financial agreement, making a profit out of this service [2]. The future of cloud broker is unquestionable and is considered to

© Springer International Publishing AG 2017
J.Á. Bañares et al. (Eds.): GECON 2016, LNCS 10382, pp. 19–32, 2017.
DOI: 10.1007/978-3-319-61920-0_2

be the single largest cloud service in 2015 [3]. According to Gartner [4], cloud broker is identified as one of the top ten technology trends of 2014 and it is expected that by year 2015, 40% of cloud services will be delivered via brokers [5]. In addition, cloud brokerage market is predicted to grow from $1.57 billion in 2013 to $10.5 billion by 2018, as illustrated in Fig. 1, which represents a compound annual growth rate of 46.2% between these years [6]. This growth of cloud broker changes constantly the cloud environment and the cloud broker model seems to hold the key of these reforms.

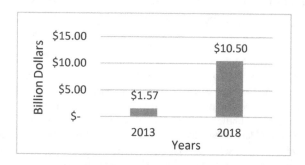

Fig. 1. The expected cloud brokerage growth (2013–2018).

The rest of the paper highlights the cloud broker's vital role and is structured as follows. Section 2 provides a description of the cloud broker business model and its services, while Sect. 3 highlights the beneficial role of the broker, exploring at the same time its drawbacks. The financial context and a comparative review of the contemporary literature on the pricing models of a cloud broker are described in Sect. 4. Finally, Sect. 5 concludes, providing directions for future research.

2   Cloud Broker and Services

A cloud broker aims at building a secure cloud management model in order to ease the delivery of cloud services to cloud clients, while it presents them the services a cloud provider can offer [7]. It mediates between clients, such as SMEs or larger scale businesses, and providers, by buying resources from providers and sub-leasing them to clients [8]. It is an entity that manages the use, performance and delivery of cloud services, and negotiates relationships between cloud providers and consumers [9].

Cloud broker plays a dual role in the context of cloud computing. When it interacts with a provider, acts as a client and it behaves as a provider when interacting with a customer [10]. Cloud brokers are considered to be the key for managing hybrid IT environments [11]. Enterprises, brokers and providers agree at a Service Level Agreement (SLA) that specifies the details of the service, according to their requirements. The SLA is agreed by all parties; it determines details about the provided services and contains penalties for violating the expectations of all parties [8].

A cloud broker manages multiple cloud services and offers technical services to businesses, focusing on managing interoperability issues among providers.

Furthermore, it negotiates contracts with cloud providers on behalf of the businesses [9]. A graphical depiction of the above is given in Fig. 2.

A cloud broker provides services in three categories:

1. Intermediation: A cloud broker acts as an intermediary between clients wishing to adopt cloud services and cloud providers [9, 12].
2. Aggregation: A cloud broker can customize and combine multiple cloud services into one or more services. An aggregation service establishes the secure data movement between businesses and multiple cloud providers and includes data integration [9, 12].
3. Arbitrage: A cloud broker assists customers to select several cloud providers according to requirements, such as cost or performance. Service arbitrage is similar to service aggregation, except that the services are being combined and are not fixed [9, 12].

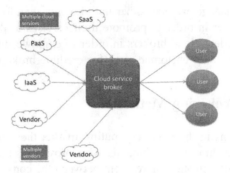

Fig. 2. Cloud service broker model

3 Cloud Broker Benefits

Businesses usually face difficulties in choosing the best provider based on service cost and other specified requirements, mainly due to lack of knowledge and time. It is also hard for clients to select services offered directly by providers, because there are no standards that can measure performance of different service providers. Every provider has its own standards, which are not necessarily widely acceptable [8]. Thus, they grant the authorization to a broker to decide on behalf of them [12].

The benefit of cloud broker for an enterprise can be realized by assisting a provider to choose the best framework, so that an enterprise can focus on its core business rather than being concerned about task deployment strategies, meeting its functional or non-functional requirements. Cloud broker offers not only the best provider but also integrates disparate services across multiple hybrid approaches. Furthermore, it helps providers adapt directly to market conditions and offer more efficient services [12]. It pioneers the integration of the entire cloud ecosystem, connecting hardware players such as IBM, HP, Dell; software players such as Microsoft, Citrix; PaaS, IaaS, SaaS providers such as Google, Salesforce, Amazon, and Rackspace, among many other prominent players in the IT and Telecom industry [3].

Cloud broker is a trusted and reliable advisor for businesses, as organizations mistakenly think that the choice of cloud services is similar to the selection of web services. However, this choice is in fact different, because there is no standardized representation of cloud providers' properties. The broker is bound to provide the guaranteed resources [8] and it also forms Service Level Agreements with the providers because the SLAs of the providers often vary in format and content, causing confusion to the non-aware clients [2].

The model of cloud broker also provides budget guidance to businesses and assists them to adopt a cost effective solution, satisfying budget requirements. It usually achieves better discounts, reduces capital costs and accesses more information from providers [12].

Some of the world's largest technology companies offer cloud services, including Google, Amazon and Microsoft. Since cloud providers deliver many services it is almost impossible to manage each customer individually, therefore providers need the intermediate cloud broker in order to promote their services to the clients [13]. They cooperate with independent cloud brokers in order to empower their relationship with enterprise customers, because customers seek for credible brokers [14].

4   Overview of Brokering Methods

A cloud broker functions in the cloud computing market the same way as it does in real-world markets, matching users demands with providers supplies [8]. It aims to succeed in settling the best financial agreement between the consumer and the provider [15]. In the next paragraphs, the most common cloud brokers pricing methods are presented, according to the contemporary corresponding literature.

4.1   Financial Brokering Method Based on Derivative Contracts

This brokering method was initially developed by HP Labs by Wu, Zhang, and Huberman (WZH). It describes the financial method of a cloud broker based on derivative contracts.

A derivative contract is a contract that derives its value from the performance of an underlying entity. Options contracts, are common types of derivatives contracts which give buyers the legal right, but not an obligation, to purchase a resource for an agreed price on some later delivery date [16]. Derivative contracts are used by the broker as a strategy to avoid the risk for uncertainty over future demand and supply [2].

Reserved instances are committed by the broker through derivatives contracts. As soon as the contract matures, the resources are delivered to clients by the broker. The broker makes a long-term reservation of resources, in fact the broker purchases obligations on resources for the next 3 years. Then the cloud broker repacks the reserved instances as one month options contracts [17]. Each month the broker accepts the resource requirements from clients. The requirements are expressed as a probability that reveals the utilization of an instance in the next month. The broker sums these probabilities that correspond to the prediction of how many instances will be required in the following period. Consequently, the broker sells to clients options contracts and decides whether or not to purchase resources [2, 17, 18].

The broker compares the performance of a reserved instance during the previous 36 month time period, $P = \{P_{t-36}, ..., P_t\}$, with the future resource capacity, such as the number of reserved instances that the broker has currently available $F = \{f_t, .., f_{t+36}\}$ during the following 3 years. The deficit profile D is estimated for each forthcoming month, by subtracting historical demand from future expected demand.

$$D = F - P \tag{1}$$

Margin Resource Utilization (MRU) describes the possible utilization of an additional reserved resource and it is the proportion of item in $D > 0$. In addition, the broker uses another metric variable, which is called threshold and is denoted by θ. Threshold advices the broker whether it is in its interest to purchase reserved instances in advance or it is better to buy on demand resources later on [2, 17, 18].

MRU and θ are combined in the following way:

1. If MRU $> \theta$, then the broker is advised to purchase additional reserved instances, which will very probably be utilized in the following months and this decision is expected to be profitable.
2. If MRU $<= \theta$, then the broker should purchase new instances on demand, estimating that it will be more profitable than purchasing reserved instances in advance.
3. The next month clients can demand instances from the broker by exercising their options contracts. If the broker has available capacity to satisfy the demand of the client, instances are sold to clients at a higher value than the purchased one. Otherwise, the broker has to buy on demand instances and provide them to the client in order to fulfill its obligation [2, 17].

The simulation was programmed in Python. Simulations were implemented with a pool of 1000 clients submitting probabilities. The drawback of this method is that if clients reveal a mistaken possibility, the broker will inaccurately forecast the reservation of the resources.

4.2   A Cloud Computing Broker Model for IaaS Resources

This brokering method is based on provider tariffs instead of providers. Tariff options constitute an open contract between the cloud provider and the client which outlines the terms and conditions of providing cloud computing services to consumers and includes rates, fees and charges [19].

Infrastructure as a Service includes control of fundamental computing resources, such as memory, computing power and storage capacity [20]. The instances of IaaS are presented by virtual machines (VMs) here. The resource (VM) is denoted as a vector $r = (\#vCPU, RAM, HDD)$ which depicts a virtual machine that includes a number of virtual CPUs (#VCPU), an amount of virtual random access memory in Gigabytes (RAM) and an amount of storage capacity in Gigabytes (HDD).

The consumer-resource demand is expressed by the following number of factors and criteria: (a) Qualitative criteria (C), such as constraints for CPU, RAM, HDD (upper and lower bound, customer service, location and legislation), (b) Load profile (L) that contains the consumer's performance priorities for CPU, RAM, HDD, (c) Time T: The total deployment time in hour of the VM, (d) ton: The number of hours the VM is running ("on-time)", (e) s: the HDD capacity required by the VM.

This brokering method can be described by 4 steps. In the first step consumers send resource requests as mentioned above. Thereafter, the model filters provider tariffs for consumer constraints, for example location, upper and lower bound and excludes tariffs which do not meet the requirements. In the third step the cost-performance ratio of each tariff is computed. The lowest cost-performance indicates the most cost-efficient solution for the consumer. In the final step the broker ranks and returns the results.

The cost-performance ratio of an IaaS instance is estimated by a benchmarking suite called UnixBench [21]. For every provider tariff, an instance (CPU, RAM, HDD) is ordered and UnixBench runs benchmarks on the system, calculating the benchmark points of the VM. The benchmark results (benchmark points BP, $\bar{X}$), the announced price of the provider (P) and L are the three factors that estimate the cost performance ratio. Especially L is a factor that can either attribute to the calculation of the ratio or not. If it is independent of the process then the performance rate (Price per BP) is calculated by the equation:

$$\text{Price per BP} = P/\bar{X} \tag{2}$$

Therefore the lowest price per BP indicates the highest performance for the given price and it is considered to be the most appropriate solution for the consumer.

If L that describes the relative importance of components (CPU, RAM, HDD) is taken into account then the brokering process is more complicated. The benchmark results are denoted by $\bar{X}_{CPU}$, $\bar{X}_{RAM}$, $\bar{X}_{HDD}$ for each component of the VM. L is considered to be (W_{CPU}, W_{RAM}, W_{HDD}). At first, P is divided into components (CPU, RAM, HDD) according to the weights of the load profile. By using the price to distribute weights, the need to make assumptions about the relation of benchmarking values between components is avoided. The performance weighed component price (PWC) for each component is presented below, as shown in Table 1.

Table 1. Performance weighed component price

CPU	RAM	HDD
WCPU*P	WRAM*P	WHDD*P

Afterwards and for each tariff, the performance weighed component price is divided by the component benchmark points, calculated by UnixBench and then the sum of them is used so that the Composed Total Weight tariff (CTW) is estimated:

$$\text{CTW} = \left(\text{PWC}_\text{CPU}/\overline{X_{CPU}}\right) + \left(\text{PWC}_{RAM}/\overline{X_{RAM}}\right) + \left(\text{PWC}_\text{HDD}/\overline{X_{HDD}}\right) \quad (3)$$

After the estimation of the cost-performance ratio the tariffs are enlisted. In previous step tariffs that do not fulfill qualitative criteria have been already excluded. The lowest price per performance unit is the most suitable solution for the consumer's task [19].

4.3 Dynamic Cloud Resource Reservation via Cloud Brokerage

As proposed in [22], the cloud brokerage service reserves a large pool of instances from cloud providers and serves users with price discounts. The broker optimally exploits both pricing benefits of long-term instance reservations and multiplexing gains, and makes instance reservations, based on dynamic strategies, with the objective of minimizing its service cost. The evaluation of the methodology was made by simulations driven by large-scale Google cluster-usage traces, revealing that the broker can achieve significant price discounts.

IaaS clouds provide users with multiple purchasing options, the most popular being "on-demand instances" and "reserved instances". On-demand instances allow users to pay a fixed rate in every billing cycle (e.g., an hour) with no commitment, paying for example $n*p$ monetary units, for n hours usage of an instance, which is charged at p monetary units per hour. Reserved instance allows users to pay a one-time fee, in order to reserve an instance for a certain amount of time. In most cases, the cost of a reserved instance is fixed. The cloud broker exploits the pricing difference between reserved and on-demand instances to reduce the expenses for the users.

The main problem to be satisfied in order to address the dynamic resource reservation corresponds to the decision regarding the number of instances the broker should reserve, the number of instances they should be launched on demand, as well as when to reserve, since the demand changes dynamically over time. The "Instance Reservation Problem" is an optimization problem, seeking to minimize the total cost of all the user demands, and can be formulated as:

$$\min \text{cost} = \sum\nolimits_{t=1}^{T} r_t \gamma + \sum\nolimits_{t=1}^{T} (d_t - n_t)^+ p, \text{ s. t. } n_t = \sum\nolimits_{i=t-r+1}^{t} r_i, \forall t = 1, \ldots, T \quad (4)$$

In the minimization formula, the first summation describes the total cost of reservations and the second the cost of all on-demand instances. In the above equation r_t is the number of reserved instances, d_t the aggregate demand and n_t the number of reserved instances that remain effective at time t = 1, 2 ,..., T. with the time in terms of billing cycle. The term $(d_t - n_t)^+$ describes the additional on-demand instances needed to be launched at time t. Moreover, r is the reservation period, γ the one time reservation fee for each reserved instance and p the price of running an on-demand instance per billing cycle.

The broker's problem is to make dynamic reservation decisions for r_t, t = 1,2 ,..., T to minimize its total cost, as described by the above equation, while accommodating all the demands. This problem is integer programming needing complex combinatorial methods to solve it. However, such kind of problems are described by the *curse of dimensionality*, the high number of possible combination and states which results into exponential time complexity seeking for solutions. In addition and in the cases of users who cannot predict their future demand, an online strategy is proposed which reserves instances based only on demand history.

The performance evaluation was based on simulations and on Google cluster-usage traces. The corresponding dataset contained 180 GB over a month's resource usage information of 933 users. According to their findings the broker can bring an aggregate cost saving at a level of 15%, when it aggregates all the user demands. The broker's benefit is different in different user groups, achieving a higher cost saving, at a level of 40% for users with medium demand fluctuation, than those with low demand fluctuation which amounts at a level of 5%.

Evaluating the price discount in each individual user who can enjoy from the brokerage service it is found that over 70% of users can save more than 30%, while the broker can bring more than 25% price discounts to 70% of users if all users are aggregated.

4.4   Dynamic Pricing Based on Quantized Billing Cycles and the Ski-Rental Problem

Quantized Billing Cycles (QBC) is the situation according to which the user pays the same price for an on-demand instance, regardless if the time of usage is smaller than the whole Billing Cycle, i.e. paying the same price of using the VM for 1 min or 1 h [23]. Users with sporadic demand are facing QBC problems and the higher the sporadic nature, the greater the loss. When a cloud broker needs to buy VMs to serve the aggregate demand faces the risk of underutilization of the VM in the subsequent time slots. So, the broker has to decide without knowledge of future demand.

The pricing method presented in this section derives from the research performed in [23] and can be used to maximize the profit of the cloud broker under QBC, in both static pricing (the selling price remains constant at nominal rate) and dynamic pricing (price varies in response to the user's demand). The idea behind dynamic pricing is: "Suffer a small loss in one interval by decreasing the demand, rather than buying a VM and then suffering a major loss in the subsequent intervals due to low demand". This is realized by decreasing the demand and not increase the revenue, so the role of dynamic pricing is to regulate the demand. Dynamic pricing turns out to make more profit than static pricing, mainly due to the underutilization of the VMs met in the latter approach.

The mathematical formulation of the optimization problem described above, considering that the user pays the cloud broker based on per-request basis is:

$$maxP = \sum_{t=1}^{T} (\gamma_t d_t - u_t) \, s.t. \sum_{i=t-r+1}^{t} u_i \geq d_t; d_t = f \, dt*, \gamma t; \tag{5}$$
$$\forall t = 1, 2, \ldots, T$$

P is the profit to be maximized, $(\gamma_t d_t - u_t)$ is the profit at t^{th} interval, γ_t is the selling price per VM per time slot, d_t is the number of VMs required to service the incoming request, u_t is the number of VMs bought at the tth interval and d_t^* is the actual demand, at t.

The equivalent minimization problem to the above is:

$$minL = \sum_{t=1}^{T} \left[\left(\gamma^* d_t^* - \gamma_t d_t \right) + u_t \right] = f \left(d_t^*, \gamma_t \right);$$

$$\text{s.t.} \sum_{i=t-\tau+1}^{t} u_i \geq d_t; \forall t = 1, 2, \ldots, T d_t$$

(6)

In the above equation, $\left(\gamma^* d_t^* - \gamma_t d_t \right)$ and u_t correspond to the demand loss and VM loss, respectively and $f(d, \gamma)$ is the demand function. If there is an unexpected increase in demand d_t^* for a short time, then the optimization problem described by (6) will increase the selling price γ_t to reduce the demand. Thereby the cloud broker will suffer a small "Demand Loss". The option of buying enough VMs to support the demand hike is a good solution only if the hike in demand persists for a long time, otherwise the cloud broker may suffer a huge "VM Loss" in subsequent intervals due to underutilized VMs. Since it is not possible to know beforehand if an increase in demand will persist or decay soon, d_t^* is needed for all t. Hence, the next step is to design online algorithms which can make such decisions online based on present and past data.

The proposed algorithms are based on the *ski-rental problem*, according to which a player faces the decision of whether to buy or rent a resource, without the a priori knowledge of the period of usage. If the period of usage is short, then renting is preferable, while for a long period buying is cheaper. The concept of *breakeven point* is used for the construction of online algorithms, suggesting the point after which buying is cheaper than renting.

The evaluation of the proposed algorithms was based on simulations and on google cluster usage traces and the generation of the demand function, while conducting comparative studies regarding the effect of demand prediction and the demand threshold for switching between renting and buying. The results revealed the importance of demand prediction and indicated the appropriate breakeven points for the different threshold values considered.

The key points of the presented pricing methods, together with the evaluation results are presented in Table 2.

Table 2. Overview of common pricing methods of a cloud broker

Name	Description	Evaluation	Results
Financial brokering method for cloud computing [2]	• Clients send to the broker probabilities revealing the utilization of instances in the following month • Reserved instances are committed by the broker through option contracts	• The simulation was programmed in Python • Use of a pool of 1000 user agents submitting probabilities	• The broker is profitable • It is more profitable for the broker to purchase long-term options contracts • The past performance of clients benefits the broker

(*continued*)

Table 2. (*continued*)

Name	Description	Evaluation	Results
	• The broker, based on the probability and the previous performance of clients, purchases reserved instances or waits to buy instances on demand		
A cloud computing broker model for IaaS resources [19]	• The model is based on provider tariffs instead of providers • Each client presents to the broker his priorities (CPU, RAM, and Storage) • The broker collects tariffs from the provider market and assesses them by calculating the cost-performance of each tariff • The lowest price per performance unit is the most suitable solution for the consumer's task	• The cost-performance ratio of an IaaS instance was estimated by UnixBench • The data of simulation was obtained from three providers: Amazon, Azure and Rackspace	• Rank of price/performance price: different from the order by price or performance alone • Performance and price deflect among providers → less performance at a higher price. • Larger instances have a worse price/performance price
Dynamic Cloud Resource Reservation via Cloud Brokerage [22]	• The broker reserves a large pool of instances from providers and optimally exploits both pricing benefits of long-term instance reservations and multiplexing gains • Users purchase instances from the broker in an "on-demand" way and are served with price discounts • Dynamic strategies are used for the	• The simulations were driven by large-scale Google cluster-usage traces • >900 users' usage traces on a 12 K-node Google datacenter were used • Users' computing demand data were converted to IaaS instance demand • Users: 3 groups based on demand fluctuation level	• Users receive a lower price when trading with the broker. There is no need for upfront payment for reservations and no money wasted on idled reservation instances • The broker makes profit by leveraging the wholesale (reservation) model

(*continued*)

Table 2. (*continued*)

Name	Description	Evaluation	Results
	broker in order to make instance reservations with the objective of minimizing its service cost • When demand predictions are unavailable, an online reservation strategy to make decisions based on history is proposed		
Quantized Billing Cycles [23]	• Quantized Billing Cycles (QBC): user pays the same price for an on-demand instance, regardless if the time of usage is smaller than the whole Billing Cycle • When a broker needs to buy VMs faces the risk of underutilization of the VM and has to decide without knowledge of future demand • The idea behind dynamic pricing is: "Suffer a small loss in one interval by decreasing the demand, rather than buying a VM and then suffering a major loss in the subsequent intervals due to low demand" • Decrease of demand and not increase of revenue, so that the role of dynamic pricing is to regulate the demand	• The proposed algorithms were based on *ski-rental problem* • It was made use of the *breakeven point*: the point after which buying is cheaper than renting • The simulations were based on google cluster usage traces and the generation of demand function • Comparative studies of demand prediction and threshold for switching between renting and buying were conducted	• Dynamic pricing turns out to make more profit than static pricing, mainly due to the underutilization of the VMs met in the latter approach • The results revealed the importance of demand prediction and indicated the appropriate breakeven points for the different threshold values considered

5 Discussion

The overview of the cloud broker discussed in this paper focuses on the numerous benefits of this widely known business model. From a business oriented perspective, the broker assists enterprises to develop themselves, makes cost savings, creating at the same time a competitive environment with more job opportunities and challenges. The cloud brokering has a substantial potential for cloud service providers and small, upstart entrepreneurs, who gain improved profitability and new revenue opportunities, resulting to the growth of the society's economy and the increase of social surplus.

Furthermore, the pricing methods adopted by a broker offer economic benefits to both consumers and providers, while creating profits for the broker as well. Into that context, a research area of high interest and importance, regarding the cloud brokering services, is the development of more intelligent and flexible pricing approaches, since the existing ones do not succeed to adequately address the pricing of cloud services.

Towards this direction, some of the most common cloud brokers pricing methods are presented in this paper. According to them, the broker reserves instances from cloud providers, based on past performance of clients, using either a probability which reveals the utilization of instances for the next month [2] or an online reservation strategy to make decisions based on history [22]. In addition, a broker may collect tariffs from the provider market and assesses them by calculating the cost-performance of each tariff always according to clients' priorities for resources [20]. Dynamic pricing is also proposed as an approach aiming to regulate clients' demand based on the underutilization of the VMs [23] or minimize the broker's service cost using dynamic programming and approximate algorithms [22].

6 Conclusions

In the market of cloud computing, a broker functions in the same way as it does in other, real-world, markets. It matches users' demands with providers' supplies, aiming to succeed in settling the best financial agreement between the supply and the demand side of the corresponding market, in order to make profit and this is the successful result of a deal in a commodity market.

The work presented in this paper describes the cloud broker and its promising future, in terms of maintaining an essential role in an increasingly complex cloud computing scenario and in profit making. It highlights the broker's vital role and the benefits that arise from the use of its services. The economic context of the cloud broker model is also examined by presenting a short review of the contemporary literature for the pricing methods that can be adopted by a cloud broker in order to achieve cost savings.

As the cloud broker business model is still developed, there are a number of important aspects to be further explored, mainly towards the direction of developing and adopting more efficient pricing methods and the role of the broker into the reduction of costs. Research must be extended to accommodate the SaaS and PaaS models as well, which are also expected to diffuse quickly in the coming years, raising the imperative need for new, innovative, business models.

References

1. Marston, S., Li, Z., Bandyopadhyay, S., Zhang, J., Ghalsasi, A.: Cloud computing—The business perspective. Decis. Support Syst. **51**(1), 176–189 (2011)
2. Rogers, O., Cliff, D.: A financial brokerage model for cloud computing. J. Cloud Comput. **1** (1), 1–12 (2012)
3. King, M.: Cloud services brokerage market to increase by 55% (2013). http://www. companiesandmarkets.com/News/Information-Technology/Cloud-services-brokerage-market-to-increase-by-55/NI6908. Accessed 8 Apr 2013
4. Rivera, J.: Gartner identifies the top 10 strategic technology trends for 2014 (2013). http:// www.gartner.com/newsroom/id/2603623. Accessed 8 Oct 2013
5. Clancy, H.: Cloud integration brokerage services mature. Next-Gen Partner (2014). http:// www.zdnet.com/article/cloud-integration-brokerage-services-mature. Accessed 15 Apr 2014
6. Marketsandmarkets: Cloud services brokerage market by types (Cloud Brokerage Enablement (Internal, External (Telecom Service Providers, System Integrators & ISVs, Hosting & Cloud Providers)), Cloud Brokerage) - Global Forecast to 2020 (2015)
7. Nair, S.K., Porwal, S., Dimitrakos, T., Ferrer, A.J., Tordsson, J., Sharif, T., Sheridan, C., Rajarajan, M., Khan, A.U.: Towards secure cloud bursting, brokerage and aggregation. In: 2010 IEEE 8th European Conference on Web Services (ECOWS), pp. 189–196. IEEE (2010)
8. Buyya, R., Yeo, C.S., Venugopal, S., Broberg, J., Brandic, I.: Cloud computing and emerging IT platforms: Vision, hype, and reality for delivering computing as the 5th utility. Future Gener. Comput. Syst. **25**(6), 599–616 (2009)
9. Pritzker, P., Gallagher, P.: NIST cloud computing standards roadmap, pp. 500–291. NIST Special Publication (2013)
10. Bohn, R.B., Messina, J., Liu, F., Tong, J., Mao, J.: NIST cloud computing reference architecture. In: 2011 IEEE World Congress on Services (SERVICES), pp. 594–596. IEEE (2011)
11. Yasin, R.: Mid-year review: 10 predictions for cloud computing. GCN (2013). https://gcn. com/articles/2013/08/21/cloud-predictions.aspx. Accessed 21 Aug
12. Geetha, D.V., Hayat, R.M., Thamizharasan, M.: A survey on needs and issues of cloud broker for cloud environment. Int. J. Dev. Res. 4(5), 1035–1040 (2014)
13. Sampson, L.: A cloud broker can be a cloud provider's best friend. SearchCloudProvider.-com (2012). http://searchcloudprovider.techtarget.com/feature/A-cloud-broker-can-be-a-cloud-providers-best-friend
14. Mihai, C.: Cloud broker or cloud provider? Or both? (2013). https:// enterprisetechnologyconsultant.wordpress.com/2013/05/07/cloud-broker-or-cloud-provider-or-both/. Accessed 7 May
15. Papazoglou, M.P., van den Heuvel, W.-J.: Service oriented architectures: approaches, technologies and research issues. VLDB J. **16**, 389–415 (2007). doi:10.1007/s00778-007-0044-3
16. Clearwater, S.H., Huberman, B.: Swing options: a mechanism for pricing IT peak demand. In: Paper Presented at the International Conference on Computing in Economics (2005)
17. Clamp, P., Cartlidge, J.: Pricing the cloud: an adaptive brokerage for cloud computing. In: 5th International Conference on Advances in System Simulation (SIMUL-2013), pp. 113–121. IARIA XPS Press, Venice (2013). Citeseer
18. Wu, F., Zhang, L., Huberman, B.A.: Truth-telling reservations. Algorithmica **52**(1), 65–79 (2008)

19. Gottschlich, J., Hiemer, J., Hinz, O.: A cloud computing broker model for IaaS resources (2014)
20. Mell, P., Grance, T.: The NIST definition of cloud computing (2011)
21. Smith, B., Grehan, R., Yager, T., Niemi, D.: Byte-unixbench: a Unix benchmark suite. Technical report
22. Wang, W., Niu, D., Li, B., Liang, B.: Dynamic cloud resource reservation via cloud brokerage. In: 2013 IEEE 33rd International Conference on Distributed Computing Systems (ICDCS), pp. 400–409. IEEE (2013)
23. Saha, G., Pasumarthy, R.: Maximizing profit of cloud brokers under quantized billing cycles: a dynamic pricing strategy based on ski-rental problem (2015). arXiv preprint arXiv: 150702545

Work in Progress on Quality of Services and Service Level Agreements

Robust Content-Centric SLA Enforcement in Federated Cloud Environments

Nikoletta Mavrogeorgi$^{(\boxtimes)}$, Athanasios Voulodimos,
Vassilios Alexandrou, Spyridon Gogouvitis,
and Theodora Varvarigou

School of Electrical and Computer Engineering,
National Technical University of Athens, Athens, Greece
{nikimav, thanosv, alexv, spyrosg}@mail.ntua.gr,
dora@telecom.ntua.gr

Abstract. In this paper we present a system for declaring and enforcing SLAs in Cloud environments. The SLAs proposed are enriched with content terms, storlets and federation capabilities and provide high degrees of customizability for clients. A mechanism for SLA enforcement has been designed and implemented which, based on policies, measurements, usage data computations, and monitoring methods permits proactive SLA violation detection and handling. SLA renegotiation is supported as well. The proposed framework has been developed and evaluated in challenging scenarios in a variety of different application domains.

Keywords: SLA schema · SLA enforcement · Monitoring · Proactive SLA violation detection · Content centric storage · Storlets · Federation · Evaluation

1 Introduction

The cloud paradigm has undoubtedly revolutionized the IT landscape given the significance of on-demand cloud services offered by increasingly powerful cloud providers. The need for secure storage and retrieval of data is shared among all types of clients who can range from a simple user who uses a cloud service to store their photos to big enterprises (in a variety of sectors, i.e. healthcare, media, IT, banking, industry, etc.), which store financial and other sensitive data. A Service-level agreement (SLA) is a contract between a (cloud) service provider and a customer that specifies, in measurable terms, what services the provider offers. A SLA often includes metrics that specify the performance, availability, and security assured to the customer, as well as penalties for violating these requirements.

SLAs in Cloud architectures have been the focus of attention of a significant number of researchers and professionals, especially with the rapid adoption of cloud based solutions in many different application domains. SLA schemas XML schemas that represent the content of an SLA. Some existing approaches for SLA schemas and the corresponding languages to define service description terms are: SLAng [1], WS-Agreement [2], WSLA [3], WSOL [4], and SWAPS [5]. Nevertheless, the proposed schemas have limitations. SWAPS is quite complex and the implementation is

© Springer International Publishing AG 2017
J.Á. Bañares et al. (Eds.): GECON 2016, LNCS 10382, pp. 35–48, 2017.
DOI: 10.1007/978-3-319-61920-0_3

not publicly available. WSLA and SLAng have not further development at least since 2009. Apart from this, SLAng does not permit to define management information such as financial terms and WSLA has not formal definition of metrics semantics. WSOL lacks SLA related functionalities, such as the capture of the relationship between service provider and infrastructure provider. The WS Agreement is a Web Services protocol for establishing agreement between two parties using an extensible XML language for specifying the nature of the agreement, and agreement templates to facilitate discovery of compatible agreement parties. It allows arbitrary term languages to be plugged-in for creating domain-specific service description terms.

Two challenging research issues are the requirements translation from high level metrics to low level requirements and vice versa and the proactive violation detection. Several proposals have been made for these issues, but very little for cloud environments. For instance, GRIA SLAs [6] suggest a solution for avoiding violations but concerns only Grid environments. The LoM2HiS framework [7] proposes the translation of low level metrics to high level terms that are used in Cloud SLAs, but not the reverse translation. Also, they are based on generic characteristics and terms (e.g. availability) which are not application specific. The LAYSI framework [8] supports two kinds of monitors sensors, the host monitor and the runtime monitor sensor. The latter senses future SLA violation threats based on resource usage experiences and predefined threat thresholds. In DesVi [9], an architecture is proposed for preventing SLA violations based on knowledge database and case-based reasoning. It also uses the LoM2HiS framework for the requirements translation.

In [10] an analysis of SLA violations in a production SaaS platform is described, while [11] presents a scalable, stochastic model-driven an interacting Markov chain based approach to quantify the availability of a large-scale IaaS cloud. In [12] the authors present an aggregation mechanism for merging service-level objectives and for guaranteeing a single SLA that specifies obligations and responsibilities of all participants in a federation. The framework in [13] uses a portfolio-based optimisation to improve SLA compliance by diversifying the selection and consequently the allocation of traded instances of web services from multiple providers. An end-to-end framework for consumer-centric SLA management of cloud-hosted databases is proposed in [14] to facilitate adaptive and dynamic provisioning of the database tier of the software applications based on application-defined policies for satisfying their own SLA performance requirements. SALMonADA [15] performs an automated monitoring configuration and it analyses highly expressive SLAs by means of a constraint satisfaction problems based technique. In [16] a new proactive resource allocation approach is proposed aiming at decreasing impact of SLA violations by using two user's hidden characteristics, i.e. willingness to pay for service and willingness to pay for certainty. In [17] an SLA implementation for Cloud services based on the CMAC (Condition Monitoring on A Cloud) platform is proposed, while in [20] decision-making with regard to availability SLAs is explored.

In this paper, we present a system for declaring and enforcing SLAs in Cloud environments where commitments for using Cloud services are defined. The SLAs are enriched with content terms, storlets and federation capabilities. Additionally, many SLOs (Service Level Objectives) are supported at different levels permitting the clients to have customized SLAs. A mechanism for SLA enforcement has been designed and implemented which, based on policies, measurements and usage data computations, permits SLA violations to be handled and imminent SLA violations to be proactively detected. Moreover, renegotiation is supported, i.e. a client can change their SLA for a variety of reasons. The system permits the SLA renegotiation and based on measurements and usage data can suggest changes to the existing SLA aiming at being more compatible to its data usage or for cost reduction. The main core of the presented framework was developed in the context of the VISION Cloud EU project [18].

2 Cloud Models and Enriched SLA

Our proposed system permits the storage of objects and their retrieval anytime and from anywhere. In order this to be achieved replicas of the objects are stored in appropriate locations. The clients of the Cloud are the tenants and their users. A tenant is the unit that subscribes to storage cloud services. A tenant defines its users. The users handle the objects that are stored in the Cloud. The objects are stored grouped by containers. Containers serve as an aggregation point for grouping related data objects together. Policies can be set on a container basis and are applied to all of the objects in the container. A container is associated with an SLA and based on it the number and the locations of the replicas of the objects are defined. The Cloud is composed of multiple data centers. Each data center is split to clusters and each cluster consists of multiple nodes which contains the servers. This hierarchy is stored in Catalogs. Each level has its own aggregated catalog and uses GPFS-SNC. A local catalog enables mapping objects to file paths and the node containing the object. The resource model can be seen in Fig. 1. The existence of a resource model in the PaaS layer of a Cloud environment serves the need of management in terms of resource allocation, services deployment and execution and finally optimization.

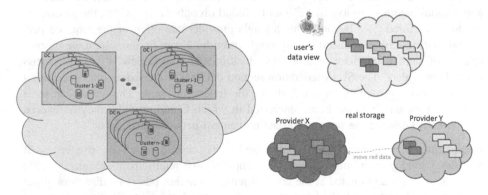

Fig. 1. Resource model.   **Fig. 2.** Federation.

The proposed SLA contains additions that are significant for Cloud provisions. Apart from the classical data of an SLA such as availability levels and responsibilities data between the provider and the tenant, our SLA is based on content terms and contains more SLO's in order to be customized as per the tenants' desires. Also, it contains federation and storlets support and commitments. Finally, it provides renegotiation with suggestions for better SLA according to the tenant's usage.

Content term addition. The innovation of declaring content terms permit the Cloud to provide content-centric services. Also, it links content with performance estimates, decisions for moving computation close to storage, pricing models, etc. Another advantage is that support more efficient capabilities, e.g. quicker search and retrieval of the objects, services regarding the content term for instance in case of media, high performance video related services are supported.

SLOs. The SLOs are not restricted in availability. There are many requirements in different levels that are selected by the tenant according to their desires. A tenant can balance the cost with the supported levels. For instance a tenant that uses data related to media can demand throughput of the highest level for the objects that concern the daily news as these are highly demanded whereas to choose lower throughput in order to have less cost. Finally, geographic constraints are supported. The tenant can choose the desired regions and black list regions where restricts its data to be stored.

Storlets. Storlets are executables which provide capabilities for supporting and improving the services that are offered to the tenants. Some storlets are: data compression, file transformation in various formats, translation, speech2text, text2speech, text2pdf, pdf2txt, transcode format, classify photos, extract data for patient, etc. Each storlet has a condition and an action that is executed when the condition is met.

Federation. Cloud federation is the practice of interconnecting the cloud computing environments of two or more service providers for the purpose of load balancing traffic and accommodating spikes in demand. Also, there is a need for interoperability that is to move data between providers without this to be visible to data usage. There are many reasons for having data in more than one Cloud providers. For instance, the SLA (or application) requires services that cannot be found on only one provider, the amount of resources required goes beyond what a single provider can offer, or the required performance cannot be guaranteed by any single provider alone. In our system we support change of storage providers without data lock-in and single view of storage across multiple providers. The SLAs federation section declares if the federation is permitted and with which providers. Figure 2 shows the federation view. The tenant can have access to their data without being interested in which Cloud provider they are stored and without knowing the process of data movement between providers.

Requirements. The requirements addressed were chosen based on use cases of VISION Cloud project and include: Throughput (some requirements require specific throughput levels aggregated at the level of tenant, whereas others require throughput per request), Durability (asked for specific durability levels), Availability, Duration (constraints regarding the duration of the requests: latency and response time), Security and privacy (Authorization, authentication and guarantee of proper use), Geographic constraints (User determines in which regions he desires to store his data), Violations checks (All the requirements should be checked and met during the SLA lifecycle),

Storlets (SLAs also provide storlet selection), CDMI (The external interfaces should be CDMI compliant), Billing, CRUD operations.

3 SLA Management and Enforcement

Our proposed SLA Management provides a robust end-to-end SLA system starting from the SLA negotiation and runtime enforcing the currents SLAs with the agreed services and commitments. The SLA enforcement apart from dealing with providing the requested services according to the agreed SLOs with the tenant, is responsible for checking for SLA violations and for detecting proactively imminent SLA violations. In case of possible SLA violations it tries to avoid them with corrective actions. The SLA enforcement is based on policies and usage data analytics that are checked based on monitoring data.

As far as the architecture is concerned, there are two main components: (a) the **SLA Negotiator** which handles the services that have to do with the external communication with the clients that is SLA negotiation, SLA renegotiation, SLA templates generation, billing etc. (see Fig. 3) and (b) the **SLA Enforcer** which deals with the enforcement of the SLA and handles services that are needed in the Cloud internally such as policies generation for monitoring and analysis, check of SLA violations, proactive detection of possible SLA violations and decisions for corrective actions (see Fig. 4). The SLA schema that is used is described in detail in [19].

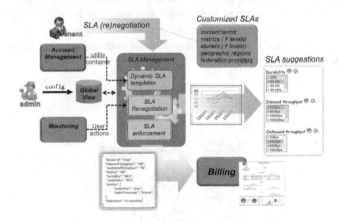

Fig. 3. SLA negotiator.

SLA Negotiator. The SLA Negotiator component is responsible for implementing the external interface of the platform with regard to SLAs.

SLA Negotiation. The negotiation of SLAs is realized by taking into account content related terms, thus reflecting the content centric approach of VISION Cloud. Different capabilities and costs are provided depending on the selected content term. To sign an SLA, a tenant chooses and fills an SLA template. SLA templates are generated dynamically according to the supported capabilities of VISION Cloud and the content terms. SLA templates contain the supported metrics with different levels, by which the SLOs are derived when the tenant chooses his desired level, the supported services, the obligations of both parties (provider and tenant), the billing rules and the penalties in case the agreed service level is not met. An SLA template also contains terms related to the federation capabilities of the platform, which define the tenant's ability to perform federation and with which providers. Additionally, a section for storlets is provided. The set of storlets available to the tenant is based on the tenant authorization and the type of the requested SLA template. Some storlets in the set might be compulsory, and some optional; besides these storlets, other optional ones are displayed and can be additionally chosen.

SLA Renegotiation. SLA renegotiation is supported. During SLA negotiation there is a section for determining which data the tenant can request to the provider to be modified during the SLA lifecycle (e.g. levels of the permitted SLO, addition of storlets, federation permissions, etc.). If both parties agree, the SLA is changed, and it is pushed to the internal system with all the necessary modifications. Also, suggestions are provided to the tenant informing of what terms may be changed in his SLA in order to better suit him (e.g. adding storlets, or using a lower level SLA which already covers his needs at a lower cost). The SLA Management component is easily modifiable, and contains an automatic way to handle changes in the SLA schema.

Reports and SLA Data. SLA Management provides a user friendly GUI, by which the user can request the creation of an SLA and can delete, edit, view an SLA or a list of SLAs that concerns the current user. Also, the user can be notified about certain events, receive reports, and view older notifications and reports (e.g. SLA violations occurred in a certain period). The GUI supports user authentication in order to enforce security and privacy policies.

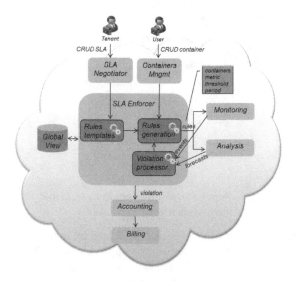

Fig. 4. SLA enforcer.

SLA Enforcer. The SLA Enforcer deals with the system configuration regarding the SLAs and the enforcement and maintenance of SLAs between tenants and providers.

Container Configuration. During container creation, the SLA Enforcer is contacted by the Container Management component to obtain the QoS requirements stemming from the chosen SLA. One responsibility is to translate the requirements translation from the high-level QoS metrics to the low-level ones and vice-versa. Translation from the high-level metrics specified in an SLA (e.g. durability) to low-level metrics by which the internal system works (e.g. number of replicas) is important during SLA management. It is also needed for checking the feasibility of the requested QoS metrics, for generating policies in order to ensure the SLA enforcement and for the placement execution. The reverse translation is needed during SLA templates generation in order to generate templates expressed in SLA metrics based on the available and supported low level metrics. Moreover, the SLA Enforcer is responsible for tuning the Monitoring and Analysis components with appropriate parameters needed for the SLA enforcement. These include the metrics that should be monitored and the threat thresholds. Also, it provides to the Container Management component placement requirements (how many replicas and in which locations) in low-level terms.

SLA Violation Handling. SLA violation is handled according to policies that are sent to Monitoring. When an SLA violation occurs, a notification is sent to the Accounting and Billing in order for the provider to be charged with the agreed penalty. Moreover, the SLA Enforcer stores appropriate information in the Global View so as to be used for preventing future SLA violations.

Proactive SLA Violation Detection. The SLA Enforcer is responsible for detecting proactively possible SLA violations. The SLA Enforcer calculates for each metric the threat threshold, which is more restrictive than the one signed and appropriate policies, and sends them to the Analysis component. The Analysis component receives monitoring information for this metric and calculates trends and patterns. The SLA Enforcer is notified by Analysis when forecasts that a metric will reach the given threshold. Then, the SLA Enforcer decides on the actions that are needed to prevent the imminent SLA violation and it reconfigures the system with new appropriate policies and monitoring parameters. Examples of corrective action are replica creation, replica movement, or request redirection to a cluster which is less loaded.

The proactive SLA violation detection is based on resource usage experiences and historical data and uses the case base reasoning (CBR). CBR is the process of solving problems based on past experience. In the knowledge database used in Global View the conditions are stored under which a violation is going to be realized, and the preventative actions and solutions that should be performed for avoiding the violations.

Analysis algorithms for proactive SLA violation detection regarding forecasting and normality are implemented based on Map/Reduce processes.

Policies Mechanism. The SLA Enforcement is based on policies that are created runtime according to the SLOs and the monitoring data. The policies concern either monitoring or forecasting metrics. Some policies examples are depicted in Fig. 5.

topic	metric	operation	predicate	threshold	aggregationMethod	filterUnit	period	rule-type
throughput-topic	transaction-throughput	PUT	<	5		ntua,niki,photos		violation
throughput-topic	transaction-throughput	PUT	<	7		ntua,niki,photos		threat-violation
latency-topic	transaction-latency	GET	>	500		ntua,niki,photos		violation
latency-topic	transaction-latency	GET	>	400		ntua,niki,photos		threat-violation
average-throughput-topic	transaction-throughput	PUT	<	5	avg	ntua,niki,photos	500	violation
sla-per-request	transaction-throughput	PUT	<	5		ntua,niki		measurement

Fig. 5. Monitoring policies examples.

Monitoring. The main responsibility of the Monitoring Component is the collection, propagation and delivery of all events generated in the system to their respective recipients. To this end, the component employs an asynchronous message delivery mechanism, and on top of it, a simple distributed rules engine to decide where each event should be transmitted and whether it should be aggregated with other events first. The system distinguishes between a number of different aggregation levels. More specifically a rule can be defined at a per node, per cluster, per datacenter or per cloud level combined with a time frame. These levels have different granularities.

The monitoring component's interactions fall into two broad categories:

Producers of Events in VISION Cloud include the Object Service, CCS, Resource Map, SRE (Storlet Runtime Environment), VM-storlets and low-level metric gathering probes. These services generate events upon user actions or at scheduled intervals. The events are passed to Monitoring which performs various aggregation operations and are finally passed on to consumers. A library provided by Monitoring is used (in python and java) for integrating with the producers.

Consumers of Events. Most management operating layer services, for example CTO, SLA Management, Accounting/Billing, Analysis and Analytics service, depend integrally on the events dispatched by Monitoring. The events can be consumed through a provided library.

The main components are the following:

Vismo-Core. This is the main monitoring instance. There is a unique instance running on each node and its main purpose is to coordinate with the other modules. In the most basic terms, it acts as a conductor of events and as such, can be seen as the backbone of the system, receiving events from the event producers and distributing them to the event consumers. Moreover, it is responsible for collecting locally produced events, performing partial (node-level) aggregation and pushing the events to consumers.

Vismo-Dispatch. The sole purpose of this library is to connect a producer to the locally running monitoring instance. In doing so, events generated in the producer are passed in instantly to the monitoring process. Under the hood the open source zmq library is used, in a pull/push fashion.

Vismo-Notify. The library is used by the various consumers to declare interest in one or more group of events, called topics. Upon registration, the library is responsible for notifying the client of the arrival of new events. The notification happens in an asynchronous fashion to the main client program, in another thread. Here, also, the zmq library is employed, using a PUBSUB mechanism.

Rule System. A basic rule system is used to evaluate every event received and trigger different processing actions, such as partial aggregation or immediate dispatching according to rules.

Aggregator. This module is used to generate new events which are the result of an aggregation method upon a list of raw events. Typically, the aggregation happens over events of the same type. Another option is to collect a number of raw events and group them by a given property field.

Rule Synchronizer. This module is responsible for synchronizing all the instances of the rules engine to contain the same rules.

Vismo-Probes. These constitute various low level probes that are external to the main instance and collect data about CPU and memory usage, network load, etc., per node.

CDMI-Queues Service. This service implements and extends the Notification queues as proposed in the CDMI specification. CDMI specifies a means to define and implement notification functionality that is based on queues.

Rules Propagation Mechanism. In order to allow for new rules to be inserted in the system a new mechanism has been developed that allows for rules to be added, updated or deleted at runtime. Moreover, the mechanism guarantees that the rules will be eventually synchronised across all the instances of the distributed rules engine of the monitoring system. The propagation mechanism works as follows: all the nodes at the cluster level form a multicast domain. A simple election mechanism is used to elect a cluster-head, a datacenter-head and a cloud-head. Once a node receives a request for a rule, it propagates the change to all other nodes in the cluster through a multicast message. Each node is responsible to send an acknowledgement to the cluster-head that the change has been received.. Once the cluster is updated the cluster-head is responsible to contact the datacenter head which in turn informs all the cluster-heads.

Implementation and Design Decisions. Our system is based on widely used protocols. For the services we use REST services. Data exchanges are done with JSON format. The database that we use is Cassandra a distributed database. The catalogs are using GPFS. The SLA schema follows the WS-Agreement. Implementation language is Java, Javascript and Python. For the policies the CDMI protocol is used and for federation OVF and OCCI interface. The technical details of the SLA Management component are abstract for other components, so they are unaware of them: RESTful web services are provided to other components in order to use the SLA Management functionality.

The SLA Management component at VISION Cloud is installed in all the nodes, but only one instance runs per cluster. This decision was taken for failover and performance reasons. Some of the SLA Management tasks are handled in different clusters. Nevertheless, synchronization and other matters should be taken into account. An alternative solution is installing the SLA Management component in one cluster and offering a centralized SLA Management. This solves any synchronization issues that may raise, but the performance is severely impacted. The source code of SLA Management was packaged in a WAR file and was deployed on a Tomcat web container, which was tested in the VISION Cloud testbed.

4   Evaluation

In this section we present an experimental evaluation of our system. The tests were executed on a machine with an AMD Phenom II x4 965 Processor running Scientific Linux 6.1. An event creation client created events with configurable event size and rate. The client used the producer library of the mechanism, which added a timestamp to every event. Each message was then propagated to the monitoring mechanism, which after processing the event forwarded to a consumer which appended a timestamp to the event. Using the two timestamps the latency and throughput were calculated in varying scenarios of event rate generation, event size and rules to be executed. The testbed examined consists of 9 machines, organized into 3 clusters.

In the first set of experiments the rate at which events were generated was kept constant at **1000 events per second** while the size of the events was gradually made larger, starting from 512 bytes up to 10240 bytes. For each specific size a set of 5000 events were generated and the mean throughput and latency were calculated. Moreover the memory used by the mechanism was measured in each run. The results can be seen in following, while a statistical analysis of each graph can be found in Fig. 6.

	1000events/sec			3000events/sec			variable events rate	
	latency	throughput	memory consumption	latency	throughput	memory consumption	latency	memory consumption
MIN	0,0281	983,3073	6,1131	0,0343	2375,4264	3,9766	0,0264	3,3901
MAX	0,0390	1001,3353	134,2253	1,6094	2998,7618	189,1281	0,6211	189,7027
AVERAGE	0,0329	992,5467	50,3893	0,6280	2841,0245	96,5134	0,1990	69,5728
STDEV	0,0029	4,7669	31,8081	0,5565	150,4115	62,3577	0,1877	46,2812
Confidence (95%)	0,0009	1,4961	9,9828	0,1746	47,2059	19,5707	0,0213	5,2459

Fig. 6.   Statistical analysis of experiments.

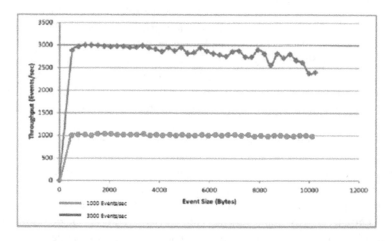

Fig. 7. Throughput with variable size of events 1000 Events/sec rate and 3000 Events/sec rate.

As the size of the events is made larger so does the latency increase, reaching approximately 0,04 s at an event size of 10240. This is considered to be adequate considering that event sizes should not in general be this large. As it is evident the mechanism easily maintains a constant throughput of 1000 events per second. Memory consumption is also affected by the size of the events reaching a maximum of 134 MBs.

In the next set of experiments and in order to stress the system we executed the same experiment with an event rate of **3000 events/sec**. As expected we see a negative impact on the measured latency and throughput (Figs. 7, 8 and 9).

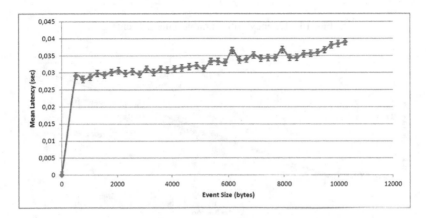

Fig. 8. Latency with variable size of events at 1000 Events/sec rate.

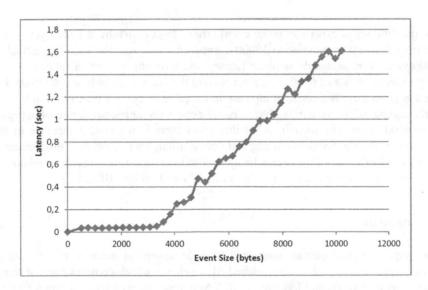

Fig. 9. Latency with variable size of events at 3000 Events/sec rate.

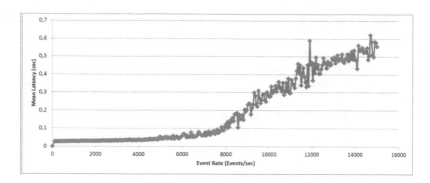

Fig. 10. Latency with variable rate of events.

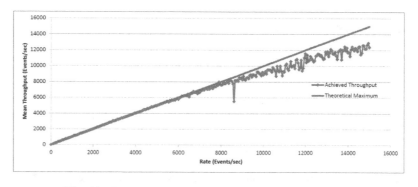

Fig. 11. Comparison of achieved to maximum throughput.

In the third set of experiments the **event size of kept constant** at 1024 bytes while event rates from 100 events/sec to 15000 events/sec were used. For each rate a total of 15000 events were sent and the mean latency and throughput were calculated.

Up to an event rate of 6000 events per second the latency is stable at around 0,04 s. After this point there is a constant increase in its value reaching a maximum of 0,62 s. The throughput of the system is able to easily cope with a generation rate of approximately 6500 events per second. After this point there is a constant increase in the difference between generation and rate and output throughput. Memory consumption is also affected by the rate of the events being similar to the consumption measured during the first two tests and reaching a maximum of 189 MBs (Figs. 10 and 11).

5 Conclusion

In this paper we proposed an automated SLA Management mechanism for content centric storage. It is based on an enriched SLA schema which contains content terms and sections for storlets and federation. SLA Management exploits the chosen content terms and supports services to the customer more efficiently and with reduced cost.

During the SLA enforcement, dynamic rules are created and updated, in order to handle proactively SLA violations. Dynamic SLAs are also supported, as SLA templates are generated according to the current supply, and renegotiation is offered.

References

1. Lamanna, D.D., Skene, J., Emmerich, W.: SLAng: a language for defining service level agreements. In: FTDCS 2003, Washington, DC, USA. IEEE (2003)
2. Andrieux, A., Czajkowski, K., Dan, A., Keahey, K., Ludwig, H., Kakata, T., Pruyne, J., Rofrano, J., Tuecke, S., Xu, M.: Web Services Agreement Specification (WS-Agreement)
3. IBM Web Service Level Agreements (WSLA) Project. http://www.research.ibm.com/wsla/
4. Tosic, V., Pagurek, B., Patel, K.: WSOL - a language for the formal specification of classes of service for web services. In: ICWS, pp. 375–381. CSREA Press (2003)
5. Oldham, N., Verma, K., Sheth, A., Hakimpour, F.: Semantic WS-agreement partner selection. In: WWW 2006, pp. 697–706. ACM, New York (2006)
6. Boniface, M., Phillips, S.C., Sanchez-Macian, A., Surridge, M.: Dynamic service provisioning using GRIA SLAs. In: Nitto, E., Ripeanu, M. (eds.) ICSOC 2007. LNCS, vol. 4907, pp. 56–67. Springer, Heidelberg (2009). doi:10.1007/978-3-540-93851-4_7
7. Emeakaroha, V.C., Brandic, I., Maurer, M., Dustdar, S.: Low level metrics to high level SLAs - LoM2HiS framework: bridging the gap between monitored metrics and SLA parameters in cloud environments. In: 2010 HPCS, pp. 48–54 (2010)
8. Brandic, I., Emeakaroha, V.C., Maurer, M., Dustdar, S., Acs, S., Kertesz, A., Kecskemeti, G.: LAYSI: a layered approach for SLA-violation propagation in self-manageable cloud infrastructures. In: 2010 IEEE 34th Annual COMPSACW, pp. 365–370, July 2010
9. Emeakaroha, V.C., Netto, M.A.S., Calheiros, R.N., Brandic, I., Buyya, R., De Rose, C.A.F.: Towards autonomic detection of SLA violations in cloud infrastructures. FGCS (2011)
10. Martino, C.D., Chen, D., Goel, G., Ganesan, R., Kalbarczyk Z., Iyer, R.: Analysis and diagnosis of SLA violations in a production SaaS cloud. In: 2014 IEEE 25th International Symposium on Software Reliability Engineering, Naples, pp. 178–188 (2014)
11. Ghosh, R., Longo, F., Frattini, F., Russo, S., Trivedi, K.S.: Scalable analytics for IaaS cloud availability. IEEE Trans. Cloud Comput. 2(1), 57–70 (2014)
12. Stanik, A., Koerner, M., Kao, O.: Service-level agreement aggregation for quality of service-aware federated cloud networking. IET Netw. 4(5), 264–269 (2015)
13. Alrebeish, F., Bahsoon, R.: Implementing design diversity using portfolio thinking to dynamically and adaptively manage the allocation of web services in the cloud. IEEE Trans. Cloud Comput. 3(3), 318–331 (2015)
14. Zhao, L., Sakr, S., Liu, A.: A framework for consumer-centric SLA management of cloud-hosted databases. IEEE Trans. Serv. Comput. 8(4), 534–549 (2015)
15. Müller, C., et al.: Comprehensive explanation of SLA violations at runtime. IEEE Trans. Serv. Comput. 7(2), 168–183 (2014)
16. Morshedlou, H., Meybodi, M.R.: Decreasing impact of SLA violations: a proactive resource allocation approach for cloud computing environments. IEEE Trans. Cloud Comput. 2(2), 156–167 (2014)
17. Galati, A., Djemame, K., Fletcher, M., Jessop, M., Weeks, M., McAvoy, J.: A WS-agreement based SLA implementation for the CMAC platform. In: Altmann, J., Vanmechelen, K., Rana, O.F. (eds.) GECON 2014. LNCS, vol. 8914, pp. 159–171. Springer, Cham (2014). doi:10.1007/978-3-319-14609-6_11

18. Kolodner, E.K., et al.: A cloud environment for data-intensive storage services. In: IEEE CloudCom 2011, pp. 357–366 (2011)
19. Mavrogeorgi, N., Gogouvitis, S.V., Voulodimos, A., Kyriazis, D., Varvarigou, T.A., Kolodner, E.K.: SLA management in clouds. In: CLOSER 2013, pp. 71–76 (2013)
20. Franke, U., Buschle, M., Österlind, M.: An experiment in SLA decision-making. In: Altmann, J., Vanmechelen, K., Rana, O.F. (eds.) GECON 2013. LNCS, vol. 8193, pp. 256–267. Springer, Cham (2013). doi:10.1007/978-3-319-02414-1_19

Structural Specification for the SLAs in Cloud Computing (S3LACC)

Waheed Aslam Ghumman$^{(\boxtimes)}$ and Alexander Schill

Technische Universität Dresden, Dresden, Germany
{Waheed-Aslam.Ghumman,Alexander.Schill}@tu-dresden.de

Abstract. Cloud service providers generally offer service level agreements (SLAs) in descriptive format which is not directly consumable by a machine/system. The SLA written in natural language may impede the utility of rapid elasticity in a cloud service. Automation of different phases of the SLA life cycle (e.g. negotiation, monitoring and management) is also dependent on the availability of a machine readable SLA. In this work, we propose a Structural Specification for the SLAs in Cloud Computing (S3LACC) for the automation of complete SLA life cycle i.e. negotiation, monitoring, management and recycling. S3LACC is specifically designed for cloud domain to meet latest standards and complex requirements of the cloud services such as service composition, dynamic negotiations, automated monitoring and formalization of qualitative parameters. Additionally, S3LACC defines a single SLA structure to be used as an SLA template and as a final agreement as well.

Keywords: Service Level Agreement · Negotiation · Monitoring

1   Introduction

Cloud computing has been established as a ubiquitous model for on-demand computing with regnant effects across IT infrastructures, software architectures, storage solutions, applications and services. Cloud services are most often bounded by an agreement between cloud service provider (CSP) and a cloud service user (CSU), termed as service level agreement (SLA), to define the quality of service (QoS) parameters, guarantees and obligations. The life cycle of an SLA generally includes requirement specification, negotiation over SLA parameters between a CSU and a CSP, monitoring and management of the SLA. Manual or semi-automated approaches for complete SLA life cycle and for its individual phases diminish true utility of cloud features like cost efficiency, timeous availability of the cloud services and lesser administrative overheads. An admissible SLA specification should fulfill some definitive requirements, e.g. composition of more than one quantitative and/or qualitative metrics into a single service level objective (SLO), an SLO may include one or more sub-SLOs to define complex business objectives, definition of a common template for all parties (CSP, CSU and third parties) or linking negotiation and monitoring parameters to an SLA template.

© Springer International Publishing AG 2017
J.Á. Bañares et al. (Eds.): GECON 2016, LNCS 10382, pp. 49–61, 2017.
DOI: 10.1007/978-3-319-61920-0_4

Also, an appropriate SLA specification should have a good trade-off between its power of expressiveness and complexity [3]. In this paper, we present a Structural Specification for the SLAs in Cloud Computing (S3LACC). The structural design of the S3LACC is rationalized considering the following standards/guidelines:

- Cloud computing service metrics description (draft) by National Institute of Standards and Technology (NIST), US Department of Commerce (2014).[1]
- Cloud service level agreement standardization guidelines by European Commission (2014).[2]

The SLA standard (ISO/IEC 19086[3]) by International Organization for Standardization (ISO) is still under development to date. The main design features of S3LACC include, (i) a single SLA document for an SLA template, SLA negotiation process and an agreed SLA, (ii) quantitative and qualitative service parameters can be defined using S3LACC, (iii) different deadline based negotiation strategies (e.g. linear, Boulware, conceder or a custom negotiation strategy) are possible to embed in SLA itself for an automated negotiation process, (iv) a dynamic negotiation strategy can be linked with the SLA for an autonomous negotiation based on opponent's behavior, demand/supply and/or other factors, (v) an automated and fully customizable scheduling based monitoring process is supported by S3LACC design, (vi) the SLA guarantees and obligations are supported by renegotiation parameters, automatic renewal of SLAs and service state transformations to achieve a fully automated SLA management and (vii) S3LACC is language or format independent, it can be implemented in most of modern programming languages.

The rest of the paper is organized as follows. Section 2 presents the detail of the proposed specification S3LACC. In Sect. 3, a brief overview of collective functioning of the S3LACC framework is discussed. A use case for S3LACC based SLA is presented in Sect. 4. An analysis of the presented SLA specification structure, related work and a comparison with existing approaches are presented in Sect. 5. Future work and conclusions are summarized in Sect. 6.

2   S3LACC Design and Specification

An SLA template is a document which consists of service description, obligations, QoS parameters (SLOs), metrics to measure those SLOs and guarantees. An SLO is a mean to measure the level of a cloud service [12]. An SLO can be quantitative (e.g. availability or throughput) or qualitative (e.g. reliability). A qualitative SLO has a value that is in a descriptive form. A **metric** is a method or scale to measure an SLO e.g. the SLO *availability* is generally measured with the

---

[1] NIST Special publication 500-307 - http://www.nist.gov/itl/cloud/upload/RATAX -CloudServiceMetricsDescription-DRAFT-20141111.pdf.

[2] https://ec.europa.eu/digital-single-market/news/cloud-service-level-agreement-standardisation-guidelines.

[3] ISO/IEC JTC 1/SC 38 - http://www.iso.org/iso/home/store/catalogue_tc/catalogue_tc_browse.htm?commid=601355.

metric *percentage*. An SLO contains a service level, metric, measurement period, measurement type and location [2]. The SLA template is a common document among the participating parties and is a basis for the negotiation process. Mostly, an SLA template is a different document than the final agreed SLA. However, in S3LACC, an SLA template and final SLA are combined into a single structure. To achieve this common structure, the SLA parameters ($P_s = \{P_1, ..., P_n\}$ such that $P_i \in P_s$ and $1 \leq i \leq n$) are divided in the following three types:

- **Template parameter** represents such information which is part of an SLA template only and is denoted by a P_i^T. The template parameters are not negotiable. An SLA with template parameters is generated by a service provider based on a mutually known format.
- **Negotiation parameter** represents such parameter which contains information about automated negotiation process and is denoted by P_i^N.
- **Agreement parameter** contains the agreed value of a negotiated parameter and is denoted by P_i^F.
- **Mix parameter** contains such information which may belong to different phases of the SLA transformation in different SLAs and is donated by P_i^ρ where $\rho \in \{T, N, F\}$.

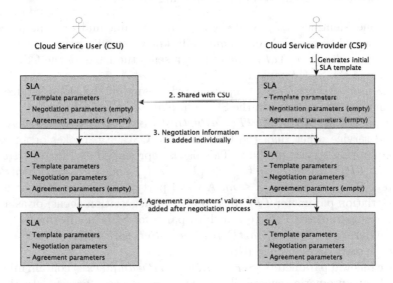

Fig. 1. S3LACC transformation process from SLA template to the final SLA.

The categorization of SLA parameters enables specification of all information in a single SLA and is adapted in different phases of the SLA life cycle. Negotiation parameters and agreed values of the negotiated parameters are added to the SLA template by the CSP and the CSU individually. An overview of this transformation from SLA template to the final SLA is shown in Fig. 1.

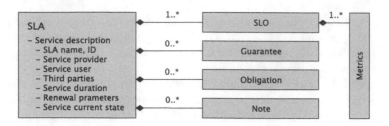

Fig. 2. UML representation of the SLA structure in S3LACC.

An SLA in S3LACC is composed of service description, one or more SLOs, zero or more guarantees, zero or more obligations and zero or more notes (containing such explanatory information and clauses which are not related to QoS parameters). A UML representation of the relationships between the SLA and its different parts is shown in Fig. 2. Detail of each SLA part is given in the following subsections.

2.1   Service Description

Service description is composed of the following parameters:

- SLA name/identifier ($SLAName^T$) is a unique name and/or a unique identifier assigned to the SLA and is mutually known to all parties
- Service provider ($ServiceProvider^T$) represents the name of the CSP and is available in the SLA template
- Service user ($ServiceUser^N$) represents the name of the cloud service user and contains empty value in the SLA template
- Third parties list with roles ($ThirdParties^\rho$) is a list of parties involved in a cloud service other than the CSP and the CSU, e.g. broker or an external monitoring service provider. This list is represented as $ThirdParties^\rho = [TP_1^\rho, ..., TP_m^\rho]$ where $m \geq 0$, $\rho \in \{T, \ N, \ F\}$ and $TP_i^\rho = \langle ThirdParty\ Name_i, \ Role_i \rangle$ where $0 \leq i \leq m$. A third party information may be added as negotiation parameter TP_i^N (e.g. broker or negotiation agent) or as a final agreement parameter TP_i^F (e.g. a third party for SLA monitoring)
- Service duration ($ServiceStartDateTime^F$, $ServiceEndDateTime^F$) represents the start date and end date of the service
- Service renewal parameters ($ServiceRenewalParameters^F$) contain information about automatic renewal of the cloud service on a preset date/time or based on a precondition. Automatic renewal may involve automatic renegotiation also. Renewal parameters are the following:
  - Precondition ($ServiceRenewalCondition^F$) represents a boolean expression that must be evaluated to *true* before the service is renewed. If the precondition is empty then service is renewed automatically on preset date/time

- Renegotiate on renewal ($RenegotiateOnRenewal^F$) is a boolean which represents whether a renegotiation is required on service renewal or not. *Renegotiation parameters* are defined in Sect. 2.3
- Service renewal date/time ($ServiceRenewalDatTime^F$) is the timestamp on which serviced is renewed
- Renew service ($ResetService()^F$) is a function that resets all agreement parameters (P_i^F) to their initial values or to renegotiated values
- Service current state ($ServiceCurrentState^F$) contains the current state of a cloud service. It may contain one of the intuitive values {*Starting, Stopping, Stopped, Started, Terminated*}.

2.2 Service Level Objectives (SLOs)

The performance of a cloud service is characterized by defining Service Level Objectives (SLOs). An SLO may depend on another SLO, may contain one or more qualitative parameters, quantitative parameters or both. One way to represent such an SLO is to divide the SLO into two separate SLOs i.e. a quantitative SLO and a qualitative SLO. In S3LACC, qualitative and quantitative parameters of the SLOs are intuitively shifted to their metrics and a single SLO may contain one or multiple metrics (qualitative, quantitative or both). Further detail of quantitative and qualitative metrics is discussed in the Sect. 2.3. An SLO contains the following parameters:

- SLO ID ($SLOID^T$) contains the unique identifier of the SLO
- Name ($SLOName^T$) contains the SLO name
- SLO weight ($SLOWeight^\rho$) is a value from the interval $[0,1]$ to represent the priority of an SLO. This value is used at the time of negotiation to generate and evaluate the negotiation bids
- Metric list ($M_s^\rho(SLOID) = \{M_1^\rho, ..., M_l^\rho\}$ where $l \geq 1$), represents list of metrics IDs associated with the $SLOID$
- SLO list ($SLO_s^\rho = \{SLO_1^\rho, ..., SLO_k^\rho\}$ where $k \geq 0$), is a list of SLOs used to combine one or more SLOs as sub-SLOs to meet composition requirements.

2.3 Metrics

A metric $M_i^\rho(SLOID)$ can have one of the value types from the set $\nu =$ {numeric, date/time, range of numeric or date/time values, boolean, qualitative/fuzzy}. A **quantitative metric** represents a metric which contains value type in set $\{\nu\} \setminus \{qualitative/fuzzy\}$. A **qualitative metric** in S3LACC has value type of qualitative/fuzzy. All possible descriptive values of the qualitative metric are defined as a well ordered set ($X_s = \{X_1, ..., X_j\}$ where $j \geq 1$, $X_i \in X_s$ and $1 \leq i \leq j$) with respect to the utility level ($U(X_i)$) of each descriptive value (X_i) such that $U(X_i) < U(X_{i+1})$ and $U(X_i) = i/j$. Semantically, utility level of a descriptive value X_i represents its worthiness level. A *qualitative metric* in S3LACC is automatically processed by converting its descriptive values to their numeric utility levels. A metric comprises of the following parameters:

- Metric ID ($MetricID^\rho$) is a unique metric identifier
- Name ($MetricName^\rho$)
- Unit of measurement ($MetricUnit^\rho$)
- Negotiation parameters
- Renegotiation parameters
- Monitoring parameters

The **negotiation parameters** of a metric are the following:

- Negotiable ($IsNegotiable^T$) is a boolean value which describes whether metric is part of the negotiation process or not. A *false* value is used when a metric is defined for monitoring or management purposes only
- Mandatory ($IsMandatory^N$) is a boolean value which is set by the CSP and the CSU in their respective template as part of the negotiation strategy. If a *true* value is assigned to this parameter then negotiation requirements (as restricted by *desired value* and *acceptable value*) for the metric must be fulfilled otherwise the negotiation process is unsuccessful. If a *false* value is assigned to this parameter then it represents that negotiation requirements are preferred to be fulfilled, however not mandatory.
- Weight ($MetricWeight^N$) is value from interval $[0, 1]$ representing the priority/importance level of the metric. A weight at SLO level and at metric level facilitates to prioritize an SLO and metrics within an SLO separately
- Desired value ($DesiredValue^N$) represents best possible single value or range of values for the metric. Depending on negotiation policy, this value is usually the starting value in the negotiation process
- Acceptable value ($AcceptableValue^N$) represents the reserve value (or worst possible value that is acceptable) during the negotiation process
- Agreed value ($AgreedValue^F$) represents the final value that is agreed between the CSP and the CSU after negotiation process
- Deadline ($Deadline^T$) is the maximum number of negotiation rounds or time limit allowed for the negotiation process for the metric. This parameter is part of the SLA template and set by the CSP. However, a CSU may set a different value if required but not exceeding the value set by the CSP
- Concession values ($CV_s^N = \{\langle D_1, CV_1 \rangle, ..., \langle D_q, CV_q \rangle\}$) is an ordered set (with respect to deadline D_i) such that $\langle D_i, CV_i \rangle \in CV_s^N$, CV_i is concession value and $1 \leq i \leq q$. If this set contains only one tuple ($\langle D_1, CV_1 \rangle$) then $D_1 = Deadline^N$ which means that in every negotiation round an equal amount of concession value CV_1 is applied to generate a new bid value for the metric. If more than one tuples are present in the set CV_s then concession value CV_i is applied until deadline D_i. After D_i, the concession value CV_{i+1} is applied until deadline D_{i+1} and so on. These values can be used to preset a negotiation strategy i.e. conceder, Boulware, linear or a custom concession strategy can be defined by varying the values in this set.
- Negotiation strategy ($NegotiationStragety()^N$) is a function which dynamically fills the negotiation parameters in set CV_s and may depend on opponent's negotiation strategy, number of competitors, demand/supply and/or

any other factor. This function is used to implement any type of automated and dynamic negotiation strategy by modifying the set CV_s on runtime.

Renegotiation parameters define a set of new values or expressions for the specified parameters of a metric for which negotiation information is to be updated for the renegotiation process. This set is defined as:
$RNP_s^F = \{RNP_1^F, ...RNP_r^F\}$ where $r \geq 0$, $RNP_i^F \in RNP_s^F$, $0 \leq i \leq r$ and $RNP_i^F = \langle RNPID, ResetParameterName, NewValueOrExpression \rangle$.
RNP_s^F enables to automate the renegotiation process in case of service failure or SLA violation by linking the $RNPID$ to the violation rules (discussed in Sect. 2.4).

Monitoring parameters are the following:

- Computation formula ($ComputationFormula^F$) is a well formed mathematical expression to compute the value of a metric which may include the observed/calculated values of other metrics in the same SLA, constants and/or variables containing values from the metrics of other SLA(s), web service(s), database value(s) or any other internal and/or external data source.
- Monitoring schedule (MS^F) is a set which contains different monitoring schedules at which monitoring of the metric is performed:
  $MS_s^F = \{MS_1^F, ..., MS_t^F\}$ where $t \geq 0$, $MS_i^F \in MS_s^F$, $1 \leq i \leq t$,
  $MS_i^F = \langle MSStartDate_i, MSEndDate_i, MSStartTime_i, MSEndTime_i,$
  $MSFreq_i, StoreLocation \rangle$ and $MSFreq_i \in \{ms, ss, mm, hh, dd, mm, yy\}$.
  $MSStartDate_i, MSEndDate_i, MSStartTime_i$ and $MSEndTime_i$ are start and end dates and times respectively at which monitoring schedule MS_i^F of a metric starts and ends. $MSFreq_i$ is the monitoring frequency which contains one of the value from the set $\{ms, ss, mm, hh, dd, mm, yy\}$ to represent monitoring of the metric every millisecond, second, minute, hour, day, month or year respectively. This flexible monitoring schedule technique allows to define the different monitoring schedules for different weekdays, for different months of the year or for a particular season to accommodate the dynamic requirements of cloud service monitoring. $StoreLocation$ contains the data storage location where the monitored value is stored.

2.4   Guarantees/Obligations

An SLA guarantee is an agreed commitment by a cloud service provider to maintain a certain service level. Guarantees are defined with respect to the agreed values of metrics in the SLOs. A guarantee has the following parameters:

- Guarantee ID ($GuaranteeID^\rho$) is a unique identifier
- Guarantee precondition ($GuaranteePrecondition^\rho$) is a combination of one or more boolean expressions (containing observed/calculated value(s) of the metric(s), variable(s) and/or constant(s) joined by boolean operators (AND, OR, NOT)

– Guarantee action $(GuranteeAction()^{\rho})$ is a function that performs predefined tasks (e.g. automatically logging of the specific information, changing $ServiceCurrentState_F$ or preparing a service claim document).

Obligations are also defined as guarantees with similar parameters as *guarantees*, i.e. $ObligationID^{\rho}$, $ObligationPrecondition^{\rho}$ and $ObligationAction()^{\rho}$. Obligations are different from guarantees in such a way that obligation may not depend on observed/calculated metric values but rather may depend on external conditions e.g. a cloud service user may be obliged to inform the cloud service provider two hours in advance if further resources are required compared to what is agreed in the SLA.

3   S3LACC Framework

S3LACC framework briefly gives an overview of the S3LACC's usage in a cloud environment. An overview of S3LACC framework is depicted in Fig. 3. Service requirements come from the CSU which starts a provider discovery process and may involve a broker/third party as a support service party. It is assumed that all CSPs for the same service have similar SLA templates. *SLA processing service* selects shortlisted CSPs, negotiation parameters are added to the SLA template and any qualitative metrics are transformed to their quantitative utility levels by *qualitative metric processor*. A custom negotiation strategy may also be embedded in the SLA as described in above sections. *Negotiation service* may involve a broker to mediate the negotiation process. Implementation and details of the negotiation process based on S3LACC is out of the scope of this paper and a state of the art negotiation strategy with implementation using S3LACC is presented in a separate paper. After negotiation process, agreed values from the SLA are communicated to the *monitoring service* component. *Monitoring service* reads real-time metric values from the specified locations on the specified time schedule. Variables are stored separately which contain up-to-date data values from different sources. Each variable contains a particular data value from a specific data source. These variable values are used as input in metric computation formula and also in condition expressions (e.g. in *GuaranteePrecondition* or in *ObligationPrecondition*). The *guarantees/obligations service* checks for service violations or obligations. An integration with external system is achieved through an integration service which transforms the SLA data to XML format.

4   Use Case

As a proof of concept, we transform a precise descriptive SLA of a cloud based customer relation management (CRM) service S1 (assumed) to the S3LACC based SLA. Let's consider the following scenario for the service S1:

A company ABC has its offices throughout the country and requires S1 to be used by its employees (S1 users). ABC requires that S1 should have availability

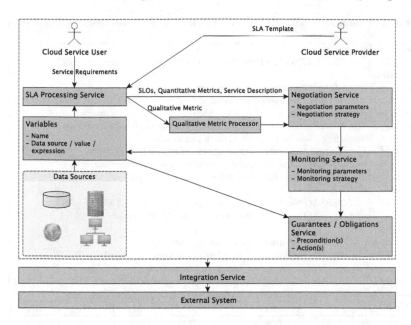

Fig. 3. An overview S3LACC framework.

from 95% to 100%. S1 may have 2 to 6 outages per month with maximum duration of 10 min per outage. The S1 users should be authenticated using one of the protocols {TACACS+, RADIUS, DIAMETER, Kerberos, OpenID}, arranged in ascending order of priority. S1 users should be authenticated within 5 seconds after submitting the login information. The cloud service providers CSP1 and CSP2 offer S1. ABC receives SLA template from CSP1 and CSP2, adds negotiation parameters according to its objectives and starts an automated negotiation process with the CSP1 and CSP2. An agreement is made with the CSP1 after negotiation process. According to the final SLA, the following terms are agreed. If monthly availability of the S1 is less than 96% then CSP1 will reimburse 20% of the monthly service cost. S1 may have upto 5 outages per month with maximum duration of 5 min per outage. ABC is responsible to provide logged information of service unavailability (date, time, duration). If average user login time is more than 3 seconds then CSP1 is liable to reimburse 7% of the monthly service cost. ABC is responsible to inform CSP1, one day in advance if ABC wants payment of the S1 to be delayed.

Above SLA description is transformed to the S3LACC based SLA as shown in Table 1. Due to space limitation, only relevant SLA parts of the S3LACC are included in this description. SLO_1 (*Availability*) contains three metrics (with metric IDs M_1, M_2 and M_3) and SLO_2 (*Authentication*) contains two metrics (a qualitative metric M_4 and a quantitative metric M_5). Assumed negotiation and agreement parameters are described for each metric in a nested table for illustration. The metric parameter $Weight^N$ is set by the ABC according to its

Table 1. Example of S3LACC based SLA for the scenario described in Sect. 4.

Service description:
$SLAName^T = S1\_SLA$, $ServiceProvider^T = CSP1$, $ServiceUser^N = ABC$
Variables:
var $x_1 = PlannedDowntime = 5 \times 5 = 25mins$
var $x_2 = TotalServiceTimeAgreed$ =<Total agreed service time in the month>
var $x_3 = ActualAvailability$ = <Monitored value>
var $x_4[\ ] = DurationPerOutageInTheMonth$ =<Array of outage durations>
var $x_5 = MonthlyServiceCost = x_3 \times$ <price per unit>
var $x_6[\ ] = UserAuthenticationTimes$ =<Array of monitored values>
var $x_7 = MonthlyLoginRequests$ =<total number of login requests>
var $x_8 = AccountBalance$ =<External value from accounting system>
SLOs:
$SLOID^T = SLO_1$, $SLOName^T = Availability$, $M_s^T(SLO_1) = \{M_1, M_2, M_3\}$
$SLOID^T = SLO_3$, $SLOName^T = Authentication$, $M_s^T(SLO_3) = \{M_4, M_5\}$
Metrics:
$MetricID^T = M_1$, $MetricName^T$ =Availability percentage
$MetricID^T = M_2$, $MetricName^T$ = Number of outages per month
$MetricID^T = M_3$, $MetricName^T$ = Duration per outage
$MetricID^T = M_4$, $MetricName^T$ = Authentication protocol
$MetricID^T = M_5$, $MetricName^T$ = Average authentication time per user

$MetricID^T$	M_1	M_2	M_3	M_4	M_5
$IsNegotiable^N$	true	true	true	true	true
$IsMandatory^N$	true	true	true	true	true
$Weight^N$	0.40	0.15	0.15	0.15	0.15
$AcceptableValue^N$	95%	6	10 mins	TACACS+	5 sec
$DesiredValue^N$	100%	2	1 min	OpenID	1 sec
$AgreedValue^F$	96%	5	6 mins	OpenID	3 sec
$Deadline^N$	20	4	10	5	5
CV_s^N	$\{\langle 0.001, 15\rangle, \langle 0.007, 20\rangle\}$	$\{\langle 1, 4\rangle\}$	$\{\langle 1, 10\rangle\}$	$\{\langle 1, 5\rangle\}$	$\{\langle 1, 5\rangle\}$
$Computation\ Formula^F$	$\dfrac{x_3 + x_1}{x_2} \times 100$	$Length(x_4)$	x_4	None	$\dfrac{Sum(x_6)}{x_7}$

Guarantees:
$GuaranteeID^F = G_1$, $GuaranteePrecondition^F = M_1 < 96\%$
- $GuaranteeAction()^F\{$
      var $ClaimAmount = 0.2 \times x_5$;
      Send claim to CSP1 of $ClaimAmount$;
      Send logged information to CSP1 for monthly service unavailability;
$\}$
$GuaranteeID^F = G_2$, $GuaranteePrecondition^F = M_5 > 3$ seconds
- $GuaranteeAction()^F\{$
      var $ClaimAmount = 0.07 \times x_5$;
      Send claim to CSP1 of $ClaimAmount$;
$\}$

Obligations:
$ObligationID^F = O_1$,
- $ObligationPrecondition^F = x_8 <$ reserve amount AND bill is due tomorrow
- $ObligationAction()^F\{$
      Inform CSP1 about delay in payment
$\}$

priority (supposed) for each metric. The negotiation process for M_4 starts from highest priority authentication protocol (i.e. $OpenID$) and if not accepted by a CSP then a lower priority protocol is suggested in next round. CV_s^N represents the list of tuples containing concession value up to a specific deadline during the negotiation process, e.g. $\{\langle 0.001, 15\rangle, \langle 0.007, 20\rangle\}$ for M_1 indicates that 0.1% concession is given on initial preferred value of 100% until 15 rounds of the negotiation process. From 16th round and until 20th round, 0.7% concession is offered. Variables (containing values of different sources) are used in computation formulae of some metrics.

5   Related Work and Analysis

Different languages and specifications have been proposed to represent an SLA in a machine readable format e.g. Web SLA (WSLA) Framework [5], SLAng for defining SLAs in IT services [8,9], Web Services Agreement (WS-Agreement) specification [1], SLA* as part of SLA@SOI project [4], CSLA (Cloud Service Level Agreement) language [7] and a formal language SLAC for SLAs in cloud computing [11]. However, as discussed by SLAC authors [11], most of these specifications are not defined specifically for the cloud services and do not fulfill specific requirements of SLAs for the cloud services e.g. scenarios involving a broker during negotiation process [11]. In [11] a comparison of different SLA specification models and languages with respect to different features such as cloud domain, multi-party, broker support, business metrics, price schemes, syntax, semantics, verification, evaluation and open-source. S3LACC includes all of these features except verification. Apart from these features, the S3LACC extends the SLA specification with additional capabilities such as a common template for the CSU and the CSP, static/dynamic negotiation support in the SLA and automated monitoring facilitation. Moreover, S3LACC is designed according to the latest available cloud SLA standards and definitions to support the complete SLA life cycle rather than its isolated phases. All information of the complete SLA life cycle is efficiently bundled in a single SLA. The quantitative and qualitative SLA parameters are possible to be grouped in a single SLO using S3LACC. Another closer approach is presented by Stamou *et al.* [10] which describes SLAs for data services as a directed graph to represent dependencies in SLA data management flow. The SLA directed graph model by Stamou *et al.* is based on WSLA Framework. The structure defined as the graph model in [10] is different from the S3LACC structure, i.e. an *SLO* and a *service object* are different entities in their model. According to [10], a *service object* contains SLA parameters like *transaction time* or *average execution time*, whereas, *SLOs* define limits for these SLA parameters through guarantees or obligations. Kotsokalis *et al.* [6] model SLAs for service computing as binary decision diagrams (BDDs) to automate the SLA negotiation, subcontracting, optimizing the utility and SLA management. An SLA in [6] is defined in terms of *facts*, *conditions* and *clauses* which evaluate to *true* or false, hence an SLA is represented as a boolean function. This boolean function is represented as BDD to eliminate redundancies.

However, as discussed in the [6], the proper recognition of *facts* requires additional attention.

6 Conclusions and Future Work

In this paper, we have proposed a specification for SLAs in cloud computing (S3LACC) with a good trade-off between complexity and expressiveness. Our specification targets specific requirements of cloud domain such as complex dependencies among different metrics and composition of different metrics in one SLO (through metric lists). Current approaches lack standardized structure definition according to international standards for the cloud computing SLAs. Also, support for automation of the complete SLA life cycle is generally ignored in most of the SLA specification languages and models. S3LACC meets all of these requirements by defining an intuitive SLA structure which can be used to implement almost all types of negotiation strategies and monitoring policies for an automated SLA life cycle. Also, renegotiations in case of QoS violations and automated recycling of the SLA is possible using S3LACC. Qualitative parameters are an important part of the cloud SLAs which are easily definable using S3LACC. Future work includes definition and implementation of an automated negotiation strategy using S3LACC, automated monitoring service utilizing S3LACC based SLAs and an automated management environment to complete the automated life cycle for the SLAs in cloud computing.

References

1. Andrieux, A., Czajkowski, K., Dan, A., Keahey, K., Ludwig, H., Nakata, T., Pruyne, J., Rofrano, J., Tuecke, S., Xu, M.: Web services agreement specification (Ws-Agreement). In: Open Grid Forum, vol. 128, p. 216 (2007)
2. Frey, S., Reich, C., Lüthje, C.: Key performance indicators for cloud computing SLAs. In: The Fifth International Conference on Emerging Network Intelligence, pp. 60–64, September 2013
3. Ghumman, W.A.: Automation of the SLA life cycle in cloud computing. In: Lomuscio, A.R., Nepal, S., Patrizi, F., Benatallah, B., Brandić, I. (eds.) ICSOC 2013. LNCS, vol. 8377, pp. 557–562. Springer, Cham (2014). doi:10.1007/978-3-319-06859-6_51
4. Kearney, K.T., Torelli, F., Kotsokalis, C.: SLA*: an abstract syntax for service level agreements. In: 11th IEEE/ACM International Conference on Grid Computing, pp. 217–224, October 2010
5. Keller, A., Ludwig, H.: The WSLA framework: specifying and monitoring service level agreements for web services. J. Netw. Syst. Manage. **11**(1), 57–81 (2003)
6. Kotsokalis, C., Yahyapour, R., Rojas Gonzalez, M.A.: Modeling service level agreements with binary decision diagrams. In: Baresi, L., Chi, C.-H., Suzuki, J. (eds.) ICSOC/ServiceWave -2009. LNCS, vol. 5900, pp. 190–204. Springer, Heidelberg (2009). doi:10.1007/978-3-642-10383-4_13
7. Kouki, Y., De Oliveira, F.A., Dupont, S., Ledoux, T.: A language support for cloud elasticity management. In: 14th IEEE/ACM International Symposium on Cluster, Cloud and Grid Computing, pp. 206–215, May 2014

8. Lamanna, D.D., Skene, J., Emmerich, W.: SLAng: a language for defining service level agreements. In: The Ninth IEEE Workshop on Future Trends of Distributed Computing Systems, pp. 100–106, May 2003
9. Skene, J., Lamanna, D.D., Emmerich, W.: Precise service level agreements. In: 26th International Conference on Software Engineering, pp. 179–188, May 2004
10. Stamou, K., Kantere, V., Morin, J.H., Georgiou, M.: A SLA graph model for data services. In: Proceedings of the Fifth International Workshop on Cloud Data Management, pp. 27–34, October 2013
11. Uriarte, R.B., Tiezzi, F., Nicola, R.D.: SLAC: a formal service-level-agreement language for cloud computing. In: Proceedings of the IEEE/ACM 7th International Conference on Utility and Cloud Computing, pp. 419–426, December 2014
12. Wu, L., Buyya, R.: Service level agreement (SLA) in utility computing systems. In: Performance and Dependability in Service Computing: Concepts, Techniques and Research Directions. IGI Global, pp. 1–25, July 2011

Load Balancing in In-Memory Key-Value Stores for Response Time Minimization

Antonios Makris$^{(\boxtimes)}$, Konstantinos Tserpes,
and Dimosthenis Anagnostopoulos

Department of Informatics and Telematics,
Harokopio University of Athens, Athens, Greece
{amakris, tserpes, dimosthe}@hua.gr

Abstract. In-memory key-value stores (IMKVS) have now turned into a mainstream technology in order to meet with demanding temporal application requirements under heavy loads. This work examines the factors that affect the load distribution in IMKVS clusters as well as migration policies that cure the problem of unbalanced loads as a means to provide response time guarantees. Experiments are conducted in a Redis deployment under various settings. The results show that the key distribution and key length are contributing factors to the load balancing problem and impact the cluster's response times. On the contrary, key popularity and query volume seem to have minor or no effect at all.

Keywords: Distributed storage · In-Memory · Stores · Load balancing · Query response time

1 Introduction

Data centers have become a critical component in enterprise systems as web services and cloud computing continue their massive growth. For example, Facebook reported having 936 million daily active users in the first quarter of 2015 and a detailed request trace from Facebook's servers in 2012, reported an average of 54 thousand requests per second [1]. Meeting hard application constraints (e.g. temporal) under these circumstances puts an enormous strain on the capabilities and limits of enterprise systems, especially in coping with the immense rate of queries in the persistence layer.

To cope with these ever-growing application requirements, the data management layer must decouple itself from the many, heavy disk IOs and add a faster persistence layer in between. This approach is implemented with in-memory storage mechanisms which maintain data views in the form of key-value pairs and respond to queries in near-real time even under heavy loads. Two of the most popular in-memory key value stores (IMKVS) are Redis and Memcached. These key-value stores are commonly used as a caching layer between a front-end web server and a backend database and the goal is to keep the most frequently accessed data in this cache so that it can be served directly from main memory.

However IMKVS suffer inherently (as any distributed system) from the problem of the uneven load distribution among the underlying nodes. The load balancing problem refers to the identification of a utility function that expresses the distribution of keys in

© Springer International Publishing AG 2017
J.Á. Bañares et al. (Eds.): GECON 2016, LNCS 10382, pp. 62–73, 2017.
DOI: 10.1007/978-3-319-61920-0_5

the IMKVS nodes and minimizes the average response times to queries or maximizes the average resource utilization or both (in which case it equals to a maximization of the throughput). The latter is in fact more realistic as intuitively there is an implicit relationship between utilization and response time, if we disregard factors external to the IMKVS such as network latency, etc.

Focusing on the intrinsic factors that affect the balanced load distribution we conclusion that a proper investigation of the problem requires the examination of at least three factors: the frequency and volume of incoming queries and the way the keys are distributed in the system. These factors are often considered in isolation in the various implementations mainly because the mitigation policy can be complex and includes a combination of operations such as migration and replication.

This work aims at validating and identifying the actual contributing factors to the load balancing problem, i.e. the metrics that are needed to be monitored in order to better distribute the load among the IMKVS nodes. A prototype deployment of the Redis IMKVS is employed and the response times in "get" queries are monitored as an indication of uneven load distribution. Multiple load configurations are tested based on the three abovementioned factors. A fourth potential factor, the key length, is also examined under the intuition that it might infuse an overhead in the hash function when the keys are distributed using a consistent hashing approach among the nodes. Finally, the paper presents a key distribution load balancing policy based on migration and discusses the results.

The document is structured as such: Sect. 2 provides details about the related work in load balancing in IMKVS presenting representative solutions from each factor class; Sect. 3 provides the details of the experimental approach and the assumptions made; Sect. 4 gives a full account of the experimental results while Sect. 5 presents the final conclusions and future work.

2 Related Work

According to the above existing load balancing mechanisms in IMKVS can be examined under three lenses if we only consider the intrinsic factors of uneven load distribution:

1. load balancing based on key popularity: The frequency that specific items are invoked seems to be related to the performance of the IMKVS node and system.
2. load balancing based on key distribution: In many systems the distribution of the keys in the available nodes are inherently posing a load balancing challenge. The examination of the problem in isolation from the previous as well as from the capabilities of the underlying nodes can be risky, however it is far more simple in terms of implementation, even though based on mere statistics.
3. load balancing based on query volume: The amount of keys requested concurrently from a IMKVS deployment and consequently from a node seems to be a metric of interest in some load balancing deployments.

In what follows we provide a brief account of existing tools that tackle the problem of load balancing under each of the abovementioned prisms.

2.1 Load Balancing Based on Key Distribution

Most of Redis and Memcached's Application Programming Interface (API) clients use a technique called consistent hashing (CH). According to CH the available keys are uniformly distributed among the servers. This has been used successfully in several kinds of applications, like caching and storage. Although CH is a very efficient technique, it is prone to unbalanced loads in a production network, causing hot spots, since it does not consider any environmental aspects nor object's characteristics, like size, link congestion or object's popularity [2].

To improve the performance of in-memory key value stores cache, the two-phase load balancing mechanism is used. This solution consists of two phases: the First-Phase Load Balancer that can operate with distinct load balancing algorithms and the Second-Phase Load Balancer that is a specialized cache that implements traffic management and replicates frequently used data items. This load balancer can be deployed on unstructured networks aiming at the replacement of the consistent hashing algorithm [2].

2.2 Load Balancing Based on Key Popularity

One more method to ensure load balancing, is by using a popularity-based small front-end cache, which directly serves a very small number of popular items in front of primary servers ("back-end nodes"), in cluster architectures. This application cache is small enough to fit in the L3 cache of a fast CPU, enabling a high-speed and efficient implementation compatible with front-end load balancers and packet processors. The cache serves the most popular items without querying the back-end nodes, ensuring that the load across the back-end nodes is more uniform and need to store only O(n log n) where n is the total number of back-end nodes entries, to provide good load balance. As an example, a key-value storage system with 100 nodes using 1 KiB entries can be serviced using 4 megabytes of fast CPU cache memory, regardless of the query distribution that it must handle leads to a cluster that use large numbers of slower, but more energy- and cost-efficient nodes to provide massive storage and high overall throughput. As a result these kind of cluster can serve high query rate with all of their code and data in the CPU cache [4].

2.3 Load Balancing Based on Query Volume

Another data rebalancing mechanism called Citrusleaf ensures that query volume is distributed evenly across all nodes, and is robust in the event of node failure happening during rebalancing itself. Rebalancing does not impact cluster behavior because the system is designed to be continuously available. The transaction algorithms are integrated with the data distribution system, and there is only one consensus vote to coordinate a cluster change. Thus, there is only a short period when the cluster internal redirection mechanisms are used while clients discover the new cluster configuration. This mechanism optimizes transactional simplicity in a scalable shared-nothing environment while maintaining ACID characteristics. Also Citrusleaf allows the configuration options to specify how much available operating overhead should be used for administrative tasks like rebalancing data between nodes as compared to running client transactions. Finally, one of the advantages is that the system can rebalance data on the fly while using real-time prioritization techniques to balance short running transactions with several classes of long running tasks [6]. Also SRDS (Service Resource Discovery System) is a system that provides scalable and configurable query support over platform by combining different P2P approaches [9].

Searching non-textual data is challenging, because of the big volumes of mixed multimedia data and the distribution of them among multiple nodes. The authors propose a system called MRoute that supports similarity search for content-based retrieval and combines the Routing Index with the Similarity Search on the Metric Spaces Approach. The system uses a P2P indexing structure. Each node (peer) stores and indexes its object and a table for every neighbor. The complex queries are easily supported while the similarity-based search exploits objects characterized by a metric space. This system offers a better scalability and the client queries are well-balanced over the network [10].

2.4 Adaptable Load Balancing Approaches

Another research output is the DBalancer, a generic distributed module that performs fast and cost-efficient load balancing on top of a NoSQL data store. The load balancing is performed by message exchanges. More specifically, the DBalancer component runs in every data store's node executing the desired load balancing algorithm. It then exchanges messages in order to find balancing partners, co-ordinate the balancing procedure and collect load information. When the appropriate nodes have been found and reserved, it utilizes the data-store's specific implementations to exchange keys and fix routing table information between balancing partners [5].

2.5 External Factors Affecting Load Balancing Based on Key Popularity

A method to do rapid load balancing of key-value stores is the Network-Assisted Lookups (NAL) which exploits the existing IP infrastructure. This method involves a distributed caching method based on dynamic IP address assignment. Keys are mapped to a large IP address space statically and each node is dynamically assigned multiple IP addresses. This leads to a system with minimal need for central coordination (no single point of failure). Instead of having fixed network service identifiers attached to data nodes and have these identifiers updated at the lookup service, whenever the location of a data block is changed due to migration, NAL employs a static key-to-location mapping created once and for all at key hash generation time and provides for accurate lookup of arbitrarily migrated data blocks by updating the network identity of the actual location of a block [3].

The load-balancing algorithm of the NAL approach works as follows: (a) at the beginning of each load-balancing iteration, the algorithm reads the eviction rates of all cache servers and computes the average eviction rate across the system, (b) no load-balancing action is taken in case no outlier is identified, (c) the algorithm enters the core of its load-balancing logic towards deciding the list of block sets (sets of key-value stores) that are to be migrated from the most overloaded to the least loaded server, (d) the choice of the destination server depends on the state of the caches, (e) the algorithm picks the block sets with the lowest number of requests per second, thus keeping the hot blocks at the overloaded data server and (f) the number of block sets to migrate is driven by the parameter N (normalization factor for deciding popularity of blocks to be migrated) [3].

3   Approach

In our approach we employed the Redis IMKVS to implement a prototype and conduct experiments mainly due to its simple architecture and adaptability in "plugging in" load balancing policies.

Redis is an in-memory data structure store that can be used as database, cache and message broker. The Redis Cluster is a distributed implementation of Redis and aims to provide high performance and scalability, availability through partition tolerance and acceptable degree of consistency.

The nodes in Redis Cluster are responsible for holding the data, capturing the state of the cluster and mapping keys to the right nodes. The nodes in the cluster are connected through a service channel using a TCP bus and a binary protocol, called the Redis Cluster Bus. To exchange and propagate information about the cluster, nodes use a gossip protocol in order to auto-discover new or other nodes, to send ping-pong packets, to detect working or non-working nodes, to send cluster messages needed to signal specific conditions and to promote slave nodes to master when needed in order to continue to operate when a failure occurs [7]. Figure 1 represents an instance of the communication between nodes themselves as well as with the clients.

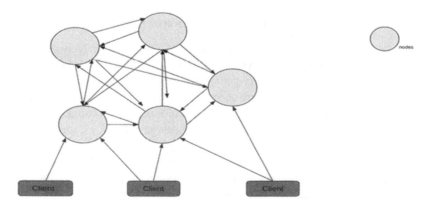

Fig. 1. Connection between nodes and client communication with them.

Cluster nodes are not able to proxy requests, thus clients redirect and talk to other nodes guided through redirection errors based on ASCII protocols. Thus, the client may be ignorant of the cluster state and employ the redirection property to reach any key.

However the performance can be improved by caching the map between keys and nodes. Instead of client redirection in the node that holds the key in every read, the client is able to hold persistent connections with many nodes (using cluster hints from nodes), cache node info (hash slot), and update his table that contains the information about the slots configuration. Clients usually need to fetch a complete list of hash "slots" and mapped node addresses at startup in order to populate the initial slots configuration. The same thing may happen when a 'MOVED' redirection notification is received [7].

According to the Redis Official Documentation, there is currently no way to rebalance automatically the cluster by checking the distribution of keys across the cluster nodes and intelligently moving slots as needed [8]. To tackle this issue, we devised an algorithm that adaptively rebalances the keys between the Redis cluster master nodes based on certain real-time measurements that trigger the migration policy for balancing the nodes' load.

3.1   IMKVS Infrastructure Setup

Initially, we installed Redis-3.0.4 version and for the needs of our experiments, we implemented a Redis cluster with 6 nodes. Three nodes were employed as masters and for each master we assigned a single slave (used mainly for fault tolerance purposes). Redis Cluster does not provide strong consistency, but has a different form of sharding where every key is part of a hash slot. In Redis there are by default 16384 hash slots. We followed the recommended reshard plan and thus, each master node was assigned an equal number of hash slots.

- Master One (M1) - allocated hash slots 0-5460
- Slave One (S1) replicates Master One, is promoted if a quorum of nodes cannot reach M1
- Master Two (M2) - allocated hash slots 5461-10922
- Slave Two (S2) - replicates Master Two, is promoted if a quorum of nodes cannot reach M2
- Master Three (M3) - allocated hash slots 10923 - 16383
- Slave Three (S3) - replicates Master Three, is promoted if a quorum of nodes cannot reach M3

Both master and slave nodes run two TCP services, the first is for normal RESP messages and the second is Cluster Bus that communicates with the Redis Cluster Gossip protocol as shown in Fig. 2.

The last step was to load keys in master nodes dissimilarly, aiming to test our algorithm.

3.2   Key Distribution Load Balancing Algorithm

Initially, we implemented a function named reshard_keys inside redis-trib.rb. In general redis-trib.rb constitutes a cluster manager program and contains all the functions

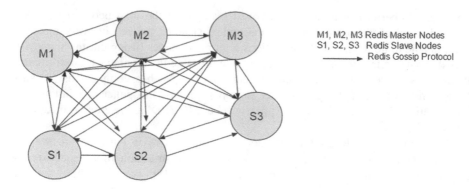

Fig. 2. Redis cluster configuration.

for the management of the cluster such as the initializer, the resharding of the hash slots, the messages between nodes, consistency checking etc. The existing support of resharding allows the user to reshard hash slots from one node to another but without the knowledge of whether there are actual keys in these hash slots. So, there is a need to create a function that moves the actual keys to the existing node to allow rebalancing. The function `reshard_keys` can be called at any point it is required by the client for load balancing the distribution of keys in cluster but the key-idea is that it runs in fixed time intervals monitoring the distribution of the keys to all master nodes.

The steps of the algorithm are as follows:

1. Find the crowd of masters
2. Obtain the total number of keys they hold
3. For each master node store the hostname, port and number of keys
4. Calculate the keys that each master must hold so that the distribution of keys to be balanced (total keys of cluster/ number of masters)
5. Find which master nodes must take or give keys and the total amount of keys that they must give/take
6. Characterize masters as source or target nodes depending on whether they are receiving or giving away keys respectively
7. Start migrating from source node to target nodes, first the hashslots and then the relevant keys and iterate until all the masters have the same amount of keys

With this implementation we achieve to balance the load of the cluster, by redistributing the keys in the master nodes. Note, that this process is performed as a background process not affecting the cluster's read/write operations. This is possible as every node knows what slots are served and what keys are held for all the nodes in the cluster therefore any change is propagated in the cluster almost in real time.

4 Experiments

The aim of the experiments was to investigate the impact of the three well-studied factors (key distribution, key popularity and query volume) to the way that the load is balanced among the nodes of a IMKVS cluster. The impact itself is measured in terms of response times to "get" queries that are generated based on the particular factor that is needed to test. Furthermore, is being tested two extrinsic factors: (a) the length of the keys and how this affects the response time, based on the intuition that the calculations that the hash function is conducting may contribute to lower response times, and (b) the volume of the values for the requested keys.

Finally, the migration policy for a uniform key distribution based on the algorithm presented in Sect. 3 was also tested.

The underlying computing infrastructure was a commodity machine with the following configuration:

- Ubuntu 14.04 LTS 64-bit
- Intel® Core™ i5-4570 CPU @ 3.20 GHz × 4
- 7,7 GiB RAM

The 3 + 3 nodes' cluster described in Sect. 3 was set up in this PC using virtualized nodes.

In the first experiment, our aim was to observe how response time (RT) changed according to the number of keys in a node, in different numbers of concurrent calls. For this experiment we created a python script that fires concurrent read calls for one particular key and calculates the RT. Three setups with 33000, 16000 and 1 keys in a node were employed and for each setup, we generated 1000, 100 and 1 concurrent client calls. The results are represented in Fig. 3.

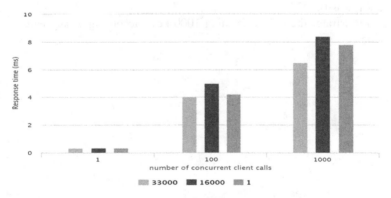

Fig. 3. Average response time to fetch one particular key for 33000 (blue), 16000 (black) and 1 (green) keys under concurrent client calls (1, 100, 1000). (Color figure online)

We observed that the RT to get one particular key hardly changed, as the number of keys changed in the node. For example the RT remained about the same in 100 concurrent client calls, for a different amount of keys loaded in the node. Furthermore, the RT was affected by the different number of client calls. Specifically, the RT increased as the number of client calls was increasing.

In our second experiment, our aim was to observe how RT changed according to the key length. We created a JavaScript script that reads all keys and calculates the RT. For the purposes of our experiment, we loaded 1000, 5000 and 10000 keys in node. The results are represented in Fig. 4.

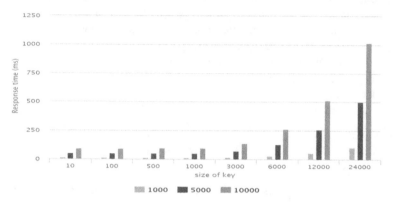

Fig. 4. Average response time considering key size (number of characters) for 10000 (green), 5000 (black) and 1000 (blue) keys. (Color figure online)

We observed that the RT grew rapidly, with an increased length of the key. In detail, for a node with 10000 keys and size of key 10, the RT was 91,7 ms and for the same node and key length 24000, the RT was 1014,3 ms. Furthermore, to retrieve one single key with size 10 the RT was 0.0127 and to retrieve one single key with size 24000 the RT was 0,102.

Figure 5 illustrates the RT for fetching 1000 keys according to key length for one specific node.

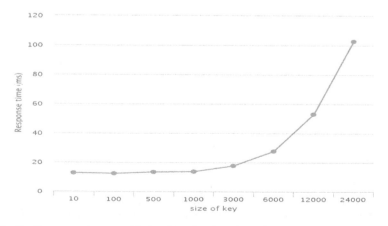

Fig. 5. Response time considering key size (number of characters) for 1000 keys.

Also, we made one more experiment to observe how RT was changed according to the value length this time. We created a JavaScript script, that reads all keys and calculates the RT. The results are represented in Fig. 6.

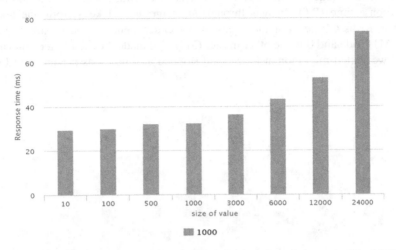

Fig. 6. Average response time considering value size (number of characters) for 1000 keys.

We observed that the difference of response times between the volumes of the values is insignificant and thus we concluded that value size does not affect RT.

In the third experiment, our aim was to observe how response time (RT) changed according to the number of keys in the node, in different numbers of concurrent calls. For this experiment we created a python script that reads all the keys at once and calculates the RT. We loaded 33000, 16000 and 1 keys in node and for each one of the above values, we made 1 and 4 concurrent client calls. The results are represented in Fig. 7 below.

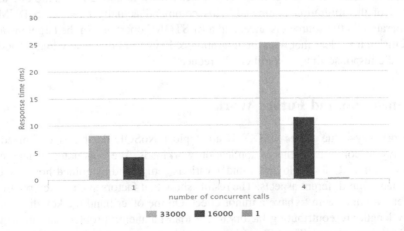

Fig. 7. Average response time to fetch all keys for 33000 (blue), 16000 (black) and 1 (green) keys under concurrent client calls (1, 4). (Color figure online)

The RT is about 3 times larger in the case of four calls. Thus, the growth rate of RT is proportional the number of client calls.

The experiments demonstrate that the distribution of the keys plays an important role in the load balancing factor. Thus, in our last experiment our aim was to observe how response time (RT) changes through the migration of keys from one node to another in Redis Cluster. For the needs of our experiment we loaded 33000 in one master (M1) node and 0 in the other master (M2). We made 4 concurrent client calls in M1 and we started migration at time 7 and stopped at time 36 as presented in Fig. 8.

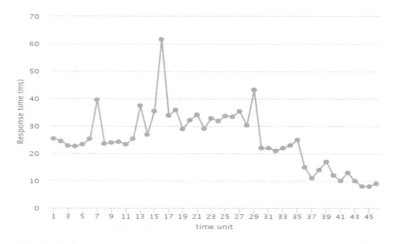

Fig. 8. Response time in time unit by migration of keys from M1 to M2.

We observed that the RT for 4 concurrent client calls averaged a 25 ms. In the beginning of the migration process the response times present a sudden increase while at the end of the process we notice a reduction in the order of magnitude of 9 ms. This improvement indicates a 3x speedup. The spikes shown in above Fig. 8 are due to the overhead of the migration command. This command actually executes a DUMP + DEL operation in the source instance, and a RESTORE operation in the target instance. In conclusion it is clear that with the migration of keys from one heavy loaded node to another the response time is significantly reduced.

5   Conclusion and Future Work

In-memory key-value stores (IMKVS) are typical NoSQL databases optimized for read-heavy or compute-intensive application workloads. We conducted a number of experiments in a Redis deployment under various setups and examined how response time varies given different aspects. The results show that factors such as key popularity and query volume seem to have a minor effect. On the other hand the key distribution and key length are contributing factors to the load balancing problem and impact the cluster's response times. The RT can be reduced by migrating the keys from one node to another, in such way that each node in the cluster has the same number of keys.

Our future plans include the creation of a mechanism for dynamic load balancing in a Redis Cluster in a dynamic context. This mechanism will be able to rebalance the cluster according to the number of keys changed over time. Eventually we will achieve the optimization of the read operations in the system in terms of RT. Also we intend to execute the migration experiment between nodes that are located in different servers and compare the results with the current implementation that comprises of a single PC with multiple virtual machines.

References

1. Facebook Company Info. http://newsroom.fb.com/company-info/
2. Trajano, A.F.R., Fernandez, M.P.: Two-phase load balancing of in-memory key-value storages using network functions virtualization (NFV). J. Netw. Comput. Appl. **69**, 1–13 (2016)
3. Cesaris, D., Katrinis, K., Kotoulas, S., Corradi, A.: Ultra-fast load balancing of distributed key-value stores through network-assisted lookups. In: Silva, F., Dutra, I., Santos Costa, V. (eds.) Euro-Par 2014. LNCS, vol. 8632, pp. 294–305. Springer, Cham (2014). doi:10.1007/978-3-319-09873-9_25
4. Fan, B., et al.: Small cache, big effect: provable load balancing for randomly partitioned cluster services. In: Proceedings of the 2nd ACM Symposium on Cloud Computing. ACM (2011)
5. Konstantinou, I., et al.: DBalancer: distributed load balancing for NoSQL data-stores. In: Proceedings of the 2013 ACM SIGMOD International Conference on Management of Data. ACM (2013)
6. Srinivasan, V., Bulkowski, B.: Citrusleaf: a real-time nosql db which preserves acid. Proc. VLDB Endow. **4**(12), 1340–1350 (2011)
7. Redis Cluster Specification. http://redis.io/topics/cluster-spec
8. Redis Cluster tutorial. http://redis.io/topics/cluster-tutorial
9. Carlini, E., et al.: Service and resource discovery supports over p2p overlays. In: 2009 International Conference on Ultra Modern Telecommunications & Workshops. IEEE (2009)
10. Gennaro, C., et al.: MRoute: a peer-to-peer routing index for similarity search in metric spaces. In: Proceedings of the 5th International Workshop on Databases, Information Systems and Peer-to-Peer Computing (DBISP2P 2007) (2007)

Fault-Tree-Based Service Availability Model in Cloud Environments: A Failure Trace Archive Approach

Alexandru Butoi[✉] and Gheorghe Cosmin Silaghi

Business Information Systems Department,
Faculty of Economics and Business Administration, Babes-Bolyai University,
Cluj-Napoca, Romania
{alexandru.butoi,gheorghe.silaghi}@econ.ubbcluj.ro

Abstract. In a cloud computing environment with capabilities such as live migration and elastic resource provisioning, with a mandatory request for critical availability of the service, our challenge consists in how to use basic fault tree analysis for assessing the health state of a node/service instance and perform load balancing in an autonomous manner. We propose a model that extracts event abstraction from the run-time logs, aiming to assess whether the primary service instance or its replica is reliable or unreliable. We employ replication or live migration processes to keep the service availability at an acceptable level. The model is a probabilistic one and is validated using the LANL HPC Failure Trace Archive (FTA) data set.

Keywords: Fault trees · Service availability · Cloud environments · Distributed computing · Failure trace · Archive

1 Introduction

This paper is a continuation of the previous work presented in [1,2]. The first one introduced the idea of using fault trees for autonomous tracing and assessment of the failures of virtual machines in cloud computing. The second paper used some XEN log traces to evaluate the model at the IaaS level with three differential modeled cases for error impacts. The current paper mainly provides an enhanced fault tree based reasoning model by introducing the scenario of event logs being dependent by the previously raised ones, tackling the problem of chained errors scenarios. Moreover we use real FTA LANL failure traces [3] as input for evaluation that changes the applicability context used by the previous publications, from infrastructure level to the service instance specific level. Compared with previous work, the paper brings the following contributions: (1) excludes the decaying error impact while simplifying and speeding the computation; (2) extends the previous fault model by taking into consideration the chained errors scenario in Sect. 3; (3) improves the computation of migration

© Springer International Publishing AG 2017
J.Á. Bañares et al. (Eds.): GECON 2016, LNCS 10382, pp. 74–86, 2017.
DOI: 10.1007/978-3-319-61920-0_6

and theoretical probabilistic indicators in Sect. 3; (4) introduces new methodology and event abstraction computation in Sect. 4; (5) the model is adapted and evaluated using Failure Trace Archive [4,5] in Sect. 5. The aim of the current work is to provide a dynamic model used to avoid and reduce the costs of penalties induced by the SLA breaches while minimizing the amount of replicated resources locked with the purpose of service unavailability avoidance, having a direct impact on associated costs.

2 Background

We consider a cloud specific distributed system such as virtual clusters, high performance systems (HPC), peer-to-peer (P2P) or grid, with a number of n nodes $N_1, N_2, ..., N_n$. Every node runs specific services in a distributed manner. The service instance node are deployed on a specific node N_i and requires specific amount of minimum resources of different types, mainly CPU's, RAM memory, Storage and Network Bandwidth. These services are delivered according to a Service Level Agreement (SLA) between the cloud provider and cloud consumer. The two essential properties of the cloud system model applicable for our problem are: (1) the availability of the service guaranteed by the SLA (known as minimum up time)- at service level, this can be expressed as a maximum accepted failure rate: for example if the guaranteed availability is 99% of the total running time, the maximum accepted failure rate is 1% of the total time running time; (2) the capacity of every service instance to be replicated or to migrate to another node at any time; the majority of cloud systems have this capacity due to elastic provisioning of resources in cloud computing, being a powerful fault tolerance mechanism for such systems. Replication and migration is used for assuring the service availability in these systems, by running a separate instance of the same service on a different node. In this case the main service running instance is further referred as *primary instance of the service*, while the replicated one is referred as *replicated instance of the service/migrated instance of the service*. If rs_1 is the replicated service instance of the s_1, rs_1 will require the same amount of resources as s_1.

3 The Enhanced Fault Tree Model

In a cloud computing environment that has all the properties and capabilities described above, if every node or service instance has a synchronized replica, the challenge is to use basic fault tree analysis for assessing the health state of a node and perform load balancing in an autonomous manner.

We build a fault tree for every service instance together with its replica. The computed probabilistic indicators of failure are constantly updated and recalculated every time an event is raised by the corresponding instance. At time t_i, the model considers four types of event logs raised in the system: (1) **run-time error events** which are raised by running service instances and describes a possible faulty state in the running process; (2) **run-time non-error events** raised by running service instances describing a (positive) non-faulty state in the running process; (3) **migration error events** raised by the migration process, describing a possible faulty state of the system which may result in an unsuccessful migration; (4) **migration non-error events** specific to the migration process, describing a (positive) non-faulty state of the migration capability of the system; The error type event abstractions are the input descriptors for a possible fault state of the instance, while the non-error event abstractions are the input descriptors for a healthy state of the source instance. Another relevant remark would be the fact that some events could be related or unrelated with each other.

The fault tree model. We further use the fault tree model depicted in Fig. 1 using the following assumptions about the entire distributed system: (1) every primary service instance has an identical state replica; (2) every primary service instance runs independently by other primary instances; (3) every instance has associated a fault tree built using the relationships of her with other replicas or migrated instances; (4) every running instance is subject of event logs produced by itself or by the underlying operating system or running environment; (5) every service instance is deployed on a virtual or physical node in the distributed system;

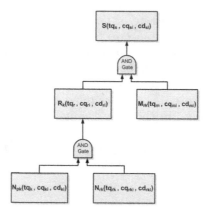

Fig. 1. Fault tree model of one replicated service instance which runs independent by others - source: [1].

The components of the fault tree presented in Fig. 1 have the same meaning as described in [1].

Every fault tree node in the tree is characterized by three probabilistic indicators that computes the probability of possible fault states at time t. The basic fault tree presented in Fig. 1 uses three probabilistic indicators to predict the faults of the corresponding instances. A basic requirement for the chosen probabilistic indicators is to be comparable and at least one of them to be designed to be used as benchmark. The gates for aggregation are AND gates, because replica and migrated instances are parallel running components of the system. The probabilistic indicators used in our model have the same definition as described in [1,2]: (1) tq_k is the theoretical fault probability of the fault node; (2) cq_{ki} is the computed independent fault probability of the fault node, after the event i was raised by the instance k; (3) cd_{ki} represents the computed dependent fault probability of the fault node after the event i was raised by the instance k; The main improvements introduced here are the introduction of dp indicator that tackles with the chained errors scenario, the migration probability computation and the theoretical probability computation. For a clear understanding of the model we present the entire enhanced model.

Computed fault probabilities cq **or** cd of a specific node are recomputed every time an event abstraction is raised by the corresponding service instance. In our fault tree model cq represents the cumulative fault probability of an instance to have a faulty state assuming that all instance related events are independent, while cd indicator represents the cumulative fault probability of an instance to crash, assuming that the instance-related events have dependency relations between each other. These indicators are computed as follows for every fault node in the tree:

1. If at time t_i an instance run-time error event $E_i(ip, dp)$ is raised by the instance k or by its replica r_k, inducing a probability ip computed with the independent events assumption and another dp probability computed with the dependent events assumption:

    I. update the cq and cd indicator of the corresponding fault node N_{pk} or N_{rk}:

$$cq_{k_i} = Min(Q_{SLA}, cq_{k_{i-1}} + ip); cd_{k_i} = Min(Q_{SLA}, cd_{k_{i\ 1}} + dp).$$

The Q_{SLA} is a constant between 0.9 and 1 referring to the maximum guaranteed service availability that can be specified in the SLA. For example if a service has a maximum guaranteed availability time of 99% the Q_{SLA} constant will be 0.99, if the maximum guaranteed up-time is 99.9% the Q_SLA will be 0.999. We can also treat this constant as a maximum agreed probability for the service not to fail: $\frac{TotalServiceAvailabilityTime}{TotalUsageTime} = \frac{99}{100} = 0.99$
This means that there is an acceptable probability for the service to not be available due to fault incidents: $\frac{TotalServiceUnavailabilityTime}{TotalUsageTime} = \frac{100-99}{100} = 0.01$

    II. recompute the cq_{r_i} and cd_{r_i} of the replication node R_k:

$$cq_{r_i} = cq_{k_i} \cdot cq_{r_{k_i}}; cd_{r_i} = cd_{k_i} \cdot cd_{r_{k_i}}$$

    III. recompute the cq_{s_i} and cd_{s_i} of the general failure node S:

$$cq_{s_i} = cq_{r_i} \cdot cq_{m_i}; cd_{s_i} = cd_{r_i} \cdot cd_{m_i}$$

2. If at time t_i an instance migration error event $E_i(ip, dp)$ is raised in the system, inducing a probability ip for the independent events assumption and another dp probability for the dependent events assumption for the migration process to fail:

   I. update the cq_{m_i} and cd_{m_i} indicators of migration node M_{r_k}:

   $$cq_{m_i} = Min(Q_{SLA}, cq_{m_{i-1}} + \frac{ip}{Rq}); cd_{m_i} = Min(Q_{SLA}, cd_{m_{i-1}} + \frac{dp}{Rq})$$

   where Rq is the probability of having enough resources to migrate at time t; in the case of the event of not having enough resources to migrate, the probability of fault will increase while the lack of available resources for the migration process will increase the chances of service unavailability.

   II. recompute the cq_{s_i} and cd_{s_i} of the general failure node S:

   $$cq_{s_i} = cq_{r_i} \cdot cq_{m_i}; cd_{s_i} = cd_{r_i} \cdot cd_{m_i}$$

3. If at time t_i an instance run-time non-error event $E_i(ip, dp)$ is raised by the instance k or by its replica r_k, with a probability ip in the case of independent events assumption and dp in the case of dependent events assumption:

   I. update the cq and cd indicators of the corresponding fault node N_{pk} or N_{rk}:
   $$cq_{k_i} = Max(0, cq_{k_{i-1}} - ip); cd_{k_i} = Max(0, cq_{k_{i-1}} - dp)$$

   II. recompute cq_{r_i} and cd_{r_i} of the replication node R_k:

   $$cq_{r_i} = cq_{k_i} \cdot cq_{r_{k_i}}; cd_{r_i} = cd_{k_i} \cdot cd_{r_{k_i}}$$

   III. recompute the cq_{s_i} and cd_{s_i} of the general failure node S:

   $$cq_{s_i} = cq_{r_i} \cdot cq_{m_i}; cd_{s_i} = cq_{r_i} \cdot cd_{m_i}$$

4. If at time t_i a migration non-error event $E_i(ip, dp)$ is raised in the system, with a probability ip in the case of independent events assumption and dp in the case of dependent events assumption:

   I. update the cq_{m_i} and cd_{m_i} indicators of migration node M_{r_k}:

   $$cq_{m_i} = Max(0, cq_{m_{i-1}} - \frac{ip}{Rq}); cd_{m_i} = Max(0, cd_{m_{i-1}} - \frac{dp}{Rq})$$

   where Rq is the probability of having enough resources to migrate
   II. recompute the cq_{s_i} of the general failure node S:

   $$cq_{s_i} = cq_{r_i} \cdot cq_{m_i}; cd_{s_i} = cd_{r_i} \cdot cd_{m_i}$$

The probability of having enough resources to migrate at time t, R_q is computed with the assumption of a unique and limited pool of resources from which every service can claim the required amount of resources. In the migration process, required resources can be of several types like CPU, RAM,

Storage, Bandwidth. Moreover, a required resource can be subject of a maximum linear increasing criteria ("as bigger the amount, as better") like CPU, RAM, Storage or a subject of minimum linear decreasing criteria ("as little as better") like latency or time for response. In this case, when $RAA(RT_i)$ stands for the "Required Amount of Resource Type i" and $TAA(RT_i)$ stands for the "Total Amount Available from Resource Type i", R_q can be computed as follows:

1. if the resource type is a linearly increasing one, $Rq_i(RT_i)$ is computed as follows:

$$Rq_i(RT_i) = \begin{cases} Q_{SLA} & \text{if } RA(RT_i) \leq TAA(RT_i) \\ \frac{RA(RT_i)}{TAA(RT_i)} & \text{if } RA(RT_i) > TAA(RT_i) \end{cases} \tag{1}$$

2. if the resource type is a linearly decreasing one, $Rq_i(RT_i)$ is computed as follows:

$$Rq_i(RT_i) = \begin{cases} Q_{SLA} & \text{if } TAA(RT_i) \leq RA(RT_i) \\ \frac{TAA(RT_i)}{RA(RT_i)} & \text{if } TAA(RT_i) > RA(RT_i) \end{cases} \tag{2}$$

A service instance will require more than one resource type to migrate defined as $RT_1, RT_2, ..., RT_k$. The probability for the event of having enough resources to migrate will be the probability of the independent events of having enough RT_1 resources AND RT_2 resources AND $..RT_i..$ AND RT_k resources: $Rq = \prod_{i=1,k} Rq_i$ where Rq is the probability of having enough required resources for every required type, in order to migrate to a new service instance. In our setup we calculate two probabilities for every raised event: the ip associated probability calculated with the assumptions that all previous events of the instance are independent by others and dp probability calculated with the assumption that previous events of the instance are dependent by each other.

Theoretical fault probability is computed once when the fault tree is built and initialized, and does not change during the entire life time of the fault tree. It is being used as a baseline in the process of decision making. The tq values for every computation nodes are the theoretical, context-free probabilities of the corresponding service instance to fail. The tq of the N_{pk} and N_{rk} nodes is: $tq = \frac{1}{ReplicationLevel}$, where the replication level represents how many possible replicas of the same service instance can be found at a certain moment in the system; in our fault tree model the replication level for tq values of the computation nodes is equal with 2, considering the primary instance and the replica. Following the fault tree aggregation rules of nodes N_{pk} and N_{rk} the theoretical fault probability of the R_k node will be: $tq_r = tq_k \cdot tq_{rk} = \frac{1}{ReplicationLevel^2}$, where R_k and M_k nodes are siblings aggregated at the general fault node level S and having the theoretical probability of fault equal to the accepted service disruption rate specified in the SLA. The accepted service disruption rate is computed as $1 - Q_{SLA}$, Q_{SLA} accordingly with SLA specification:

$$tq_s = tq_r \cdot tq_m = 1 - Q_{SLA},$$

Knowing the tq_s and tq_r, the theoretical probability of the migration node is computed indirectly:

$$tq_m = \frac{1 - Q_{SLA}}{tq_r} = \frac{1 - Q_{SLA}}{\frac{1}{ReplicationLevel^2}} = ReplicationLevel^2(1 - Q_{SLA})$$

The general fault probability of the system at the general fault node has to be lower than or equal with the accepted service disruption rate in order to avoid SLA breaches.

The decision model is the same as in previous work [1,2]: at time t_i, given a threshold fi, $0 < fi < 1$, fi is the percent or ratio of independent probability computed indicators in theoretical probability of a fault node, and fd, $0 < fd < 1$, fd is the percent or ratio of dependent probability computed indicators in theoretical probability of a fault node; if the computed probabilistic indicators are approaching the theoretical fault indicator within a fixed threshold the service instance might enter in a fault state and a replication or migration decision has to be made. The possible decisions taken by the fault agent are: (1) REPLICATED - the control has to be transferred to replica - taken based on primary instance corresponding node; (2) MIGRATED - the primary instance and its replica are unreliable - taken upon replication node; (3) OK - a computation node is in a reliable state; (4) REPLICATED to OK/MIGRATED to OK - when a service instance is becoming reliable again and can be reversed from its previous state (replicated/migrated) to its normal state; (5) SYSTEM UNRELIABLE - when replication and migration strategy has not succeeded, the service enters in an unreliable state - taken based on the general failure fault nodes;

4   Methodology and Experimental Setup

The Failure Trace Archive is a centralized and standardized repository which provides availability traces of some of the known distributed systems [4]. The tabbed format contains several columns like *platform, node, eventtrace, creator, eventtrace* and *eventstate* [5]. The most relevant columns used in our setup were the *node* indicator for identifying the instance, *eventstate* indicating an availability/unavailability state and *eventtrace* consisting of *eventstarttime* and *eventendtime* used to compute availability and unavailability times of the components for event abstractions. While currently the FTA does not provide a failure trace archive for a real cloud system, we used the FTA tabbed format for LANL High Performance Computer [3] as the HPC systems are similar to cloud systems used for intensive and long-time computation jobs.

Based on FTA archive we used distinct node topologies that have traces in the input tabbed file. For every node we parsed the associated event traces from the failure trace archive into the simulation framework, transforming them in event objects abstraction. All the output was saved in a delimited format file, which was further analyzed. We analyzed the fault probabilistic evolution for every type of fault node in the fault trees together with the fault agent decisions.

Every event has associated two probabilities of fault:

1. *EIP* - the probability of the independent event, calculated with the assumption that the corresponding event log took place independently by other events; At time t if the service state is unavailability, we consider the event as an error event: $EIP = \frac{TotalUnavailabilityTime}{TotalRunningTime}$. For all unavailability events raised before time t, $TotalUnavailabilityTime$ is: $TotalUnavailabilityTime = \sum(EventStopTime - EventStartTime)$. At time t if service is in an availability state, we have a non-error event: $EIP = \frac{TotalAvailabilityTime}{TotalRunningTime}$. For all availability events raised before time t, $TotalAvailabilityTime$ is: $TotalAvailabilityTime = \sum(EventStopTime - EventStartTime)$. In both cases the $TotalRunningTime$ is expressed as:

$$TotalRunningTime = \sum(EventStopTime - EventStartTime)$$

2. *EDP* - the probability of the dependent event, calculated with the assumption that the corresponding event log was influenced or triggered by other events. The EDP indicator is computed for those events that have the same type (error or non-error), are raised by the same node and all considered events are raised before the current event; At time t if service state is unavailability, we have an error event and: $EDP = \prod_{k=1}^{n} \frac{TotalUnavailabuility - TimeSpan(E_k)}{TotalRunningTime - TimeSpan(E_k)}$, where $TimeSpan(E_K)$ represents the time span of unavailability induced by the current event computed as: $TimeSpan(E_k) = EventStopTime(E_k) - EventStartTime(E_k)$. At time t if the service state is availability, we have an error event and: $EDP = \prod_{k=1}^{n} \frac{TotalAvailabuility - TimeSpan(E_k)}{TotalRunningTime - TimeSpan(E_k)}$ and $TimeSpan(E_k)$ represents the time span of availability induced by the current event: $TimeSpan(E_k) = EventStopTime(E_k) - EventStartTime(E_k)$

5   Experimental Results for LANL Traces

In this section we present a relevant experiment based on LANL high performance computing traces. We ran a sample of 500 experiments for the LANL failure trace dataset, provided by the Failure Trace Archive. We analyzed the structure of the event failure probabilities, the evolution of the primary node, replication node, migration node and general failure node probabilistic indicators. The plots in Fig. 2 presents the event associated fault probabilities computed for (a) the independent events assumption and for (b) the dependent events assumption. We observe that the distribution of these probabilities is a uniform one in the specific interval, with a strong variation for the event probabilities values. We also analyzed the evolution of fault probabilities of the replication at the primary service fault node level and at the replication fault node level in a given observation time span. Figure 3 depicts the evolution in time of the computed values for probabilistic indicators on computation nodes. The red line is the theoretical probability used as a benchmark. All the values that are bellow the red line, indicate that the node is in a reliable state, while all

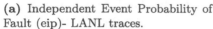

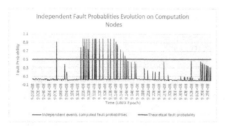

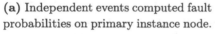

(a) Independent Event Probability of Fault (eip)- LANL traces.

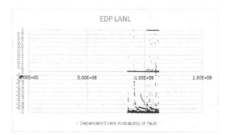

(b) Dependent Event Probability of Fault(edp) - LANL traces.

Fig. 2. Probabilistic event indicators for LANL sample.

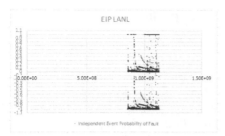

(a) Independent events computed fault probabilities on primary instance node.

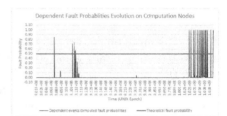

(b) Dependent events computed fault probabilities evolution on primary instance node.

Fig. 3. Computed probabilistic indicators evolution for the instance specific nodes.

the values which are in the proximity and above the red line indicate a possible state of fault. If at time t an event triggers the probabilistic indicators above the red limit in both (a) and (b) charts, the fault agent will trigger an unreliable state of the corresponding fault node. We can observe the "healing" effect of the non-error raised events, which lowers the computed probabilities of fault turning, the node state from UNRELIABLE to OK. Moreover, when both probability values are above the theoretical value, the fault agent takes the decision for REPLICATION.

The evolution of aggregated fault probabilistic indicators on replication node are depicted in Fig. 4. When the fault indicators in both cases are above the line, live migration strategy is needed, if the migration process is reliable and enough resources are available.

Figure 5 depicts the fault probabilistic indicators for migration indicating whether the migration is feasible or not. At the general fault node level, the replication and migration nodes are aggregated to assess the capacity of the system to maintain it's availability state after the replication and migration strategy were employed. The important thing here is timing: in order for the fault agent to decide the GENERAL FAILURE state, the four indicators of the

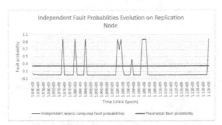

(a) Independent events computed fault probabilities evolution on replication node.

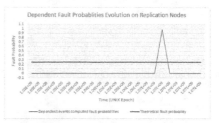

(b) Dependent events computed fault probabilities evolution on replication node.

Fig. 4. Computed probabilistic indicators on replication nodes.

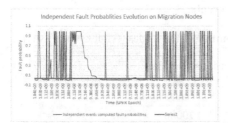

(a) Independent events computed fault probabilities evolution on migration node.

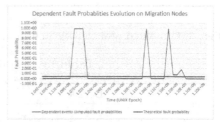

(b) Dependent events computed fault probabilities evolution on migration node.

Fig. 5. Computed probabilistic indicators on migration nodes.

migration and replication node has to be positive and higher enough for their aggregation product to be above or in the proximity of theoretical value (0.01 in this case) at the same moment of time t.

Figure 6 depicts the scatters of the computed indicators for replication node together with the migration node. We can observe that in sub-figure (a) we have 4 cases when migration and replication indicators are above the line, while in sub-figure (b) we have two similar cases. The agent declared the SYSTEM UNRELIABLE state in three cases (the ones marked with red), when the independent and dependent computed values are both above the line at the same moment. The fault agent decisions are summarized in Table 1.

Computing the unavailability of the system we have Total Running time = 179414800500 UNIX EPOCHS, Total DownTime = 16941060 UNIX EPOCHS and the unavailability percent is 0.01% obtaining 99.99% availability. If we used only the replication mechanism we would obtain a Total Down Time = 8484500500 UNIX and an unavailability percent of 4.72% resulting a 95.27% availability.

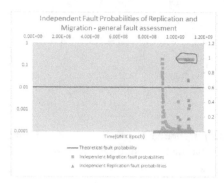
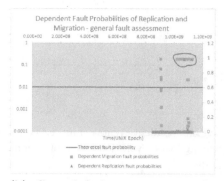

(a) General fault assessment at the general fault node level - independent events.

(b) General fault assessment at the general fault node level - dependent events.

Fig. 6. Computed probabilistic indicators on migration nodes. (Color figure online)

Table 1. Agent decisions overview.

Decision	Fault nodes
OK	79056
REPLICATED	605
REPLICATED to OK	291
MIGRATED	8
MIGRATED to OK	2
SYSTEM UNRELIABLE	3

6   Related Work

Literature offers many abstractions for describing the ability of a distributed system to cope with failures. In this paper, we describe the failure behavior of a fault tolerant system using fault tree models [6] which seems to be well fit to present the different levels of errors interdependence specific to distributed computing infrastructures [7,8].

The cloud services impose conditions for which the hardware is not incipiently created [9]. Applications deployment on cloud instances within clouds adds more risks while failures in data centers cannot be controlled by the client being the responsibility of the cloud provider. Traditional approaches in fault tolerance challenges require the users to have very good knowledge of the base mechanisms.

We have identified a gap in using the fault tree analysis applied in the fault management of distributed systems. Although some examples can be summarized here like [6] which states that the behavior of servers can be analyzed through fault tree models. The fault trees present the different levels of errors interdependence inherent to the cloud computing infrastructure [7,8].

Examples for using fault tree analysis in computing science are tackling the problem in a combination with neural networks [10]. Moreover fault tree analysis has been recently used in fault-tolerant parallel processor [11] and GPU speed-up [12]. Failure Trace Archive approaches are relatively new in today's literature: for example [4] comparatively presents statistical analysis of nine FTA data sets, mitigating the specific limitations of fault algorithms built using specific data sets while [13] propose a reliable provisioning model of spot instances based on traces extracted from Parallel Workload Archive.

7 Conclusions

We presented the results when applying our model for LANL failure traces, but the model has been successfully applied on P2P, Grid, Web and DNS FTA archives. The main advantage of the above approach is that the third replica is created only on demand and the required resources are not used from the start, resulting a more efficient mechanism for resource allocation with the capability of higher service availability. The main disadvantage of the strategy is timing: for a successful migration process, the migrated instance should be in a healthy state implying the usage of probabilistic provisioning system to be able to predict future fault states and to be able to start migration while is feasible. Future work could focus on producing and applying the model on a new failure trace archive for a real cloud system and analyze the cost reduction when using the fault strategy compared to existing approaches.

Acknowledgements. We acknowledge support from UEFISCDI under project PN-II-PT-PCCA-2013-4-1644.

References

1. Butoi, A., Stan, A., Silaghi, G.C.: Reliable management of virtualized resources using fault trees. In: 2014 16th International Symposium on Symbolic and Numeric Algorithms for Scientific Computing (SYNASC), pp. 309–316. IEEE (2014)
2. Butoi, A., Stan, A., Silaghi, G.C.: Autonomous management of virtual machine failures in IaaS using fault tree analysis. In: Altmann, J., Vanmechelen, K., Rana, O.F. (eds.) GECON 2014. LNCS, vol. 8914, pp. 206–221. Springer, Cham (2014). doi:10.1007/978-3-319-14609-6_14
3. Schroeder, B., Gibson, G.A.: A large scale study of failures in high-performance-computing systems. In: International Symposium on Dependable Systems and Networks (DSN) (2006)
4. Javadi, B., Kondo, D., Iosup, A., Epema, D.: The failure trace archive: enabling the comparison of failure measurements and models of distributed systems. J. Parallel Distrib. Comput. **73**(8), 1208–1223 (2013)
5. Kondo, D., Javadi, B., Iosup, A., Epema, D.: The failure trace archive: enabling comparative analysis of failures in diverse distributed systems. In: 2010 10th IEEE/ACM International Conference on Cluster, Cloud and Grid Computing (CCGrid), pp. 398–407. IEEE (2010)

6. Jhawar, R., Piuri, V.: Fault tolerance management in IaaS clouds. In: 2012 IEEE First AESS European Conference on Satellite Telecommunications (ESTEL), pp. 1–6 (2012)
7. Guerraoui, R., Yabandeh, M.: Independent faults in the cloud. In: Proceedings of the 4th International Workshop on Large Scale Distributed Systems and Middleware, LADIS 2010, pp. 12–17. ACM, New York (2010)
8. Undheim, A., Chilwan, A., Heegaard, P.: Differentiated availability in cloud computing SLAs. In: Proceedings of the 2011 IEEE/ACM 12th International Conference on Grid Computing, GRID 2011, pp. 129–136. IEEE Computer Society, Washington, DC (2011)
9. Feller, E., Rilling, L., Morin, C.: Snooze: a scalable and autonomic virtual machine management framework for private clouds. In: 2012 12th IEEE/ACM International Symposium on Cluster, Cloud and Grid Computing (CCGrid), pp. 482–489 (2012)
10. Bartlett, L.M., Andrews, J.D.: Choosing a heuristic for the "fault tree to binary decision diagram" conversion, using neural networks. IEEE Trans. Reliab. **51**(3), 344–349 (2002)
11. Xiang, J., Yanoo, K., Maeno, Y., Tadano, K.: Automatic synthesis of static fault trees from system models. In: 2011 Fifth International Conference on Secure Software Integration and Reliability Improvement (SSIRI), pp. 127–136 (2011)
12. Aghassi, F., Aghassi, H., Sheykhlar, Z.: A speed-up algorithm in Monte Carlo simulation for fault tree analysis with GPU computing. In: 2011 International Conference on Soft Computing and Pattern Recognition (SoCPaR), pp. 469–474 (2011)
13. Voorsluys, W., Buyya, R.: Reliable provisioning of spot instances for compute-intensive applications. In: 2012 IEEE 26th International Conference on Advanced Information Networking and Applications, pp. 542–549 (2012)

Work in Progress on Cloud Economics

An Economical Security Architecture for Multi-cloud Application Deployments in Federated Environments

Mathias Slawik[1]([⊠]), Begüm Ilke Zilci[1], Axel Küpper[1], Yuri Demchenko[2],
Fatih Turkmen[2], Christophe Blanchet[3], and Jean-François Gibrat[3]

[1] Telekom Innovation Laboratories, Service-centric Networking,
Technische Universität Berlin, Berlin, Germany
{mathias.slawik,ilke.zilci,axel.kuepper}@tu-berlin.de
[2] System and Network Engineering,
University of Amsterdam, Amsterdam, The Netherlands
{y.demchenko,f.turkmen}@uva.nl
[3] CNRS, UMS 3601; Institut Français de Bioinformatique, IFB-core,
Avenue de la Terrasse, 91190 Gif-sur-Yvette, France
{christophe.blanchet,jean-francois.gibrat}@france-bioinformatique.fr

Abstract. Contemporary multi-cloud application deployments require increasingly complex security architectures, especially within federated environments. However, increased complexity often leads to higher efforts and raised costs for managing and securing those applications. This publication establishes an economical and comprehensive security architecture that is readily instantiable, pertinent to concrete users' requirements, and builds upon up-to-date protocols and software. We highlight its feasibility by applying the architecture within the CYCLONE innovation action, deploying federated Bioinformatics applications within a cloud production environment. At last, we put special emphasis on the reduced management efforts to highlight the economic benefit of following our approach.

Keywords: Cloud federation · Architecture design · Security

1 Introduction

There is widespread usage of cloud technologies within contemporary application deployments. Examples include using VMs and containers for componentization of applications, relying on highly scalable public cloud infrastructures, and embracing the immutable infrastructure paradigm to structure scalable cloud services, possibly deployed to multiple clouds. As the architecture of these applications becomes more complex, securing them also presents many new challenges that we address in this publication.

Our contribution was devised in the CYCLONE innovation action that focuses on two main application characteristics: multi-cloud deployment, e.g.,

© Springer International Publishing AG 2017
J.Á. Bañares et al. (Eds.): GECON 2016, LNCS 10382, pp. 89–101, 2017.
DOI: 10.1007/978-3-319-61920-0_7

for increased resiliency or reduced latency, and authentication and authorization using federated identities, e.g., academic and social identities (Google, Facebook, etc.). We previously gave an overview about CYCLONE in [9]. The project deliverables[1] complement this publication with information about the architecture (D4.1), the APIs and data formats (D4.3), as well as the Bioinformatics Use Case (D3.1). This publication extends our previous work in the following ways: in contrast to expansive project deliverables, it summarizes key aspects in a short and concise way. It furthermore consolidates information about the practical application of our work from diverse sources. At last, we thoroughly analyze its economic benefit as well as highlight its feasibility through the deployment in a production environment.

As a methodology we apply "Design Science in Information Systems Research" by Hevner et al. [3] that also structures our presentation: first, in order to define the application area of our contribution we define the stakeholders and analyze their requirements in Sect. 2. Afterwards, to ensure research rigor, we give a comprehensive overview about related works in Sect. 3. Then, we describe the architecture and its provided functionalities in detail in Sect. 4 before evaluating it in Sect. 5. The evaluation also incorporates a discussion on the economic benefit. We conclude the paper by explicating the future extensions and open issues in Sect. 6 before summarizing it in Sect. 7.

2   Stakeholders and Requirements

This section provides the involved stakeholders and concludes with an analysis of their requirements for the security architecture. We consider three stakeholder groups: *Cloud Infrastructure Providers* who provide cloud resources to *Application Service Providers* to deploy applications for *Cloud Application End Users*. In the following, we describe the three main requirements that are most pertinent to our contribution:

Requirement 1: Federated authentication and authorization. Federated identities, for example, academic identities, are quite common in cloud environments. They are used, for example, by scientific online libraries and shared research infrastructures. Using Facebook and Google identities to access personal cloud applications is also quite popular. We see that all stakeholder groups require using them: *Cloud Infrastructure Providers* for reuse of preexisting identities for administrative log-ins as well as *Application Service Providers* to attract *End Users* who can reuse their identities in a practical and secure manner. Especially for data sharing by *End Users*, authorization by federated identities can be way more trusted than anonymous username/password pairs. To sum up, the security architecture has to provide functionalities to authenticate and authorize federated user identities in a secure manner.

Requirement 2: Secure multi-cloud application deployment. Multi-cloud deployment by *Application Service Providers* provides many benefit, for example, lower latency through global server distribution, and higher resiliency if

---

[1] http://www.cyclone-project.eu/deliverables.html.

using more than one cloud provider. The security architecture should therefore allow the deployment of applications in multiple clouds while still providing all of the security properties.

Requirement 3: Unified logging for distributed systems. As both the cloud infrastructure as well as many cloud applications are extensively distributed, gathering diagnostic messages and performance metrics from all of these applications in a unified system is very challenging. Without, debugging these systems and providing an audit trail becomes a tedious endeavour. Therefore, the security architecture should provide unified logging capabilities for highly distributed systems.

Nonfunctional requirements. We address the following four main solution qualities as nonfunctional requirements: **Relevance:** Through the requirements analysis with concrete use cases we create a relevant architecture for contemporary cloud environments. **Immediate instantiability:** Since we publish all components as open source[2], our security architecture becomes almost instantly instantiable. **Comprehensibility:** We provide a large volume of comprehensible supporting material, making it easy to follow and take up our ideas. **Maturity:** We use established software as well as common protocols and libraries to create a stable and mature environment. We highlight this by applying the architecture within a production environment.

3   Related Technologies

After establishing the stakeholders and their requirements, we now give an overview about the technologies related to our contribution.

OpenID, OAuth, and OpenID Connect. Accessing resources on Web 2.0 platforms on behalf of other resource owners - without handing over usernames and passwords - provided the first use case for federated web-authentication and authorization. For this purpose, *OAuth*, *OpenID*, and the recent *OpenID Connect* were introduced: **OpenID**[3] specifies how *relying parties* "prove that an end user controls an identifier" without disclosing credentials to *relying parties*. Resource access requests can be expressed by *OAuth* [2]. **OAuth** enables "a third-party application to obtain limited access to an HTTP service, either on behalf of a resource owner [...] or by allowing the third-party application to obtain access on its own behalf", most commonly through the OAuth Authorization Code Grant flow[4]. The most recent authentication protocol, **OpenID Connect**, focuses on solving security issues when using *OAuth* for authentication[5].

---

[2] https://github.com/cyclone-project/.

[3] http://openid.net/specs/openid-authentication-2_0.html.

[4] Basically, *relying parties* use HTTP redirection to request an access token from the resource server. If users accept this request, the resource server issues a token that allows relying parties access to users' resources (see 4.1 of [2]).

[5] For a comprehensive discussion, see http://oauth.net/articles/authentication.

OpenID Connect uses JSON Web Tokens (JWTs)[6] for transmitting user claims. As a result, the OpenID Connect Authentication Code Flow (OIDCACF) combines JWT and OAuth to provide secure web-based single sign-on for contemporary web applications.

SAML and eduGAIN. The OASIS *Security Assertion and Markup Language (SAML)*[7] "defines the syntax and processing semantics of assertions made about a subject by a system entity". It incorporates Web Service technologies, such as XML, XML Encryption & Signature, and SOAP. Version 2.0 adds HTTP bindings to use SAML without SOAP. The GÉANT *eduGAIN* service "interconnects identity federations around the world", i.e., it provides a metadata aggregator for inter-federation service access between 38 participating federations, 2093 Identity-, and 1208 Service Providers.

Notable Compatible Implementations. *Shibboleth*[8] is an open source Discovery Service, Identity-, and Service Provider implementation, based on SAML 2.0, extensively deployed in academic institutions worldwide. The *SimpleSAMLphp*[9] Identity- and Service Provider additionally supports *OpenID* and *OAuth*. *Keycloak*[10] provides "Integrated SSO and IDM for browser apps and RESTful web services" and implements all standards previously mentioned. It offers an Identity Broker, integration with Active Directory and LDAP, as well as a rich set of libraries for different implementation platforms.

PAM, XACML & Moonshot. The Linux *Pluggable Authentication Modules* (PAM)[11] subsystem provides a simple API to offer policy-compliant authentication, authorization, and accounting to relying software, such as Secure Shell Server (SSH) or getty processes. The *Extensible Access Control Markup Language (XACML)*[12] provides an XML-based policy language and a distributed access control architecture. It enables *attribute-based authorization*, that is, it uses a set of subject *attributes*, e.g., group membership or confidentiality level, to authorize *actions* carried out on arbitrary *resources*. The *Moonshot* project[13] "aims to enable federated access to virtually any application or service". One of its main components is a federation-enabled version of OpenSSH. However, relevant work ceased at the end of the last pilot in March 2015. Now, Moonshot-provided software packages are outdated and insecure due to a lack of patches for recent vulnerabilities and therefore unsuitable for CYCLONE production environments.

---

[6] See http://jwt.io and [4].
[7] http://saml.xml.org/saml-specifications.
[8] http://shibboleth.net/.
[9] https://simplesamlphp.org/.
[10] http://keycloak.jboss.org/.
[11] http://www.linux-pam.org/.
[12] https://www.oasis-open.org/committees/xacml/.
[13] https://wiki.moonshot.ja.net/.

4   Security Architecture and Security Functionalities

We now describe the security architecture and its functionalities. Figure 1 presents the architecture. The main component is the **Federation Provider**[14] that issues uniform user claims to relying applications, e.g., users' identifiers, email addresses, and their home organizations. These claims are contained within JWTs retrieved using the OIDCACF. The *Federation Provider* contains the **Identity Broker** as well as the **Backend Modules** implementing SAML 2.0 and OpenID Connect. The SAML 2.0 functionality is used to communicate with the Shibboleth-based *Identity Providers*, using eduGAIN as a **Metadata Provider**. As the end user's **User Agents** communicate directly with the **Identity Providers**, credentials are never transmitted to 3rd parties. Furthermore, end users can reuse their login sessions to achieve web-based *single sign-on*.

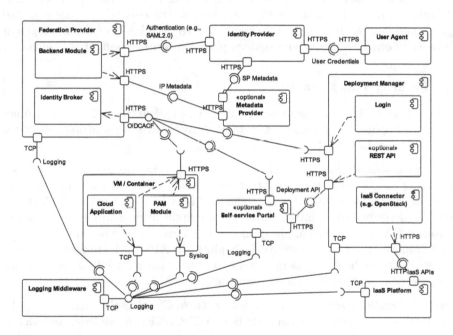

Fig. 1. UML component diagram of the security architecture.

The **Logging Middleware** unifies distributed log messages, supporting, besides others, TCP-based and Syslog-compatible loggers. Not shown are the *Logging Frontend*, allowing end user log consumption, as well as the *Logging Backend*, e.g., a database or flat files, to persist the logs.

---

[14] We use this term as "Federated Identity Provider" would be ambiguous: "provider of a federated identity" or "identity provider in a federation"?.

Deployed **Cloud Applications** rely on the OIDCACF to authenticate and authorize users - both on the *application layer*, through OpenID Connect libraries, as well as the *OS layer*, through the **PAM Module**. Depending on the concrete requirements, the PAM module maps identities either to a respective local user account, or to a shared user account. In contrast to Moonshot, the **PAM Module** does not need a modified SSH client or server.[15] They also log to the **Logging Middleware** and rely on the **Deployment Manager** to be deployed on the **IaaS Platform**. The **Deployment Manager** should support multi-cloud application deployment, e.g., it should model application topologies, connect to different IaaS APIs, and offer a web- and a RESTful interface. It should also allow end users to use the OIDCACF for logging in and should write its log messages to the *Logging Middleware*.

There is an *optional* architectural element, the **Self-service Portal**. It allows end users without technical background to use the **Deployment Manager** for instantiating VMs on the IaaS platform. This Portal uses OIDCACF for authentication and authorization and logs to the network interfaces of the logging middleware. It communicates with the RESTful API of the *Deployment Manager* in order to deploy and scale applications on preconfigured clouds.

4.1   Security Functionality

We now describe how the components interact to realize the main security functionalities *application deployment, federated authentication and authorization,* and *distributed logging.*

Application deployment. First, *deployment descriptions* need to be created containing all the steps necessary to create new application instances. Nuv.la, for example, uses base images (e.g., "Ubuntu Linux LTS") as well as deployment scripts to describe how to install the respective application components on newly instantiated VMs. After all application modules have been prepared, the *Deployment Manager* calls the respective IaaS platform APIs to instantiate the base images and runs the deployment scripts on them, either for initial deployment, for subsequent scaling, or to tear down the application.

Federated authentication and authorization. Cloud applications rely on the OpenID Connect authentication code flow (OIDCACF) to use federated identities for authentication and authorization. They transmit signed authentication requests and retrieve signed user identity claims to and from the *Federation Provider*. There is a set of attributes recommended for every eduGAIN identity provider[16], for example, display name and home organization. The research institutions are free to implement any number of these attributes and can also introduce additional attributes, for example, group membership. At last, the Federation Provider also supports creating local user accounts and using an LDAP server for special cases not involving federated identities.

---

[15] More details at https://github.com/cyclone-project/cyclone-python-pam.

[16] https://wiki.edugain.org/IDP_Attribute_Profile:_recommended_attributes.

Distributed Logging. The *Logging Middleware* should be quite flexible in the formats it accepts for logging as well as the structure of the log messages. For example, the Logstash middleware used by CYCLONE supports 49 different input plugins[17]. As the logging system is multi-tiered (front-end, middleware, database), it can be clustered and scaled quite flexibly, thus supporting a wide range of different deployment topologies. We created a filter for the ELK stack[18] that we use in production to filter log messages based on clients' ids. Together with an OIDCACF-compliant logging dashboard, this provides a flexible multi-tenant logging system.

5   Evaluation

This chapter presents the evaluation of the production deployment of the architecture within the CYCLONE innovation action, emphasizing three aspects:

1. **Functionality.** We evaluate how the architecture enables new functionality within the CYCLONE innovation action.
2. **Economics.** We evaluate how the architecture lowers efforts and therefore provides economic benefit to its users.
3. **Security.** We apply a formalized security threat analysis of the *Federation Provider* to assess the level of security.

5.1   Securing the CYCLONE Bioinformatics Use Case

The CYCLONE Innovation Action is funded by the European Commission in the Horizon 2020 framework and aims at integrating cloud management software in order to create a holistic cloud application management platform. A project cornerstone is the direct implementation of innovative developments within production environments, such as the CYCLONE bioinformatics use case. This use case extends an established self-service cloud platform[19] with new functionalities addressing the challenge areas of CYCLONE. The self-service cloud platform allows bioinformaticians to initiate the deployment of VMs containing related software, for example, to analyze human biomedical data and microbial genomes. We deployed the security architecture in production and detail the main implementation tasks in the following:

Establishing the federation provider. First, we set up and registered the Federation Provider with eduGAIN. The process is different for each NREN, in our case it meant registering the Federation Provider metadata[20] as a Service Provider (SP) through the DFN, the German NREN. To allow attribute retrieval we followed the "Data Protection Code of Conduct Cookbook"[21]. However, we

---

[17] See: https://www.elastic.co/guide/en/logstash/current/input-plugins.html.
[18] See: https://github.com/cyclone-project/cyclone-logging.
[19] https://cloud.france-bioinformatique.fr/cloud/.
[20] https://technical.edugain.org/show_entity_details.php?entity_row_id=213.
[21] https://wiki.edugain.org/Data_Protection_Code_of_Conduct_Cookbook.

faced two major difficulties: first of all, not every Identity Provider (IdP) is fully accustomed with all of the accompanying technologies and procedures - requiring manual coordination effort. Second, there are only recommendations but no requirements for the attribute release. Some IdPs chose to release all attributes, some only when SPs follow the Data Protection CoC, some implement approval processes, and some release no attributes at all. These circumstances make it nearly impossible to offer a Federation Provider for *all* of the 2091 Identity Providers.

Federated authentication for the biomedical data analysis VM. The Biomedical data analysis VM allows Bioinformaticians to upload data and retrieve analysis results at a later point in time, both via HTTP. Extending this upload form with federated authentication proved quite straightforward: as the form was presented using the Apache HTTP server, we used the HTTP server module mod_auth_openidc[22] for implementing the OIDCACF.

PAM-based federated authorization. Bioinformaticians collaboratively use the "microbial genomes analysis" as well as the "live remote cloud sequencing data processing" VMs and require simple data sharing between them. As they access the VMs using SSH and X2Go (which relies on SSH), enforcing access control using Linux file system ACLs was obvious. We integrated the PAM module into the VMs to map federated identities to local user accounts. Now the bioinformaticians can, for example, securely assign access rights to any collaborator using their email address.

5.2   Economic Benefits

This section discusses the economic benefit of applying the security architecture, contrasting them with the required upfront efforts. We strive to lower these upfront costs by preparing ready-to-deploy modules, providing practical demos, as well as writing comprehensive documentation. However, not every user will realize all of the benefit as this depends on a number of factors that we cannot control, e.g., how many relying applications there are and how well are the users versed in the technologies.

Once the Federation Provider is initially set-up and registered in eduGAIN, further applications are registered in minutes instead of weeks. Before introducing the Federation Provider, registering every cloud application instance with eduGAIN was simply not feasible for a large number of applications: first, the process itself is manual and can take days to complete. In fact, registering the first Federation Provider instance took us weeks, a duration deemed typical by other project partners that have completed such an undertaking before. Second, eduGAIN requires publishing every Service Provider's metadata[23]. Adding every cloud application instance would enlarge this document considerably, raising memory and processing requirements for all eduGAIN

---

[22] https://github.com/pingidentity/mod_auth_openidc.
[23] Currently 1206 SPs, see https://technical.edugain.org/entities.

participants. In contrast, registration of new OpenID Connect clients at the Federation Provider is a much more straightforward process: logging into the administrative interface and entering the details of the new client.

After investing effort in learning the technologies, using OpenID Connect libraries and handling JWTs proves far more easier than using the Shibboleth SP and SAML. This observation is based on our own experience as well as those of our use case partners. Reasons include: the token format is simpler, the documentation is more abundant and comprehensive, there is a larger number of libraries available for a wider range of platforms, and the protocol is less complex.

After setting up the Federation Provider and integrating all relying applications through OpenID Connect, the extensive identity brokering available at the Federation Provider saves the effort of integrating, e.g., a social login into each application. The Federation Provider can broker identities from eduGAIN, LDAP, Google, Facebook, Twitter, GitHub, LinkedIn, Microsoft, and Stack Overflow. The economic benefit of using the Federation Provider as a kind of authentication proxy are most extensive if there are a large number of applications in need of this functionality, as it needs to be integrated *just once into the Federation Provider* instead of *into every application.*

After the PAM module is installed and set-up, end users reuse their existing identities instead of learning about SSH, or remembering yet another credential. Furthermore, federated authorization management is very simple: modifying a plain text file. Before CYCLONE, Bioinformaticians were required to either learn how to manage SSH keys or memorize yet another local account in order to access their VMs. Now, they can just reuse their existing federated identities, thus reducing identity management overheads and simplifying account management on the cloud provider's side. This effect is magnified when there are a large number of machines where the end users have access to. Permitting access to a VM is also very simple: VM owners just need to add the mail address of the other account to a certain file on the VM.

After setting up the distributed logging and changing the configuration of logging applications, debugging distributed applications becomes far more easy. Merging application- as well as infrastructure log messages eases the debugging process considerably. As the logging middleware supports a large number of input sources, integrating the distributed logging into applications is oftentimes as easy as changing some lines of a configuration file, for example, when using the popular Log4j Java library.[24]

---

[24] https://www.elastic.co/guide/en/logstash/current/plugins-inputs-log4j.html.

5.3   Security Analysis of the Federation Provider

We use the OWASP Application Threat Modelling (ATM) methodology[25] to analyze the Federation Provider. Our goal was to assess the current level of security, to find out security threats, and to strengthen the architecture. While all details of this process can be found in the CYCLONE Deliverable 4.1, this subsection gives an overview about the four main steps and their results:

Step 1: Application decomposition. In order to provide a comprehensive base for the next steps, we decomposed the Federation Provider.

Step 2: Definition of dependencies, trust levels, and entry points. Next, we identified: **External Dependencies**, such as the deployment on a hardened VM and the use of an H2 database, **Trust Levels**, such as "Anonymous Web User", and "Federation Provider Admin", and system **Entry Points** such as the OpenID Connect API and the Federation Provider log-in screen.

Step 3: Modeling the Federation Provider data flows. Figure 2 shows the modeling of the data processes, -stores, -flows, as well as the environment boundaries as a data flow diagram. We modeled the current project environment,

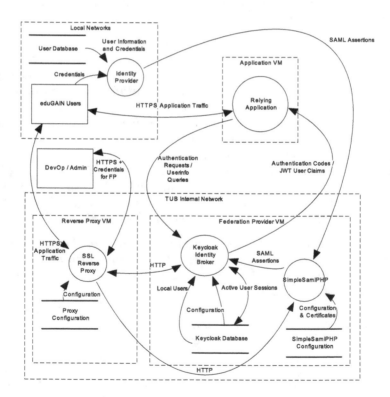

Fig. 2. Federation provider data flow diagram.

[25] https://www.owasp.org/index.php/Application_Threat_Modeling.

where the Federation Provider is installed on a VM hosted in the internal cloud of TU Berlin. It uses the Keycloak Identity Broker for implementing OpenID Connect and integrates SimpleSamlPHP for eduGAIN access.

Step 4: Determining and ranking threats. As the most valuable step, we then compiled an extensive list of threats, their possible causes, a mitigation strategy, and the attacker type, applying the DREAD threat-risk model[26] and the Thread Rating Table[27] provided by Microsoft. We saw that some threats can be mitigated by following the Open ID Connect standard, others by following industry best practice. For brevity reasons, the three top threats are: impersonation of eduGAIN users, impersonation of Federation Provider admins, as well as further exposure to security and privacy threats by unintended authentication request disclosure.

6   Extensions and Open Issues

This section highlights a number of future extensions and open issues associated with the security architecture.

Automated Registration of OpenID Connect Clients. Creating new OpenID Connect clients for each cloud application deployment is a manual process. In the future, we will implement an API that can be used to automatically register newly deployed applications as OpenID Connect clients. This includes the secure exchange of OpenID Client identifiers and associated secrets.

End-to-End Data Security in Cloud Environments. Our previous work [7] establishes the Trusted Cloud Transfer Protocol (TCTP), an end-to-end data security protocol, based on TLS. In [8] we have already demonstrated that it can be successfully deployed in production environments. To enable the users of the security architecture to also benefit from its additional security characteristics, we will work on integrating TCTP into the security architecture.

Attribute-Based Access Control and Secure Trust Bootstrapping. While the PAM module is sufficient for most CYCLONE use cases, there are advanced scenarios requiring more flexible authorization schemes. Our past work [1,6] shows that a XACML-based distributed attribute-based access control infrastructure provides many benefit in dynamically provisioned cloud environments. In the future we will integrate this work into the security architecture to create opportunities for new use cases as well as a further reduction of management effort. We will also employ a secure trust bootstrapping mechanism [5] for the establishment of trust between provisioned cloud resources, enabling the dynamic configuration of access control attributes for VMs during deployment.

Open Issue: Federated authentication using non-browser software. OpenID Connect and SAML are aimed for browser usage, leading to a lot of

---

[26] https://www.owasp.org/index.php/Application_Threat_Modeling#DREAD.

[27] https://msdn.microsoft.com/en-us/library/ff648644.aspx (see Table 3.6).

issues when using them with, e.g., RESTful API clients. OpenID Connect provides the Direct Access Grant flow[28] to retrieve an identity token using a username/password combination, although this has negative security implications. SAML2.0 provides the "Enhanced Client or Proxy"[29] that supports *non-browser* clients. There is a working implementation in the Shibboleth IP, however none of the 2000+ eduGAIN identity providers has enabled it.

Federated access delegation to cloud resources. While the PAM module allows people to use their federated identities for logging into systems, allowing these systems access to other cloud resources on behalf of the federated identity is still an ongoing issue. There are related technologies, such as Kerberos, however we did not find a simple to use and economically feasible solution to apply in this scenario.

7   Summary and Outlook

By deploying the architecture presented in this publication in production we significantly reduce the effort to provide federated multi-cloud application security. This publication contains more than just the interaction of contemporary technologies: we provide a design rationale in form of stakeholders and requirements, evaluate the resulting architecture through both real-world application and a thorough analysis, and provide readily instantiable components in our public code repository[30]. In the future, we will work together with the community on extending the architecture as well as deploying it to new use cases.

Acknowledgements. The authors wish to thank the members of the bioinformatics platforms Centre Léon Bérard (Lyon, France) and IFB-MIGALE (Jouy-en-Josas, France) to provide their bioinformatics applications as respective use cases "Biomedical data analysis" and "Bacterial genomes analysis". This work is supported by the CYCLONE Horizon 2020 Innovation Action CYCLONE (http://www.cyclone-project. eu), funded by the European Commission under grant number 644925.

References

1. Demchenko, Y., de Laat, C., Lopez, D.R., Garcia-Espin, J.A.: Security services lifecycle management in on-demand infrastructure services provisioning. In: Qiu, J. (ed.) Proceedings of the IEEE Second International Conference on Cloud Computing Technology and Science (CloudCom 2010). IEEE, Piscataway, NJ (2010)
2. Hardt, D.: The OAuth 2.0 authorization framework. RFC 6749 (Proposed Standard), October 2012. http://www.ietf.org/rfc/rfc6749.txt
3. Hevner, A.R., March, S.T., Park, J., Ram, S.: Design science in information systems research. MIS Q. **28**(1), 75–105 (2004)

---

[28] https://keycloak.github.io/docs/userguide/keycloak-server/html/ direct-access-grants.html.
[29] https://wiki.shibboleth.net/confluence/display/CONCEPT/ECP.
[30] https://github.com/cyclone-project.

4. Jones, M., Bradley, J., Sakimura, N.: JSON Web Token (JWT). RFC 7519 (Proposed Standard), updated by RFC 7797, May 2015. http://www.ietf.org/rfc/rfc7519.txt
5. Membrey, P., Chan, K.C.C., Ngo, C., Demchenko, Y., de Laat, C.: Trusted virtual infrastructure bootstrapping for on demand services. In: Seventh International Conference on Availability, Reliability and Security, Prague, ARES 2012, Czech Republic, 20–24 August 2012, pp. 350–357 (2012)
6. Ngo, C., Membrey, P., Demchenko, Y., de Laat, C.: Policy and context management in dynamically provisioned access control service for virtualized cloud infrastructures. In: Proceedings of the Seventh International Conference on Availability, Reliability and Security (ARES2012). IEEE, Piscataway, NJ (2012)
7. Slawik, M.: The trusted cloud transfer protocol. In: IEEE 5th International Conference on Cloud Computing Technology and Science (CloudCom), vol. 2 (2014)
8. Slawik, M., Ermakova, T., Repschläger, J., Küpper, A., Zarnekow, R.: Securing medical SaaS solutions using a novel end-to-end encryption protocol. In: Avital, M., Leimeister, J.M., Schultze, U. (eds.) ECIS 2014 Proceedings. AIS Electronic Library (2014)
9. Slawik, M., Zilci, B.I., Demchenko, Y., Aznar Baranda, J.I., Branchat, R., Loomis, C., Lodygensky, O., Blanchet, C.: CYCLONE: unified deployment and management of federated, multi-cloud applications. In: Proceedings of the 5th Workshop on Network Infrastructure Services, pp. 453–457 (2015)

Efficient Context Management and Personalized User Recommendations in a Smart Social TV Environment

Fotis Aisopos[1](✉), Angelos Valsamis[2], Alexandros Psychas[1], Andreas Menychtas[1], and Theodora Varvarigou[1]

[1] Distributed, Knowledge and Media Systems Group,
National Technical University of Athens, Athens, Greece
{fotais, ameny, alps}@mail.ntua.gr,
dora@telecom.ntua.gr
[2] Department of Informatics and Telecommunications,
National and Kapodistrian University of Athens, Athens, Greece
ang.valsamis@gmail.com

Abstract. With the emergence of Smart TV and related interconnected devices, second screen solutions have rapidly appeared to provide more content for end-users and enrich their TV experience. Given the various data and sources involved - videos, actors, social media and online databases- the aforementioned market poses great challenges concerning user context management and sophisticated recommendations that can be addressed to the end-users. This paper presents an innovative Context Management model and a related first and second screen recommendation service, based on a user-item graph analysis as well as collaborative filtering techniques in the context of a Dynamic Social & Media Content Syndication (SAM) platform. The model evaluation provided is based on datasets collected online, presenting a comparative analysis concerning efficiency and effectiveness of the current approach, and illustrating its added value.

Keywords: Smart TV recommendations · Social media · Second screen · Context management · Graph analysis

1 Introduction

Recent studies show that mobile devices are gradually employed more and more in parallel with TV usage, creating the so called second screen phenomenon[1]. Users comment or rate TV shows on Social Media and search for related information about actors, places and all other sorts of information related to the show they are watching. This phenomenon is expected to grow exponentially, creating a huge impact on the way content is created and delivered, not only through regular broadcasting but also thought mobile devices. However, there are still no second screen standards, protocols or ever common practices for users to discover and access additional information related to the consumed content [1].

---

[1] Second Screen Society: http://www.2ndscreensociety.com/.

J.Á. Bañares et al. (Eds.): GECON 2016, LNCS 10382, pp. 102–114, 2017.
DOI: 10.1007/978-3-319-61920-0_8

The lack of such attributes drives them to search intuitively in the social media or online search engines for content. Moreover, despite the popularity of products like Vizrt Social TV[2] or Beamly social content network, building a custom user experience, including context management and recommendations, is inefficient and not scalable[3]. The continuing growth of online content though led to a need for the creation of systems that manage it, to provide quality of service, content syndication and recommendations. The main motivation of the current work is to provide an efficient model that captures and manages Social TV-related context data, to provide smart recommendations to the users.

In the context of the SAM Project [2], a Social Media-aware content delivery platform for syndicated data to be consumed in a contextualised social way through second screen devices has been provided. The former, out-dated model of users searching for the information they desire is replaced with a new approach, where information reaches users on their second screen using content syndication. This paper focuses on user interaction history with first and second screen and the related behavioural models applied in SAM, to form an innovative Context Management mechanism, based on a graph database. To this end, users, Social Media items (e.g. widgets appearing in second screen) as well as related interactions are saved in the form of a nodes/edges, where graph analysis models and correlation techniques are employed to properly assess the relevance of each media item to every user. As a result, a relevance rating list for each first/second screen user is produced, allowing personalized recommendations of videos and related assets. Thus, user's Social TV experience is enriched as such: upon interaction with first screen, a relevant list of videos is recommended to her, while upon watching a specific video only relevant information widgets (like Wikipedia articles) appear in second screen.

More specifically, the current paper contributions are summarized below:

- Scalable and timely efficient Social Media user profiling and Context Management using an appropriate graph model (visualizing users, assets, interactions)
- Intelligent data analysis based on a combination of graph analysis and collaborative filtering
- Multi-level Social TV personalized user recommendations via relevance rating approach for root assets (videos) in first screen and sub-assets (video-related sources of information) in second screen
- A comparative analysis of commonly used machine learning algorithms and clustering techniques, applied to Social TV user context-based recommendations

The rest of the document is organized as follows: Sect. 1 is the current one and serves the purpose of the introduction. Section 2 presents related work on graph-based and collaborative filtering techniques, investigating the existing Social TV user context modelling and recommendations. Section 3 introduces the SAM context management approach, while Sect. 4 elaborates on graph analysis and collaborative filtering. Finally, Sect. 5 analyzes the experimental results and Sect. 6 presents the conclusions.

---

[2] http://www.vizrt.com/solutions/social-tv-solution/.

[3] http://adexchanger.com/digital-tv/social-tv-platform-beamly-learns-the-second-screen-is-a-feed/.

2   Related Work

Graph databases have been extensively used lately to optimize storage and processing of highly connected data. For example, authors in [3–5] provide insights into Neo4j graph database and its performance advantages, illustrating the various cases it is used, including recommender systems that apply "item-to-item" and "user-to-user" (i.e. collaborative filtering) correlation. Demovic et al. [6] presented an interesting context-based graph recommendation approach, saving multimedia-related data in a graph structure and using Graph Traversal Algorithms to efficiently address user preferences. This work uses explicit user "likes" for movies or genres, but does not collect any other contextual or social data. Focusing on Social TV Platforms, works in [7, 8] highlight the concept of context management and analysis in the frame of social enabled content delivery to multi-screen devices. These papers present a novel solution for media content delivery, based on the idea of fusing second screen and content syndication, exploiting the advancements in the area of social media.

Recommender systems for eCommerce [9, 10] usually follow a personalised recommendation approach, based on users' clustering and correlation, as well as behavior factorization [11]. When it comes to TV-related personalised recommendations, a substantial amount of work has been performed, focusing on TV programs and movies' context evaluation. Krauss et al. [12] introduced personalized TV program recommendations based on users' viewing behavior and ratings, combining various data mining approaches. A ten-fold cross validation over a user-generated dataset aggregated from the operation of the TV Predictor software resulted into a promising program prediction accuracy. Kim et al. [13] on the other hand, presented an automatic recommendation scheme based on a user clustering approach that did not require explicit ratings from TV viewers, but rather the watching history logs. The proposed rank model used a collaborative filtering technique, taking into account the watching times, to illustrate effectiveness with rich experimental results over a real usage history dataset.

Collaborative filtering techniques are frequently used by online recommender systems [14] in domains such as web services [15], social networks [16] or movies [17] selection. Kwon and Hong [18] propose a personalized program recommender for smart TVs using memory-based collaborative filtering, employing a novel similarity method that is robust to cold-start conditions and faster than existing approaches. The evaluation uses an own-built crawling agent to retrieve movie reviews by real users and predict ratings for non-viewed programs. On the other hand, work in [19] proposes improvements to two of the most popular approaches to Collaborative Filtering, introducing a new neighborhood based model, as well as extensions to SVD-based latent factor models and integrating implicit feedback into the model. Those are evaluated with a very limited form of implicit feedback, available on Netflix. Efficient methods for collaborative filtering like Item-to-Item or SVD [20] decrease the impact of noise and improve the ability for high quality recommendations systems, such as movie recommenders [21]. However in our case, the high performance of the graph analysis that will be presented is supported by a Pearson correlation technique, only in the case the user has not interacted with neighboring multimedia items, in which case Item-to-Item approaches would not provide sufficient results.

SAM Context Management for Smart Social TVs attempts to progress beyond the state-of-the-art solutions presented above, by providing a personalized multi-level recommendation mechanism (applying both for first and second screen content), based on an efficient graph-based approach. The localization of the graph analysis, in contrast with the global machine learning or collaborative filtering models, yields a high scalability for a big datasets of multimedia items and interactions.

3 SAM Context Management Approach

3.1 Platform Architecture and Data Collected

SAM aims at the development of a context-centric middleware that acts supportively to its advanced federated social media delivery platform, providing open and standardised way of defining, characterising, discovering, syndicating and consuming media assets interactively. In the context of SAM Platform, the generic components of Context Control are responsible for storing and managing context information. Figure 1 [22] shows the subcomponents realising the Context Representation operations along with the connections between them and other SAM components. The core component for context-related operations is the Context Manager, collecting contextual information from Social Media, including SAM dynamic communities exposed by Community Structure Analyser, as well as the Syndicator and the Dashboard. Based on the analysis of those data, the Context Manager produces ranked lists of assets (videos or widgets)

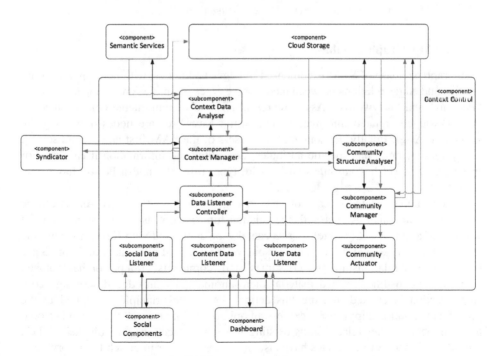

Fig. 1. SAM context control components.

per user and forwards those to the Syndicator that uses them to send smart recommendations to first and second screen, after a user logs in to the SAM Dashboard.

The SAM Dashboard connects to specific Data Listeners capturing and storing all interactions according to an extended W3C Social Web Working Group context model (successor to the OpenSocial format). The aforementioned Data Listeners (Social Data Listener, Content Data Listener, User Data Listener) are managed by a Data Listener Controller and forward to the Context Manager all data related to the Social TV context, including Social Media posts on SAM multimedia and user interactions with first and second screen. The interactions which are useful for the Context Data Analyser are the ones illustrating user's relevance or satisfaction with the content provided, such as "likes" or "scrolls", as well as text comments or online posts, further evaluated with the support of Semantic Services for sentiment analysis, so as to enrich the user profile with contextual information.

In specific, the following user interaction items (Table 1) are collected from Generic Dashboard listeners and sent to SAM Context Management component to support the analysis:

Table 1. User interactions collected from Generic Dashboard.

Root asset interactions	Widget interactions
Consume root asset	Scroll widget
Scroll root asset	Dismiss widget (Close window)
Fullscreen root asset	Like widget
Comment root asset	Dislike widget

3.2   SAM's Graph Database

The Graph database of SAM is composed of edges and nodes, with nodes representing entities and edges relations between them. Three types of entities are defined: "Assets", "Persons" and "Keywords". Assets represent all kind of multimedia content in SAM (video, widgets, related information etc.), while Keywords are nodes describing the tags of an Asset. Finally, Persons represent users of the SAM first and second screen. Every type of node has specific attributes, describing the information it enfolds. For instance, an Asset has attributes such as id, type, title, etc. and a Person has name, identifier, etc.

Nodes are connected to each other with edges called relationships. Assets can be connected with other Assets with the relationship "is root asset of", signifying the widgets of a root Asset (movie). Assets can also be connected with Keywords with the relationship "has keywords" or with Persons via a variety of relations. For Root Assets (movies), these relationships are "consumes" and "comments". If a person has watched a movie or consumed related material then automatically an edge describing "consume" action is created to store this action. The same principle is applied to the "comment" relationship: if users express an opinion about an asset, the action is stored as "comment". Other relationships existing in such connections are "dislike", "like", "fullscreen" and "scroll". Edges have also attributes in order to enrich the information

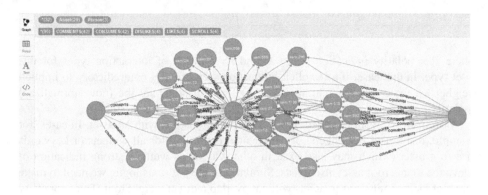

Fig. 2. SAM context manager graph database example.

about the entities' relationships. For example the edge "comment" contains information about the intensity of a comment, its type (if it is a negative or a positive comment) and the comment itself. An instance of the SAM graph DB with some initial records can be seen in Fig. 2:

Note that the same person can change her mind on an asset (e.g. dislike what she liked in the past). Thus, we decided to replace the explicit interactions (like/dislike, comment) with the latest one received from the SAM Dashboard, so that the relevance score to be calculated is efficient and properly updated.

4 Context Analysis and Recommendations

4.1 Graph Analysis

A basic part of the graph analysis is the application of "weights" to the interactions between users and assets. Setting +1 and −1 as absolute values of relevancy and irrelevancy respectively, we apply those values to user-asset relations that explicitly show such a rating ("like" weights for +1, "dislike" weights for −1). Moreover, comments on assets are saved along with their sentiment polarity and intensity (percentage of positivity or negativity), thus we can apply decimal weights, ranging from (0, +1] for positive comments and from [−1, 0) for negative comments. Zero values obviously express neutrality.

However, consuming or scrolling a root asset also indicates some interest by the user. The same applies for clicking or scrolling a specific widget in second screen, while dismissing it before it automatically closes indicates lack of interest. To capture those implicit patterns, we need to make sure that they will not totally overlap the explicit ones already mentioned. For example, if a user has "liked" an asset, but on the other hand dismissed it early on, this implies a weaker "like" or "interest" relation. The approach that we follow to make sure the overall weight (sum of weights) is mainly defined by "likes"/"dislikes" and only partly affected by other interactions is to apply to the latest a weight of

$$w_i = \frac{p_i}{t-1} \tag{1}$$

where p_i = polarity indication (+1, −1) and t = number of interaction types for this asset type. In this case, if an explicit interaction weight w_e is contradictory to implicit weights w_i, the overall weight $W = w_e + \sum w_i$ will still bare the (now normalized) "polarity" of w_e

Moreover, we want to collect indirect user relationships with an asset. In cases, for example, that a user has "liked" or commented positively for all widgets or keywords of a root asset (which may also exist in other videos as well), a strong indication of relevance to this root asset also exists. Similarly to the previous logic, we need to make sure that indirect relations to assets will not overlap a direct weight to it. Thus, for every rating to a connected asset/keyword we apply a weight of

$$w_x = \frac{r_x}{a+k+1} \tag{2}$$

where r_x = rating of neighbouring node, a = number of neighbouring assets and k = number of the initial asset's keywords. The overall relevance weight of a person for an asset now becomes:

$$W = w_e + \sum w_i + \sum w_x \Leftrightarrow W = w_e + \sum \frac{p_i}{t-1} + \sum \frac{r_{xi}}{a+k+1} \tag{3}$$

Running this process recursively for connected assets, we conclude to the following general algorithm:

Algorithm 1. Pseudo-code of Context Management graph analysis to rate the relevance of an asset for a user.

```
procedure AssetRelevance (user, asset, graph)

    RelevanceWeights we, wi, wx;
    InteractionList I;
    InteractionTypes types= Interaction.getTypes();
    t = types.length();

    if user.hasRated(asset) then
        we = user.getExplicitRating (asset);

    if user.hasInteracted(asset) then
        I = user.getInteractions(asset);
        foreach interaction ∈ I do
            wi = wi + interaction.getPolarity()/(t-1);

    A=asset.getNeighbours();
    n = A.length();
    foreach neighbour_asset ∈ A do
        rx = AssetRelevance (user, neighbour_asset, (graph-asset));
        wx = wx + rx /(n+1);

    return we + wi + wx;
```

Note that keywords are also treated as assets in the following algorithm for simplicity purposes.

To provide a rated list of assets to a user, based on her relevance to those, we need to calculate a user's node weights with existing assets. Thus, the algorithm shown above must be run for all assets in the graph which implies a complexity of $O(n^2)$. However, given the fact that recursive calls only need to apply for depth 2 in order to make sense (when shortest path between assets equals 2 to bare some meaningful relevance), complexity is further reduced to $O(n)$.

4.2   Collaborative Filtering Analysis

In cases of more "isolated" assets in the graph, when the user analyzed has not interacted with those or their neighbours (e.g. a new movie), it is obvious that the aforementioned analysis will not identify any meaningful relevance. In such cases, it was decided to use collaborative filtering among different users, in order to estimate the user relevance with the specific assets, based on her correlation with other users.

A most common approach used for collaborative filtering, having a dataset of simple numeric ratings [15], is using the Pearson Correlation Coefficient:

$$c_{au} = \frac{\sum_{i=1}^{h}(r_{ai} - \bar{r}_a) \times (r_{ui} - \bar{r}_u)}{\sqrt{\sum_{i=1}^{h}(r_{ai} - \bar{r}_a)^2 \times \sum_{i=1}^{h}(r_{ui} - \bar{r}_u)^2}} \tag{5}$$

between users a and u, where in our case $h = |I_{au}|$ is the amount of assets having been rated by both users, r_{ai} is user a's weight for asset i and $\bar{r}_a = average(r_{a1}, r_{a2}, \ldots, r_{ah})$.

Having calculated the correlation coefficients of a user with other users, collaborative filtering analysis can provide a prediction, rating her relevance with an asset j, based on other users' relevance for the specific asset and their correlation:

$$p_{aj} = \bar{r}_a + \frac{\sum_{u=1}^{g}(r_{uj} - \bar{r}_u) \times c_{au}}{\sum_{u=1}^{g} c_{au}} \tag{6}$$

where g is the number of users that consumed j and P_{aj} is the predicted rating of relevance for user a.

4.3   Personalised Recommendations

The results of the analysis processes described above for every user is two-fold:

- A rated list of root assets, consisted of pairs of videos and relevancy scores for the user, similar to top-k ranking approach presented in [16].
- A rated list of sub-assets of any root asset (appearing as widgets in second screen), consisted of pairs of widgets and relevancy scores for the user.

Thus, personalized recommendations can be provided to first and second screen Syndicator component, to prioritize or even disappear irrelevant movies and related widgets of a movie upon consumption.

This results into the following two-level recommendation mechanism that provides:

- Smart recommendations of root assets (videos) to user.
- Smart recommendations of second screen widgets to user, while watching a Smart TV program on first screen.

5 Experiments and Evaluation

5.1 Dataset and Configuration

The presentation of the analysis methods above makes the performance advantages of the graph-based approach evident. For example, when retrieving for users having consumed a specific asset in the graph, Neo4j just returns the neighbours of the corresponding node, in contrast with the latency resulting from a respective SQL query. To acquire a meaningful and extended dataset, in order to form the SAM experimental Context Management graph, the authors decided to search online for available related data (users, movies, keywords, likes etc.).

Our experimental dataset is comprised of a big movie rating dataset found online [23], comprising a huge database of movies and user ratings, as well as keywords linked with those movies. To get most correlated users and movies in order to make a meaningful graph collaborative filtering and analysis, we selected the 30 most popular movies, in terms of number of ratings, rated by 619 users (overall 7038 ratings) and the 5 most popular keywords for each movie. This sampling assures that many common keywords exist between movies, so that the aforementioned graph weighting will apply. The dataset imported was interpreted into the SAM logic, directly importing SAM users and assets (movies and keywords) into the graph. Unfortunately the original dataset does not contain real life user interaction data, thus ratings were used to simulate comment sentiments and likes/dislikes based on their values, without any other interactions (scroll, fullscreen etc.) captured in the graph. With no widgets and relevant interactions existing, the current evaluation results are limited only to the first screen. The analysis in the context of the current experiments results into a movie relevance evaluation, which can then produce movie recommendations (one level evaluation) for users based on their movie relevance.

The dataset was split into training and testing sets (70% and 30% of the original rating respectively), with the first one to be fed into various data analysis algorithms and the later to be used as ground truth. Experiments conducted mostly focused on the accuracy of the aforementioned technique, in contrast with mainstream machine learning approaches, for estimating users' relevance with movies of the testing set. The graph analysis, supported by the Pearson Collaborative filtering presented above, was applied and compared with a k-nearest neighbours (K-NN) algorithm run over Neo4j[4],

---

[4] https://neo4j.com/graphgist/8173017/.

as well as various machine learning algorithms (SVM, C4.5, MLP etc.) employed in Weka software, version 3.7[5], taking the initial dataset as an .arff file input. Experiments operated on a desktop machine with Intel Core TM i5-3400 Processor 2.80 GHz and 12 GB of RAM memory, running 64-bit Windows 10 Pro.

5.2 Experimental Results

In Table 2 an analytical report of results per approach is provided, for predicting users' relevance to the assets (movies) of the training set. The mean errors refer to the difference between the calculated values and the real original ratings, ranging from −1 to 1, which represent the current evaluation's ground truth.

Table 2. Accuracy and mean errors of SAM predictions, compared to State-of-the-Art machine learning techniques.

	Mean absolute error	Root mean squared error	Mean percentage error
SVM with linear kernel	**0.1099**	0.3315	**5.5%**
C4.5 w/10 Bagging	0.1253	0.2688	6.3%
Best-first decision tree	0.1274	0.2626	6.4%
Logistic regression	0.1269	0.2612	6.4%
LAC lazy associative classifier	0.1306	0.2563	6.5%
Bayes net with K2 search	0.1263	0.2559	6.3%
Naive Bayes	0.1283	0.2551	6.4%
Naive Bayes tree	0.1334	0.2652	6.7%
MLP 100 neurons	0.1324	0.2632	6.6%
CNN 100 neurons	0.1269	**0.2530**	6.4%
CNN 1000 neurons	0.1202	0.2578	6.0%
Hoeffding tree	0.1499	0.2684	7.5%
Hidden Markov model	0.1653	0.2875	8,3%
K-nearest neighbour on Neo4j	0.3226	0.4108	16,1%
SAM (graph + CollabFiltering)	**0.1312**	**0.2604**	**6.6%**

Note that time comparison between algorithms running in batch mode that do not connect to a database and algorithms that return results on-demand, like the one we implement in SAM, is irrelevant. For example the Naive Bayes approach trains its model instantly but requires the full dataset available in memory. When considering our dataset of 7038 ratings this is feasible, however it is apparent that this is not a scalable solution. The motivation behind the decision to get metrics from

---

[5] http://www.cs.waikato.ac.nz/ml/weka/.

state-of-the-art machine learning algorithms is mainly to evaluate the accuracy of our proposed algorithm.

As can be observed in the experimental results, SAM's approach scores relatively well, taking into account the low performance cost introduced by the graph database, as well as its multilevel capabilities. The authors compared our graph-based analysis approach with variations of some known algorithms. In particular, we used Breiman's Bagging technique [24] with 10 iterations (C4.5) and also tried different neural network models (Convolutional Neural Network with 100 and 1000 neurons, Multi-layer Perceptron). Probabilistic models (Logistic Regression, Naive Bayes, Bayesian network with K2 search algorithm) and simple tree implementations (C4.5, Best-first) were also used, yielding competitive results. In terms of mean absolute error the SVM with a linear kernel was superior but with a weak root mean squared error, for which the 100 neurons CNN produced the best results. We approached the problem as a classification problem because the dataset has discrete values in ratings (1–5); however we report the error metrics because in our case we are interested in how close the predictions were to the ground truth. Since our data is ordinal and have an inherent order, it is a safer metric to ensure generalization of models.

Beyond comparing SAM Context Management approach with other machine learning techniques in terms of effectiveness, we also present a comparison of the two algorithms running on top of the graph database (SAM, K-NN) time-wise. Resulting from those algorithms, SAM's Context Management component exposed two recommendation web services respectively. Stress-testing our approach performance, as a commercial deployed service, we used JMeter [25] to generate requests for all ratings of the testing set to those services. The response times of the first 1000 requests can be seen in Fig. 3:

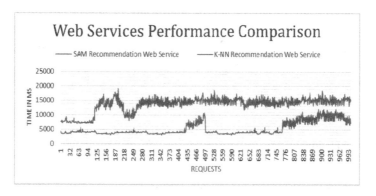

Fig. 3. A time performance comparison between K-NN and SAM recommendation web services.

SAM Recommendation Web Service evidently outperforms K-NN, one of the most popular clustering approaches for recommendations using graphs. Results above validate the current model's low complexity and illustrate its scalability. Results can be explained by the locality of the data needed for SAM. In both recommendations levels the algorithms start from the user's node and travel in his near neighbours to find interactions without the need of prior knowledge that is needed in the K-NN case.

6 Conclusions

In this paper, we presented an efficient Context Management approach for Social TV users, collecting context-related data and actions to provide personalized multi-level recommendations via a hybrid method combining graph paths analysis and Pearson collaborative filtering. Experiments used a real movie rating dataset found online and illustrated promising results in one level recommendations, in terms of accuracy and performance. The effectiveness of the current model will be more evident with the addition of an extended user interaction dataset, which can be aggregated from the SAM second screen listeners during the final trials of the project in the upcoming months. Thus, in the future the authors plan to aggregate Social TV-related datasets, in order to evaluate the current model end to end in both levels (first and second screen). The validity of the results will be better illustrated using more diverse datasets, in terms of user relevance scores, thus training sets where ratings are distributed more widely must be included, so that correlation techniques can generate more concrete and meaningful user clusters. Lastly, as long as such a solution will go commercial, privacy-related issues should be also tackled, employing user anonymisation and privacy-preserving item-based collaborative filtering [26].

Acknowledgements. This work has been supported by the SAM project and funded from the European Union's 7th Framework Programme for research, technological development and demonstration under grant agreement no 611312.

References

1. Heino, N., Tramp, S., Auer, S.: Managing web content using linked data principles-combining semantic structure with dynamic content syndication. In: Computer Software and Applications Conference (COMPSAC), pp. 245–250. IEEE (2011)
2. Socialising Around Media (SAM) Project: Dynamic Social and Media Content Syndication for 2nd Screen. http://samproject.net/
3. Vicknair, C., et al.: A comparison of a graph database and a relational database: a data provenance perspective. In: Proceedings of the 48th Annual Southeast Regional Conference. ACM (2010)
4. Holzschuher, F., Peinl, R.: Performance of graph query languages: comparison of cypher, gremlin and native access in Neo4j. In: Proceedings of the Joint EDBT/ICDT 2013 Workshop (2013)
5. Miller, J.J.: Graph database applications and concepts with Neo4j. In: Proceedings of the Southern Association for Information Systems Conference, Atlanta, GA, USA, March 2013
6. Demovic, L., et al.: Movie recommendation based on graph traversal algorithms. In: 2013 24th International Workshop on Database and Expert Systems Applications (DEXA). IEEE (2013)

7. Menychtas, A., Tomás, D., Tiemann, M., Santzaridou, C., Psychas, A., Kyriazis, D., Vidagany, J.V., Campbell, S.: Dynamic social and media content syndication for second screen. Int. J. Virtual Communities Soc. Netw. (IJVCSN) **7**, 50–69 (2015)
8. Santzaridou, C., Menychtas, A., Psychas, A., Varvarigou, T.: Context management and analysis for social tv platforms. In: eChallenges e-2015 (2015)
9. Sarwar, B.M., et al.: Recommender systems for large-scale e-commerce: scalable neighborhood formation using clustering. In: Proceedings of the Fifth International Conference on Computer and Information Technology, vol. 1 (2002)
10. Wei, K., Huang, J., Fu, S.: A survey of e-commerce recommender systems. In: 2007 International Conference on Service Systems and Service Management. IEEE (2007)
11. Zhao, Z., et al.: Improving user topic interest profiles by behavior factorization. In: Proceedings of the 24th International Conference on World Wide Web (2015)
12. Krauss, C., George, L., Arbanowski, S.: TV predictor: personalized program recommendations to be displayed on smarttvs. In: Proceedings of 2nd International Workshop on Big Data, Streams and Heterog. Source Mining: Algorithms, Systems, Programming Models and Applications (2013)
13. Kim, E., Pyo, S., Park, E., Kim, M.: An automatic recommendation scheme of TV program contents for (IP) TV personalization (2011)
14. Schafer, J.Ben, Frankowski, D., Herlocker, J., Sen, S.: Collaborative filtering recommender systems. In: Brusilovsky, P., Kobsa, A., Nejdl, W. (eds.) The Adaptive Web. LNCS, vol. 4321, pp. 291–324. Springer, Heidelberg (2007). doi:10.1007/978-3-540-72079-9_9
15. Tserpes, K., Aisopos, F., Kyriazis, D., Varvarigou, T.: Service selection decision support in the internet of services. In: Altmann, J., Rana, O.F. (eds.) GECON 2010. LNCS, vol. 6296, pp. 16–33. Springer, Heidelberg (2010). doi:10.1007/978-3-642-15681-6_2
16. Chen, H., Cui, X., Jin, H.: Top-k followee recommendation over microblogging systems by exploiting diverse information sources. Future Gener. Comput. Syst. **55**, 534–543 (2016)
17. Salter, J., Antonopoulos, N.: CinemaScreen recommender agent: combining collaborative and content-based filtering. IEEE Intell. Syst. **21**(1), 35–41 (2006)
18. Kwon, H.-J., Hong, K.-S.: Personalized smart TV program recommender based on collaborative filtering and a novel similarity method. IEEE Trans. Consum. Electron. **57**(3), 1416–1423 (2011)
19. Koren, Y.: Factorization meets the neighborhood: a multifaceted collaborative filtering model. In: Proceedings of the 14th ACM SIGKDD International Conference on Knowledge Discovery and Data Mining. ACM (2008)
20. Ekstrand, M.D., Riedl, J.T., Konstan, J.A.: Collaborative filtering recommender systems. Found. Trends Hum. Comput. Interact. **4**(2), 81–173 (2011)
21. Koren, Y.: Collaborative filtering with temporal dynamics. Commun. ACM **53**(4), 89–97 (2010)
22. SAM deliverable D6.9.2 – Context Analysis & Dynamic Creation of Social Communities Public Report (second version). http://samproject.net/sam-community/
23. Harper, F.M., Konstan, J.A.: The movielens datasets: history and context. ACM Trans. Interact. Intell. Syst. (TiiS) **5**(4) (2015). Article 19
24. Breiman, L.: Bagging predictors. Mach. Learn. **24**(2), 123–140 (1996)
25. Apache JMeter, an open source Java application designed to load test functional behavior and measure performance. http://jmeter.apache.org/
26. Li, D., Chen, C., Lv, Q., Shang, L., Zhao, Y., Lu, T., Gu, N.: An algorithm for efficient privacy-preserving item-based collaborative filtering. Future Gener. Comput. Syst. **55**, 311–320 (2016)

When Culture Trumps Economic Laws: Persistent Segmentation of the Mobile Instant Messaging Market

Maria C. Borges[✉], Max-R. Ulbricht, and Frank Pallas

Information Systems Engineering Group, TU Berlin, Berlin, Germany
{m.borges, mu, fp}@ise.tu-berlin.de

Abstract. This paper discusses the general characteristics of the mobile instant messaging market from a competition point of view. Positive feedback and indirect network effects, which strongly influence the mobile instant messaging market, tend to facilitate the development of one quasi-monopoly. Even after several years of market maturation, however, no mobile instant messaging application has yet established such a monopoly, seemingly contradicting economic theory. In order to resolve this contradiction, this paper deconstructs the global instant messaging landscape using theoretical insights into local bias and distinct cultural needs. We find that differences between high- and low-context cultures provide the most compelling explanation for market fragmentation and derive possible strategies for single applications' global market expansion.

Keywords: Instant messaging · Network economics · Information economics · Monopoly · Shared market

1 Introduction

Instant messaging, often abbreviated simply to IM, first became popular in the late 1990s with desktop applications like ICQ, AIM, or MSN Messenger. Recently, due to the widespread use of smartphones and the increasing diffusion of mobile Internet access [1], mobile IM has become predominant.

Instant messaging applications are, according Shapiro and Varian's definition [2], information goods. They are software that can be encoded into a stream of bits which is costly to produce but involves very low marginal costs. They are also products driven by the network economy, where the number of users directly and indirectly affects utility and thus consumer adoption, resulting in a so-called positive feedback loop [3, 4]. Markets with such characteristics, in turn, are usually so called winner-takes-all markets which tend to tip in favor of the company or technology that is ahead [2, 5]. In other digital markets such as social networks or the e-commerce market, such near-monopolies obviously occur [6, 7].

In the mobile instant messaging market, however, we are not able to identify one service that is dominating the market on a global level even almost 11 years after the first mobile IM service, Blackberry Messenger (BBM), launched in 2005. Instead, the mobile IM landscape is still a highly fragmented space, with multiple applications offering similar value propositions, competing to increase their market share.

© Springer International Publishing AG 2017
J.Á. Bañares et al. (Eds.): GECON 2016, LNCS 10382, pp. 115–126, 2017.
DOI: 10.1007/978-3-319-61920-0_9

When the necessary mobile technologies became widely available, the market allowed for a lot of new competitors to enter the market. *WhatsApp, LINE, WeChat, Kakao Talk, Snapchat* and *Viber* all entered the market after 2009, while veterans like Facebook Messenger or Tencent QQ successfully transition to mobile as well. Today, there are more than 10 different mobile IM applications with more than 100 million users[1], and while not all of them grow at the same rate, market competition shows no signs of slowing down.

From a global perspective, WhatsApp currently leads, having recently reported more than one billion users[2]. It may thus appear as the frontrunner and the foreseeable monopolist to most. The Asia-Pacific market, however, has demonstrated itself impenetrable for the application. Similarly, LINE and WeChat are also having trouble expanding beyond their respective regional markets.

This paper seeks to explain the apparent discrepancy between economic theory and the observed structure of the mobile IM market. The instant messaging market lacks any significant objective data, which companies try to leverage for competition reasons. Accordingly, instead of a quantitative analysis, we strive to find compelling explanations using theoretical insights. For this aim, we first analyze how (direct and indirect) network effects influence the instant messaging market in Sect. 2. We then briefly introduce the most important mobile IM applications and their specific characteristics in Sect. 3 and illuminate global and local market structures of mobile IM in Sect. 4. On top of that, we provide possible explanations for the observable market fragmentation in defiance of network effects in Sect. 5. In particular, we see variables like local bias and different cultural givens to significantly moderate competition in network markets. Finally, we discuss possible strategies for overcoming cultural obstacles to market expansion pursued by different mobile IM players in Sect. 6. Section 7 concludes.

2 Networks Effects in Instant Messaging

Network economics largely rest upon four main concepts: direct network effects, indirect network effects, switching costs, and lock-ins [8]. In order to establish a common ground for our discussion, these concepts shall be described and applied to the instant messaging market in brief.

2.1 Direct Network Effects

In a network subject to direct network effects, the value of connecting to it depends on the number of people already connected [2]. Communication networks are the prime example for such network effects, since the user can't extract any use from the product if the network isn't there [9]. According to Metcalfe's law, the value of the communication network increases as the square of the number of users. The more users a

---

[1] WhatsApp, LINE, WeChat, Kakao Talk, Snapchat, Viber, Kik, Tango, Facebook Messenger, Tencent QQ and iMessage have all individually reported having more than 100 million users .

[2] https://blog.whatsapp.com/616/One-billion.

network already has, in turn, the more will it attract further users. This so-called positive feedback, where a system feeds itself to become stronger, is ignited once technologies reach a certain threshold of users – the so-called critical mass [2]. As different players in a market try to reach this critical mass at, a battle between them ensues. Markets with strong positive feedback usually tend to tip in favor of the company or technology that is ahead [2], while players that lag behind eventually slump. These are so-called winner-takes-all markets. Figure 1 shows the typical evolution of such markets.

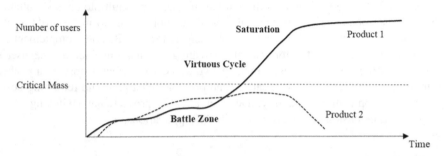

Fig. 1. Evolution of a winner-takes-all market over time, according to [2, 10].

Mobile IM is in its very nature a telecommunication technology. Users can communicate with others who use the same instant messaging application and consequently build a communication network subject to strong direct network effects and positive feedback. The value of a mobile IM application to the individual user depends on how many potential communication partners already use the same application or a compatible one.

Wang et al. [3] proved that the perceived number of users in instant messaging networks directly influences behavioral intention to use. Other research [4, 11] provides similar results.

2.2   Indirect Network Effects

Indirect network effects refer to the dependency between the size of a network and the availability of complementary products and services [8]. When the size of a network increases, more complementary goods are developed as producers see more potential in the market. The availability of more complementary goods, in turn, makes more users want to join the network.

In the mobile IM market, complementary goods particularly exist in the form of so-called "stickers", which are digital images that can be obtained as "add-ons" used in conversation to express emotions. They are usually developed by third-party designers or advertisers and therefore subject to indirect network effects: more stickers will be developed with increasing size of the network, which in turn makes the network more attractive to users considering adoption. This positive in instant messaging applications has been shown in [4]. Other examples for complementary products in instant messaging are in-app games or additional services.

2.3   Switching Costs and Lock-in

Switching costs and lock-ins refer to the disadvantages (in terms of monetary costs or effort, for example) that a user faces if he decides to switch to a new technology [9]. Complementary products typically heighten these switching costs as long as they are not transferable across different networks. When the switching costs are so high that they keep the user from switching at all, then the user is locked-in [2].

Switching costs are especially critical for instant messaging applications, as most applications cost nothing to download and join. Users can run multiple applications on their phones, but have to deal with the burden of managing multiple apps simultaneously. As continuous use is a prerequisite for these applications to make profit at all, applications try to lock-in their users in order to ensure loyalty. Besides complementary products, switching obstacles for instant messaging applications include the user's established relations with other users in the network, the user's chat history or any other data that binds the user to the application, and possible relearning and retraining costs regarding the applications usability. Deng et al. [12] proved that switching costs directly influence customer loyalty to mobile IM applications.

3   Applications

Most mobile IM applications share the same basic features, but as competition in the market increased, established players and new entrants started offering new services and value propositions. While it is clear that people use mobile IM applications to communicate with other people, the features that mediate the communication differ. In the following, we will thus introduce some of the most popular mobile IM applications and identify their defining features.

3.1   WhatsApp

WhatsApp launched in 2009. It is a simple and straightforward app that relies heavily on the basic chatting functionality and cross-platform compatibility. Users can communicate through text and simple Unicode emojis. They can share contact information, images, video, audio, documents and their location, just like in all of the other apps mentioned below. WhatsApp also provides group chat functionality and recently introduced the ability to make voice calls.

3.2   Facebook Messenger

Facebook Messenger spun out of the company's desktop messenger, Facebook Chat, which launched in 2008. In April 2014, Facebook removed the messaging feature from the main app, in order to force users to the separate Messenger application. Since then, it has evolved into a feature-rich application. In addition to WhatsApp's features, Messenger also has "stickers" and GIFs that can be used in conversations. Moreover, the mobile version has recently added a third-party app platform. Furthermore, users can also chat with businesses and organizations that have a Facebook page.

3.3 WeChat

WeChat has basically the same features as Facebook Messenger: it also offers stickers and allows users to chat with official business and organization pages. WeChat's platform is, however, significantly more advanced. It offers payment services and businesses can run whole e-commerce shops on the platform.

3.4 LINE

LINE first launched in Japan in 2011, as a response to the damaged telecommunications infrastructure in Japan caused by an earthquake. Since then, it has evolved into a rich platform that provides many multimedia features, similar to WeChat. It allows users to talk to strangers in the same way, and also enables business to connect to users through the app.

3.5 Kakao Talk

Kakao Talk offers a rich user experience. The messaging app has expanded into a social platform that provides not only the messaging feature, but also games, social-network-like user feeds, music-streaming and e-commerce. It was an innovator when it came to expanding the platform to integrate new features.

Table 1 summarizes how the aforementioned apps differentiate each other in terms of features. What is noteworthy is the extreme simplicity of WhatsApp, as well as the richness of the Asian applications. Facebook Messenger also provides some of the features of its Asian competitors, though they only adopted them after the features had shown success in the Asian market (e.g. stickers in instant messaging took off in 2012 when LINE introduced them. Facebook Messenger followed in 2013).

Table 1. Distinguishing features of the top applications.

Features	WhatsApp	Facebook Messenger	WeChat	LINE	Kakao Talk
Stickers		✓	✓	✓	✓
Business pages		✓	✓	✓	✓
Third-party apps		✓	✓	✓	✓
User feed		(Facebook)	✓	✓	(KakaoStory)
Share location	✓	✓	✓	✓	✓
Group chat	✓	✓	✓	✓	✓
Payments		✓	✓	✓	✓

4 Local Markets and the Global Instant Messaging Landscape

As already laid out above, markets with strong positive feedback usually end up tipping and become so-called winner-take-all markets. Shared markets on the other hand, don't tip and competitors share the market with predictable market shares [5]. Furthermore, we also showed in Sect. 2 that the mobile IM market is strongly influenced by positive feedback. Accordingly, one provider should eventually emerge as the winner and conquer the global market for mobile IM. Nonetheless, almost 11 years have passed since the first market entry (BBM in 2005) and there is still no winner in sight. WhatsApp leads in matters of the total number of users and recently passed the 1 billion milestone but, as Fig. 2 shows, other applications like Facebook Messenger and WeChat also continue to gain users at comparable speeds.

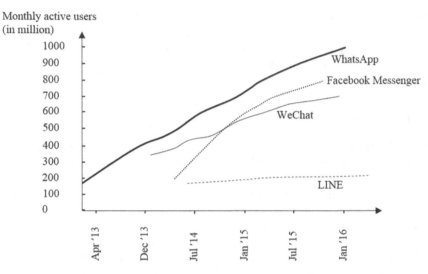

Fig. 2. Evolution of the instant messaging market over the last 3 years[3].

At closer inspection, it turns out that different mobile IM applications prevail in different regions of the world: WhatsApp controls the European market, as well as the South American market. In countries like Spain, Germany, Italy and the Netherlands, it is hugely popular. However, WhatsApp has barely had any traction in the Asia-Pacific region[4]. The application failed to attracts a substantial share of the market in key countries like Japan, Taiwan, Thailand and South Korea. It is the only popular foreign application not forbidden by the Chinese government, but the application has not found much of a user base there either (aside from Hong Kong). After failing to cooperate with a criminal investigation, WhatsApp saw its services temporarily banned in Brazil, a move that left many users scrambling for alternatives.

---

[3] Numbers according to https://www.techinasia.com/wechat-697-million-monthly-active-users, http://www.forbes.com/sites/niallmccarthy/2016/02/02/whatsapp-reaches-one-billion-users-infographic/#244ac6a8520b, http://fortune.com/2016/04/07/facebook-messenger-900-million/, https://www.techinasia.com/line-annual-revenue-2015.

[4] https://ondeviceresearch.com/blog/messenger-wars-how-facebook-climbed-number-one.

In fact, governmental regulations also shaped the Chinese Market considerably. WeChat, in turn, currently has more than 700 million users, the majority of which are from mainland China. The app has benefitted from China's increasing smartphone penetration and the relative lack of competition in the market. A variety of laws and regulations prevent several websites and applications from functioning, which leads to the development and popularity of their domestic products [13].

LINE dominates the markets of Japan, where it first launched, Taiwan and Thailand. The application recently made a big push into the Indonesian market, and managed to attract a significant share of the market (see also Sect. 6), though BBM still dominates there. The application managed to attract a large user base in the first year, and introduced stickers less than a year after launch, a feature that has shown to be very popular and profitable in the Japanese market.

Facebook Messenger has recently reached 900 million users. The application is especially popular in North America, where it is for example the most downloaded Android app after Facebook's main app[5].

Kakao Talk, a Korean product, is South Korea's market leader in the instant messaging market. South Korea is currently ranked as the country with the highest smartphone penetration in the world[6], which makes them an interesting, mature and developed market for mobile-instant messaging services. With more than 38 million monthly active users in the country in 2015, Kakao Talk reports a penetration of more than 97%[7]. That figure becomes even more remarkable when compared to the penetration rate of other applications. Facebook Messenger has less than half of Kakao Talk's market share, and WhatsApp barely exists in South Korea with a 1% install rate[8].

Altogether, market structures of mobile IM significantly differ across the world. Instead of one single global monopoly, we see different regions to be dominated by different mobile IM players: WhatsApp in South America and Europe, Facebook Messenger in North America, Kakao Talk in South Korea, LINE in Japan, Taiwan and Thailand, and WeChat in China.

5 Explanation Approaches

As we see, the market for mobile IM is much more fragmented than suggested by economic network theory. A possible approach for resolving this discrepancy between theory and the observable situation in mobile IM markets lies in the local-bias-theory laid out by Lee et al. [14]. According to this theory, local bias occurs when a user only maintains relationships with a small number of acquaintances that do not adopt the leading technology, but rather one of the lagging competitors, thus preventing a winner-takes-all market from actually developing. If all friends of a certain user live in

---

[5] https://www.quettra.com/research/mobile-app-landscape-2015-q3-report/.

[6] http://www.pewglobal.org/2016/02/22/smartphone-ownership-and-internet-usage-continues-to-climb-in-emerging-economies/.

[7] http://www.kakaocorp.com/en/pr/pressRelease_view?page=2&group=1&idx=8255.

[8] https://www.quettra.com/research/mobile-app-landscape-south-korea-insights-NOVEMBER-2015/.

South Korea and use Kakao Talk, for example, the user could be unaffected by the network effects of WhatsApp or another big network, as he doesn't perceive value in connecting to a network not adopted by his peers. Local bias tends to be preserved in highly clustered networks, but if many links between the clusters exist, then the effect of local bias is usually damped down [14].

As established in Sect. 4, instant messaging popularity tends to differ significantly according to geographical location. Different countries or cultures thus build different clusters. However, many opportunities for links between the clusters exist: the world is becoming gradually more interconnected as people increasingly tend to interact across the boundaries of such clusters (that is, communicate with people from other regions of the world where other mobile IM applications prevail). This would speak against the prospect of local bias persisting in the mobile IM market. The social network market is a good example: It is relatively similar to the mobile IM market and it is also a market fueled by network effects. As opposed to mobile IM, however, the social networking market eventually tipped in favor of Facebook, even in countries where there had been an established local alternative (studiVZ in Germany, Mixi in Japan). While it may moderate the market to some degree, local bias is therefore not a powerful enough variable to fully explain the current state and evolution of the mobile IM market.

Another variable that moderates a market's likelihood to tip is different customer needs. When different users have very different requirements, then the market is less likely to tip [2]. In this regard, different communication styles are an important factor in the mobile IM market. Hall's theory of high and low context cultures [15] may thus be another valuable explanation approach. It attempts to categorize cultural orientations and represents the extent to which different cultures contextualize information. High-context cultures rely heavily on situational information such as nonverbal behavior or the relationship between participants to facilitate understanding [16]. As much of the communicative content is already given by the respective context and thus does not need to be codified explicitly, communication tends to be economical, efficient and satisfying [15]. Low-context cultures, on the other hand, typically communicate primarily through verbal information [16].

Putting this dichotomy in relation to mobile IM, several studies have shown that stickers or emojis are highly important for users in high-context cultures [16, 17] as they allow users to express certain feelings or emotions that cannot be easily articulated in words. Both, emojis and stickers originated in Japan. They tend to be really popular in high-context cultures like Japan, Taiwan, South Korea and China. LINE claims that its users send close to two billion stickers a day[9]. In cultures where languages tend to have thousands of characters and tricky input methods, it's not hard to understand how applications that offer stickers got so big.

The distinction between high- and low-context cultures and the resulting differences in communication style may thus provide an explanation for the lack of traction of some mobile IM applications in specific low-context markets. Applications like

---

[9] https://nmk.co.uk/2014/03/19/next-in-line-for-mobile-messaging-interview-with-line/.

WhatsApp, that do not provide the necessary support for visual or non-verbal communication are not suited for that communication style and thus fail to attract users.

Shapiro and Varian [2] also identified the legacy of an earlier system and the tendency to favor domestic firms as possible reasons that might keep a global market from tipping. The latter certainly seems to be the case in some local markets, for example in South Korea. Tang and Lee [18] theorize that Kakao Talk's success might be due to Korean's loyalty to domestic products or services. They favor Korean search engine *Naver* over *Google, Samsung* and *LG* phones over *Sony* and *iPhones,* while also favoring Korean social network services like *KakaoStory* and *NaverStory* over Facebook.

Across Europe, in turn, WhatsApp seems to have attracted a large user base because its simplistic and straightforward design caters to the more low-context communication style of cultures like Germany, Netherlands and the Scandinavian countries. But that doesn't tell the whole story. WhatsApp now benefits from its legacy. BlackBerry Messenger preceded it four years, yet Whatsapp was the first one to offer cross-platform compatibility, which gave them a considerable advantage in Europe's very diverse mobile OS market. In the first year after launching in 2009, WhatsApp was already available on Apple, Android, BlackBerry and Symbian phones. Furthermore, the creators made the application available not just to smartphone users, but also for Nokia feature-phones, who at the time still controlled a considerable share in the European market. BBM is another example of a legacy system having a lasting effect on the mobile IM market. The application dominates in Indonesia, where historically BlackBerry held a large share of the device market. Because the app came preinstalled, Indonesians started using it, and when they switched to modern smartphone brands like Samsung, they continued to use the app (which was ported to other platforms in 2013) there.

Lock-in and Apple's legacy also has significant repercussions for the mobile IM market. iMessage is an instant messenger service integrated almost seamlessly in iPhone's traditional SMS and MMS application. iOS users usually start using the application by default and are therefore less likely to seek other instant messaging applications like WhatsApp, which ranks consistently higher in the US's Android application store than in the iOS store.

As shown in Sect. 2, lock-in and switching costs are a powerful driver for user loyalty to IM applications. The legacy systems mentioned above have secured high switching costs and lasting lock-in effects for their users. This suggests a certain inertia in the market, where switching costs may be too high to overcome.

Altogether, we can thus identify different communication needs in high- vs. low-context cultures as the most compelling explanation for the observed fragmentation of the mobile IM market in defiance of what economic network theory suggests. In addition, the structure of the smartphone market in a given region may have a significant indirect effect on the local instant messaging market, as legacy systems have managed to hold on to the lock-in associated with their IM application. The local bias theory, however, does not satisfy as the only explanation for the segmentation of the market, even though it may influence the market to some degree.

6   Strategies and Implications

Given the above analysis, it is crucial to recognize different cultural environments within various local markets for companies looking to expand beyond their established region. In the literature (e.g. [19]) on market internationalization, two general strategies have emerged: globalization and localization. Globalization involves selling the same products or services in the same way everywhere, while localization involves operating in a number of countries and adjusting products and practices accordingly [20]. In the following, we will discuss both strategies for the mobile IM market.

6.1   Globalization

Pursing globalization as a strategy has many advantages. For one, providers are able to save costs, because they don't have to adapt the product according to local markets. The product also benefits from stronger network externalities, as a network with more users has a higher perceived value. On the other hand, globalization also faces challenges: no local market is like any other, so adaptation to local needs may be necessary to attract more users and maximize profits.

Facebook Messenger is perhaps the application that is most aggressively pursuing the global market. From 2013 onwards, Facebook Messenger started to venture away from its messaging core capabilities and also introduced stickers and platform features – with the obvious intention of making the app more appealing to the Asia-Pacific market.

Western markets seem unaffected by Facebook Messenger's feature expansion, as users continue to use the app. The move proved to be successful in the Philippines, where it is the most frequently used mobile IM app[10]. However, its diversification efforts haven't yielded promising returns in South Korea, Japan and Taiwan, where local applications still dominate. Perhaps users don't see a reason to switch, as the applications they're using already provide the features Facebook is now implementing. As Facebook Messenger shows, expanding an existing application with features addressing specific needs of multiple cultures can be a viable strategy for expanding market share in yet unexploited regions.

6.2   Localization

The localization strategy is associated with higher marketing costs, as it requires product customization and extensive market research, but may prove to be advantageous in the instant messaging market, which, as established in Sect. 5, has to cater to very distinct cultural needs. LINE's expansion into the Indonesian market is a fine example of this.

The company developed stickers that show characters fasting and celebrating Ramadan, which appeals to the country's large Muslim population. LINE also made

---

[10] http://thenextweb.com/asia/2014/07/09/facebook-messenger-outguns-whatsapp-asias-chat-apps-philippines/#gref.

their application available for the BlackBerry operating system, as they recognized the large number of users who still had a BlackBerry device. Recently, though, there has been some backlash regarding some stickers in the app depicting LGBT themes. Indonesia is a very socially conservative nation. After governmental ban, LINE removed LGBT-themed stickers from the app, which shows how important it is to cater to the market's culture.

While the localization strategy can thus also prove viable in general, LINE's expansion to new markets has been comparably slow and the company is struggling to grow their user base further (see Fig. 2). This raises doubts about whether, in a market as dynamic as mobile IM, the costly and time-consuming localization strategy may be suitable.

7 Conclusion

Altogether, mobile IM applications operate in a market driven by network economics. Economic theory tells us that such markets should eventually tip and become winner-takes-all markets. This is what finally ended up happening with the social network market: after market entry in 2004 and global launch in 2006, Facebook first controlled the North American market, but eventually managed to dominate in local markets where other applications once ruled.

The same *tippyness* would be expected of the mobile IM market. However, as shown in Sect. 4, the market still seems very fragmented. Insights into cultural differences suggest that one of the reasons the market hasn't tipped yet is the distinct communication style of different cultures. Lock-ins and a tendency to favor domestic firms have also been observed in the instant messaging market. Basically, two different strategies can be pursued for addressing these factors in order to open up new markets: a globalization strategy, where different culture-specific features are joined in one product, and a localization strategy, where culturally different markets are targeted individually. In the mobile IM market, both strategies can currently be observed, with the globalization approach appears to be more agile and successful.

It will be interesting to see how the same cultural challenges will be addressed in other markets beyond mobile IM in the future. In particular, the market for business messaging faces comparable challenges. Internationalization and remote work has increased interculturality within companies. Players in the business messaging world thus also have to address barriers in cross-cultural communication.

References

1. Smith, A.: Mobile Access 2010. Pew Internet & American Life Project, Washington, DC (2010)
2. Shapiro, C., Varian, H.: Information Rules. Harvard Business School Press, Boston (1999)
3. Wang, C., Hsu, Y., Fang, W.: Acceptance of technology with network externalities: an empirical study of Internet instant messaging services. J. Inf. Technol. Theor. Appl. (JITTA) 6(4), 15–28 (2005)

4. Zhou, T., Lu, Y.: Examining mobile instant messaging user loyalty from the perspectives of network externalities and flow experience. Comput. Hum. Behav. **27**(2), 883–889 (2011)
5. Arthur, W.: Positive feedbacks in the economy. Sci. Am. **262**(2), 92–99 (1990)
6. Haucap, J., Heimeshoff, U.: Google, Facebook, Amazon, eBay: is the Internet driving competition or market monopolization? IEEP **11**(1–2), 49–61 (2013)
7. Baran, K., Fietkiewicz, K., Stock, W.: Monopolies on Social Network Services (SNS) markets and competition law. In: 14th International Symposium on Information Science (ISI 2015), pp. 424–436 (2015)
8. Katz, M., Shapiro, C.: Network externalities, competition, and compatibility. Am. Econ. Rev. **75**, 424–440 (1985)
9. Shy, O.: The Economics of Network Industries. Cambridge University Press, Cambridge (2001)
10. Dietl, H., Royer, S.: Management virtueller Netzwerkeffekte in der Informationsökonomie. Zeitschrift Führung und Organisation **69**(6), 324–331 (2000)
11. Lin, C., Bhattacherjee, A.: Elucidating individual intention to use interactive information technologies: the role of network externalities. Int. J. Electron. Commer. **13**(1), 85–108 (2008)
12. Deng, Z., Lu, Y., Wei, K., Zhang, J.: Understanding customer satisfaction and loyalty: an empirical study of mobile instant messages in China. Int. J. Inf. Manage. **30**(4), 289–300 (2010)
13. Deans, P., Miles, J.: A framework for understanding social media trends in China. In: Paper Presented at the 11th International DSI and APDSI Joint Meeting, pp. 12–16 (2011)
14. Lee, E., Lee, J., Lee, J.: Reconsideration of the winner-take-all hypothesis: complex networks and local bias. Manage. Sci. **52**(12), 1838–1848 (2006)
15. Hall, E.: Beyond Culture. Anchor Books, New York (1976)
16. Kayan, S., Fussell, S., Setlock, L.: Cultural differences in the use of instant messaging in Asia and North America. In: Proceedings of the 2006 20th Anniversary Conference on Computer Supported Cooperative Work - CSCW 2006, pp. 525–528 (2006)
17. Lim, S.: On stickers and communicative fluidity in social media. Soc. Media + Soc. **1**(1), 1–3 (2015)
18. Tang, N., Lee, Y.: A comparative study on user loyalty of mobile-instant messaging services. In: Proceedings of the 17th International Conference on Electronic Commerce 2015 - ICEC 2015 (2015)
19. Coskun Samli, A., Wills, J., Jacobs, L.: Developing global products and marketing strategies: a rejoinder. J. Acad. Mark. Sci. **21**(1), 79–83 (1993)
20. Levitt, T.: The globalization of markets. Harvard Bus. Rev. **61**(3), 92–102 (1983)

Energy Consumption

Energy Efficiency Support Through Intra-layer Cloud Stack Adaptation

Karim Djemame[1]([✉]), Richard Kavanagh[1], Django Armstrong[1],
Francesc Lordan[2], Jorge Ejarque[2], Mario Macias[2], Raül Sirvent[2],
Jordi Guitart[2,3], and Rosa M. Badia[2,4]

[1] School of Computing, University of Leeds, Leeds, UK
{k.djemame,r.kavanagh,d.j.armstrong}@leeds.ac.uk
[2] Barcelona Supercomputing Center, Barcelona, Spain
[3] Universitat Politecnica de Catalunya, Barcelona, Spain
[4] Artificial Intelligence Research Institute (IIIA) - Spanish
National Research Council (CSIC), Barcelona, Spain

Abstract. Energy consumption is a key concern in cloud computing. The paper reports on a cloud architecture to support energy efficiency at service construction, deployment, and operation. This is achieved through SaaS, PaaS and IaaS intra-layer self-adaptation in isolation. The self-adaptation mechanisms are discussed, as well as their implementation and evaluation. The experimental results show that the overall architecture is capable of adapting to meet the energy goals of applications on a per layer basis.

Keywords: Cloud computing · Energy efficiency · Self-adaptation · Programming models

1 Introduction

The rapid growth of cloud computing and the use of the Internet have produced a large collective electricity demand which is expected to increase by 60% or more by 2020 as the online population steadily increases [9]. Although currently moderate energy consumers, cloud data centres are continuously increasing their energy consumption share as compared to other sectors. Cloud computing offers the potential for energy saving through centralisation of computing and storage technologies at large data and computing centres. Some mechanisms are exploited to reduce energy consumption (e.g. server consolidation) but mainly operate at the data centre, hardware and virtual infrastructure level and do not include the platform and software application in their energy reduction approaches.

Previous work has characterised the factors which affect energy efficiency in the design, construction, deployment, and operation of cloud services [8]. The approach focused firstly on the identification of the missing functionalities to support energy efficiency across all cloud layers (SaaS, PaaS and IaaS), and secondly on the definition and integration of explicit measures of energy requirements into the design and development process for software to be executed on

© Springer International Publishing AG 2017
J.Á. Bañares et al. (Eds.): GECON 2016, LNCS 10382, pp. 129–143, 2017.
DOI: 10.1007/978-3-319-61920-0_10

a cloud platform. This paper adds the capabilities required in the architecture in order to achieve dynamic energy management for each of the cloud layers thanks to adaptation, which is supported by an *intra-layer* approach. The key research challenge is the ability to take adaptive actions based upon factors such as energy consumption, cost and performance within each layer of the architecture and examine the effect that these have upon the running applications. Therefore, the paper's main contribution are:

1. an energy efficiency aware cloud architecture, which is discussed in the context of the cloud service life cycle: construction, deployment, and operation.
2. an intra-layer self-adaptation methodology tailored for: (1) the SaaS Programming Model to make use of advanced scheduling techniques that consider different versions of an application's Core Elements, target platform and consumption profile; (2) the Self-Adaptation Manager that manages applications at runtime and maintains performance and energy efficiency at the PaaS layer, and (3) the Self-Adaptation Manager that performs re-scheduling of Virtual Machines (VMs) to maintain energy efficiency and performance at the IaaS layer.

The remainder of the paper is structured as follows: Sect. 2 describes a proposed architecture to support energy-awareness. Section 3 explains how self-adaptation is supported within the SaaS, PaaS, and IaaS layers of the architecture. Section 4 presents the experimental design, and Sect. 5 discusses the evaluation results of intra-layer self-adaptation within the layers. Section 6 reviews some related work. In conclusion, Sect. 7 provides a summary of the research and plans for future work.

2   Energy Efficient Cloud Architecture

Methods and tools that consider energy efficiency are needed to manage the life cycle of cloud services from requirements to run-time through construction, deployment, operation, and their adaptive evolution over time. Their availability will result in an implementation of a software stack for energy efficient-aware clouds. Thus, an architecture supporting energy efficiency and capable of self-adaptation while at the same time aware of the impact on other quality characteristics of the overall cloud system such as performance is proposed in [8]. Figure 1 provides an overview of this architecture, which includes the high-level interactions of all components, is separated into three distinct layers and follows the standard cloud deployment model.

In the **SaaS** layer a set of components interact to facilitate the modelling, design and construction of a cloud application. The components aid in evaluating energy consumption of a cloud application during its construction. A number of plug-ins are provided for a frontend *Integrated Development Environment* (IDE) as a means for developers to interact with components within this layer. A number of packaging components are also made available to enable provider agnostic deployment of the constructed cloud application, while also maintaining

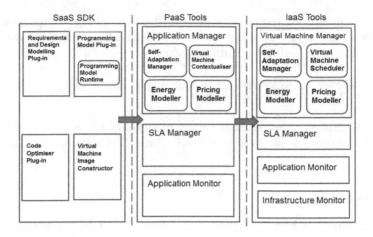

Fig. 1. Energy-aware architecture.

energy awareness. The *Programming Model Plug-in* (PM plug-in) provides a graphical interface to use the Programming Model and supporting tools to enable the development, analysis and profiling of an application in order to improve energy efficiency. On the other hand, the *Programming Model* provides the service developers with a way to implement services composed of source code, legacy applications executions and external Web Services [11].

The **PaaS** layer provides middleware functionality for a cloud application and facilitates the deployment and operation of the application as a whole. Components within this layer are responsible for selecting the most energy appropriate provider for a given set of energy requirements and tailoring the application to the selected provider's hardware environment. The *Application Manager* (AM) manages the user applications that are described as virtual appliances, formed by a set of interconnected VMs. Application level monitoring is also accommodated for here, in addition to support for Service Level Agreement (SLA) negotiation.

In the **IaaS** layer the admission, allocation and management of virtual resource are performed through the orchestration of a number of components. The *Virtual Machine Manager* (VMM) is responsible for managing the complete life cycle of the virtual machines that are deployed in a specific infrastructure provider. The IaaS layer monitors the energy consumed by the virtual machines, and is able to aggregate them by application. These infrastructure-level information is used to optimize the energy consumption at a VM level (by means of server consolidation mechanisms), and gathered to the PaaS level in conjunction with application-level metrics provided from software probes installed in the VMs.

The *Energy Awareness* provision is an important step in the architecture implementation plan as it concentrates on delivering energy awareness in all system components. Monitoring and metrics information are measured at IaaS level and propagated through the various layers of the cloud stack (PaaS, SaaS). The *Cloud Stack Adaptation* with regard to energy efficiency will focus on the addition of capabilities required to achieve dynamic energy management per each of the cloud layers, in other words *intra-layer* self-adaptation. *Inter-layer* self-adaptation is the subject of future work.

3   Intra-layer Self-adaptation

This sections explains how dynamic energy management is achieved by the individual cloud layers (SaaS, PaaS and IaaS) through a self-adaptive intra-layer approach.

3.1   SaaS Layer

The **Programming Model (PM)** is based on the COMPSs Model [5]. This architectural component enables applications including a single Core Element (CE) to have different implementations together with the possibility of implementing energy-aware policies in the PM Runtime. Details on these techniques can be found in [11] where a greedy policy is provided as a proof-of-concept.

To support self-adaptation at the SaaS layer more complex policies are implemented as optimization algorithms to adapt the execution of the application at run time. The algorithm is an optimization of one parameter, but filtering out the options that surpass the boundaries defined for the rest of parameters and searches for a local optimal in the discrete search space in every scheduling step. As will be shown in Sect. 6, self-adaptation at software development level has already been considered in other frameworks, but have not taken into account the three parameters considered here for optimization: energy, performance and cost. Therefore, the scheduling policies at application-level to optimize these three parameters are the key novelty in this layer. More precisely, the policies proposed are: (1) Minimise energy consumption (total Wh used) of the application run, with instant boundaries for price (EUR/h) and performance (s per CE); (2) Minimise cost (total EUR spent) of the application run, with boundaries for power (W) and performance (s per CE), and (3) Maximise performance (total execution time) of the application run, with boundaries for power (W) and price (EUR/h).

The three parameters are dynamic during the execution of an application when they are calculated for a specific CE. This is especially important in the case of cost because a fixed price would not allow any optimisations. In the proposed architecture in Fig. 1 the IaaS Pricing Modeller implements a dynamic pricing scheme, where the price of a physical host is divided between its running VMs and applications, allowing the PM runtime to optimize it. More specifically, the price of a host is divided between the VMs running there at the same time, the price of a VM is divided between the applications running together on that VM, and in the PM case the application price can be even divided among all CEs running.

Instant boundaries, such as maximum power, maximum EUR/hour and maximum execution time for a CE are considered for the adaptation. This is due to the nature of the PM applications. Depending on the application the complete workflow may not always be available to make the scheduling plan in advance. In addition, service-like applications as opposed to batch-like applications do not have a clear completion time. These boundaries will drive the optimization of either: energy, performance or cost, which will be specified by the end user before the execution of the application. It is also worth mentioning that these optimization algorithms mixed with the versioning capabilities presented in [11] enable interesting options for deciding how to execute an application in a set of resources, thus, not only having different machine choices to make that optimization, but also different pieces of software implementing the same functionality.

3.2 PaaS Layer

The **PaaS Self-Adaptation manager (PaaS SAM)** is the principle component in the PaaS layer for deciding on the adaptation required to maintain SLAs. The overall aim of this component is to manage the trade-offs between energy, performance and cost during adaptation at runtime. The PaaS SAM is notified of the need to take an adaptation by the SLA manager, see Fig. 1.

In this the PaaS SLA Manager, detects a breach of the SLA terms. It then notifies the PaaS SAM of the SLA breach. Notifications of SLA breaches principally contain the following information: (1) *Time*: the timestamp of the detected violation; (2) *Type of violation* message: This is either a "violation" if the violation is detected, or "warning" message if the guarantee is near the violation threshold; (3) *SLA Agreement Term*: used to distinguish between different constraint terms, and (4) *SLA Guaranteed State*: provides information on the border conditions of the SLA: (1) Guarantee Id: the metric to be monitored; (2) Operator: such as greater than, less than, equal, and (3) Guaranteed Value: the value of the threshold.

The adaptation rules then run in two stages. The first stage indicates the type of adaptation to make such as: add/remove VMs by assessing the causes of the SLA breach. This runs as a match making process by which the notification of the SLA term is matched against the adaptation rules. The PaaS SAM thus matches the decision rules that map between the event notifications and the potential actuators. In its most basic mode of operation a tuple of <Agreement Term, Direction, Response Type> is utilised in a match against the SLA violation notification to determine the form of adaptation to take, e.g. <energy_usage_per_app,LT, REMOVE_VM>. The types of events that the PaaS SAM can respond to are for the guarantees on the application's power consumption and the overall energy consumption of an application.

The rules includes an overall threshold value, which determines how many events are required before a rule fires, assuming that temporary reporting of SLA breaches can be ignored. An example of this would be if VM power was to become too high due to a short burst of CPU utilisation. This setting of this threshold value depends on the rate at which the SLA Manager reports SLA violations events and upon how responsive the PaaS SAM is required to be to these violations. A history of recent adaptations is also recorded to ensure that the PaaS SAM will not react a second time in short succession to the same violation event, this history is kept for a shortwhile and once a recent log of adaptation has timed out the PaaS SAM is able to respond again to the same SLA term been violated. This thus puts important limits upon how quickly the PaaS SAM will perform adaptation. In a more advanced mode of operation *fuzzy logic* is used with the following input parameters: (1) Current metric difference: between the guaranteed value and the actual measured value; (2) Trend difference: between the first detected breaches value and the current detected breaches value, and (3) Energy usage/power usage per Application: counts the number of times the event has fired.

The second stage indicates the exact nature of this adaptation such as what type of VM to add or which VM should be deleted. The principal actuators made available to the PaaS SAM are the ability to: (1) add and remove VMs from an application; (2) scale the VM vertically in terms of its allocated memory and CPUs, and (3) terminate the application as a whole. The engine that makes the decision of the scale of adaptation can be varied but is required to look at the application's Open Virtualization Format (OVF) document to determine constraints such as the minimum and maximum allowed VMs of a given image type. It then needs to make the selection of which VM to modify or which new type of VM to start.

3.3   IaaS Layer

The VMM is the component responsible for the deployment and life cycle of the VMs, as well as for their disk images. It also allows the IaaS layer to select different scheduling policies such as: energy-aware, cost-aware, distribution and consolidation of VMs.

The policies are implemented as scoring functions that evaluate an allocation scenario towards the desired policies. The scorers are injected in the OptaPlanner constraint optimisation solver [4], which applies heuristics to decide in a reasonable time which is the best allocation for a set of VMs in the available nodes. The administrator can choose the local search heuristic from Simulated Annealing, Hill Climbing, and Late Acceptance [3]. The ability to self-adapt at operation time which is supported by the **Self-Adaptation Manager (SAM)** is needed to keep the cloud infrastructure in an optimal state during its operation. To maximise the objective scores while keeping acceptable performance, the VMM needs to be able to live migrate VMs. To effectively enable live migration it is required that the VM images are stored in a shared disk space that is accessible by the source and destination hosts. For memory-intensive applications it is also required a fast local network infrastructure (e.g. 100GbE or Infiniband) to allow copying the main memory without having to stall the VM.

The migration decision takes into account information about the infrastructure and comes from several architectural components: the Energy Modeller, the Pricing Modeller, the Infrastructure Monitoring, and the SLA Manager (see Fig. 1). The information from the aforementioned is used as input into the scoring functions used by OptaPlanner.

The VMM administrator can choose which scoring function will be used by OptaPlanner as a heuristic to perform a local search through all the possible VM/host allocations. Currently, four policies are supported:

Distribution. The VMs are distributed equally along all the available hosts. This policy maximises the performance of the applications but minimises the energy efficiency.

Consolidation. The VMs are allocated to the minimum number of hosts (without overselling resources). This policy is energy-efficient but does not consider the particularities of the applications that must coexist in the hosts, and how the VMs can interfere between them.

Energy-Efficiency. The VMM asks to the Energy Modeller [8] about the predicted consumption for a VM into a given host, and chooses the allocation that minimises such consumption.

Price Minimisation. Similar to the Energy-Efficiency policy, but asking to the Price Modeller for the allocation whose price is the lowest. The Price Modeller gets a prediction of the energy from the Energy Modeller and ponders it with the expected energy prices for a given time range.

4 Experimental Design

This section presents the experimental design. The objective of the experiments is to ascertain that the self-adaptation at SaaS, PaaS and IaaS when monitoring a service in an operation achieves dynamic energy management in each of the cloud layers.

Application. Two applications are used: (1) a compute intensive simulation application of buildings to optimize their energy, thermal quality and indoor comfort and thus achieve a sustainable design. This is performed by the jEPlus application [2], which is the EnergyPlus [1] simulation manager, a well-known simulation tool in the real estate sector. The jEPlus application implements a parameter-sweep algorithm which performs large scale executions of the Energy-Plus simulator with several configurations to find out the optimal setup, and (2) a 3-tier Web application comprising of 5 VMs: one MySQL database VM, one HA Proxy load balancing VM, 2 JBoss Instances/worker nodes and one JMeter based VM that acts as a set of users inducing load onto the system.

Metrics and KPIs. A number of metrics and KPIs are used to drive the intra-layer self-adaptation: (1) *Application Run Time*: KPI which the PM tries to optimise when an application is deployed in a Performance mode; (2) *Application Energy Consumption*: KPI which the PM optimises when an application is deployed in a energy efficient mode. At PaaS level, the proposed architecture is able to provide the current energy consumption of a deployed application by monitoring the total energy consumed by the different VMs, see *Application Monitor* in Fig. 1; (3) *Application Execution Cost*: KPI which is optimized when the PM deploys an application in a cost efficient mode. The PaaS layer also provides the current application total cost thanks to the *Pricing Modeller*, see Fig. 1. Other metrics include: (1) *Estimated Task Execution Time* by the PM Runtime based on historic data of executions; (2) *Estimated Task Execution Power/Energy Consumption* by the PaaS Energy Modeller; (3) *Estimated Task Execution Price/cost* by PaaS Pricing Modeller, see Fig. 1. At the IaaS level, KPIs include: (1) *VM power*, (2) *physical host power* and (3) *Datacentre power*, as the spot measurement in watts for VM, host and the whole data centre.

Cloud Testbed. The cloud testbed is located at the *Technische Universität Berlin*. The computing cluster consists of 32 nodes with the following attributes: Quadcore Intel Xeon CPU E3-1230 V2 3.30 GHz, 16 GB RAM, 3x1TB HD and 2x1 GBit Ethernet NIC. Each node is connected to a storage area network usage where storage nodes are accessible through a Distributed File Systems, *CephFS*. Virtual Infrastructure Management is supported through an OpenStack Ice House distribution with Neutron and the OpenDaylight software-defined networking (SDN) controller. Power consumption on each node is measured thanks to identical energy-meters to guarantee comparative measurements. The actual devices are *Gembird EnerGenie Energy Meters* that share their measurements in the local network. These devices can measure power up to 2,500 W with an accuracy of ±2% and are able to deliver two measurements per second.

5   Results

5.1   SaaS Layer

In order to evaluate the new functionality implemented in the Programming Model (PM), we executed the same jEPlus calculation with different configurations. The selected jEPlus calculation generates 100 Energy+ runs executed in 5 VMs with 8 vCPUS (equivalent to a 4 real cores) an 8 GB of RAM which allows to run 20 tasks in parallel. Each experiment run has been repeated several times to ensure its statistical significance, and no large standard deviations have been found. Firstly, we executed the application with the original COMPSs-based PM which is used as the baseline for comparisons. The execution is then repeated adding the different PM improvements (the efficient execution mechanism, task versioning support and multi-mode self-adapted scheduling capabilities). In the first part of the experiment, we executed the application twice: one with the sequential version of the Energy+ task and another one with a threaded version as the original PM runtime does not support task versioning. Table 1a shows the KPIs obtained for each of these baseline executions. The minimum elapsed time achieved with the baseline is 750 s, minimum cost is 68 Euro-cents and the minimum energy consumption is 93.10 Wh. While the execution time metric for the CEs is controlled directly by the PM, the power and energy values are requested to the PaaS Energy Modeller component, and the price and cost values to the PaaS Pricing Modeller. Essentially the energy/power is obtained from real measurements, mapped to VMs, applications, and CEs, and the cost/price

Table 1. Application KPI measurements with different configurations.

(a) Measurements without ASCETiC PM Improvements.

Execution	Elapsed Time	Energy Consum.	Cost
Only Threaded Tasks	750 seconds	108.70 Wh	68 Euro-cents
Only Sequential Tasks	1152 seconds	93.10 Wh	72 Euro-cents

(b) Measurements with efficient execution improvements.

Execution	Elapsed Time	Energy Consumption	Cost
Only Threaded Tasks	662 seconds (-11.7%)	95.70 Wh (-12%)	60 Euro-cents(-11.8%)
Only Sequential Tasks	1008 seconds (-12.5%)	81.10 Wh (-12.9%)	63 Euro-cents (-12.5%)

(c) Single Task metrics estimations.

Task Version	Mean Exec. Time	Estim. Mean Power	Estim. Energy Consum.	Estim. Cost
Threaded	125 seconds	26.10 W	0.90 Wh	0.57 Euro-cents
Sequential	193 seconds	14.47 W	0.78 Wh	0.60 Euro-cents

(d) Measurements with self-adaptation.

Deployment Mode	Elapsed Time	Energy Consumption	Cost
Performance Mode	735 seconds	94.37 Wh	61 Euro-cents
Energy-efficiency Mode	882 seconds	83.80 Wh	63 Euro-cents
Cost-efficiency Mode	751 seconds	94.45 Wh	61 Euro-cents

(e) Application Execution KPI comparison.

Execution	Elapsed Time (w/o ASCETiC)	Energy Consum. (w/o ASCETiC)	Cost (w/o ASCETiC)
Only Threaded	662 secs (750 secs)	95.70 Wh (108.70 Wh)	0.60 Euros (0.68 Euros)
Performance	+9.9% (-2%)	-1.4% (-13.2%)	+1.7% (-10.3%)
Energy-efficiency	+25% (+15%)	-12.9% (-22.9%)	+5% (-7.3%)
Cost-efficiency	+11.8% (0%)	-1.3% (-13.1%)	+1.7% (-10.3%)
Only Sequential	1008 secs (1152 secs)	81.10 Wh (93.10 Wh)	0.63 Euros (0.72 Euros)
Performance	-27% (-36.2%)	+14%(+1.3%)	-3.2% (-15.27%)
Energy-efficiency	-12.5% (-23.4%)	+3.2% (-9.9%)	0% (-12.5%)
Cost-efficiency	-25.5% (-34.8%)	+14.1% (+1.4%)	-3.2% (-15.27%)

is calculated using fixed factors, and variable factors, such as the cost of the energy used. Afterwards, we introduced the efficient execution improvements in the PM runtime which includes the non-blocking I/O communication and persistent workers. We ran the same executions and measured the same KPIs which are shown in Table 1b. A general gain of 12% in all KPIs can be observed.

With the architecture tools, we are also able to extract the monitored metrics for each type of executed tasks (duration, power, energy and cost). The values obtained for these metrics are shown in Table 1c. In this table, the threaded version is shorter, but consumes more power and energy. In the case of cost, it is calculated by a combination of the resource usage, duration and energy consumption. As the duration term is the one which has more effect in this cost calculation, the threaded version is cheaper. These metrics are used by the PM runtime to perform the application level self-adaptation. In the last part of the experiment, we introduced the task versioning and the multi-mode self-adapted scheduling. In this case, we have executed the application in the three possible modes: the Performance mode, where the elapsed time is optimized;

the Energy-efficient mode, where the energy consumption is optimized; and the Cost-efficient mode, where the cost of the execution is optimized. For each of these runs, we measured the same KPIs which are shown in Table 1d. We can observe that the Performance mode gives the smaller elapsed time, the Energy-efficient mode gives the best energy consumption and the Cost-efficient mode gives the cheaper. Note that, cost and performance gives almost the same values because the sequential version has a similar behavior for duration and cost. Therefore, the solution found by the PM runtime in both cases is almost the same.

Finally, Table 1e compares the KPI values obtained in the different experiments with baseline. When we compare the versions with the improved PM, we can observe the cost of using the self-adaptation mechanisms. The *Only Threaded* execution is the most efficient for the Elapsed time and Cost because it only uses the version which has the best performance and cost. In contrast, the *Only Sequential* execution is the most energy-efficient because it only executes the version with the best energy consumption. When we compare with the values obtained with *Performance*, *Energy-efficient* and *Cost-efficient* modes, we can see that the KPI are degraded by a 9.9%, 3.2% and 1.7% respectively. This is due to the initial execution of different versions to obtain the first metric values. If we compare the results with the ones obtained without the PM improvements, we can observe that this overhead has been mitigated with the general gain obtained by the efficient execution mechanism. It is important to highlight that all the different improvements are obtained only by doing actuations at the SaaS layer, which means distributing the tasks execution in the available VMs, without changing either VMs or physical hosts, and we are able to improve some of the metrics even up to a 36%. In addition, the mechanisms give an extra degree of freedom to users, who can decide in advance if their application run will be done chasing minimum execution time, energy or cost.

5.2 PaaS Layer

The PaaS SAM listens for notification events of SLA violation breaches. These events arrive over an ActiveMQ interface. Messages can be submitted to the appropriate queue causing the PaaS SAM to invoke adaptation. This is achieved by calling either the Application manager or in the case of the experimentation below the Virtual Infrastructure Manager Open Nebula via a connector interface that invokes the required changes. A 3-tier Web application is used to perform the experimentation. It comprises of 5 VMs: one MySQL database VM, one HA Proxy load balancing VM, 2 JBoss Instances/worker nodes and one JMeter based VM that acts as a set of users inducing load onto the system. The experiment is structured in such that 5 VMs are started initially, then during the course of the experimental run, violation notification events are submitted to the PaaS SAM. This in turn causes the PaaS SAM to invoke adaptation which causes one of the VMs to be shutdown. The PaaS SAM is required to decide what action to take and when multiple messages are received it is expected to only make an adaptation to the application once, within a short space of time.

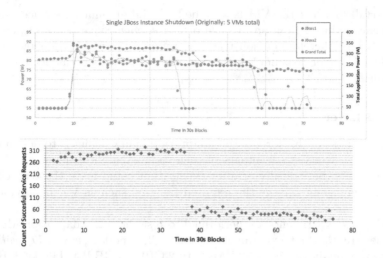

Fig. 2. VMs Trace - 30s time units division (top); Count of successful service request by JMeter (bottom).

The PaaS SAM as part of the experimentation used its rule based threshold system, with the threshold set to first event arriving would trigger adaptation. This threshold could be configured to be higher, especially in cases where the IaaS layer is also expected to adapt. Thus the PaaS SAM could wait n time intervals of warnings from the SLA manager, thus giving the IaaS layer time to adapt before the PaaS intervenes. It has a poll interval of 5 s in which it observes the message queue for new events as well as cleans up any historical log of past events that had become too old to consider as still relevant. The PaaS SAM keeps a history of events that last 30 s. This time-span is relatively short but it allows the experiment to run smoothly without multiple adaptation events taking place simultaneously. This also limits the time to wait until any additional adaptation can be demonstrated. The PaaS SAM on deciding to remove a VM, in the mode of operation selected for the experiment removes the last VM that was created of the appropriate type. This is done to ensure which VM to be removed is predictable.

In Fig. 2 (top), the JMeter and HAProxy instances can be seen to be very stable in their overall power consumption. The SQL database is less stable in its measured values. The total application power initially is around 276 W. It then increases at time unit 10 under increased system load by the JMeter instance to 327 W. This is then reduced by the removal of one of the VMs at time unit 36 to 243 W where the JBoss instance is turned off due to the arrival of several SLA violation notification events. At time unit 56 the load is stopped and the power goes to 221 W. This demonstrates how the PaaS SAM can invoke change which can result in a reduced power consumption thus saving energy. The count of successful service requests is shown in Fig. 2 (bottom). It can be seen in the initial phase a short loading period where the induced load increases. In time interval 36 when the VM is switched off the amount of service requests is drastically reduced from an average of 294 service requests to 42 per every 30 s block. This therefore demonstrates a trade-off in combination by showing that although power consumption can be reduced there is an associated loss in performance.

5.3 IaaS Layer

The main purpose of this form of self-adaptation management is to demonstrate how the VMM uses the advantages of migration capabilities to reorganize the VMs at runtime, periodically or after events that could leave the testbed in a sub-optimal status to achieve the required policies, such as VM deployment or removal.

Two jEPlus experiments are performed to test the Self-Adaptation Manager capabilities. In the first experiment, three 8-CPU nodes (*wally159*, *wally162*, *wally163*) progressively start a 12 VMs with 2 CPUs, 1 GB RAM and, 1 GB Disk executing a 4-thread CPU load generator that performs floating-point matrix multiplications. The VMM is configured with a consolidation policy to deploy the VMs on the lowest number of physical nodes. The OptaPlanner component is configured to look for the optimum allocation by means of Hill Climbing algorithm, though with a reduced number of hosts any other local search algorithm would quickly converge to an optimum solution. The intention is to save energy when it is combined with mechanisms to turn off the idle physical nodes and turn them on again when they are required. Every 5 min, a VM from a physical host (selected alternatively) is destroyed and the self-adaptation policy is triggered to re-consolidate the other VMs. The second experiment is simulated using an Energy Modeller. A set of 30 VMs are deployed progressively in 10 physical hosts and then destroyed. The objective is to compare the same execution with three policies: Consolidation (but without self-adaptation), Power-Aware (allocate VMs in the host that the Energy Modeller predicts it will consume less energy) and Power-Aware with runtime self-adaptation.

First Experiment. Figure 3 shows the effects of self-adaptation in the three physical nodes. In the first third of the experiments, the energy consumption of the three physical serves generally decreases as VMs are removed. In some points, the energy is slightly increased because the policy calculations decide that is more efficient to migrate a VM to such host. In the second third (from 16:38 to 16:42), all the running VMs fit in two hosts. Consequently, the VMM decides that is better to consolidate all the VMs in two physical hosts. This is the reason for wally163 to have a plain, low consumption from that time. Such consumption would be near 0 if the testbed had available a mechanism for remote sleep/wakeup. Analogously, in the last third of the experiments, only 4 VMs are in the system, and all are consolidated in wally162. The IaaS layer demonstrated the feasibility of live migration for generic VMs in order to maximize the overall performance of the system in terms of energy efficiency. The VM migration process typically took 10–20 s.

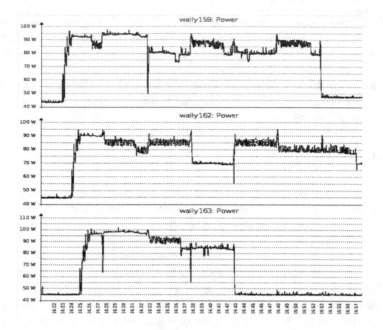

Fig. 3. Historic of power consumption for the three servers.

Second Experiment. Figure 4 shows the evolution of the overall power consumption since the beginning of the experiment, with no VMs deployed, until the end, where all the VMs have been undeployed. The measured results show that Power-Aware policy consumes 21% less energy than Consolidation. Savings are higher during the first half of the experiment and later, when the VMs are undeployed, the system becomes non-optimal since the VMs are not consolidated. With Power-Aware with Self Adaptation policy, the system status is optimized when the VMs are destroyed. The overall power consumption is 16% lower with self adaptation with respect to Power-Aware without self-adaptation.

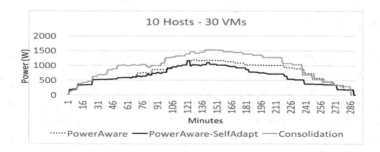

Fig. 4. Overall power consumption for three different policies.

Cost of migrations must not be underestimated. Migrations of memory-intensive VMs are expensive in terms of network and memory usage for the physical nodes. 10–20 s is not significant for batch applications, but may decrease the QoS for web services. Future versions of the self-adaptation policy penalise migrations in the scoring functions. To maximise energy efficiency, nodes should provide remote sleep/wake up to allow energy saving when a host becomes idle thanks to consolidation.

6   Related Work

Research effort has targeted energy efficiency support at various stages of the cloud service lifecycle (construction, deployment, operation). Regarding self-adaptation capabilities at software development level, tools such as Green-Pipe [13] consider energy as a parameter to be optimised, but it is provided by the user and tailored for a particular type of applications. The PaaS SAM is similar to the SHoWA framework's recovery planner [12]. The recovery planner is likened to a disease database, with a set of rules on how to treat certain anomalies in performance. The PaaS SAM manager goes further and specifies conditions such as the recent violations of a similar nature and recent adaptation responses. It also avoids pure thresholds and utilises fuzzy logic in order to give a more refined response during adaptation. The Synthesis of Cost-effective Adaptation Plans (SCOAP) framework [15] is a similar PaaS/application oriented adaptation framework which focuses on the economic costs of utilising Cloud infrastructures under various pricing models. Mistral [10] is a controller framework that optimizes power consumption, performance benefits as well as the impact of adaptations but with a focus on the IaaS layer. In the service *operation* stage, energy efficiency has been extensively studied and has focused for example on approaches towards energy management for distributed management of VMs in cloud infrastructures, where the goal is to improve the utilization of computing resources and reduce energy consumption under workload independent quality of service constraints. This approach has been faced during VM allocation [6] and runtime migration [7,14].

7   Conclusion

This paper has described an energy-aware cloud architecture along side an intra-layer self-adaptation methodology tailored for SaaS, PaaS and IaaS. The self-adaptation implementation has been showcased in two applications and results show that dynamic energy management is achieved for each of the Cloud layers. Future work focuses on the *inter-layer self-adaptation* where each layer monitors relevant energy efficiency status information locally and shares this with the other layers, assesses its current energy status and forecasts future energy consumption as needed. Self-adaptation actions can then be decided and executed according to this assessment in a coherent and consistent way.

Acknowledgements. This work is partly supported by the European Commission under FP7-ICT-2013.1.2 contract 610874 (ASCETiC project), by the Spanish Goverment under contract TIN2015-65316-P and BES-2013-067167 and by the Generalitat de Catalunya under contract 2014-SGR-1051. Thanks to GreenPreFab Italia for providing the jEPlus application and TU Berlin for their technical support.

References

1. EnergyPlus Building Energy Simulation Program. https://energyplus.net/
2. JEPlus: EnergyPlus Simulation Manager for Parametrics. http://www.jeplus.org/
3. OptaPlanner User Guide, July 2016. http://docs.jboss.org/optaplanner/release/6. 4.0.Final/optaplanner-docs/html/index.html
4. OptaPlanner Web Site, May 2016. http://www.optaplanner.org
5. Badia, R.M., Conejero, J., Diaz, C., Ejarque, J., Lezzi, D., Lordan, F., Ramon-Cortes, C., Sirvent, R.: Comp superscalar, an interoperable programming framework. SoftwareX **3**, 32–36 (2015)
6. Beloglazov, A., Abawajy, J., Buyya, R.: Energy-aware resource allocation heuristics for efficient management of data centers for cloud computing. Future Gener. Comput. Syst. **28**(5), 755–768 (2012)
7. Dargie, W.: Estimation of the cost of VM migration. In: 23rd International Conference on Computer Communication and Networks (ICCCN), pp. 1–8 (2014)
8. Djemame, K., Armstrong, D., Kavanagh, R., et al.: Energy efficiency embedded service lifecycle: towards an energy efficient cloud computing architecture. In: Proceedings of the 2nd International Conference on ICT for Sustainability 2014, vol. 1203, Stockholm, Sweden, pp. 1–6, August 2014
9. Greenpeace: clicking clean: how companies are creating the green internet, April 2014
10. Jung, G., Hiltunen, M.A., Joshi, K., Schlichting, R., Pu, C.: Mistral: dynamically managing power, performance, and adaptation cost in cloud infrastructures. In: 2010 IEEE 30th International Conference on Distributed Computing Systems (ICDCS), pp. 62–73 (2010)
11. Lordan, F., Ejarque, J., Sirvent, R., Badia, R.M.: Energy-aware programming model for distributed infrastructures. In: Proceedings of the 24th Euromicro International Conference on Parallel, Distributed, and Network-Based Processing (PDP 2016), Heraklion, Greece, February 2016
12. Magalhaes, J.P., Silva, L.M.: A framework for self-healing and self-adaptation of cloud-hosted web-based applications. In: Proceedings of the 5th IEEE International Conference on Cloud Computing Technology and Science (CloudCom), pp. 555–564 (2013)
13. Mao, Y., et al.: GreenPipe: a Hadoop based workflow system on energy-efficient clouds. In: 26th International Parallel and Distributed Processing Symposium Workshops, pp. 2211–2219. IEEE (2012)
14. Murtazaev, A., Oh, S.: Sercon: server consolidation algorithm using live migration of virtual machines for green computing. IETE Tech. Rev. **3**(28), 1–8 (2011)
15. Perez-Palacin, D., Mirandola, R., Calinescu, R.: Synthesis of adaptation plans for cloud infrastructure with hybrid cost models. In: Proceedings of the 2014 40th EUROMICRO Conference on Software Engineering and Advanced Applications, pp. 443–450 (2014)

Energy-Aware Pricing Within Cloud Environments

Alexandros Kostopoulos(✉), Eleni Agiatzidou, and Antonis Dimakis

Network Economics and Services Research Group, Department of Informatics,
Athens University of Economics and Business,
76 Patission Street, 10434 Athens, Greece
{alexkosto, agiatzidou, dimakis}@aueb.gr

Abstract. The Adapting Service lifeCycle towards EfficienT Clouds (ASCE-TiC) project aims to provide novel methods and tools to support software developers aiming to optimize energy efficiency resulting from designing, developing, deploying and running software at the different layers of the cloud stack architecture, while maintaining other quality aspects of software to meet the agreed levels. The *Pricing Modeler* is a component within the ASCETiC architecture, which is responsible for the price estimation and billing of cloud applications or Virtual Machines (VMs) based on their energy consumption. In this paper, we propose a set of novel energy-aware pricing schemes implemented within the Pricing Modeler component, as well as a set of envisaged service plans which aim to facilitate the gradual adoption of the ASCETiC architecture.

Keywords: Cloud economics · Pricing · Energy efficiency

1 Introduction

The ASCETiC project [1] complements cloud computing developments by addressing the energy efficiency of the software, which runs on cloud infrastructures. Although energy use is of relevance across all software development phases from design and implementation, we make specific reference to energy used during cloud-based service operations. The emergence of cloud computing with its emphasis on shared software components which are likely to be used and reused many times in many different applications makes it imperative for cloud service software to be developed in the most energy-efficient and eco-aware manner.

The ASCETiC approach focuses firstly on the identification of the missing functionality to support energy efficiency across all cloud layers and secondly on the definition and integration of explicit measures of energy and ecological requirements into the design and development process for software to be executed on a cloud platform.

Our main goal is to characterize the factors, which affect energy efficiency in software development, deployment and operations. The main novel contribution is the incorporation of an approach that combines energy-awareness related to cloud environments with the principles of requirements engineering and design modelling for self-adaptive software-intensive systems. This way, the energy efficiency of both cloud

© Springer International Publishing AG 2017
J.Á. Bañares et al. (Eds.): GECON 2016, LNCS 10382, pp. 144–159, 2017.
DOI: 10.1007/978-3-319-61920-0_11

infrastructure and software is taken into consideration in the cloud service development and operation lifecycle.

Therefore, ASCETiC addresses the total characterization of software energy with respect to the impact of the software structure on energy use, which is not incorporated into any current models. It is this gap in the research agenda, which ASCETiC addresses. Determining the relationship between software structure and its energy use allows the definition of a set of software energy metrics similar in concept to those for hardware. By associating these metrics with software components and libraries, it is possible to populate a software development framework with information to predict the energy requirements of applications, thereby allowing alternative selections of software components to be made, using energy as a selection criterion.

The proposed architecture measures how software systems actually use cloud resources, with the goal of optimizing consumption of these resources. In this way, the awareness of the amount of energy needed by software will help in learning how to target software optimization where it provides the greatest energy returns. To do so, all three layers in cloud computing, namely Software, Platform and Infrastructure, will implement a MAPE (*Monitor, Analyse, Plan and Execute*) loop. Each layer monitors relevant energy efficiency status information locally and shares this with the other layers, assesses its current energy status and forecasts future energy consumption as needed. Actions can then be decided and executed according to this assessment. Hence, ASCETiC intends to make significant contributions to software engineering, programming models and adaptive architectures for clouds.

One solution for accomplishing energy efficiency could be the adoption of energy-aware pricing by the cloud service providers. Charging cloud services based on energy, will provide the necessary incentives to the customers for achieving a more efficient resource usage. In response to this challenge, the *Pricing Modeler* component, incorporated within the ASCETiC architecture, is responsible for providing energy-aware price estimation and billing related to the operation of applications or VMs associated with them.

In this paper, we propose novel pricing schemes and charging services based on actual consumption and energy efficiency of cloud resources. The energy models and the real-time monitoring mechanisms and measurements by ASCETiC make possible the creation of new pricing schemes that will charge users based on their actual consumption and energy efficiency of cloud resources. Our aim is to adapt existing pricing schemes, as well as develop new ones, thus creating an energy-efficient and at the same time economically sustainable ecosystem.

The paper is organized as follows. Section 2 gives a brief overview of the three-layer ASCETiC architecture. Section 3 provides a cloud market analysis with respect to the pricing schemes adopted by the cloud providers. In Sect. 4, we propose a set of novel energy-aware pricing schemes implemented within our Pricing Modeler component. Section 5 introduces a set of envisaged service plans intending to facilitate the gradual adoption of the ASCETiC architecture. We conclude our remarks and present our future work in Sect. 6.

2   ASCETiC Architecture

In this Section, we provide an overview of the ASCETIC Architecture. It complies with the standard cloud architecture [2] and considers the classical Software-as-a-Service (SaaS), Platform-as-a-Service (PaaS) and Infrastructure-as-a-Service (IaaS) layers, supporting a wide range of components, including the Pricing Modeler component.

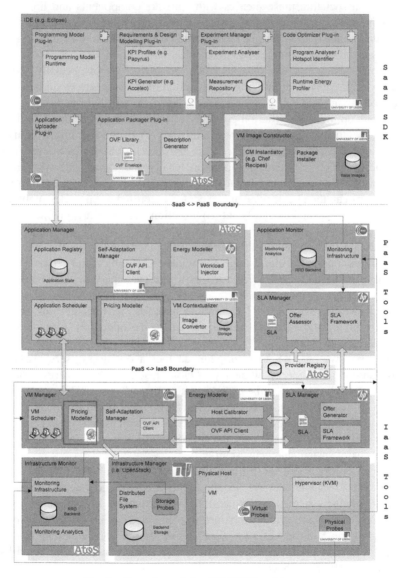

Fig. 1. Overview of the ASCETIC architecture.

In the SaaS Software Development Kit (SDK) layer, a collection of components interact to facilitate the modelling, design and construction of a cloud application. The components assist in evaluating energy consumption of a cloud application during its constructions. A number of plug-ins are provided for a frontend Integrated Development Environment (IDE) as a means for developers to interact with components within this layer. Lastly, a number of packaging components are made available that enable provider-agnostic deployment of the constructed cloud application, while also maintaining energy awareness.

The PaaS layer provides middleware functionality for a cloud application and facilitates the deployment and operation of the application as a whole. Components within this layer are responsible for selecting the most energy appropriate provider for a given set of energy requirements and tailoring the application to the selected provider's hardware environment.

Finally, in the IaaS layer, the admission, allocation and management of virtual resources are performed through the orchestration of a number of components. Energy consumption is monitored, estimated and optimized using translated PaaS level metrics. These metrics are gathered via a monitoring infrastructure and a number of software probes.

Figure 1 provides an overview of the ASCETiC architecture [3]. It includes the high-level interactions of all components, is separated into three distinct layers and follows the standard cloud deployment model.

A fully functional architecture demands the existence of a component that is dedicated to support the financial operations of the provider. Such a component focuses on the *cost function* and the *pricing schemes* of the cloud provider. Hence, as part of the presented architecture, we implement two different Pricing Modeler components.

The *PaaS Pricing Modeler* is situated in the PaaS layer of the cloud stack, and its main functionality is to estimate the price per hour and charges of an application before deployment, as well as to calculate its charges after its operation.

The *Iaas Pricing Modeler* is situated in the IaaS layer of the cloud stack, and it is used to estimate the price per hour and the charges of a VM before deployment, as well as to calculate its charges after its operation. The goal of the IaaS Pricing Modeler is to provide energy-aware price estimation related to different IaaS level operations that may be envisioned in order to take the most energy-efficient course of action.

A variety of cost functions and pricing models can be implemented within the Pricing Modeler components. A *cost function* calculates the costs that a provider faces during its operation in order to offer his services. It is a mathematical formula associated with a certain action. The providers forecast their expenses associated with their services, to determine what pricing strategies to use in order to achieve the desired profit margins. A *pricing scheme* is another mathematical function that dictates the way of making revenues from the customers. For the determination of the right pricing strategy, the decision on the objectives of the strategy and good market knowledge are a necessity. The prices resulting from the model are used as part of the Service Level Agreement (SLA) that is contracted with the customer. Thus, they are needed both during the negotiation phase with the customer and during the billing phase.

The basic purpose of the Pricing Modeler components is to enable the use of appropriate cost and price functions for the provider of the corresponding cloud layer. The cost function of a PaaS provider differs from that of an IaaS one, which is straightforward. A PaaS provider neither pays the electricity bill, nor owns any physical machine. However, a PaaS provider could act as a broker providing cloud services from different IaaS providers. Thus, the costs of a PaaS provider are based on the contract that he has with the IaaS provider(s), and the licenses of the operation systems and administration operations. We envision that our proposed energy-aware pricing schemes (Sect. 4) and service plans (Sect. 5) make sense mainly for the IaaS providers, since there are direct cash flows between them and energy providers, but at the same time motivate the upper layers to become energy-efficient.

3 Adopted Pricing Schemes

Let us provide a brief overview of the current pricing schemes adopted within the cloud market. We studied twelve well-known worldwide providers that offer cloud services. Most of them are IaaS providers but many of them are also PaaS. The most common pricing scheme is the "*pay-as-you-go*" one, but monthly or yearly subscriptions can be found too. Furthermore, Amazon provides one different scheme; the "*spot instances*".

In the "pay-as-you-go" scheme the customer pays only for the resources that he uses. There is no minimum fee and the total price that the customer pays depends on the resources needed, as well as on the operating system used on top. The charge is made per hour, while usually 740 h correspond to one month. When the "pay-as-you-go" scheme is used, the customer can choose the amount of a variety of characteristics that will compose his VMs. The basic characteristics of the VMs are the capacity of the CPU and the memory. Depending on the service that the customer is running, more resources can be purchased. Such resources may be storage, data transfer and the operating system, depending on the provider. The pricing is done differently per resource. Usually, the *capacity* is charged per hour, while the *data transfer* and the *storage* per GB per month. Some companies also charge for each request, or per million I/O requests, or per HTTP request, or per GB of data processed. The latter scheme is used mostly when the applications running are short-term and their workloads are unpredictable or changing over time.

The other popular scheme used is the *periodic payment* (e.g., monthly, semester, yearly subscriptions, etc.) or *pre-payment*. The customers pay or pre-pay the use of specific resources, having a discount on the hourly charges. Usually under these schemes, if the needs of the customer change, the resources reserved for him cannot be returned and the amount is not refunded. But on the other hand, if the customer needs more resources, he can always purchase under the "pay-as-you-go" scheme.

It is worth noting that some providers offer an on-line cost calculator to their potential customers. Such tools allow on-the-fly addition of the type and amount of resources needed and the upper bound of the amount of money that the customer will pay at the end of the month under 100% utilization of the resources and the "pay-as-you-go" scheme (or the exact amount on the monthly one). The estimates for the "pay-as-you-go" scheme are done based on 730–750 h per month. This scheme is used mostly for applications with more predictable usage patterns.

Most of the IaaS/PaaS providers nowadays use the "pay-as-you-go" scheme. *AT&T* is a representative example. The customer may choose the size of the processing capacity, the memory and the system storage that will compose his VM. For AT&T's PaaS, the customer selects a package based on his needs, builds his application and begins using it. The packages may include networking tools, email, web-based support and the option to add mobile users. The customer pays a per-device per-month fee [4]. *GoGrid* is an IaaS provider of computing, network and storage resources. It offers hourly, monthly, and annual cloud server pricing. Under the hourly "pay-as-you-go" option, there is no commitment, and the customer pays per hour for the resources used. The resources can be increased or decreased depending on the needs. Monthly or annual cloud server plans provide discounts in hourly charges, since the customer commits to a specific period of time of resource use [5]. In *Terremark* also the hourly price depends on the virtual processors (VPUs), the memory, the system storage configuration, and the operating system used [6]. *Microsoft* charges its VMs by the minute. In case of a monthly or yearly subscription the discount can fluctuate from 20 to 32%. Microsoft also offers a

Table 1. Comparison of cloud providers' pricing schemes.

Provider	Pricing scheme	Provided cloud services
Amazon [9]	On-Demand Instances, Reserved Instances, Spot Instances	Standard, Second Generation, Micro, High Memory, High CPU, Cluster Compute, High Memory Cluster, High I/O, High Storage, and according to the operating system
RackSpace [10]	Pay-as-you-go	Cloud Servers: Size, Disk, vCPUs, Public/Internal Network, operating system
GoGrid [5]	Hourly, monthly, semiannual, and annual cloud	RAM, Cores, Storage
Microsoft [7]	Pay-as-you-go, semester, year	CPU, RAM
Terremark [6]	Pay-as-you-go	Memory, VPU
AT&T [4]	Pay-as-you-go	Capacity, memory and system storage
Google [11]	Pay-as-you-go	Virtual Cores, Memory, Local disk
OpScource [8]	Pay-as-you-go, monthly	Size, Disk, vCPUs, Public/Internal Network, operating system
SoftLayer [12]	Pay-as-you-go, monthly	Core, RAM, storage, operating system
HP [13]	Pay-as-you-go	Core, RAM, storage, operating system
Engine Yard [14]	Pay-as-you-go	Core, RAM, storage
Acquia [15]	Pay-as-you-go	Core, RAM, storage

larger discount under the pre-paid monthly fee [7]. *Opsource* bills the customer only when the server is actually running [8]. For servers that are in a non-running state (stopped), the customer pays only for the storage that the server is using.

"On-demand instances" of *Amazon* correspond to the "pay-as-you-go" pricing scheme mentioned before. The customers pay for compute capacity by the hour with no long-term commitments. The notion behind the "reserved instances" is the reservation of the resources before their use for a specific amount of time. The customers can make a low, one-time payment for each instance that they reserve and in turn receive a significant discount on the hourly charge for that instance. Amazon provides three types of instances; for *light*, *medium*, and *heavy* utilization.

However, Amazon also provides the "*spot instances*" scheme. The customer buys the unused Amazon EC2 capacity and runs it until the price of the instances bought becomes higher than his bid. The *spot price* changes periodically based on supply and demand, and customers whose bids meet or exceed it, gain access to the available spot instances [9].

In the following table we present the providers examined, the employed pricing scheme, as well as the different VM features that the customer pays for (Table 1).

4   Energy-Aware Pricing

In this section, we propose novel pricing schemes for charging services based on their actual consumption to ensure energy efficiency of cloud resources. The energy models and the real-time monitoring mechanisms and measurements by ASCETiC make possible the creation of new energy-aware pricing schemes.

4.1   Why Energy-Based Pricing?

In Sect. 3, we observed that cloud IaaS providers mainly charge for their resources — which come in the form of VMs with specific performance characteristics— on the basis of fixed rates per unit of time. The rate levels depend on specific VM characteristics, such as CPU speed, memory, network bandwidth, etc. In certain cases, the pricing varies dynamically in time and depends on bids made by other IaaS customers. In any case, IaaS prices do not depend on energy usage —at least not explicitly, since IaaS providers strive to recover their factor (e.g., energy) costs through the appropriate selection of pricing levels—.

At the same time, applications take decisions which can have an important impact on both energy consumption and performance. An example of such a decision is the level of parallelism in the event of multiple tasks scheduled on many different VMs: the application has the choice of the parallel execution of a number of tasks on many different VMs instead of using only a few. Choosing a large number may prevent server consolidation from reaping all the potential energy gains. Actually, since pricing is not energy-dependent as discussed above, applications would go after the maximum level of parallelization possible, i.e., they will utilize all available VMs (or, at least it will not be in their interest not to do so). Thus, even though the great level of parallelism makes an application to have unnecessary low latency, it may incur unnecessarily high energy costs (by requiring a large number of physical servers to host the VMs). These increased energy costs are carried over to increased IaaS prices and so lower profit levels for the IaaS providers.

We propose to use IaaS prices which dynamically depend on the energy usage of applications. Under such a scheme the applications will be aware of the economic impact of their decision and so they will have the incentive to take energy costs into account, e.g., when they decide on the level of parallelism. Applications will themselves trade energy for performance according to their preferences, and not let other entities such as IaaS providers do it instead (through server consolidation) on the basis of guesswork about their preferences. Indeed, task scheduling at the application level may be more energy and performance effective than server consolidation by the IaaS providers since it is the applications which know what should be run in parallel and what should not.

Another reason that makes energy usage based prices desirable is that it is common for energy prices to vary in time for various reasons (e.g., varying availability of energy sources, time-of-day pricing, demand-response schemes).

4.2   Energy-Aware Pricing Schemes

In Table 2, we define some useful notions to be used in what follows:

Table 2. Terminology for energy-aware pricing.

Term	Description
Price	The (time) average charge incurred by a VM (or an application) per unit of time measured in euros per hour
Charge	The total charges incurred by a VM (or an application) measured in euros
Energy price	The price per a unit of energy, in euros per Watt seconds
Static price	The portion of price not explicitly depending on energy consumption; usually it depends on the static characteristics of a VM (e.g., CPU speed, Memory, maximum network bandwidth, etc.). It could be also the result of a market mechanism, e.g., auction for computing resources
Static charge	The total charge due to static prices
Billing	The calculation of a price or charge incurred by a specific VM based on past usage
Prediction	The calculation of a price or charge estimate concerning the future usage of a specific VM, given a prediction of its energy (or power) consumption
Pricing scheme	A formula for computing the price

The pricing schemes we present below are based on the costs of an IaaS Provider during its operation or on predicted charges based on estimates of future usage. Such costs take into account the energy consumption of a VM.

4.2.1 Two-Part Tariff Pricing

The actual form of IaaS price could be comprised by two parts: a fixed one, a, depending only on static information of a VM, and a dynamic one, b which depends on the average power usage. As an example we have the following simple scheme: a is a fixed part based on static VM characteristics, and b is the average power usage multiplied with the price per watt-hour (Wh).

Thus, the price p of a VM (starting at time 0 and up to time T) is computed by the formula

$$p = \frac{1}{T} \int_0^T p_{static}(VM, t)dt + \frac{1}{T} \int_0^T p_{energy}(t)W(t)dt \tag{1}$$

where,

VM: a parameter identifying the characteristics of the VM
$p_{static}(VM, t)$: the static price of VM at time t
$p_{energy}(t)$: the energy price at time t
$W(t)$: the power usage of the VM at time t.

We assume that the energy price changes only at the time instants $T_0 = 0 < T_1 < T_2 < \ldots$, and let the energy consumption during the corresponding time period be as given by the red curve in Fig. 2.

Then the total charges $C(T) = \int_0^T p_{energy}(t)W(t)dt$ incurred up to time T can be calculated from $C(T_k)$ as

$$C(T) = C(T_k) + p_{energy}(T_k) \int_{T_k}^T W(t)dt \tag{2}$$

Thus, in order to be able to calculate the charge for any VM one must keep track of $C(T_k)$, i.e., the charges incurred up to the last price change, the current energy price $p_{energy}(T_k)$ and the energy $\int_0^{T_k} W(t)dt$ consumed (by this VM) up to the last price change. Then the energy consumption $\int_{T_k}^T W(t)dt$ appearing in (1) can be computed as the difference $\int_0^T W(t)dt - \int_0^{T_k} W(t)dt$. Hence, on a price change one must iterate through all the VMs in the infrastructure and update $C(T_k), \int_0^{T_k} W(t)dt$. The energy price p is computed from the total charge $C(T)$ as $p = C(T)/T$.

The term $\frac{1}{T}\int_0^T p_{static}(VM,t)dt$ represents the static price of the VM based on its own characteristics. If the static price does not vary in time, i.e., $p(VM,t)$ is constant in the time parameter t then no time averaging is necessary. If it does vary then similarly to the above analysis, the total static charge $\int_0^T p(VM,t)dt$ up to time T can be written as

$\int_0^{T_k} p(VM,t)dt + p(VM,T_k)(T - T_k)$, i.e., the total static charges incurred up to time T_k plus the static charges from that point onwards. Thus, in order to keep track of the static charges incurred by any VM, the total static charge up to the last static price change[1] should be stored (for each VM). Consequently, every time the static prices changes one must update the static charges for each VM in the infrastructure. The static price up to time T is computed from the static charges as $\int_0^T p(VM,t)dt/T$.

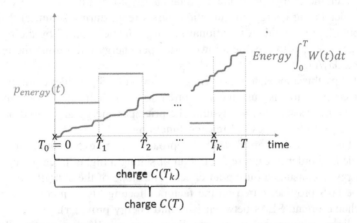

Fig. 2. Recursive calculation of energy charges $C(T)$ up to time T by the energy charges $C(T_k)$ and the energy charge during the time period from T_k up to T, where T_k is the last instant the energy price changed prior to T (Color figure online).

4.2.2 Two-Part Tariff with Energy Saving Discounts

A disadvantage of the dynamic usage price presented in Sect. 4.2.1 is that the actual energy that an application may use is not known by the developers at the time the SLA is established. A simple alternative is to pay a lump sum and then apply a discount based on the actual power consumption. Hence, we could use the following two-part price: a is a fixed price based on static info of a VM which also incorporates energy costs through the historical average power consumption, and b is a price discount depending on the level of power savings below the historical average. In this way it is not possible to pay more than the lump sum initial payment.

---

[1] For example, if the static price is the spot price of a market mechanism.

More specifically, the price p is computed by the formula

$$p = \frac{1}{T}\int_0^T p_{static}(VM,t)dt + \min\left\{\frac{1}{T}\int_0^T p_{energy}(t)W(t)dt - \frac{1}{T}\int_0^T p_{energy}(t)W_{nominal}dt, 0\right\} \quad (3)$$

where, $W_{nominal}$: the nominal average power consumption, i.e., the power consumption already accounted for in the static price. Any average power consumption above $W_{nominal}$ does not increase price above the (time average) static price. Deviations below $W_{nominal}$ result into a proportional discount.

4.3   Linearly Increasing Energy-Based Pricing

In both aforementioned pricing schemes, we assumed that the price of energy could potentially vary in each epoch. However, such schemes do not consider any direct relation between the energy price and the total energy consumption. Let us consider an energy provider facing energy consumption bursts (e.g., during summer) that he reasonably would like to avoid. A traditional pricing scheme adopted by the majority of the energy providers, is to provide a lower price per energy unit during the less bursty periods (e.g., day/night).

Motivated by this approach, we investigate how an IaaS provider could provide the necessary incentives to his customers in order to shift their energy demand to less bursty periods. In this scheme, we assume the price per energy unit based on the total consumed energy to be a linear increasing function.

It should be mentioned here that other approaches (e.g., exponential function) may also be applied, in order to capture the notion of setting a higher price per energy unit, as more energy is consumed during an epoch. The slope of the charging function will be set by the IaaS provider based on the factors affecting his own cost function (e.g., charging scheme or/and SLAs between IaaS and energy provider).

For the linear assumption, p_{energy} can be written as $cW(t)$, assuming that c is a constant parameter set by the IaaS provider, showing how aggressively p_{energy} will increase with respect to the total energy consumption. In order to prevent IaaS provider to charge arbitrarily high prices, we set an upper bound, such that $cW(t) \leq p_{energy\_upper}$.

Thus, the price p is computed by the formula

$$p = \frac{1}{T}\int_0^T p_{static}(VM,t)dt + \min\left\{\frac{1}{T}\int_0^T cW^2(t)dt, \frac{1}{T}\int_0^T p_{energy\_upper}(t)W(t)dt\right\} \quad (4)$$

4.4   95th Percentile Rule

The 95th percentile rule is a widely used pricing scheme in telecommunications for charging the transit traffic sent by lower-tier ISPs. By employing this scheme, transit ISPs intend to penalize lower-tier ISPs in case of traffic bursts.

A similar pricing scheme could be employed by IaaS providers for penalizing bursts of the consumed energy. To implement this scheme, it is assumed that the energy consumption within the infrastructure of an IaaS provider is measured or sampled and recorded (e.g., log file)[2]. At the end of each billing cycle (e.g., every month), the energy consumption samples are sorted from highest to lowest, and the top 5% of data is thrown away. The next highest measurement is the 95th%, and the customer will be billed based on that energy consumption.

We let $l^*(t)$ denote the 95th% measurement of the energy consumed by the customer at time t. Then, l^* is defined as $max\{l|P(W > l) \geq 0.05\}$.

Thus, the price p is computed by the formula

$$p = \frac{1}{T}\int_0^T p_{static}(VM, t)dt + \frac{1}{T}\int_0^T p_{energy}(t)l^*(t)dt \qquad (5)$$

5   Service Plans

In this section, we introduce service plans for the IaaS/PaaS provider to facilitate the evaluation of opportunity costs by offering multiple mutually exclusive service plans to its customers. The plans are intended to form the basis of business level contracts between layers by clearly specifying the responsibilities between the participating layers. Service plans is just one example of a method which IaaS/PaaS providers may use to facilitate energy-aware adoption, and others may exist. They are given here to complement the discussion on ASCETiC adoption implied by the energy-based pricing schemes proposed in Sect. 4.

The proposed service plans are intended to form the basis of business level contracts between cloud layers by clearly specifying the responsibilities between the participating layers. These responsibilities are the combination of

a. an SLA agreement,
b. a pricing scheme, and
c. a clear understanding of adaptation semantics, i.e., a specification of the originator and the means of corrective actions on the event of an SLA violation or just before it happens.

It is important to note that the plans need not be part of the ASCETiC architecture as such, as they are defined by combinations of instances of (a, b, c) above.

---

[2] For example, in the ASCETiC framework, the *IaaS Energy Modeler* component is the principle component for predicting energy usage and generating historic logs of usage [3].

On the other hand, the service plans are essential in evaluating opportunity costs and therefore affect business and technological decisions.

A key idea is that multiple plans should be offered at the same time, with multiple choices existing along two axes: the degree of adoption of energy-aware functionality, and the level of service performance.

Adoption axis: A successful adoption strategy should include plans similar to the ones offered in legacy architectures in order to not exclude customers (i.e., layers, applications) which

i. do not want to change method they are charged with to an energy-based one, and/or
ii. are not capable of exploiting the additional features of an energy-aware architecture.

Non-legacy plans which take information on energy into account, i.e., when either constituent of (a, b, c) involves energy-related terms, should be offered alongside with legacy ones. This coexistence will allow the gradual adoption of energy-aware elements of the architecture. The menu of plans offered should accommodate all customer types in respect to their adoption degree. For example, we could identify three degrees of adoption:

(1) legacy customers, i.e., described by (i, ii) above,
(2) non-legacy customers which prefer legacy payments, i.e., described by (i) but not (ii), and
(3) non-legacy customers which do not belong to either (i) or (ii), i.e., they have fully adopted the architecture and energy-aware payment models.

Performance axis: The second axis along which customers are categorized is performance. If multiple performance measures exist, such as response delay and reliability then the second axis is actually multidimensional. Higher performance means lower latency and/or higher throughput and is normally associated with costlier plans, while low performance is a budget option.

Figure 3 depicts these two axes along with five illustrative service plans which intend to cover most of the space defined by the axes:

HiPerf: geared towards high performance legacy customers. Normally it is associated with SLAs with performance-related terms. As these customers are not energy aware, the lower layer is solely responsible for adaptation actions.

Budget: a budget plan for legacy customers, which usually comes with loose or no performance guarantees specified in the SLA. Again the lower layer is solely responsible for adaptation.

Vegan: a budget plan for type (2) customers, i.e., non-legacy customers with legacy payment plan. SLA terms impose strict limits on maximum power usage (within a specific time window). The lower layer is responsible for ensuring these limits are never violated. Other than that, the customer is free to adapt in order to make best use

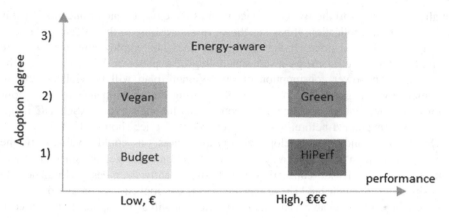

Fig. 3. Adoption degree of service plans with respect to the charging method and performance.

of system resources without exceeding the power limits. As the payment plan is legacy (i.e., not depending on energy consumption) the customer has the incentive of doing the most out of its energy-aware capabilities for the amount of price it is paying.

Green: a more high-end plan than Vegan, for type (2) customers. The share of responsibilities is the same as Vegan the only differences being that the power limits are higher at a higher price. Because the power limits are higher, this plan can be used by customer seeking higher performance.

Energy-Aware: a plan for non-legacy customers with energy aware payments. Since energy consumption is charged by the lower layer, it is the sole responsibility of the customer to make good use of energy-efficient actions. SLA terms could prevent overcharging due to excessive energy consumption, by either limiting the maximum power usage or maximum energy-related charge. (In the case the latter is exceeded the provision of service by the lower layer could temporarily be suspended until energy charges drop below the limit.) Both high and low performance can be accommodated under this plan, as the performance/cost tradeoff is determined by the customer's adapting actions.

These plans are defined such that they span most of the space defined by the two axes. This is to ensure that as many customers as possible are accommodated within a system employing this architecture. The existence of intermediate adoption degrees (customer type (2)) also allows gradual adoption in smaller steps, instead of a single big one. This reduces the adoption costs at each step and makes full adoption more likely.

Finally, the pricing strategy, i.e., the selection of prices in the pricing schemes, should be such that services higher in the adoption degree axis are more competitive than lower ones. In other words, the pricing of service plans should provide incentives for adoption of energy-aware technologies by the customer. Thus the service plan price differences could offset part of the adoption costs and act as subsidies by the IaaS/PaaS provider. Of course pricing should also consider competition with legacy clouds.

As an example of an adoption path towards full energy-awareness, consider an application which does not require small response times and desires a low cost service.

Initially it subscribes to the Budget service plan as the closest match. Since low cost is important for the application, it has the choice of subscribing to the "Vegan" plan at a smaller but still fixed price. If the application does not employ any energy-aware capabilities through e.g., energy-aware scheduling of requests on VMs, then soon the tight bounds on power consumption of the "Vegan" plan will be violated and so performance will degrade. The only way of avoiding this to happen is for the application to develop energy awareness. Of course this involves extra "ASCETiC adoption" costs as explained before, but the lower "Vegan" price should offset these.

Once the application develops energy-awareness, it could evaluate if the "Energy-aware" plan is better. It may be a better solution than "Vegan" since there will be times, e.g., cloud-wide congestion, which significantly degrades performance. In these situations, through the "Energy-aware" plan, the application can avoid big performance drops by being able to use more resources at will at a temporarily higher cost.

6   Conclusions and Future Work

The ASCETiC project aims to provide novel methods and tools to support software developers aiming to optimize energy efficiency at the different layers of the cloud stack. The Pricing Modeler is a component within the ASCETiC architecture, which is responsible for providing energy-aware cost estimation related to the operation of applications, as well as billing information.

From our market analysis on cloud service pricing, we observed that cloud providers mainly charge for their resources on the basis of fixed rates per unit of time, without taking explicitly into account the energy usage. In response, we proposed four novel energy-aware pricing schemes to enhance IaaS providers choosing their optimal pricing strategy, reflecting also our target for incentivizing the customers to be energy-efficient. The proposed pricing schemes differ in terms of aggressiveness with respect to the charging of energy consumption bursts. Furthermore, we presented a set of envisaged service plans intending to facilitate the gradual adoption of the ASCETiC architecture.

Our future work will focus on proposing new energy-aware pricing schemes, as well as evaluating them based on different scenarios. For example, each pricing scheme could be selected by a cloud operator based on the type of the applications running within its infrastructure. Another dimension of our research is to investigate and evaluate scenarios assuming competition among cloud providers employing different pricing schemes, as well as consider the equilibriums (if any) in the cloud market.

Acknowledgements. This work is partly supported by the European Commission under FP7-ICT-2013.1.2 contract 610874 - Adapting Service lifeCycle towards EfficienT Clouds (ASCETiC) project.

References

1. ASCETiC, EU FP-7 project. http://ascetic-project.eu/
2. Mell, P., Grance, T.: The NIST definition of cloud computing. Nat. Inst. Stand. Technol. **53**(6), 50 (2009)
3. ASCETiC Deliverable D2.2.3 Architecture Specification – Version 3, Public Deliverable, December 2015
4. AT&T Cloud Services website. http://www.business.att.com/enterprise/Portfolio/cloud
5. GoGrid website. http://www.gogrid.com
6. Terramark website. http://vcloudexpress.terremark.com
7. Microsoft Windows Azure website. http://www.windowsazure.com/en-us/pricing/calculator
8. Opsource website. http://www.opsource.net
9. Amazon Elastic Compute Cloud website. http://aws.amazon.com
10. Rackspace website. http://www.rackspace.com/cloud
11. Google Cloud Pricing website. https://developers.google.com/storage/pricing
12. Softlayer website. http://www.softlayer.com
13. HP cloud website. http://www.hpcloud.com/pricing
14. Engine Yard website. https://www.engineyard.com/products/cloud
15. Acquia website. http://www.acquia.com/cloud-pricing

Energy Prediction for Cloud Workload Patterns

Ibrahim Alzamil[1,2(✉)] and Karim Djemame[1]

[1] School of Computing, University of Leeds, Leeds, UK
{sclliaa, K.Djemame}@leeds.ac.uk
[2] College of Science and Humanities, Majmaah University,
Alghat, Kingdom of Saudi Arabia
I.Alzamil@mu.edu.sa

Abstract. The excessive use of energy consumption in Cloud infrastructures has become one of the major cost factors for Cloud providers to maintain. In order to enhance the energy efficiency of Cloud resources, proactive and reactive management tools are used. However, these tools need to be supported with energy-awareness not only at the physical machine (PM) level but also at virtual machine (VM) level in order to enhance decision-making. This paper introduces an energy-aware profiling model to identify energy consumption for heterogeneous and homogeneous VMs running on the same PM and presents an energy-aware prediction framework to forecast future VMs energy consumption. This framework first predicts the VMs' workload based on historical workload patterns using Autoregressive Integrated Moving Average (ARIMA) model. The predicted VM workload is then correlated to the physical resources within this framework in order to get the predicted VM energy consumption. Compared with actual results obtained in a real Cloud testbed, the predicted results show that this energy-aware prediction framework can get up to 2.58 Mean Percentage Error (MPE) for the VM workload prediction, and up to −4.47 MPE for the VM energy prediction based on periodic workload pattern.

Keywords: Cloud computing · Energy efficiency · Energy-aware profiling · Energy prediction · Workload prediction · Cloud workload patterns

1 Introduction

With the wide adoption of Cloud Computing, energy consumption has become one of the main issues for Cloud providers to maintain. A Cloud infrastructure along with its cooling resources consume a large amount of energy in order to operate, which may cause ecological and economic issues. The ICT industry is responsible for about 2 percent of the global CO2 emission, which is similar to the amount caused by the aviation industry, as stated by Gartner [1]. For economic aspects, a data centre may consume about 100 times more energy compared to a typical office with the same size [2]. In terms of maintenance, Cloud providers consider energy consumption as one of the largest cost factors [3] with a big impact on the operational cost of a Cloud infrastructure [4]. Therefore, various energy efficient techniques have been introduced recently to help the Cloud providers reduce the energy consumption cost of their

© Springer International Publishing AG 2017
J.Á. Bañares et al. (Eds.): GECON 2016, LNCS 10382, pp. 160–174, 2017.
DOI: 10.1007/978-3-319-61920-0_12

infrastructure, which can then lead to reducing the cost of operational expenditure (OPEX) and having less impact on the environment.

The impact of energy consumption is not only dependent on the efficiency of the physical resources, but also on the efficiency of the tools deployed to manage these resources as well as the efficiency of the applications running on these resources [5]. Different methods have been used to efficiently manage the Cloud resources, all of which can be based on certain thresholds, called reactive, or based on prediction, called proactive. For example, once exceeding a certain threshold, 80% of CPU utilisation, some actions take place by reactive methods to add more resources and avoid performance degradation. With prediction, proactive methods have the advantage of taking some actions at earlier stages to avoid getting that threshold and maintain the expected performance. To enable such optimisation and the energy efficient design of Cloud applications, the applications' designers and developers should be provided with energy-aware information to support their programming decisions. Also, the deployment tools should incorporate energy-ware information to make energy-efficient decisions when deploying these applications on the Cloud resources. As discussed in [6], having appropriate tools for energy monitoring and profiling is essential to get better energy-awareness and then help for energy optimisation at all layers of such large-scale system. Also, predicting the workload of a Virtual Machine (VM) can help make effective deployment strategies and energy efficient resource allocation methods [7]. Thus, managing the Cloud paradigm in all different levels and reducing the energy consumption has been an active area of research as it can result in reduction of OPEX costs for the Cloud providers.

Cloud applications can experience different workload patterns based on the users' usage behaviours, and these workload patterns are depicted by the utilisation of the resources hosting these applications. As stated in [8], there are mainly five Cloud workload patterns, namely: *static* workload experiencing the same and stable resource utilisation over a period of time; *periodic* workload experiencing repeated resource utilisation peaks in time intervals; *continuously changing* workload experiencing a resource utilisation that continuously decreases or increases over time; *unpredicted* workload experiencing a resource utilisation randomly over time, and *once-in-a-lifetime* workload experiencing a resource utilisation peak once over time. These different workload patterns consume energy differently based on the resources they utilise. Thus, it is important to have reactive and proactive methods to efficiently manage these resources when being utilised. In order to do that, current energy usage for physical and virtual resources has to be profiled so that such reactive methods can rely on it. Consequently, future energy usage can be predicted so that such proactive methods make use of. Energy consumption can be directly measured at the Physical Machine (PM) level, but it is difficult and not directly measured at the VM level. Thus, enabling energy-awareness at different levels is a key aspect towards efficiently managing the Cloud paradigm.

In our previous work [9], we proposed and implemented a system architecture to enable energy-aware profiling for Cloud infrastructure resources at both physical and virtual levels. In this paper, we extend our work to consider heterogeneity when profiling energy consumption for different sizes of VMs running on a single PM. Also, we extend this architecture to enable energy prediction for the VMs requested to run Cloud applications by considering previously profiled and stored data as well as the incoming workload's characteristics before service deployment. The outcomes of this work can help and add value to enhance the energy efficiency of Cloud environment by feeding into other deployment models or scheduling strategies to enable energy efficient management of Cloud resources, which can lead to lowering the cost of OPEX for Cloud providers. This paper's main contributions are:

- Energy-aware profiling model that enables energy-awareness for homogeneous and heterogeneous VMs in Clouds.
- Energy-aware prediction framework that forecasts the future energy usage for VMs prior to deployment.

This paper is structured as follows: a discussion of the related work is summarised in the next section. Section 3 presents the system architecture followed by a discussion of the energy-aware profiling model for attributing PM's power consumption to heterogeneous and homogeneous VMs, and a discussion of the energy-aware prediction framework for forecasting the future VMs' energy usage before their deployment. Section 4 discusses the experimental set up followed by results and evaluation in Sect. 5. Finally, Sect. 6 concludes this paper and discusses future work.

2   Related Work

Djemame et al. [10] emphasised the importance of optimising the energy efficiency of the Cloud paradigm at different layers and proposed an architecture that addresses energy efficiency at all Cloud layers and all through Cloud application life-cycle. Monitoring and profiling as well as forecasting the energy consumption is a key step towards enhancing and optimising the energy efficiency in the Cloud paradigm. However, VMs' energy consumption cannot be measured and profiled directly as they do not have direct hardware interfaces. Therefore, their energy information can be indirectly identified via modelling the energy consumed by the servers in which they are hosted [9, 11–13].

Further, uncertainty issues associated with the Cloud environment makes it more difficult to do such prediction, like predicting job runtime. Tchernykh et al. [14] have emphasised the difficulty of dealing with uncertainty in Cloud environment especially since its workload can change dramatically over time. So, they have reviewed and classified the uncertainty issues associated with a Cloud environment and discussed some approaches to mitigate them. For example, some looked at the historical data of applications to predict the runtime job of similar applications to be executed [15].

Tchernykh et al. [16] have presented an experimental study for several online scheduling strategies in a Cloud environment with different workloads. In the experimental results, they used and analysed eight allocation strategies based on three group categories, namely, knowledge-free, energy-aware, and speed-aware. The energy model used in their work simply considers summing up the machine's idle power and the extra variable power, which depends on the workload. However, they do not consider the workload in their model when calculating the variable power consumption. Also, the workload used in their work is based on HPC jobs for parallel and grid environments and not precisely on real Cloud environments that should also consider the complexity of virtualisation aspects.

Some work focuses on predicting power consumption based on historical data while others use performance counters, which are queried from chips or OS. But, relying on performance counters would not work appropriately in heterogeneous environments with different server's characteristics, as argued by Zhang et al. [17]. Therefore, they presented a best fit energy prediction model BFEPM that flexibly selects the best model for a given server based on a series of equations that consider only CPU utilisation [17]. Dargie [18] proposed a stochastic model to estimate the power consumption for a multi-core processor based on the CPU utilisation workload and found out that the relationship between the workload and power is best estimated using a linear function in a dual-core processor and using a quadratic function in a single-core processor. Further, Fan et al. [19] have introduced a framework to estimate the power consumption of servers based on CPU utilisation only and argued with their results that the power consumption correlates well with the CPU usage. As their framework produced accurate results, they argued that it is not necessary to use more complex signals, like hardware performance counters, to model power usage. Their work also indicates that the activity of other system components, other than CPU, may have either small effect on power usage or their activity correlates well with the CPU activity.

In terms of future prediction based on historical data, estimating the energy consumption of a Cloud application prior to deployment on VMs would require understanding the characteristics of the underlying physical resources, like idle power consumption and variable power under different workload, and the projected virtual resources usage, as stated in [20]. Thus, it is essential to get the predicted VMs' workload first in order to get their predicted energy. Some work has predicted future workload in a Cloud environment based on Autoregressive Integrated Moving Average (ARIMA) model [21–24]; nonetheless, their objectives do not consider predicting the energy consumption. For example, Calheiros et al. [24] introduced a Cloud workload prediction module based on the ARIMA model to proactively and dynamically provision resources. They define their workload as the expected number of requests received by the users, which are then mapped to predict the number of VMs needed to execute users' requests and meet the Quality of Service (QoS).

Compared with the work presented in this paper, ARIMA model is used to predict the VM workload, defined as VM CPU utilisation, which is then mapped within the energy-aware prediction framework to get the forecasted VM energy consumption for the next time interval. Then, having predicted the VM workload and its energy consumption, other methods can rely on this information to help introduce a proactive resource provisioning and scheduling that aim to not only utilise resources efficiently and meet the demands, but also consider the energy efficiency aspects as well. This can drive towards a cost reduction of the energy consumption and OPEX for Cloud service providers.

3 Energy-Aware Profiling and Prediction

Enabling energy-awareness in the Cloud paradigm is a key step towards optimising its energy efficiency. An energy-aware profiling model is introduced for Cloud infrastructures where the service operation takes place in order to understand how the energy has been consumed; this profiled information can then be used to help the software developers and reactive management tools make energy-efficient decisions when optimising the applications and efficiently managing the Cloud resources. Also, an energy-aware prediction framework is proposed to predict the energy consumption of VMs, requested to execute the application, prior to service deployment, which can help and facilitate such proactive deployment tools with energy-awareness to efficiently manage the Cloud resources. The overall system architecture of this work will be discussed in the next subsection, followed by a detailed discussion of the energy-aware profiling and prediction within this architecture.

3.1 System Architecture

The system architecture is aimed at enabling energy-awareness at the deployment and operational levels of the Cloud paradigm. As depicted in Fig. 1, this architecture consists of a number of components, mainly, the Resource Monitoring Unit (RMU), Energy-aware Profiling Unit (EPU), Reporting and Analysis Unit, and Energy-aware PREdiction Unit (EPREU). The highlighted components, EPU and EPREU, are the main focus of this paper.

Starting at the bottom layer when the Cloud infrastructure is operating to run the Cloud services, the resources' usage and physical energy consumption along with the number of assigned VMs to each PM are dynamically collected by RMU. EPU has an appropriate energy model that takes as input the monitored data from RMU and outputs.

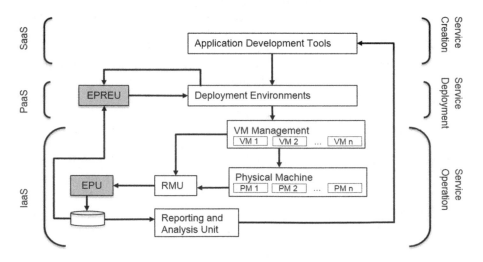

Fig. 1. System architecture.

The attribution of the energy consumption to each VM based on the energy consumption of their physical hosts. Then, EPU profiles and populates these measurements to a knowledge database, which can be further used by the Reporting and Analysis Unit to provide energy-aware reports to the application developers to help them learn how their applications consume energy and make such energy-efficient decisions accordingly to optimise their applications. Also, these measurements can be very useful for such resource management tools by enhancing their energy-awareness and making energy-efficient decisions when, for example, scheduling the tasks and balancing the workload. Further, this energy-related information of VMs, which can be used by different customers and run on the same PM, can help the service providers introduce a new pricing mechanism that charge the customers based not only on their IT resources usage, but on their energy usage as well.

Moving up to the middle layer when the Cloud services are about to be deployed, EPREU has a framework consisting of a number of models that predict the energy consumption of VMs prior to service deployment by considering the type of these VMs and their historical data. The predicted energy consumption for VMs can help other deployment strategies make energy-efficient decisions proactively.

3.2 Energy-Aware Profiling Model

The energy consumption of PMs can be directly measured and mainly consists of two parts, idle and active. The idle energy is consumed when the PM is turned on but not running any workload. The active energy is the extra energy added to the idle when the PM is busy and running some workload. As the case with the PM, the total energy consumption of the VM equals its idle energy consumption plus its active energy consumption. Yet, the energy consumption of VMs is difficult to identify and not directly measured.

In our previous work [9], we introduced an energy-aware profiling model that attributes the PM's energy consumption to VMs. It attributes the PM's idle energy evenly among the number of VMs running on it, and attributes the active energy based on VM CPU utilisation mechanism. This model enables a fair attribution of a PM's energy consumption to homogeneous VMs.

In this paper, we extend our work and introduce a new energy-aware profiling model that fairly attributes the energy consumption to homogeneous and heterogeneous VMs running on the same PM. This new model works by fairly attributing the PM's idle energy to VMs based on the number of Virtual CPUs (VCPUs) assigned to each VM, and the active energy to VMs based on the VM CPU utilisation mechanism as well as the number of VCPUs assigned to each VM.

As shown in Eq. 1, VM_{xPwr} is the power consumption of the targeted VM; $PM_{IdlePwr}$ is the idle power consumption of the PM where the VMs are hosted; VM_{xVCPU} and VM_{xUtil} are the number of assigned VCPUs and the CPU utilisation of that VM; VM_{Count} is the number of VMs running on the same PM; VM_{yVCPU} and VM_{yUtil} are the number of assigned VCPUs and the CPU utilisation of a member of the VMs set hosted by the same PM, and the active power consumption of the PM is the total PM's power PM_{Pwr} minus its idle power.

$$VM_{xPwr} = PM_{IdlePwr} \times \frac{VM_{xVCPU}}{\sum_{y=1}^{VM_{Count}} VM_{yVCPU}} + (PM_{Pwr} - PM_{IdlePwr})$$
$$\times \frac{VM_{xUtil} \times VM_{xVCPU}}{\sum_{y=1}^{VM_{Count}} \left(VM_{yUtil} \times VM_{yVCPU} \right)} \tag{1}$$

Hence, the new energy-aware profiling model can now fairly attribute the idle and active energy consumption of a PM to the same or different sizes of VMs in terms of the allocated VCPUs for each VM. For instance, when both a small VM with 1 VCPU and a large VM with 3 VCPUs are being fully utilized on the same PM, the large VM would have triple the value in terms of energy consumption as compared to the small VM; so that the energy consumption can be fairly attributed based on the actual physical resources used by each VM.

3.3   Energy-Aware Prediction Framework

As measuring the current energy consumption is difficult and cannot be performed directly at the VM level, predicting the future energy consumption is even more difficult at this level because it would rely on the estimated PM's energy to be used. Therefore, an energy-aware prediction framework that aims to forecast the energy consumption for the new VMs prior to service deployment is presented. This framework includes a model that first predicts the workload at the VM level. After that, this predicted VM workload is correlated to physical workload in order to estimate the new PM energy consumption, from which the predicted VM energy consumption would be based on. As depicted in Fig. 2, this energy-aware prediction framework includes four main steps in order to forecast the VMs' energy consumption.

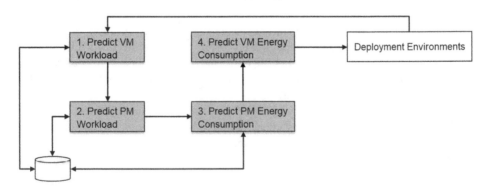

Fig. 2. Energy-aware prediction framework.

Step 1: This framework starts by receiving from the deployment environment pre-requisite information, which is the requested number of VMs along with their capacity in terms of VCPUs to execute the application, before such deployment process takes place. Then, by using the ARIMA model, the VM workload, which is VM CPU utilisation, is predicted based on historical static and periodic workload patterns.

The ARIMA model is a time series prediction model that has been used widely in different domains, including finance, owing to its sophistication and accuracy; further details about the ARIMA model can be found in [25]. Unlike other prediction methods, like sample average, ARIMA takes multiple inputs as historical observations and outputs multiple future observations depicting the seasonal trend. It can be used for seasonal or non-seasonal time-series data. The type of seasonal ARIMA model is used in this work as the targeted workload patterns are reoccurring and showing seasonality in time intervals. In order to use the ARIMA model for predicting the VM workload in our work, the historical time series workload data has to be stationary, otherwise Box and Cox transformation [26] and data differencing methods are used to make these data stationary. The model selection can be automatically processed in R package [27] using the **auto.arima** function, which selects the best fit model of ARIMA based on Akaike Information Criterion (AIC) or Bayesian Information Criterion (BIC) value.

Step 2: Once the VM's workload is predicted, the next step is to understand how this workload would be reflected on the physical resources and predict the new PM's workload, which is PM CPU utilisation, with consideration of its current workload as the PM may be running another VM already. Therefore, the relationship between the number of VCPUs and the PM's CPU utilisation is characterised for each PM in the Leeds Cloud testbed (this testbed is discussed in Sect. 4). For instance, Fig. 3a shows a linear relation between the number of VCPUs and CPU utilisation for a single physical host. Thus, using this relation equation can help estimate the new increment of PM's CPU utilisation based on the used ratio of the requested VCPUs for the VM, $VM_{xReqVCPUs}$, identified by the predicted VM CPU utilisation, $VM_{xPredUtil}$. This new increment of PM's utilisation would be also added to the current PM's CPU utilisation, $PM_{xCurrUtil}$, in order to identify the new total of the predicted PM's CPU utilisation, $PM_{xPredUtil}$, as described in Eq. 2. The PM's idle CPU utilisation, $PM_{xIdleUtil}$, is subtracted from the current because the relation equation already considers this idle value.

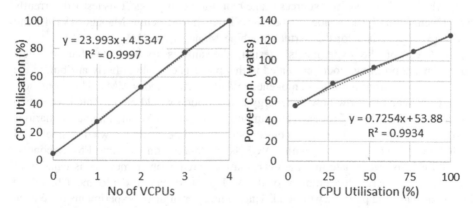

Fig. 3. (a) On the left: Number of VCPUs vs. CPU utilisation for a single host. (b) On the right: CPU utilisation vs. power consumption for a single host.

$$PM_{xPredUtil} = \left(23.993 \times \left(VM_{xReqVCPUs} \times \frac{VM_{xPredUtil}}{100}\right) + 4.5347\right) \tag{2}$$
$$+ \left(PM_{xCurrUtil} - PM_{xIdleUtil}\right)$$

Step 3: After predicting the PM's workload, the next step is to predict the PM's energy consumption based on the correlation of this predicted workload with PM energy consumption. For example, Fig. 3b shows a linear relation between the power consumption and the CPU utilisation on the same physical host.

Considering this relation, Eq. 3 is used to predict the PM's power consumption, $PM_{xPredPwr}$, based on the predicted PM's CPU utilisation.

$$PM_{xPredPwr} = 0.7254 \times PM_{xPredUtil} + 53.88 \tag{3}$$

Step 4: The final step within this framework is to profile and attribute the predicted PM's energy consumption to the new requested VM and to the VMs already running on that physical host based on the energy-aware profiling model introduced in Sect. 3.2. Hence, the energy consumption for the new VM prior to deployment will be predicted for the next interval time using Eq. 1, but substituting the VM_{xVCPU} with $VM_{xReq_{VCPU}}$, PM_{Pwr} with $PM_{xPredPwr}$, and VM_{xUtil} with $VM_{xPredUtil}$.

4 Experimental Set up

This section describes the environment and the details of the experiments conducted in order to evaluate the work presented in this paper. In terms of the environment, the experiments have been conducted on the Leeds Cloud testbed, discussed in details in [9]. Briefly, this testbed includes a cluster of commodity Dell servers, and one of these servers with a four core X3430 Intel Xeon CPU was used. The server has a WattsUp meter [28] attached to directly measure the energy consumption and push it to Zabbix [29], which is also used for resources usage monitoring purposes. This testbed currently uses OpenNebula [30] version 4.10 as the Virtual Infrastructure Manager (VIM), and KVM [31] hypervisor for the Virtual Machine Manager (VMM).

In terms of the experiments' design, the aim is to evaluate that the new energy-aware profiling model presented in this paper is capable of fairly attributing the PM's energy consumption to homogeneous and heterogeneous VMs. Thus, one scenario is designed to show how the energy consumption would be attributed when two small VMs with 1 VCPU for each are running on the same PM, and another scenario is designed to show how the energy consumption would be attributed when a small VM with 1 VCPU and a large VM with 3 VCPUs are running on the same PM. Secondly, the aim is also to evaluate that the energy-aware prediction framework is capable of predicting the energy consumption of the VM prior to service deployment based on historical static and periodic workload. Thus, a number of direct experiments have been conducted on the testbed to synthetically generate static and periodic workload by stressing the CPU on different types of VMs, like a small VM with 1 VCPU and a large VM with 3 VCPUs. The generated workload of each VM type has four time intervals of 30 min each. The first three intervals will be used as the historical data set for prediction, and the last interval will be used as the testing data set to evaluate the predicted results. The prediction process starts by firstly predicting the VM workload offline using the **auto.arima** function in R package [27] and then completing the cycle of this framework and considering the correlation between the physical and virtual resources to predict energy consumption of the VM prior to deployment on a single PM. This single PM is expected to host this VM only, so this VM would have the same energy consumption as the PM.

5 Results Discussion and Evaluation

Starting with evaluating the capability of the energy-aware profiling, Figs. 4a and b show the results of attributing the PM's energy consumption to two homogeneous and heterogeneous VMs. The first part of Figs. 4a and b shows the attribution of the PM's idle energy when the VMs are running but not generating any workload, and the second part shows the attribution of the PM's total energy when the VMs are running the same workload at 80% of CPU utilisation.

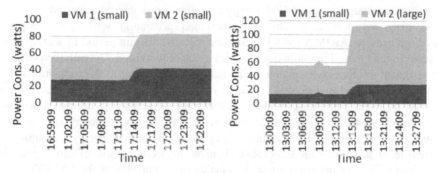

Fig. 4. Energy consumption of a single host attributed to two homogeneous VMs shown on the left (a) and to two heterogeneous VMs shown on the right (b).

Figure 4a shows the results of attributing the PM's energy consumption to two homogeneous small VMs, each with 1 VCPU. Based on the results shown on Fig. 4a, both of the VMs have the same energy consumption as they are homogeneous and have the same usage of the actual physical resources. Figure 4b shows the attribution of PM's energy consumption to heterogeneous VMs, one small with 1 VCPU and another large with 3 VCPUs. As having triple the size in terms of VCPUs, the large VM's energy consumption during the idle and active states is three times larger than the energy consumption of the small VM. Overall, the results show that the energy-aware profiling model is capable of fairly attributing PM's energy consumption to homogeneous and heterogeneous VMs based on their utilisation and size, which reflect the actual physical resources' usage.

In terms of evaluating the energy-aware prediction framework, Fig. 5 presents the predicted results for a large VM based on a historical static workload pattern at 80% of

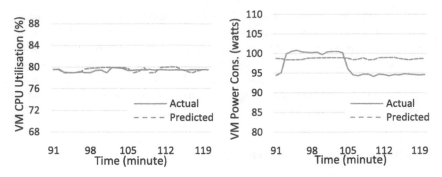

Fig. 5. Prediction results for a large VM based on static workload pattern. (a) On the left: results of workload prediction. (b) On the right: results of energy prediction.

CPU utilisation, and Fig. 6 presents the predicted results for a large VM based on a historical periodic workload pattern with two utilisation peaks.

For the prediction based on the historical static workload pattern, Fig. 5a shows the results of the predicted versus the actual VM workload. Figure 5b shows the results of the predicted versus the actual VM energy consumption over a time period.

As discussed previously, the VM workload prediction within the proposed framework uses the ARIMA model to forecast the next 30 min period of workload, as shown in Fig. 5a, based on three historical intervals of workload. Overall, the predicted VM workload results closely match the actual workload owing to the sophistication of the ARIMA model. Based on this predicted workload, the VM energy consumption is predicted using the remaining models, as previously discussed, within the proposed framework (see Sect. 3.3). Figure 5b shows the predicted VM energy consumption results, which have a small variation as compared to the actual energy consumption. The reason of this variation is because there is an accumulation of error from the previous steps within the framework, especially when correlating the PM CPU utilisation to PM power consumption. As seen on Fig. 5b, the actual energy consumption increases in the first part of the interval; this may be due to the thermal energy, which is not captured in this work, causing the machine's fan to run faster and thus leading to an increase of PM energy, which is then attributed to the VM. Despite this accumulation of error, the proposed framework can predict the VM energy consumption accurately.

In terms of prediction accuracy, a number of metrics, as summarised in Table 1, are used to evaluate the predicted VM workload and energy consumption based on static workload. As previously discussed in Sect. 4, the actual data of the VM workload and energy consumption are used as the testing data set for evaluation purposes.

As shown in Table 1, the accuracy of the predicted VM workload is very high as its metrics' values are close to zero. The predicted VM energy consumption is less accurate as compared with the predicted VM workload, but still achieves a good prediction accuracy, with −1.89 of MPE. The reason of the predicted VM energy consumption being less accurate than the predicted workload when compared to the actual data is due to the accumulated error when correlating this VM workload to physical resources.

Table 1. Prediction accuracy for a large VM based on static workload pattern.

Accuracy metric	Predicted VM workload	Predicted VM energy consumption
Mean Error (ME)	−0.11	−1.75
Root Mean Squared Error (RMSE)	0.42	3.28
Mean Absolute Error (MAE)	0.33	3.04
Mean Percentage Error (MPE)	−0.14	−1.89
Mean Absolute Percentage Error (MAPE)	0.42	3.17

In terms of prediction based on the historical periodic workload pattern, Fig. 6a shows the results of the predicted versus the actual VM workload. Figure 6b shows the results of the predicted versus the actual VM energy consumption over a period of time.

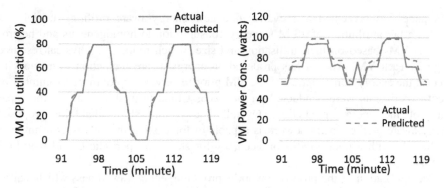

Fig. 6. Prediction results for a large VM based on periodic workload pattern. (a) On the left: results of workload prediction. (b) On the right: results of energy prediction.

Despite the periodic utilisation peaks, the predicted VM workload results are closely matched with the actual results, which reflect the capability of the ARIMA model to capture the historical seasonal trend and give a very accurate prediction accordingly. The proposed framework is also capable of predicting the energy consumption of the VM with only a small variation as compared to the actual. As shown in Fig. 6b, the actual VM energy consumption in the middle of the interval has a small peak, which was not followed by the predicted VM energy consumption. This is again can be due to the thermal energy which is not considered in the proposed framework.

For evaluating the accuracy of the predicted VM workload and energy consumption based on periodic workload, different accuracy metrics are used, as shown in Table 2.

Despite the high variation of the workload utilisation in the periodic pattern, the accuracy metrics, as shown in Table 2, indicate that the predicted VM workload achieves a good accuracy, with 2.58 of MPE. As previously discussed, the accumulated error when correlating the predicted VM workload to the physical resources in order to get the energy affects the accuracy of the predicted VM energy consumption.

Table 2. Prediction accuracy for a large VM based on periodic workload pattern

Accuracy metric	Predicted VM workload	Predicted VM energy consumption
ME	−0.02	−3.04
RMSE	1.51	5.76
MAE	0.81	4.61
MPE	2.58	−4.47
MAPE	5.30	6.43

Therefore, the predicted VM energy consumption is less accurate as compared with the predicted VM workload, but still achieves a good prediction accuracy, with −4.47 of MPE.

6 Conclusion and Future Work

This paper has presented and evaluated a new energy-aware profiling model that enables a fair attribution of a PM's energy consumption to homogeneous and hetero-geneous VMs based on their utilisation and size, which reflect the physical resource usage by each VM. Also, it has proposed an energy-aware prediction framework to forecast the energy consumption of the VM prior to service deployment. A number of direct experiments were conducted on the Leeds Cloud testbed to evaluate the capability of the energy prediction. Overall, the results show that the proposed energy-aware prediction framework is capable of forecasting the energy consumption for the VM with a good prediction accuracy for static and periodic Cloud workload patterns.

The application of the proposed work is providing energy-awareness which can be used and incorporated by other reactive and proactive management tools to make enhanced energy-aware decisions and efficiently manage the Cloud resources, leading towards a reduction of energy consumption, and therefore lowering the cost of OPEX for Cloud providers and having less impact on the environment.

In future work, we aim to facilitate the proposed prediction framework and make an online modeller on the Leeds testbed to make the prediction process dynamic. Also, we will consider the scalability aspects with different prediction scenarios to further show the capability of the proposed work, like predicting the energy usage for a number of VMs to be run on a single or multiple PMs already hosting other running VMs, and predicting the energy usage for these VMs to run all together. Further, we aim to consider the thermal energy and its impact on the energy consumption. With the evolving technologies of containers, further work will investigate the applicability of using this research in that context and consider attributing the system's energy consumption to container instances instead of VM instances.

References

1. Gartner: Gartner Estimates ICT Industry Accounts for 2 Percent of Global CO2 Emissions. http://www.gartner.com/newsroom/id/503867
2. Scheihing, P.: Creating energy-efficient data centers. In: Data Center Facilities and Engineering Conference, Washington, DC, 18 May 2007
3. Mukherjee, T., Dasgupta, K., Gujar, S., Jung, G., Lee, H.: An economic model for green cloud. In: Proceedings of the 10th International Workshop on Middleware for Grids, Clouds and e-Science - MGC 2012, pp. 1–6 (2012)
4. Conejero, J., Rana, O., Burnap, P., Morgan, J., Caminero, B., Carrión, C.: Analyzing hadoop power consumption and impact on application QoS. Futur. Gener. Comput. Syst. **55**, 213–223 (2016)
5. Beloglazov, A., Buyya, R., Lee, Y.C., Zomaya, A.Y.: A Taxonomy and Survey of Energy-Efficient Data Centers and Cloud Computing Systems. CoRR. abs/1007.0 (2010)
6. Bagein, M., Barbosa, J., Blanco, V., Brandic, I., Cremer, S., Karatza, H.D., Lefevre, L., Mastelic, T., Oleksiak, A.: Energy efficiency for ultrascale systems: challenges and trends from nesus project. Supercomput. Front. Innov. **2**, 105–131 (2015)
7. Jheng, J.-J., Tseng, F.-H., Chao, H.-C., Chou, L.-D.: A novel VM workload prediction using Grey Forecasting model in cloud data center. In: 2014 International Conference on Information Networking (ICOIN), pp. 40–45 (2014)
8. Fehling, C., Leymann, F., Retter, R., Schupeck, W., Arbitter, P.: Cloud Computing Patterns. Springer, Wien (2014)
9. Alzamil, I., Djemame, K., Armstrong, D., Kavanagh, R.: Energy-aware profiling for cloud computing environments. Electron. Notes Theor. Comput. Sci. **318**, 91–108 (2015)
10. Djemame, K., Armstrong, D., Kavanagh, R., Juan Ferrer, A., Garcia Perez, D., Antona, D., Deprez, J.-C., Ponsard, C., Ortiz, D., Macías Lloret, M., Guitart Fernández, J., Lordan Gomis, F.-J., Ejarque, J., Sirvent Pardell, R., Badia Sala, R.M., Kammer, M., Kao, O., Agiatzidou, E., Dimakis, A., Courcoubetis, C., Blasi, L.: Energy efficiency embedded service lifecycle: Towards an energy efficient cloud computing architecture. In: Joint Workshop Proceedings of the 2nd International Conference on ICT for Sustainability 2014, pp. 1–6. CEUR-WS.org (2014)
11. Kavanagh, R., Armstrong, D., Djemame, K.: Towards an energy-aware cloud architecture for smart grids. In: 12th International Conference on Economics of Grids, Clouds, Systems, and Services, Cluj-Napoca, Romania, pp. 1–14 (2015)
12. Gu, C., Huang, H., Jia, X.: Power metering for virtual machine in cloud computing-challenges and opportunities. IEEE Access. **2**, 1106–1116 (2014)
13. Yang, H., Zhao, Q., Luan, Z., Qian, D.: iMeter: an integrated VM power model based on performance profiling. Futur. Gener. Comput. Syst. **36**, 267–286 (2014)
14. Tchernykh, A., Schwiegelsohn, U., Alexandrov, V., Talbi, E.: Towards understanding uncertainty in cloud computing resource provisioning. Procedia Comput. Sci. **51**, 1772–1781 (2015)
15. Ramírez-Alcaraz, J.M., Tchernykh, A., Yahyapour, R., Schwiegelsohn, U., Quezada-Pina, A., González-García, J.L., Hirales-Carbajal, A.: Job allocation strategies with user run time estimates for online scheduling in hierarchical grids. J. Grid Comput. **9**, 95–116 (2011)
16. Tchernykh, A., Lozano, L., Schwiegelsohn, U., Bouvry, P., Pecero, J.E., Nesmachnow, S., Drozdov, A.Y.: Online bi-objective scheduling for IaaS clouds ensuring quality of service. J. Grid Comput. **14**, 5–22 (2016)

17. Zhang, X., Lu, J., Qin, X.: BFEPM: best fit energy prediction modeling based on CPU utilization. In: 2013 IEEE Eighth International Conference on Networking, Architecture, and Storage, pp. 41–49 (2013)
18. Dargie, W.: A stochastic model for estimating the power consumption of a processor. IEEE Trans. Comput. **64**, 1311–1322 (2015)
19. Fan, X., Weber, W.-D., Barroso, L.A.: Power provisioning for a warehouse-sized computer. In: Proceedings of the 34th Annual International Symposium on Computer Architecture, pp. 13–23. ACM, New York (2007)
20. Armstrong, D., Kavanagh, R., Djemame, K.: ASCETiC Project: D2.2.2 Architecture Specification - Version 2 (2014)
21. Fang, W., Lu, Z., Wu, J., Cao, Z.: RPPS: a novel resource prediction and provisioning scheme in cloud data center. In: 2012 IEEE Ninth International Conference on Services Computing (SCC), pp. 609–616 (2012)
22. Han, Y., Chan, J., Leckie, C.: Analysing virtual machine usage in cloud computing. In: 2013 IEEE Ninth World Congress on Services (SERVICES), pp. 370–377 (2013)
23. Huang, Q., Su, S., Xu, S., Li, J., Xu, P., Shuang, K.: Migration-based elastic consolidation scheduling in cloud data center. In: 2013 IEEE 33rd International Conference on Distributed Computing Systems Workshops (ICDCSW), pp. 93–97 (2013)
24. Calheiros, R.N., Masoumi, E., Ranjan, R., Buyya, R.: Workload prediction using ARIMA model and its impact on cloud applications' QoS. IEEE Trans. Cloud Comput. **3**, 449–458 (2015)
25. Box, G.E.P., Jenkins, G.M., Reinsel, G.C.: Time Series Analysis: Forecasting and Control. John Wiley & Sons, Hoboken (2008)
26. Box, G.E.P., Cox, D.R.: An analysis of transformations. J. R. Stat. Soc. Ser. B. **26**, 211–252 (1964)
27. R Core Team: R: A Language and Environment for Statistical Computing. https://www.r-project.org/
28. Watts Up? Plug Load Meters. www.wattsupmeters.com
29. ZABBIX: The Enterprise-Class Monitoring Solution for Everyone. http://www.zabbix.com/
30. Moreno-Vozmediano, R., Montero, R.S., Llorente, I.M.: IaaS cloud architecture: from virtualized datacenters to federated cloud infrastructures. Computer (Long. Beach. Calif.) **45**, 65–72 (2012)
31. KVM: Kernel-based Virtual Machine. http://www.linux-kvm.org/

An Energy Aware Cost Recovery Approach for Virtual Machine Migration

Muhammad Zakarya[1,2(✉)] and Lee Gillam[1]

[1] Department of Computer Science, University of Surrey, Guildford, UK
{mohd.zakarya,l.gillam}@surrey.ac.uk
[2] Abdul Wali Khan University, Mardan, Pakistan

Abstract. Datacenters provide an IT backbone for today's business and economy, and are the principal electricity consumers for Cloud computing. Various studies suggest that approximately 30% of the running servers in US datacenters are idle and the others are under-utilized, making it possible to save energy and money by using Virtual Machine (VM) consolidation to reduce the number of hosts in use. However, consolidation involves migrations that can be expensive in terms of energy consumption, and sometimes it will be more energy efficient not to consolidate. This paper investigates how migration decisions can be made such that the energy costs involved with the migration are recovered, as only when costs of migration have been recovered will energy start to be saved. We demonstrate through a number of experiments, using the Google workload traces for 12,583 hosts and 1,083,309 tasks, how different VM allocation heuristics, combined with different approaches to migration, will impact on energy efficiency. We suggest, using reasonable assumptions for datacenter setup, that a combination of energy-aware fill-up VM allocation and energy-aware migration, and migration only for relatively long running VMs, provides for optimal energy efficiency.

Keywords: Datacenters · Resource management · Server consolidation

1 Introduction

Cloud service providers are looking for opportunities to make cost-effective use of energy [1]. Costs of operating large datacenters are substantial, largely due to energy costs, and are suggested to be in the billions of dollars per year for all datacenters in the United States [2]. There are also environmental reasons for decreasing the amount of energy used by datacenters, with predictions that the ICT industry will be accountable for an estimated 2–3% of the global CO_2 emissions by 2020 [3]. Both environmental and economic reasons motivate scholars and industrialists to explore effective methods for saving energy in datacenters. This is more profound for Cloud service providers who have large numbers of such datacenters. In Infrastructure Clouds, datacenters comprise large numbers of hosts that cloud customers can use in the amounts they require for as long as they are willing to pay. When a cloud customer makes a request for

© Springer International Publishing AG 2017
J.Á. Bañares et al. (Eds.): GECON 2016, LNCS 10382, pp. 175–190, 2017.
DOI: 10.1007/978-3-319-61920-0_13

(part of) a host, a VM is launched on a host selected by the Cloud service provider. The user decides how long to run the VM for. The unpredictability of users in such on-demand environments can lead to a number of hosts either being idle or running a minimal VM loading – in principle, wasting energy as an idle host may still consume 60% of its peak power usage [4]. When hosts are not needed because demand is low, it may be possible to switch hosts off or enable lower energy states. However, hosts would need to be powered back on, or up, quickly when demand spikes. Switching hosts off has the potential to offer operational cost savings with some resource management efforts, but a researcher from one Cloud provider [5] suggests it is unreasonable to switch hosts off due to demand variation. Power cycling a host also carries costs in energy and may cause performance degradation if the boot time is quite long. Similarly, if the workload demand for resources (CPU) is low, then running a host in a lower energy state, for example using Dynamic Voltage and Frequency Scaling (DVFS), can reduce energy consumption but with non-trivial performance loss [6]. Those paying for Cloud services are unlikely to be keen on resources of diminished performance, unless costs are correlated with performance.

Virtualization allows several VMs to be run on a single host, making server consolidation possible [7], and virtualization is a key component of most Infrastructure Clouds. Taken over a number of hosts, server consolidation attempts to find a minimum number of hosts that would still be able to run all of the VMs in the datacenter, offering further potential to make energy savings. In [8] the authors show that in Google's cluster [9], hosts are not highly utilized and some significant power can be saved through consolidation techniques. Similarly, task runtime distributions show that the majority of tasks run only for a short duration − which could lead to unnecessary migrations that should be avoided. Server consolidation is similarly achieved through server (here, VM) migration. However, server migration also has a cost and may impact on Service Level Agreements (SLAs). Further, with unpredictable VM runtimes in an on-demand environment it is possible that the cost is never recovered through increased efficiency if the VM is terminated during, or even just after, migration.

In this paper, we investigate how migration decisions can be made such that the energy costs involved with the migration are recoverable, after which energy is saved. We explore the impact on energy efficiency of VM allocation heuristics such as Round Robin (RR), Random (R), Best Resource Selection (BRS) [10], Minimum Power Difference (MPD) [11], First Fit (FF) and Fill Up (FU) when combined with different approaches to migration. Key to this exploration is the recovery of costs incurred by a migration. This exploration is conducted through simulations that use the Google workload traces for 12,583 hosts and 1,083,309 tasks [9] in combination with CloudSim [12].

The rest of the paper is organized as follows. In Sect. 2 we explain VM migration, its energy overhead, and how to measure (virtualized) host efficiency. In Sect. 3, we discuss server consolidation as a binpacking problem, and propose as Consolidation with Migration Cost Recovery (CMCR) technique that avoids migrating VMs which would not recover the energy used in migration.

We validate CMCR using real workload traces from Google cluster in Sect. 4 and show that CMCR can reduce the migration energy overhead with reduced numbers of migrations, and that the majority of migrated VMs now recover their migration cost and continue to save energy and therefore cost. We offer an overview of related work in Sect. 5, and Sect. 6 concludes the paper.

2 Background

The migration of a VM may happen for a number of reasons within a data-center, including host maintenance or load balancing. Migrations can still be useful where renewable energy is used to reduce datacenter energy costs and CO_2 footprint. Energy sources like solar and wind are intermittent and require policies to tackle the variability in supply [13]. There are at least three benefits: (i) all oversupply of renewables allows for more energy to be provided back to the electricity grid; (ii) low supply of renewables means lessened demand on non-renewable sources from the electricity grid; (iii) lessened reliance on means to store renewable energy reduces the costs of management and replenishment of storage mechanisms, such as batteries, and extending the life of these mechanisms.

During VM migration, the running VM is moved from one host to another. This means migrating memory pages and, depending on the underlying approach to storage, data on disk. This leads to two kinds of migration: (i) live/on-disk migration, where a VM image is run from shared storage, for example in Amazon's Elastic Block Storage (EBS), and only memory is copied; (ii) block live/over-Ethernet migrations, where a VM image is run from a local disk, for example Amazon's Instance Store, and both memory and disk are copied. Since the VM image may itself be large, this latter form of migration may take rather longer.

If we perform migrations for reasons of energy efficiency, there will be an energy cost in the additional VM running on the source host for the duration of migration. The cost will relate to the source host's power profile P. We assume P of each host is a linear function of its utilization level – the more the host is utilized, the more energy it will consume, according to the power model proposed in [14]. The relationship of CPU utilization to power consumption can be expressed as shown in Eq. (1).

$$P(u) = P_{idle} + (P_{max} - P_{idle}).u \tag{1}$$

where $P(u)$ is the estimated power consumption, P_{idle} is static power consumed when host is idle, P_{max} is the power consumed when the host is fully utilized, and u is the current CPU utilization. The portion $(P_{max} - P_{idle}).u$ is called dynamic power consumption, and is treated as a linear function of utilization. This simplified model predicts non-virtualized host power consumption with less than 5% error, but requires modification to account for virtualization. In the first part of this section, we extend this power model to address virtualized hosts; in the second part we discuss measuring the migration energy cost.

2.1 Comparing Hosts Efficiencies

Our work explores migration cost recovery, which is only possible if two conditions are both met: (i) a VM is migrated to a more efficient target host; (ii) the migrated VM then runs for a sufficient length of time on the target host. In this section we discuss measuring the efficiency of hosts in order to address these conditions.

In non-virtualised platforms, if one host consumes less power than another to execute a specific workload, it is more efficient. However, efficiency should be addressed across a range of workloads as there may be other workloads that run less efficiently. In virtualised environments, multiple VMs can be running different workloads on a single host, and so several factors must be considered in order to compare power efficiency; we consider, first, division of the host to VMs and so the total power consumption of a virtualized host is characterised by:

$$P_{host} = P_{idle} + \sum_{i=1}^{n} P_i^{vm} \qquad (2)$$

where P is the total power consumed by the host, n is the number of active VMs on host, P_{idle} is the host static power consumption and P_i^{vm} is the dynamic power consumption of VM i which is calculated by the linear power model discussed in Sect. 2:

$$P_{vm} = W_{vm}.P_{dynamic} \qquad (3)$$

where W_{vm} is the fraction of host total CPU allocated to the VM. This allows us to simplify concerns by considering each VM equivalent with respect to a host; in an Infrastructure Cloud, VM size may be equally divided by the number of allocated (hyperthreaded) cores out of m cores on the host, or by allocation of an amount of memory. For simplicity, we use the number of (hyperthreaded) cores.

$$W_{vm} = \frac{cores_{vm}}{m} \qquad (4)$$

Including static power, the total power consumed by a single VM will be given by:

$$P_{vm} = \frac{P_{idle}}{n} + W_{vm}.(P_{max} - P_{idle}).u \qquad (5)$$

where n is the total number of VMs running on host, u is the utilization level of vm. Hence, efficiency of a host can be related to the number of VMs that are allocated to it and, if need be, to their individual efficiencies.

In this model, due to P_{idle}, the energy used in order to run a single VM is going to be at its highest, and the more VMs that are run on the host, the more power efficient each VM is. We also make use of the notion of VM density, used elsewhere both to address the number of VMs running on a host, and the maximum number that can be run whilst avoiding resource starvation; we combine these to understand VM density as the present fraction of the maximum for a host.

Suppose there are n VMs allocated to host H_1 and m VMs allocated to host H_2. Each VM is utilizing 100% of its proportional resources allocated. The per VM power consumption of each VM on H_1 and H_2 are $P^{H_1}_{vm_{i=1:n}}$ and $P^{H_2}_{vm_{j=1:m}}$ respectively according to above equation. The total power consumption of each host H_1 and H_2 is given by $P_{H_1} = \sum_{i=1}^{n} P_i^{vm}$ and $P_{H_2} = \sum_{j=1}^{m} P_j^{vm}$ respectively. For a VM vm_k selected for migration from H_1, with sufficient space to allocate on H_2, and provided that $P^{H_1}_{vm_k} > P^{H_2}_{vm_k}$, then H_2 is more power efficient than to H_1 with a factor of E_f given by:

$$E_f = \frac{P_{H_1}}{P_{H_2}} \qquad (6)$$

2.2 The Migration Model

During a live VM migration [15], an extra VM is created on the target host and is progressively synchronized. Once synchronized, the VM is started on target host and its copy is terminated on the source host. This means that a migration costs roughly double the resources for the duration of migration. If the VM terminates during the migration process, or before this resource cost is recovered, this effort is wasted. A number of studies [7,11,16] discuss consolidation but appear to ignore the cost that is due to the migration energy overhead, and with the notable exception of [17] this is rarely addressed. The migration cost is dictated by the cost of the most expensive VM (at source host) running for the duration of migration, plus any associated network cost during migration. The overhead also includes some marginal extra costs of migration C_m if this requires changes in power state of either or both hosts [18].

For homogeneous hosts, the time required for a migration can be given by:

$$t_{mig} = \frac{V_{mem} + V_{disk}}{B} \qquad (7)$$

where t_{mig} is dependent on VM memory size V_{mem}, VM ephemeral disk image V_{disk} (in case of block live migration) and the available network bandwidth B for data transfer. For live migration, V_{disk} is zero and V_{mem} is calculated using the VM memory size and the dirty pages that are continuously copied in multiple rounds n, during the migration process. If the VM is idle then the dirty pages are zero and hence the network traffic is only equal to V_{mem} measured in MB, otherwise:

$$V_{mem} = \sum_{i=0}^{n} V_i \qquad (8)$$

$$V_i = D.T_{i-1} \qquad (9)$$

where i denotes the round, D is the rate at which the memory pages are being dirtied in MB/s, T is round duration in seconds and V represents the size of dirty pages in MB. In our experiments, VM load remains the same, hence D is constant. However, if D varies for a VM, it may be more realistic to simulate using a distribution around a mean or with reference to historical data.

Two migration models as offer alternatives, based on (i) average (AVG) and (ii) history based (HIST), are proposed and validated in [19] with 90% accuracy. The migration energy overhead $Cost_{mig}$ is given by:

$$Cost_{mig} = t_{mig}.(P_{source} + P_{net}) + C_m \tag{10}$$

where C_m denotes the marginal cost needed to switch on/off hosts, P_{net} is the network power consumption and P_{source} is the cost of the most expensive VM running at source host. For the present paper, we simplify concerns by $C_m = 0$; subsequently we would need address this as part of the overall energy use. The amount of data transferred $data_t = V_{mem} + V_{disk}$ has a significant effect on t_{mig}. In [17], the authors have validated a model for measuring the energy consumption of a live migration with 0.993 R^2 value, which is proportional to $data_t$.

$$Cost_{mig} = 0.512 * data_t + 20.165 \tag{11}$$

Based on experimental results, the authors claim that migration is I/O intensive with energy mostly consumed in data transfer. Because of this simplicity and accuracy, we use this directly to compute migration cost. Another approach is proposed in [20], which offers a linear relationship between V_{mem} and B, hence the energy consumed is equal to $\alpha.V_{mem} + \beta.B + C$. This model does not take load into account, so only suits scenarios when the migrating VM is idle.

3   Problem Description

Server consolidation with migration can be considered as a multidimensional bin-packing problem that tries to minimize the number of hosts needed to accommodate a set of VMs [7]. Such NP-complete problems are typically solved using Linear Programming (LP) or heuristics. Dynamic consolidation is typically suggested to be an improvement on doing nothing, allowing: (a) to switch off the underutilized host if the accommodated VMs can be relocated to other hosts; (b) to withdraw hosts from an overloaded state if the sum of accommodated VMs becomes larger than its capacity [15]. Besides the trade-off involved between migrating VMs and decreasing the number of hosts to accommodate VMs, live VM migration can be completed without needing downtime, and ideally without impacting performance (and, specifically, SLAs).

If every VM can first recover the migration cost, and then continues to run on the energy efficient host, then the migration is effective in energy saving and hence in cost reduction. Dynamic consolidation can be considered as an optimization problem in minimizing the amount of energy consumed by avoiding migrations. We describe the problem as CMCR, further explained in Sect. 3.1, and address it by exploring the effect of VM runtimes. In an on-demand environment, VM runtimes are unknown, so we can only consider the past runtime R_{past} in order to decide on migration.

3.1 CMCR

We consider migrations for the purpose of consolidating to fewer hosts to minimize the cost of energy consumption. The migration cost must be considered as part of the migration decision. If the target host is similar or less energy efficient than the source host, based on the total number of accommodated VMs, then the migration cost cannot be recovered. Otherwise the migration cost will eventually be earned. Using the efficiency factor of the source and target hosts, we can find a time point t_{off} on the target host at which the VM has earned back the cost of migration $Cost_{mig}$ and will now be saving energy if it continues to run.

Consider a VM vm_1 that runs on source host H_1. A migration decision is triggered to target host H_2 at time t. Assume that we know H_2 is more energy efficient than H_1 with a factor of E_f. If there are no VMs running on both hosts, then the host with less static power consumption is considered more energy efficient. If there are some VMs running on source and target hosts then the efficiency of each host depends on the number of running VMs (n VMs on source host and m VMs on target host). The E_f as explained in Sect. 2.1, can be computed as:

$$E_f = \frac{P_{VM_{source}}}{P_{VM_{target}}} \tag{12}$$

If $E_f = 1$, it means that the power profile is identical and we cannot recover the migration cost. If $E_f < 1$, the target host is less efficient. The offset of migration cost and further savings can only be made if $E_f > 1$. $Cost_{mig}$ is measured in

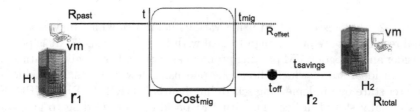

Fig. 1. CMCR technique description.

Watts per hour and is computed as explained in Sect. 2.2. The difference between the power consumption values of both source and target hosts is:

$$\triangle x = P_{VM_{source}} - \frac{P_{VM_{source}}}{E_f} = P_{VM_{source}} - P_{VM_{target}} \tag{13}$$

And so t_{off} is given by:

$$t_{off} = \frac{t_{mig} \cdot Cost_{mig}}{\triangle x} \tag{14}$$

For vm_1 with past runtime R_{past} on source host, and migration to target host started at time t, migration completes in time t_{mig} as shown in Fig. 1. vm_1 total runtime on the source host is $r_1 = R_{past} + t_{mig}$, and the remaining runtime on target host is $r_2 = R_{total} - (t - t_{mig}) = R_{total} - r_1$. If $r_2 > t_{off}$, then it means vm_1 has recovered $Cost_{mig}$ and subsequently runs more efficiently to save energy. The remaining runtime of vm_1 on the target host after the t_{off}, is given by:

$$t_s = r_2 - t_{off} \tag{15}$$

The savings $P_{savings}$ with an energy efficient migration are then only:

$$P_{savings} = t_s.\triangle x \tag{16}$$

Hence the minimum value for $r_1 + r_2$ (Fig. 1) which is sufficient to offset $Cost_{mig}$ at time t is $R_{offset} = t_{mig} + t_{off}$. For any VM running for R_{past}, the R_{offset} is given by:

$$R_{offset} = R_{past} + t_{mig} + t_{off} \tag{17}$$

If $R_{offset} \geq t_{off}$, then the migration is energy efficient. If the vm_1 is terminated before t_{off}, migration cost is not recovered. If R_{offset} is not sufficient to recover $Cost_{mig}$ then t can be estimated to make a migration efficient, using $t = t - t_{off}$ and $R_{past} = R_{past} - t_{off}$.

In the above formulation R_{total} denotes the time for which the VM will run, which is unknown. To make the scenario realistic for on-demand systems, we only consider the past runtime R_{past} of VMs in order to determine if a VM is a suitable candidate for migration.

4   Performance Evaluation

Bin-packing problems are solved using various heuristics which may not ensure optimal results but are fast enough to deal with large problems [7]. It is possible to consider an analogous VM packing problem as moving from a given datacenter state to an ideal state, which should be one using fewest hosts. We achieve a datacenter state by implementing scheduling heuristics (RR, R, BRS, MPD, FF, FU, as initially stated in Sect. 1), with VM packing then needing to guarantee energy efficiency is assured (as explained in Sect. 2.1) and migration cost can be recovered. To evaluate the effect of this, we consider (i) no migration; (ii) dynamic consolidation (all possible migrations); and (iii) CMCR (runtime-based migration).

4.1   Experimental Setting

We use real workload traces from Google to study the feasibility of our approach within the event driven simulator CloudSim [12]. The Google dataset comprises 12,583 hosts in one datacenter and 1,083,309 tasks and as explained in [9] a task runs in a Linux container (Sect. 4.2), its CPU requirements are measured in core seconds per second, and the values are normalized to the maximum cores host available in the Google's cluster.

To address a Cloud context, each task is assigned a single, notional, VM that maps to Google instance types. We assume that hosts are comparable by a single measure which allows for performance ranking, for which we adopt CloudSim's use of Million of Instructions Per Second (MIPS) as a proxy; we would not endorse this as a good performance indicator for real systems for a number of CPU architecture and workload comparability reasons. One approach is to assign a VM as a single core for the maximum value 1, half a core (hyperthread) for 0.5, and assume that higher VM gearing leads to a quarter of a core for 0.25. But to address allocation more flexibly, along lines of certain Cloud providers, we map CPU frequency for the hosts given to Google Compute Engine Units (GCEUs) as: 2 GHz CPU, 1.25GB RAM, giving types A1 (0.5 GCEU), B1 (0.25 GCEU) and C1 (1 GCEU). The GCEU then maps MIPS for consistency with CloudSim, and we assume that every instance needs at most 1 GCEU. Memory requirements then also map to these types, as shown in Table 1.

Table 1. Instance types.

Class	Instance name	GCEUs	Memory (GB)
A1	a1.tiny	0.5	0.03
	a1.xtiny	0.5	0.06
	a1.micro	0.5	0.12
	a1.small	0.5	0.25
	a1.medium	0.5	0.5
	a1.large	0.5	0.75
	a1.xlarge	0.5	0.97
B1	b1.small	0.25	0.25
C1	c1.medium	1.0	0.5
	c1.large	1.0	1.0

When a task is submitted, the task scheduler finds the most suitable instance type and the allocation policy places it on a host: RR allocation policy places the VM on the next available host; R allocation policy selects a suitable host randomly; MPD [11] is a modified Best Fit Decreasing (BFD) off-line heuristic that (at 1 second interval – to mimic on-line behavior) sorts all VMs in decreasing order of CPU utilization and allocates each VM to a host that increases energy consumption the least – selecting the most energy efficient host first, based on the linear power model (Sect. 2, Eq. 1); BRS [10] places a VM on a host with the least free capacity to maximize resource utilization; FF and FU are both on-line heuristics and place the VM on the first available host, with FU selecting the most efficient host based on the model proposed in Sect. 2.1. The host efficiency model and the on-line behavior of FU differentiate it from MPD. The task scheduler implements a First In First Out (FIFO) mechanism to dispatch submitted tasks for execution. A cluster of 12,583 heterogeneous hosts, which consists of three different architectures and characteristics as shown in Table 2, is available. The heterogeneous hosts available in datacenter are set up based on assumptions that Google had certain kinds of commonly available machines in their datacenters in May 2011, when the trace was captured [21].

The power consumption values for these hosts are taken from SPEC power benchmarks [22]. The tasks are submitted according to arrivals in the Google dataset. When VMs terminate, slots are made available to the scheduler and are also available for migrations. The migration policy regularly (every 5 min) checks all host utilizations, and if a host utilization level goes below a predefined lower threshold value e.g. 20%, VMs can be migrated to other hosts to consolidate the current demand on fewer hosts to save energy. In principle, if host utilization exceeds a predefined upper threshold value i.e. 100%, some VMs are migrated from the overloaded host to less utilized hosts to avoid SLA violations. We assume, here, that sensible ways of addressing VM density will not lead to overloading. A migration decision is based on only the lower utilization threshold value, current state of the datacenter (consolidation opportunities) and other constraints as explained in Sect. 3.1. If several VMs are selected for migration, the list is sorted in decreasing order of their past runtimes, and migrated in order until all VMs in the list are migrated. For the sake of simulation, migration duration is computed by dividing the VM memory size by network bandwidth (set at 1Gbps) as discussed in Sect. 2.2. The migration energy overhead and host efficiency factor is calculated as discussed in Sect. 2, Eq. 7.

4.2   Experimental Results

The simulated infrastructure is composed of 12,583 hosts with configuration shown in Table 2. We first run the simulation with a single day of data from the Google trace. We assume that the VM workload is homogeneous and so it does not change even when a VM is migrated from one host to another. The selected trace (day 2) comprises 1,083,309 tasks with average arrival rate of 12.54 tasks per second and terminations at 12.24 tasks per second. After each 5 min interval, CMCR checks for consolidation opportunities, and selects VMs

Table 2. Host characteristics and number suggested to be in Google's cluster in May 2011 [21].

Host type	Host name	Speed (GHz)	No. of cores	No. of GCEUs	Memory (GB)	P_{IDLE} (Wh)	P_{MAX} (Wh)	Amount
A	Intel Xeon E3110	3.0	2	3	4	75.2	117	4,195
B	Intel Xeon X3470	2.9	4	5.75	8	41.6	113	4,194
C	Intel Xeon E5540	2.5	8	10	8	67.0	218	4,194

running for longer times from a list of migration possibilities. Each experiment was performed with five different values for past VM runtime given in hours [0, 0.5, 1, 2, and 4], where 0 means migrate all – dynamic consolidation – and 0.5 means migrate only those VMs which are running for 30 min or longer, 1 means running for 1 h, and so on.

Metrics. The metrics are the number of migrations, average number of hosts used to run the VMs and total datacenter energy consumed. An overall calculation of datacenter efficiency, D measures the efficiency of a scheduling approach on datacenter level. This accounts for the load proportion (% slots filled i.e. VM density – explained in Sect. 2.1), the number of hosts 'switched on', the number of idle hosts that still consumes significant energy (idle power consumption), and factor of energy efficiency in respect to whether more or less efficient hosts were in use.

$$VM_{density} = \frac{VMs_{onHost}}{Host_{capacity}} \tag{18}$$

$$D = \frac{\sum_{hosts} VM_{density} * E_f}{Hosts_{used}} + \frac{\sum_{hosts} Hosts_{unUsed} * E_f}{Hosts_{unUsed}} \tag{19}$$

The host efficiency model presented in Sect. 2.1, is used to calculate E_f for each host. Lower values for D represent efficient datacenter resource management with maximum VMs running on a minimum number of the most efficient hosts, and hence also offers potential for hosts to be powered off in the second term.

Discussion. Figure 2 presents the results obtained from running the Google cluster's tasks submitted on day 2 using different scheduling heuristics. The results show that efficient scheduling techniques would be more economical than consolidation techniques. For example, without migration a 52.43% decrease in energy consumption was achieved using FU instead of RR. But using FU, only 3.04% decrease in energy consumption was achieved with dynamic consolidation. The metric D shows an average decrease of 16.10% in energy consumption for FU compared to R scheduler. Similarly for CMCR, FU is on average 0.49% more cost efficient as compared to FF scheduler. We also note that no migration can be more economical than the dynamic consolidation if an efficient scheduling approach is used. CMCR beats both techniques as it allocate VMs to the most efficient hosts first, minimizes the total number of migrations (runtime-based migration) and increases the probability that a VM recovers its migration cost.

Table 3 shows the mean number of hosts in use, and datacenter utilization, measured in 5 min intervals. For each allocation policy, CMCR have reduced the total number of migrations and migration energy. The D value (Sect. 4.2) shows that in terms of scheduling approach, FU is effective in using a minimum number of most efficient hosts: FU did not allocate VMs to host type A which has larger idle power consumption and is less energy efficient compared to types B & C. As MPD is an off-line heuristic, higher D values confirm inability to address online problems. For each scheduling approach, cost savings are compared to a

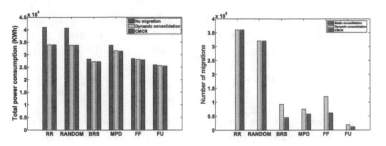

Fig. 2. Power consumption & no. migrations for Google trace day 2.

Table 3. Experimental mean results for different approaches (5 min interval).

Scheduling approach	Consolidation technique	Total hosts used			Avg used hosts	Datacenter Util (%)	D (KWh)	Cost savings (%)
		A	B	C				
RR	No migration	4,195	4,194	3,351	3,157	24.81	870.7	0
	Dynamic	4,195	4,194	2,750	2,228	47.40	859.64	25.77
	CMCR	4,195	4,194	2,750	2,228	47.40	859.64	25.77
RANDOM	No migration	4,195	4,194	3,835	3,005	25.18	870.14	0
	Dynamic	4,195	4,194	3,713	2,148	48.64	860.95	23.75
	CMCR	4,195	4,194	3,713	2,148	48.64	860.95	23.75
BRS	No migration	2,664	2,662	2,667	1,157	50.31	861.58	0
	Dynamic	2,504	2,888	2,658	1,095	69.61	860.41	5.87
	CMCR	2,612	2,899	2,683	1,089	62.95	859.82	6.04
MPD	No migration	4,195	4,194	1,908	2,412	28.21	858.17	0
	Dynamic	4,195	4,194	2,227	1,965	33.09	861.08	9.96
	CMCR	4,195	4,194	2,581	1,984	34.84	856.68	10.66
FF	No migration	2,665	2,664	2,666	1,212	51.61	860.45	0
	Dynamic	2,619	2,790	2,620	1,219	61.22	859.85	1.69
	CMCR	2,636	2,790	2,635	1,190	61.64	859.4	2.85
FU	No migration	0	4,194	2,700	1,241	48.61	855.75	0
	Dynamic	0	4,194	2,700	1,167	67.21	855.26	2.96
	CMCR	0	4,194	27,00	1,166	66.74	855.19	3.04

baseline no-migration policy. On average, CMCR reduces the number of hosts in use, with a reduced number of migrations. The runtime of VMs migrated depends on the scheduling heuristics. RR scheduler equally distributes VMs among the available hosts, keeping all the hosts active and less-utilized most of the time – making more consolidation opportunities. Similarly, R scheduler al-mostly selects a different host for VM placement randomly, which results in more energy consumption and increased number of migrations – as all hosts are switched on but less utilized. The optimal value for these two algorithms is always achieved with dynamic consolidation, i.e. past runtime ≥ 0 min. BRS, MPD and FF were able to give minimum power consumption results by migrating VMs with past runtime ≥ 30 min. The most efficient heuristic, FU, produces optimal results by migrating VMs with past runtime ≥ 60 min.

The data and migration statistics produced in Table 4, show that combining CMCR and FU means only 1.1% of VMs are migratable and 99.5% of these were able to recover their migration cost. For FU with dynamic consolidation, 1.71% VMs were migrated with 98.98% of recovering migration cost. The migration statistics given in Table 4, also include multiple entries for VMs that were migrated multiple times during their lifetime. If we now assume a PUE [23] of 1.2 and energy cost of $0.08kWh, dynamic consolidation would save $47.38 per hour for this cluster (a little over $1.1k per day) in comparison to a no-migration approach. Using above assumptions, CMCR would further save $18.85 per hour compared to dynamic consolidation. Hence, CMCR makes total savings of $66.23 per hour (almost $1.6 k per day) as compared to a no-migration approach. Over a year, this suggests a saving of some $0.58m annually, which compares favourably to a maximum projected usage of the same 12,583 hosts cluster of $1.58m/year.

For 5,48,584 tasks submitted on the first day of Google trace [9], with the same simulation, we see that no-migration technique would be more economical than dynamic consolidation if efficient VM scheduling heuristics are used. Our second finding is that migrating relatively long running VMs to more energy efficient hosts to recover their migration cost, are more economical and energy efficient.

Table 4. Cost recovery with Dynamic Consolidation (DC) & CMCR.

Scheduling approach	RR		R		BRS		MPD		FF		FU	
	DC	CMCR	DC	CMCR	DC	CMCR	DC	CMCR	DC	CMCR	DC	CMCR
Migratable VMs (%)	33.2	33.2	29.6	29.6	8.5	4.2	6.9	5.3	11.0	5.6	1.71	1.1
VMs recovered $Cost_m$ (%)	98.9	98.9	98.6	98.6	98.5	99.0	98.5	99.5	98.5	99.4	99.0	99.5

5   Related Work

Researchers elsewhere have addressed various aspects of energy savings, mindful in some cases that idle hosts consume up to 60% of the power of the fully loaded host. Khanna et al. [15] perform migration to avoid overloading leading to SLA violations, and also to switch of underloaded hosts. The specification of a compute unit such as GCEU should help to avoid overcommitting resources and avoid overloading, except where resource contention exists. Our datacentre measure offers a means to measure the gain by switch off. Wood et al. offer Sandpiper [24], a system to monitor and detect hotspots, also remap and reconfigure VMs when required. The proposed system migrates VMs based on high memory, network and CPU loads; again, not overcommitting should help to avoid migrations in the first place. Bobroff et al. [25] investigate estimating demand based on historical data in order to address dynamic server consolidation. Revisiting this work with respect to the Google data could certainly offer interesting insights for pre-empting demand, and help to reduce costs incurred due to unnecessary power state changes, which is beyond the scope of the present paper. Beloglazov [26] discusses adaptive thresholds for VM consolidation, but this does not address the migration cost, and nor does Tiagos [7] work on minimizing the number of VM migrations by not migrating VMs with steady usage, which might be considered a counterpoint to our findings. Similar to our approach, Dabbagh [27] proposed an energy-efficient migration framework which uses the model in [17] plus the marginal migration cost (host switch on) to decide a migration (migrate a VM with minimum energy cost), but these authors do not address host efficiency and migration cost recovery. Rather than for overall efficiency reasons, the migration policy in [28] selects a VM for migration based on its load, and 'scattered' [29] migrates VMs to underutilized hosts to mitigate host overload; but neither addresses the energy consumed in migration nor the need for cost recovery. Speitkamp [16] describes static and dynamic server consolidation and introduces segregation based VM placement through migration which does not guarantee energy efficiency [30], nor address migration cost.

All of these techniques are focused on live migration, but power consumed in migration and its recovery through runtime is not addressed. When a significant proportion of tasks are relatively short-lived, as is the case in the Google data, the inability to recover such costs would appear quite detrimental. The ReCon system [31] and pMapper [32] are notable exceptions in addressing migration costs, and this should motivate further appraisal of their techniques with respect both to short-lived tasks and also to block/live migration.

6   Conclusion and Future Work

Consolidation with migration is often claimed to increase the energy efficiency in datacenters. Analysis of Google workload data shows that most tasks run only for a short time, and allowing all possible migrations could create additional costs in energy. In this paper, we considered combinations of scheduling approaches and consolidation methods with knowledge of the past runtime of VMs to investigate energy saving potential. Under certain circumstances, we found that not migrating would be more energy-efficient than using dynamic consolidation, and the best approach overall limits migrations to 1.1% of VMs, of which 99.5% recover their migration cost.

The immediate priority is to investigate whether these findings would be consistent over time by evaluating using the whole Google trace (29 further days).

We also need to be able to account for both heterogeneous hosts, which cause variability in runtimes for a workload, and the impact of the marginal energy costs involved due to power state changes in respect to unused hosts.

Acknowledgements. This work is supported by Department of Computer Science, University of Surrey, UK and Abdul Wali Khan University, Mardan, Pakistan.

References

1. Garg, S.K., Buyya, R.: Green cloud computing and environmental sustainability. Harnessing Green IT: Principles and Practices, pp. 315–340 (2012)
2. NRDC. America's Data Centers Are Wasting Huge Amounts of Energy: critical action needed to save billions of dollars and kilowatts. IB:14-08-A, pp. 1–6 (2014)
3. Zeadally, S., Khan, S.U., Chilamkurti, N.: Energy-efficient networking: past, present, and future. J. Supercomput. **62**(3), 1093–1118 (2012)
4. Meisner, D., Gold, B.T., Wenisch, T.F.: Powernap: eliminating server idle power. ACM Sigplan Not. **44**, 205–216 (2009)
5. https://www.youtube.com/watch?v=7MwxA4Fj2l4. Accessed 3 Oct 2015
6. Beloglazov, A., Buyya, R., Lee, Y.C., Zomaya, A., et al.: A taxonomy and survey of energy-efficient data centers and cloud computing systems. Adv. Comput. **82**(2), 47–111 (2011)
7. Ferreto, T.C., Netto, M.A.S., Calheiros, R.N., De Rose, C.A.F.: Server consolidation with migration control for virtualized data centers. Future Gener. Comput. Syst. **27**(8), 1027–1034 (2011)
8. Reiss, C., Tumanov, A., Ganger, G.R.: Towards understanding heterogeneous clouds at scale: Google trace analysis. ... *Center for Cloud* ... (2012)
9. Reiss, C., Wilkes, J., Hellerstein, J.L: Google cluster-usage traces: format+ schema. Google Inc., Mountain View, CA, USA, Technical report (2011)
10. do Lago, D.G., Madeira, E.R.M., Bittencourt, L.F.: Power-aware virtual machine scheduling on clouds using active cooling control and DVFS. In: Proceedings of the 9th International Workshop on Middleware for Grids, Clouds and e-Science, pp. 2:1–2:6 (2011)
11. Beloglazov, A., Buyya, R.: Managing overloaded hosts for dynamic consolidation of virtual machines in cloud data centers under quality of service constraints. IEEE Trans. Parallel Distrib. Syst. **24**(7), 1366–1379 (2013)
12. Calheiros, R.N., Ranjan, R., Beloglazov, A., De Rose, C.A.F., Buyya, R.: CloudSim: a toolkit for modeling and simulation of cloud computing environments and evaluation of resource provisioning algorithms. Softw. Pract. Experience **41**(1), 23–50 (2011)
13. Stewart, C., Shen, K.: Some joules are more precious than others: managing renewable energy in the datacenter. In: Proceedings of the Workshop on Power Aware Computing and Systems, pp. 15–19. IEEE (2009)
14. Fan, X., Weber, W.-D., Barroso, L.A.: Power provisioning for a warehouse-sized computer. ACM SIGARCH Comput. Architect. News **35**, 13–23 (2007). ACM
15. Khanna, G., Beaty, K., Kar, G., Kochut, A.: Application performance management in virtualized server environments. In: 2006 IEEEIFIP Network Operations and Management Symposium NOMS 2006, vol. 20(D), pp. 373–381 (2006)
16. Speitkamp, B., Bichler, M.: A mathematical programming approach for server consolidation problems in virtualized data centers. IEEE Trans. Serv. Comput. **3**(4), 266–278 (2010)

17. Liu, H., Jin, H., Xu, C.-Z., Liao, X.: Performance and energy modeling for live migration of virtual machines. Cluster Comput. **16**(2), 249–264 (2011)
18. Luiz André Barroso and Urs Hölzle: The case for energy-proportional computing. Computer **40**(12), 33–37 (2007)
19. Akoush, S., Sohan, R., Rice, A., Moore, A.W., Hopper, A.: Predicting the performance of virtual machine migration. In: 2010 IEEE International Symposium on Modeling, Analysis and Simulation of Computer and Telecommunication Systems, pp. 37–46. IEEE (2010)
20. Strunk, A., Dargie, W.: Does live migration of virtual machines cost energy? In: 2013 IEEE 27th International Conference on Advanced Information Networking and Applications (AINA), pp. 514–521 (2013)
21. Google-cluster-data. https://groups.google.com/. Accessed 7 May 16
22. Lange, K.-D.: Identifying shades of green: the specpower benchmarks. IEEE Comput. **42**(3), 95–97 (2009)
23. Belady, C., Rawson, A., Pfleuger, J., Cader, T.: Green Grid Data Center Power Efficiency Metrics: PUE and DCIE (2008)
24. Wood, T., Shenoy, P., Venkataramani, A., Yousif, M.: Sandpiper: black-box and gray-box resource management for virtual machines. Comput. Netw. **53**(17), 2923–2938 (2009)
25. Bobroff, N., Kochut, A., Beaty, K.: Dynamic placement of virtual machines for managing SLA violations. In: 10th IFIP/IEEE International Symposium on Integrated Network Management 2007, IM 2007, pp. 119–128 (2007)
26. Beloglazov, A., Buyya, R.: Adaptive threshold-based approach for energy-efficient consolidation of virtual machines in cloud data centers. In: Proceedings of the 8th International Workshop on Middleware for Grids, Clouds and e-Science, December 2010, p. 6 (2011)
27. Dabbagh, M., Hamdaoui, B., Guizani, M., Rayes, A.: Efficient datacenter resource utilization through cloud resource overcommitment. In: 2015 IEEE Conference on Computer Communications Workshops (INFOCOM WKSHPS), pp. 330–335. IEEE (2015)
28. Andreolini, M., Casolari, S., Colajanni, M., Messori, M.: Dynamic load management of virtual machines in cloud architectures. In: Avresky, D.R., Diaz, M., Bode, A., Ciciani, B., Dekel, E. (eds.) CloudComp 2009. LNICSSTE, vol. 34, pp. 201–214. Springer, Heidelberg (2010). doi:10.1007/978-3-642-12636-9_14
29. Zhang, X., Shae, Z.-Y., Zheng, S., Jamjoom, H.: Virtual machine migration in an over-committed cloud. In: 2012 IEEE Network Operations and Management Symposium, pp. 196–203. IEEE (2012)
30. Verma, A., Pedrosa, L., Korupolu, M., Oppenheimer, D., Tune, E., Wilkes, J.: Large-scale cluster management at Google with Borg. In: Proceedings of the Tenth European Conference on Computer Systems - EuroSys 2015, pp. 1–17 (2015)
31. Mehta, S., Neogi, A.: ReCon: a tool to recommend dynamic server consolidation in multi-cluster data centers. In: IEEE/IFIP Network Operations and Management Symposium: Pervasive Management for Ubiquitous Networks and Services, NOMS 2008, pp. 363–370 (2008)
32. Verma, A., Ahuja, P., Neogi, A.: pMapper: power and migration cost aware application placement in virtualized systems. In: Issarny, V., Schantz, R. (eds.) Middleware 2008. LNCS, vol. 5346, pp. 243–264. Springer, Heidelberg (2008). doi:10.1007/978-3-540-89856-6_13

Resource Allocation

The Design and Evaluation of a Heaviness Metric for Cloud Fairness and Correct Virtual Machine Configurations

Patrick Poullie$^{(\boxtimes)}$ and Burkhard Stiller

Communication Systems Group (CSG), Department of Informatics (IfI),
University of Zürich, Binzmühlestrasse 14, 8050 Zürich, Switzerland
{poullie,stiller}@ifi.uzh.ch

Abstract. Fairness problems in data centers have been pointed out frequently over the last years. To enforce fairness in data centers, the application of job/Virtual Machine (VM) scheduling impels the traditional solution. Scheduling determines the order in which VMs/jobs are started. However, it is insufficient to enforce fairness, when jobs/VMs run over long periods and/or their PR utilization is highly fluctuant. Clouds form a special case of data centers in which this can be observed.

To overcome this shortcoming, previous work suggested to enforce fairness by handicapping VMs of heavy users and prioritizing VMs of light users during runtime. The Greediness Metric (GM) was developed and shown to be a well suited heaviness measure for that purpose. This work here defines an allocation to be GM Fair (GMF) if all users have the same greediness and resources are allocated efficiently. GM is refined such that enforcing GMF provides incentives to users to configure virtual resources of their VMs in-line with the VMs' subsequent resource PR utilization allowing cloud providers to schedule these VMs more efficiently. Finally, this work here proves that GMF provides for the same desirable characteristics as Dominant Resource Fairness, including especially sharing incentive, strategy proofness, envy-freeness, and Pareto-efficiency.

Keywords: Fairness · Multi-resource · Resource allocation · Incentives · Cloud · Data center

1 Introduction

Cloud Computing enables data centers to provide their combined computing power to numerous users, such as end-users and companies, in a highly flexible manner. To process a workload, cloud users start Virtual Machines (VM) that (i) process the users' workloads, (ii) are defined by Virtual Resources (VR), e.g., virtual CPU and virtual RAM [1,5], and (iii) are hosted by the cloud's nodes. Since cloud nodes are shared by VMs of different users, users contend for the nodes' Physical Resources (PR), such as CPU time, RAM, disk I/O, and network access. In commercial clouds Service Level Agreements (SLA) [3] prescribe

© Springer International Publishing AG 2017
J.Á. Bañares et al. (Eds.): GECON 2016, LNCS 10382, pp. 193–207, 2017.
DOI: 10.1007/978-3-319-61920-0_14

the performance a VM has to deliver. Therefore, conflicts over PRs are ruled such that these SLAs are not violated. However, private clouds, clusters, grids, and other data center types are often commodities that are shared without any contracts, wherefore, no (legal) guidelines on how scarce PRs must be allocated exist. This allows heavily loaded VMs to impair the performance of other VMs on the same node. In order to ensure fairness in such case, it is desirable to limit VMs of heavy users to prioritize VMs of more moderate users. Such prioritization scheme, would also allow for introducing novel charging schemes for commercial clouds, such as cloud flat rates [14], where SLAs apply per user and not per VM.

Cloud resources are allocated in two steps that are conducted continuously and in parallel. The first step is termed *scheduling*. In this step the cloud's orchestration layer decides which VM is started next and which node hosts this VM. Also live migrating VMs, *i.e.*, moving running VMs between nodes, is part of scheduling. The second step is termed *runtime prioritization*. In this step, each node allocates its PRs to the hosted VMs. In particular, CPU time, disk I/O, and network access are time-shared, wherefore runtime prioritization allows to efficiently allocate these PRs. Thus, the second step allows to flexibly change the performance of running VMs by altering VM priorities and, thus, PR allocation. For example, a VM scheduled to a powerful node may perform worse than when scheduled to a weak node, if the weak node prioritizes this VM. Runtime prioritization is particularly useful to control the resource allocation, when VMs run over long periods. The reason is that the longer VMs run, the less effective scheduling becomes to alter the allocation, as it only allows for influencing the resource allocation before VMs' (long) runtime.

The best known approach to (multi-resource) data center fairness, Dominant Resource Fairness (DRF) [7], introduces fairness via scheduling. DRF defines how fair allocations look like under the simplifying assumption that resources are required in static ratios, *i.e.*, Leontief utility functions are assumed (a user's *utility function* maps each bundle to a number quantifying the user's valuation for the bundle). This work here differentiates itself from DRF, as it focuses on fair runtime prioritization (and not scheduling) and is, therefore, complemental to DRF. While even during scheduling ratios in which resources are required may change, this is even more likely during runtime prioritization, where utility functions are highly fluctuant or even unavailable due to technical or privacy constraints.

Therefore, in contrary to DRF, the fairness approach taken in this paper avoids any assumptions about utility functions entirely by defining fairness as the procedure of "handicapping VMs of heavy users during runtime to allocate more PRs to VMs of light users". Developing the best suited definition of heaviness for this purpose is the core contribution of this paper. The contribution is achieved by refining the Greediness Metric (GM) [14], which maps multi-resource utilization profiles to heaviness/greediness scalars. An allocation is GM Fair (GMF), if (i) all users have the same greediness, (ii) the utility of no user can be increased by allocating resources that are currently not allocated, and

(iii) no user c receives resources that c could release without decreasing c's utility. Enforcing GMF provides the *configuration incentive*, which means that it is always best for users to chose the VRs of their VMs such that the VRs best match the VMs subsequent PR utilization. Furthermore, the *uncertainty incentive* provided by enforcing GMF ensures that even in case cloud users are unable to precisely predict the PR utilization of their VMs, they still have incentive to configure VMs to the best of their knowledge (and not tend to configure VMs with too many or too few VRs). Due to these incentives, VMs' VRs become a good predictor of the VMs' upcoming PR utilization. This allows the cloud operator to determine the best suited host for a VM during scheduling. Although GMF is developed for runtime prioritization, the avoidance of utility functions allows GMF to achieve a much wider range of application cases. Therefore, just like DRF, GMF can be enforced during scheduling.

The remainder of this paper is structured as follows: Sect. 2 discusses related work leading to the problem statement. Section 3 introduces GM and discusses its refinement such that GMF provides the configuration and uncertainty incentive. Section 4 evaluates GMF by simulations and proves that under the assumptions made by DRF, GMF has the same desirable properties as DRF. Finally, Sect. 5 summarizes and concludes the paper.

2   Related Work and Problem

The most prominent definitions of data center fairness are DRF [7] and BBF [4]. Especially DRF motivated many follow up works, which are not referenced here due to space constraints, and comes with many desirable properties under simplifying assumptions. A third approach to data centers fairness is the extension of Proportional Fairness to multiple resources [2]. All three approaches assume that resources are required in static ratios. Thus, these approaches cannot be applied to runtime prioritization of VMs, as here resource dependencies are unpredictable. Only [15] describes how to theoretically achieve BBF among running processes with varying demands on a node but is unsuited to be applied to coordinate PR allocation across nodes.

Because resources during runtime have to be allocated by assigning priorities to VMs, functions that map (multi-resource) utilization vectors to (priority) scalars are better suited. [9,10] present such priority functions and apply these functions to scheduling. Although these functions are generally applicable to runtime prioritization, they do not allow taking VRs of VMs into account, as they only operate on utilization vectors but not VR vectors. However, taking VRs into account is important to give incentive to users to configure their VMs correctly and, thereby, allow for most efficient cloud utilization.

[11] Allows users to trade resources with other users and adapt their VM runtime priorities. The adopted fairness notion is asset fairness. [11] requires trading mechanisms and VM demand prediction.

Thus, those existing approaches either (i) make assumptions on utility functions that are unrealistic for runtime prioritization, (ii) prohibit giving incentives to users to configure VMs properly, or (iii) require multiple complex mechanisms. These three aspects are addressed by [12,14].

2.1 Previous Work

[14] conducts a questionnaire among more than 600 individuals to investigate an intuitive understanding of fairness and to show that the greediness of users can be defined and quantified based on their multi-resource self-servings. The questionnaire specified real-life scenarios in terms of three questions Q1, Q2, and Q3 to not distract participants by technical terms and let them fully concentrate on the question of fairness and greediness. Q1 and Q3 were relevant to designing GM. Q1 presented four allocations A11, A12, A13, and A14 as illustrated in Table 1 and participants had to select the allocation they regarded as "most fair". A11 and A14 were selected by 0.4% and 1.1% of participants, respectively. A12 and A13 were selected by 30.0% and 68.5%. Q3 described three scenarios, where common heterogenous resources are split among individuals with different demands by letting them serve themselves. This implies mutual trust and poses the question of how individuals, who could try to exploit the system, can be identified, that is, how disproportionate utilization can be defined. The transferability to clouds is evident, where VMs serve themselves from their node's PRs. The portions individuals had served themselves were presented to participant, who had to rank individuals according to their perceived greediness. GM was developed to formalize the most frequent participant reasoning in both questions. Accordingly GM identifies A13 in Q1 as most fair allocation and also results in the most frequently selected user ranking for each of the three scenarios of Q3. No other metric, including the price and dominant-resource metric, achieves this favorable result.

Table 1. The four options A11, A12, A13, and A14 of the questionnaire [14] to allocate two resources r_1 and r_2 to three users c_1, c_2, and c_3.

User	A11		A12		A13		A14	
	r_1	r_2	r_1	r_2	r_1	r_2	r_1	r_2
c_1	2	0	3	0	4	0	5	0
c_2	0	2	0	3	0	4	0	5
c_3	4	4	3	3	2	2	1	1

[12] implements an OpenStack service called *nova-fairness*, which practically achieves GMF by runtime prioritization. In particular, nova-fairness periodically (i) quantifyies the heaviness of VMs by GM, (ii) sums up the heaviness of each user's VMs to calculate the user's heaviness, and (iii) assigns priorities to VMs inversely proportional to the heaviness of their owner. CPU, disk I/O, network access and RAM are the resources which are monitored to calculate the heaviness in

(i) and for which priorities are assigned in (iii). The libvirt API is used for both of these activities, making nova-fairness compatible with a multitude of hypervisors. The performance overhead of nova-fairness is mainly determined by the frequency with which the three steps are conducted and the number of VMs on a node and sublinear in both parameters.

2.2   Basics

A cloud budgets a certain amount of PRs for a VM based on the VM's VRs. Therefore, during scheduling, a node to host the VM will be selected that can best serve the budgeted PRs. For example, placing "small" VMs on nodes with less remaining capacity increases the utilization of these nodes and leaves nodes with more remaining capacity free to accommodate "large" VMs that cannot be hosted by nodes with less remaining capacity. Accordingly, a VM with a PR utilization that strongly deviates from what is budgeted based on the VM's VRs, leads to either over-loaded or under-utilized PRs on the VM's host, *i.e.*, higher stress for the cloud. Therefore, the heaviness of a VM must increase, when the VM's VRs are chosen poorly with respect to its PR utilization, such that users aiming to minimize their heaviness have incentive to configure their VMs properly. This is referred to as the *configuration incentive*. However, users are not always able to precisely predict the PR utilization of their VMs or the PR utilization will be fluctuant. In order to give incentive to users to configure their VMs to the best of their knowledge in such case, a heaviness metric must neither give incentive to configure a VM with too many or too few VRs in case of uncertainty. This is referred to as the *uncertainty incentive*.

2.3   Problem Statement

Besides GMF's ability to support cloud resource allocation in terms of runtime prioritization (and not scheduling), the relaxation of assumptions on utility functions being available leads to a much broader application range, especially to cover scheduling. Thus, the question on how GMF performs compared to the state-of-the-art of fair scheduling (typically considered to be DRF) leads to the problem statement:

1. Extend GM [14] to provide configuration and uncertainty incentives, *i.e.*, a GMF allocation must not only be intuitively fair, but users also must receive the more resources, the better their VMs' VRs conform with these VMs' PR utilizations.
2. Compare GMF to DRF in terms of major properties (i) strategy proofness, (ii) envy freeness, (iii) Pareto efficiency, and (iv) sharing incentives. Especially, prove that GMF achieves these properties under exactly similar assumptions made to prove these properties for DRF.

3   Greediness

A cloud consists of a set of users $U = \{u_1, u_2, \ldots, u_u\}$, a set of nodes $N = \{n_1, n_2, \ldots, n_n\}$, and a set of VMs $V = \{v_1, v_2, \ldots, v_v\}$. A VM is owned by a user and hosted by a node, whereat the cloud's scheduling policy (and not the user) decides which node hosts the VM. Function $o: U \rightarrow \mathcal{P}(V)$ maps user $u \in U$ to the set of VMs u owns and $n: V \rightarrow \mathcal{P}(V)$ maps $v \in V$ to the set of VMs that run on v's host. VMs share their host's PRs, such as CPU time, RAM, disk I/O, and network access. Let $R = \{r_1, r_2, \ldots, r_r\}$ be the set of PRs to be considered for a fair allocation. VMs are defined by VRs, which are often chosen from a range of *flavors*, *i.e.*, a VM flavor is a set of VRs that a VM of that flavor has. Especially in private clouds, resources may be managed by quotas, *i.e.*, each user has a quota that defines a maximum of VRs that the user's VMs may have in total. Function $r: V \cup N \cup U \rightarrow \mathbb{R}^m_{\geq 0}$ maps (i) VMs to their VRs, (ii) nodes to their PRs, and (iii) users to their quota. Function $u: V \rightarrow \mathbb{R}^m_{\geq 0}$ maps VMs to the PRs they utilize (at a distinct point in time). Function $e: V \rightarrow \mathbb{R}^m_{\geq 0}$ maps a VM to its *endowment*, which is the amount of PRs that are budgeted for the VM. The endowment is determined by the VM's VRs and the clouds overcommit ratios. In particular, the more VRs a VM has, the more PRs are budgeted for the VM, and the higher the overcommit ratios in the cloud are, the fewer PRs are budgeted for the VM. In general, $e(v_j) \leq r(v_j)$ holds. It is assumed that the supply of every PR in the cloud is normalized to 1, *i.e.*, $\sum_{j=1}^{n} r(n_j)_i = 1$ for every $1 \leq i \leq r$. Arithmetic operations on vectors are applied point-wise.

3.1   User Greediness

For $u_i \in U$, the user greediness metric $g_u: U \rightarrow \mathbb{R}$ quantifies u_i's heaviness by

$$g_u(u_i) := \left(\sum_{v_j \in o(u_i)} g_v(v_j) \right) - \sum_{l=1}^{r} \left(\frac{\sum_{j=1}^{n} r(n_j)}{\sum_{k=1}^{u} r(u_k)} \cdot r(u_i) \right)_l . \tag{1}$$

The minuend in Eq. 1 sums up the greediness of u_i's VMs, which is defined in Sect. 3.2. The subtrahend is u_i's share of the cloud's PRs that is proportional to u_i's quota (the sum of user quotas may exceed the cloud's PRs). The reason that this quota is subtracted is that cloud users are heterogenous in terms of their quota. In particular, depending on the payment of users or other differentiation criteria, users can have different quotas. Let two users $u_1, u_2 \in U$ operate identical VMs. Let u_1 have a greater quota than u_2. Then, $g_u(u_2)$ must be greater than $g_u(u_1)$, as u_1 and u_2 produce the same stress on the cloud but u_2 has a smaller entitlement to the cloud's resources.

3.2   VM Greediness

The VM greediness metric is stated in Eq. 2 and defines the greediness of a VM v_j depending on $u(v_j)$, $r(v_j)$ or rather $e(v_j)$, and these two parameters of the VMs that run on the same node as v_j.

$$g_v(v_j) := \sum_{i=1}^{r} \mathfrak{e}(v_j)_i + (\mathfrak{u}(v_j)_i - \mathfrak{e}(v_j)_i) \cdot$$

$$\begin{cases} \beta & \text{if } \mathfrak{u}(v_j)_i \geq \mathfrak{e}(v_j)_i, \\[2ex] \gamma \cdot \min\left(1, \dfrac{\overbrace{\sum_{v_k \in \mathfrak{n}(v_j)} \max(0, \mathfrak{u}(v_k)_i - \mathfrak{e}(v_k)_i)}^{\text{Dynamic Ceding Factor (DCF)}}}{\sum_{v_k \in \mathfrak{n}(v_j)} \max(0, \mathfrak{e}(v_k)_i - \mathfrak{u}(v_k)_i)}\right) & \text{else.} \end{cases} \quad (2)$$

The generic structure of this definition is motivated in all detail in [14]. The first summand $\mathfrak{e}(v_j)_i$ inside the sum function of Eq. 2 ensures that $g_v(v_j)$ increases with v_j's VRs, independent of v_j's PR utilization.

In case v_j's PR utilization exceeds v_j's endowment, the difference is scaled by factor $\beta > 1$ and added to $g_v(v_j)$ (if-part). This scaling of the difference is necessary, because otherwise, $g_v(v_j)$ were minimized by configuring v_j with as few VRs as possible, as this would minimize the first summand. Thus, it is important that exceeding the endowment increases $g_v(v_j)$ more than increasing v_j's endowment by that difference.

In case v_j's utilization of a PR remains under v_j's endowment, v_j's greediness is decreased by the amount that is ceded to other VMs scaled by $0 \leq \gamma \leq 1$ (else-part). The amount that is ceded to other VMs is determined by the Dynamic Ceding Factor (DCF). In particular, the DCF sums up the amount by which VMs running on v_j's host exceed their endowments and divides this number by the amount that VMs running on v_j's host do not utilize of their endowment. The mimimization of this fraction and 1 is necessary, as it is possible that the endowments of VMs do not partition the node's PRs entirely. If this were the case and the minimization were not in place, ceding a PR could be "rewarded" stronger than what is actually ceded of the PR. The introduction of γ is motivated by findings in [14] and it is necessary to counter balance β (cf. Sect. 3.3).

3.3   Choosing β and γ to Provide Appropriate Incentives

Due to the first summand inside the sum function of Eq. 2, v_j's greediness increases linearly with v_j's endowment. Let $r_i \in R$. If v_j's utilization of r_i exceeds v_j's endowment to r_i, v_j's greediness increases by the according difference scaled by β. That is, if $\mathfrak{u}(v_j)_i > \mathfrak{e}(v_j)_i$, v_j's greediness increases by $\beta \cdot (\mathfrak{u}(v_j)_i - \mathfrak{e}(v_j)_i)$. Because $\beta > 1$, v_j's greediness were less, if v_j's endowment to r_i were increased. However, increasing v_j's endowment to r_i such that it exceeds v_j's utilization of r_i is unfavorable: if v_j's endowment to r_i is greater than v_j's utilization of r_i, v_j's greediness decreases by the according difference scaled by γ and DCF. That is, if $\mathfrak{e}(v_j)_i > \mathfrak{u}(v_j)_i$, v_j's greediness decreases by $\gamma \cdot \text{DCF} \cdot (\mathfrak{e}(v_j)_i) - \mathfrak{u}(v_j)_i)$. Because $\gamma \cdot \text{DCF} \leq 1$, v_j's greediness were less (or at least not greater), if v_j's endowment to r_i were decreased. It follows that $g_v(v_j)$ is minimized, if v_j's PR utilization is equal to v_j's endowment, i.e., $\mathfrak{e}(v_j) = \mathfrak{u}(v_j)$, in which case $g_v(v_j) = \sum_{i=1}^{r} \mathfrak{u}(v_j)_i$. It follows that Eq. 2 provides the configuration incentive.

To measure how well v_j is configured, the Unnecessary Greediness Increase (UGI) of v_j is defined as the difference between the greediness of v_j and the lowest greediness possible given v_j's PR utilization, $i.e.$,

$$\text{UGI}(v_j) = g_v(v_j) - \sum_{i=1}^{r} \mathfrak{u}(v_j)_i. \tag{3}$$

Assume that, when v_j's PR utilization remains $z\%$ under v_j's endowment, the UGI is z and, when v_j's PR utilization exceeds v_j's endowment by $z\%$, the UGI is $2 \cdot z$. Thus, configuring v_j with $z\%$ too few VRs is twice as "costly" than configuring v_j with $z\%$ too many VRs. Thus, users have incentive too configure VMs too large, if they are uncertain about the PR utilization. Consequently, the uncertainty incentive is not provided, as the uncertainty incentive requires, that configuring a VM with $z\%$ too many or too few VRs results in the same UGI.

Without loss of generality, assume that there is one resource r and that the DCF is α with $0 \leq \alpha \leq 1$. Let $x > y > 0$. Let $\hat{v} \in V$ with $\mathfrak{e}(\hat{v}) = x$ and $\mathfrak{u}(\hat{v}) = x + y$, $i.e.$, $\hat{v}$ exceeds its endowment of x by y. Then $g_v(\hat{v}) = x + \beta \cdot y$ and $\text{UGI}(\hat{v}) = y \cdot \beta - y$ holds. Let $\check{v} \in V$ with $\mathfrak{e}(\check{v}) = x$ and $\mathfrak{u}(\check{v}) = x - y$, $i.e.$, $\check{v}$ leaves y of its endowment of x unutilized. Then $g_v(\check{v}) = x - \gamma \cdot \alpha \cdot y$ and $\text{UGI}(\check{v}) = y - \gamma \cdot \alpha \cdot y$ holds. In order to provide the uncertainty incentive, β and γ must be determined, such that $\text{UGI}(\hat{v}) = \text{UGI}(\check{v})$. This is the case for

$$\beta = 2 - \gamma \cdot \alpha. \tag{4}$$

3.4 Determining Concrete Values for β and γ

The GM was designed based on results of the questionnaire presented in [14]. In this section concrete values for γ and β are determined based on these results as well. In particular, the results of Q1 are chosen to determine γ and β. As A13 was the most frequent choice and was selected by roughly twice as many participants (cf. Sect. 2.1), as the second frequent choice A12, the dependency of γ and β is determined, such that the greediness metric qualifies $A13$ as twice as fair as $A12$, whereat fairness of an allocation is quantified by the (maximal) difference of user greediness for this allocation.

Because the questionnaire specified real-life scenarios, no endowments were specified. Thus, to apply GM, all endowments (function $\mathfrak{e}$ in Eq. 2) are defined as $(2, 2)$, as this is the share, when all resources are split equally.

For A12, GM results in $g_v(c_1) = g_v(c_2) = \beta - 2\gamma$ and $g_v(c_3) = 2\beta$. For A13, GM results in $g_v(c_1) = g_v(c_2) = 2\beta - 2\gamma$ and $g_v(c_3) = 0$. Thus, for A12 the greediness range is $\beta + 2\gamma$ and for A13 it is $2\beta - 2\gamma$.

Accordingly, β and γ must be determined, such that the greediness range of A12 is twice the greediness range of A13, $i.e.$,

$$\beta + 2\gamma = 2 \cdot (2\beta - 2\gamma). \tag{5}$$

Inserting Eq. 4 into Eq. 5 yields

$$\beta = \frac{4}{\alpha + 2} \quad \text{and} \quad \gamma = \frac{2}{\alpha + 2}. \tag{6}$$

When β and γ are determined according to Eq. 6, α determines how strongly a deviation of PR utilization and endowment is penalized: For $\alpha = 0$, ceding is rewarded most strongly (γ is maximized) and, accordingly, exceeding the endowment is also penalized most strongly (β is maximized). The opposite holds for $\alpha = 1$.

α has to be estimated based on the cloud's overcommit ratios. In particular, the higher overcommit ratios are, the more likely it is that PRs are ceded. Accordingly, estimates of α, which represents the DCF, increase with the cloud's overcommit ratios.

Because Eq. 6 is deduced from Question 1 of the questionnaire, the GMs conformance with all other relevant results of the questionnaire was verified numerically, when β and γ are determined by Eq. 6 for any $0 \leq \alpha \leq 1$. The results show GMs perfect compliance also with these other questionnaire results. Subsequently, g_u^x and g_v^x denote that β and γ of the GM are determined by Eq. 6 for $\alpha = x$.

3.5   GM Filling

GMF allocations for Leontief utility functions are determined by a progressive filling algorithm, termed *GM filling*. However, GMF is not constrained to Leontief utility functions but has a much broader application range.

4   Evaluation

Different GMF allocations are analyzed in order to prove that GMF gives incentive to correctly configure VMs and to show how different values of β and γ affect GMF allocations and encourage different VM configuration strategies. Furthermore, a proof of GMF's desirable properties is presented. It is assumed that (i) all resources are provided by one monolithic node n, (ii) users have Leontief utility functions with strictly positive demands for every resource, and that (iii) all overcommit ratios are 1. Therefore, the sum of quotas is at most as large as n's resources and for every VM v, $\mathfrak{r}(v) = \mathfrak{e}(v)$ holds. These simplifying assumptions are made to ease the discussion and clearly show that the extension of GMF developed in this paper has the designated effects. However, GMF is neither restricted to the case that all resources are provided by one node nor that users have Leontief utility functions. A numerical evaluation of GMF for the assumption that resources are provided by different nodes and users operate different numbers of VMs on these nodes is provided in [13]. Furthermore, [12] evaluates GMF by experiments, where (i) users operate different numbers of VMs, (ii) the VMs are hosted by different nodes, (iii) the VMs utilize different amounts of CPU time and disk I/O, and (iv) the PR utilization varies over time.

4.1   Incentives

The *ratio scenario* presented in this section shows how the GM provides incentives to users to configure VMs correctly. Let $q \mod 3 = 0$. There are $q+1$ VMs

$v_0, v_1, v_2, \ldots, v_q$ and two PRs r_1 and r_2. Every VM requests an infinite amount of PRs in ratio 2:1, $i.e.$, every VM requests twice as much of r_1 than of r_2. The VRs of VM v_j are $\mathfrak{r}(v_j) = (j, \mathsf{q} - j)$ and $\mathfrak{r}(n) = (\frac{\mathsf{q}^2 - \mathsf{q}}{2}, \frac{\mathsf{q}^2 - \mathsf{q}}{2}) = \sum_{j=0}^{\mathsf{q}} \mathfrak{r}(v_j) = \sum_{j=0}^{\mathsf{q}} \mathfrak{e}(v_j)$, $i.e.$, the VMs' endowments completely partition the host's PRs. Each VM belongs to a different user. All users have the same quota, wherefore the results presented below are independent of the amount of this quota.

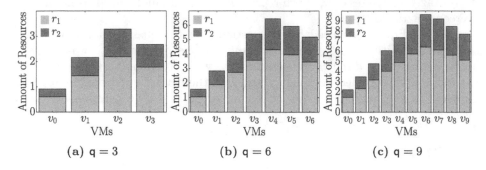

(a) q = 3   (b) q = 6   (c) q = 9

Fig. 1. GMF allocations for the ratio scenario for different numbers of VMs (q).

Figure 1 illustrates the GMF allocations for $\mathsf{q} \in \{3, 6, 9\}$. While the choice of α influences the absolute greediness of VMs, it does not influence the allocation. For example, for $\mathsf{q} = 6$, $g_v^0(v_j) = 0.920$, $g_v^{0.25}(v_j) = 0.818$, $g_v^{0.5}(v_j) = 0.736$, $g_v^{0.75}(v_j) = 0.669$, $g_v^1(v_j) = 0.614$ for all $v_j \in V$ holds. This reflects that for smaller α, deviating from the endowment increases the greediness stronger.

Although all VMs have the same sum of VRs, Fig. 1 shows that VMs receive different amounts of PRs, because the ratios of their VRs are different. In particular, the better a VM's VR ratio is aligned with the actual PR requirement, the more PRs the VM receives. Accordingly, $\mathfrak{r}(v_0) = (0, \mathsf{q})$ is the worst configuration to request PRs in ratio $(2, 1)$ and, thus, v_0 receives the least PRs for all q. In contrast, VM $v_{2\mathsf{q}/3}$'s VRs have the perfect ratio, wherefore v_2, v_4 and v_6 receive the most PRs for $\mathsf{q} = 3, 6, 9$, respectively. Although v_0 and v_q have one VR configured with 0, v_q receives significantly more PRs than v_0, because it has a high endowment to the stronger requested PR.

4.2   Effects of β and γ

The *strategy scenario* presented in this section compares two strategies to configure VMs and demonstrates the effects of different values of β and γ. Node n provides one PR r in quantity 2, $i.e.$, $\mathfrak{r}(n) = 2$. Node n is shared by two users u_a and u_b, who have a quota of 1, $i.e.$, $\mathfrak{r}(u_a) = \mathfrak{r}(u_b) = 1$. Both users have four VMs running on n and a different strategy to configure these VMs. u_a's entire quota is partitioned to u_a's VMs $v_1^a, v_2^a, v_3^a, v_4^a$, $i.e.$, $\mathfrak{r}(v_x^a) = 0.25$ for $1 \leq x \leq 4$. u_b's VMs $v_1^b, v_2^b, v_3^b, v_4^b$ are configured 80% smaller than u_a's VMs, $i.e.$, $\mathfrak{r}(v_x^b) = 0.05$

for $1 \leq x \leq 4$. The PRs that the two users attempt to utilize are equal. In particular, the first VM of both users attempts to utilize as much of r as possible. These VMs are referred to as busy VMs. The six other VMs each attempt to utilize 0.05 of r and are, therefore, referred to as idle VMs. Furthermore, this PR utilization matches exactly the VRs of u_b's VMs.

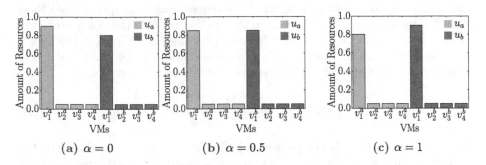

(a) $\alpha = 0$ (b) $\alpha = 0.5$ (c) $\alpha = 1$

Fig. 2. GMF allocations for the strategy scenario to align the greediness of users for different α.

Table 2. GM values for GMF allocations of Fig. 2.

Allocate for	$\alpha = 0$		$\alpha = 0.5$		$\alpha = 1$		$\alpha \in \{0, 0.5, 1\}$	
	v_1^a	v_1^b	v_1^a	v_1^b	v_1^a	v_1^b	$v_{2,3,4}^a$	$v_{2,3,4}^b$
Allocation	0.90	0.80	0.85	0.85	0.80	0.90	0.05	0.05
g_v^0	1.55	1.55	1.45	1.65	1.35	1.75	0.05	0.05
$g_v^{0.5}$	1.29	1.25	1.21	1.33	1.13	1.41	0.09	0.05
g_v^1	1.12	1.05	1.05	1.12	0.98	1.18	0.12	0.05
	u_a	u_b	u_a	u_b	u_a	u_b		
Allocation	1.05	0.95	1.00	1.00	0.95	1.05		
g_u^0	0.70	0.70	0.60	0.80	0.50	0.90		
$g_u^{0.5}$	0.56	0.40	0.48	0.48	0.40	0.56		
g_u^1	0.47	0.20	0.40	0.27	0.33	0.33		

Figure 2 (backed by full numerical details as of Table 2) shows those GMF allocations that align g_u^0, $g_u^{0.5}$, and g_u^1 of both users. The figure shows that all idle VMs are allocated all requested PRs. However, PRs allocated to the two busy VMs differ depending on α.

Figure 2a shows that for $\alpha = 0$, v_1^a receives more PRs than v_1^b. The reason is that DCF $= 1 = \gamma$ and, therefore, the over-configuration of v_2^a, v_3^a, v_4^a is not penalized. Accordingly, Table 2 shows that the idle VMs of both users have the same g_v^0 values. However, $\mathfrak{r}(v_1^a) = 5 \cdot \mathfrak{r}(v_1^b)$, wherefore, v_1^a receives more PRs than v_1^b. When α increases, the over-configuration of u_a's idle VMs is penalized stronger and the under-configuration of u_b's busy VM is penalized less. Accordingly, Fig. 2b and Table 2 show that $\alpha = 0.5$ is the tipping point, where the VMs of both users receive the same amount of PRs. Table 2 shows that $\alpha = 1$ maximizes the greediness of u_a's idle VMs. Accordingly, v_1^a receives less PRs than v_1^b to align the greediness of both users.

The strategy scenario can be altered in two dimension: the number of idle VMs and the amount of PRs the idle VMs request (while adapting the VRs of u_b's VMs accordingly). Let $s \in \mathbb{N}_{\geq 1}$ be the number of VMs that each user owns and $0 \leq t \leq 1$, such that t/s is the PR utilization of all idle VMs and the VRs of u_b's VMs. For example, in the scenario discussed above $s = 4$ and $t = 0.2$. The difference between what v_1^a and v_1^b receive under a GMF allocation is

$$u(v_1^a) - u(v_1^b) = \frac{((\gamma - 1) \cdot s + \gamma) \cdot (1 - t)}{s \cdot \beta}. \tag{7}$$

The derivation of Eq. 7 is not presented here due to space constraints. The formula shows that wether u_a's or u_b's strategy is superior depends on a combination of α (which determines β and γ) and s, whereat, increasing s and α make u_b's strategy preferable. Notably, t only changes the difference in the allocations but does not influence, which strategy is superior. Furthermore, for $\alpha = 0$ the first factor of the dividend is always positive, which reflects that u_a's strategy is always superior (as over-configuring VMs is not penalized).

4.3   Properties Achieved

GM filling is (i) strategy prove and the resulting GMF allocation is (ii) envy free, (iii) Pareto efficient, and (iv) provides sharing incentive, as proven in this section. To simplify the discussion, it is assumed that every user u_j starts one VM v_j with $r(u_j) = r(v_j)$, i.e., v_j is configured with u_j's entire quota. Therefore, $g_u(u_j) = g_v(v_j)$.

Sharing Incentive. Sharing incentive demands that each user u has a utility that is at least as high as when u had exclusive access to the resources that correspond to u's quota. Assume GM filling results in an allocation that does not provide sharing incentive. Then a VM v_p exists that receives strictly less of every resource than v_p's VRs, i.e., $u(v_p) < r(v_p)$. Because (i) $u(v_p) < r(v_p)$, (ii) $\gamma > 0$, and (iii) at least one resource is saturated, $g_v(v_p) < 0$. As $\beta > \gamma$, the sum of VM/user greediness is at least zero. Accordingly, a VM v_s exists with $g_u(u_s) = g_v(v_s) > 0 > g_v(v_p) = g_u(u_p)$. Then the greediness of users is not equal.

Pareto-Efficiency. Because Leontief utilties are assumed and at least one resource is saturated, this characteristic is trivially achieved [8].

Strategy Proofness. Assume that lying about v_j's requirement vector, *i.e.*, the vector that specifies the ratio in which VM filling allocates resources to v_j, can increase u_j's utility. Because strictly positive Leontief utility functions are assumed, v_j has to receive more of every resource, in order to increase u_j's utility. Because GM filling provides sharing incentive, v receives at least its endowment of at least one resource r. Receiving more of r increases v_j's greediness. Since GM filling aligns the greediness, the greediness increase caused by receiving more of r has to be compensated by receiving less of another resource r'. Thus, in order to receive more of r, u_j has to request/receive less of r'. Then u_j's utility decreases.

Envy-Freeness. Envy-freeness only has to hold among users with the same quota. In particular, the configuration incentive demands to allocate VMs different amounts of resources, depending on their VR, *i.e.*, envy is unavoidable between VMs with different VRs. Thus, assume two VMs v_a and v_b have the same VRs. Assume u_a envies v_b's resource allocation. Then v_b receives strictly more than v_a of at least one resource. Since both VMs have the same greediness, v_b has to receive strictly less than v_a of another resource. However, because progressive VM filling is strategy prove, u_a has stated the true requirement of v_a. Therefore, when v_b receives less of a resource than v_a, u_a cannot envy the resources v_b receives.

4.4   Assumptions and Practice

Leontief utility functions model dependencies among time shared resources well. For example, when the bandwidth of a server is reduced, the server's disk I/O utilization decreases equivalently, as requests reach the server slower and, thus, stored data is fetched at a lower rate. In contrast, the dependency between time shared resources and RAM, which is space shared, is often different. For example, assume a program has a fixed number of variables that are stored in RAM. Allocating more CPU time will execute to the program faster, while the number of variables and, thus, required RAM remains constant. What further complicates depedencies among PRs are substitutabilities: For example, (i) paging reduces RAM requirements by use of CPU time or (ii) compression saves storage or bandwidth by use of CPU time [4]. Consequently, Leontief utility functions do not cover the whole range of PR dependencies. However, because GMF is defined without access to utility functions, GMF is well suited to be enforced, when complex resource dependencies apply.

VMs' PR utilization may follow well defined but bursty patterns. For example, databases usually write in periodic large bursts to disk. However, users cannot specify this burstiness, as they only configure VRs of their VMs. Nonetheless, nova-fairness (cf. Sect. 2.1) does not penalize bursty PR utilization, when enforcing GMF. The reason is that nova-fairness measures the cumulated PR utilization over a customizable period x. Therefore, it does not matter, if within a period resource are utilized smoothly or in bursts. Only when the inter-burst time is greater than x, bursts are penalized.

5   Summary and Conclusions

This paper has applied GM to achieve fair runtime prioritization in clouds. GM has been backed by a survey among more than 600 individuals, to ensure that, when the greediness of different users is aligned, the resulting allocation is intuitively fair [14]. Accordingly, the newly defined GMF determines allocations that align the greediness of all users and are efficient. Enforcing GMF during runtime prioritization provides incentives to cloud users to configure their VMs, such that the VMs' VR conform with the VMs' subsequent PR utilization. Therefore, a VM's VRs become a predictor for this VM's upcoming PR utilization and, accordingly, allows cloud operators to place VMs efficiently on nodes.

GMF's practical applicability has been proven in practice in [12] by the nova-fairness service, which extends the OpenStack implementation. Since GMF leverages runtime prioritization, GMF is complementary to cloud fairness approaches, which introduce fairness by scheduling. And since GMF was defined on purpose without the knowledge of any utility functions, GMF offers a very wide application range, especially including scheduling. Therefore, GMF was proven to provide for (i) strategy proofness, (ii) envy freeness, (iii) Pareto efficiency, and (iv) sharing incentives, which are the four main assets of the state-of-the-art fair scheduling policy DRF.

Resources, a cloud user effectively utilizes, depend on the PR utilization of the user's VMs. Accordingly, even when users have instantiated VMs with the same VRs, PRs these users utilize effectively can be different. Contrary to scheduling schemes, runtime prioritization and, therefore, GMF especially allows for managing and, thus, streamlining this amount of utilized PRs. Therefore, GMF is more effective to establish fairness between cloud users than existing scheduling schemes, especially, when VMs run over long periods. Since resource allocations in private clouds are typically not guided by Service Level Agreements, as it is the case in commercial clouds, fairness and GMF become very important in private clouds. Nevertheless, GMF may also be deployed to define fair cloud flat rate payment schemes to enable renting a quota in a commercial cloud [14] from which VMs are instantiated. This defines in particular a very practical approach, since the telecommunications sector has shown that customers often prefer flat rates over volume based pricing models due to their predictability.

Acknowledgements. This work was supported partially by the FLAMINGO [6] project, funded by the EU FP7 Program under Contract No. FP7-2012-ICT-318488.

References

1. Arcangeli, A., Eidus, I., Wright, C.: Increasing memory density by using KSM. In: 2009 Linux Symposium, vol. 1, pp. 19–28, July 2009. http://landley.net/kdocs/ols/2009/ols2009-pages-19-28.pdf
2. Bonald, T., Roberts, J.: Multi-resource fairness: objectives, algorithms and performance. In: 2015 ACM SIGMETRICS International Conference on Measurement and Modeling of Computer Systems SIGMETRICS 2015, New York, NY, USA, pp. 31–42, June 2015. http://doi.acm.org/10.1145/2745844.2745869

3. Breitgand, D., Dubitzky, Z., Epstein, A., Glikson, A., Shapira, I.: SLA-aware resource over-commit in an IaaS cloud. In: 8th International Conference on Network and Service Management (CNSM) and 2012 Workshop on Systems Virtualization Management (SVM), Las Vegas, NV, USA, pp. 73–81, October 2012
4. Dolev, D., Feitelson, D.G., Halpern, J.Y., Kupferman, R., Linial, N.: No justified complaints: on fair sharing of multiple resources. In: 3rd Innovations in Theoretical Computer Science Conference, ITCS 2012, Cambridge, MA, USA, pp. 68–75, January 2012
5. Etsion, Y., Ben-Nun, T., Feitelson, D.G.: A global scheduling framework for virtualization environments. In: 2009 IEEE International Symposium on Parallel Distributed Processing, IPDPS 2009, pp. 1–8, May 2009
6. FLAMINGO Consortium: FLAMINGO: Management of the Future Internet, December 2014. http://www.fp7-flamingo.eu/
7. Ghodsi, A., Zaharia, M., Hindman, B., Konwinski, A., Shenker, S., Stoica, I.: Dominant resource fairness: fair allocation of multiple resource types. In: 8th USENIX Conference on Networked Systems Design and Implementation, NSDI 2011, Berkeley, CA, USA, pp. 323–336, March 2011
8. Gutman, A., Nisan, N.: Fair allocation without trade. In: 11th International Conference on Autonomous Agents and Multiagent Systems, AAMAS 2012, Valencia, Spain, vol. 2, pp. 719–728, June 2012
9. Klusáček, D., Rudová, H.: Multi-resource aware fairsharing for heterogeneous systems. In: Cirne, W., Desai, N. (eds.) JSSPP 2014. LNCS, vol. 8828, pp. 53–69. Springer, Cham (2015). doi:10.1007/978-3-319-15789-4_4
10. Klusáček, D., Rudová, H., Jaroš, M.: Multi resource fairness: problems and challenges. In: Desai, N., Cirne, W. (eds.) JSSPP 2013. LNCS, vol. 8429, pp. 81–95. Springer, Heidelberg (2014). doi:10.1007/978-3-662-43779-7_5
11. Liu, H., He, B.: F2C: enabling fair and fine-grained resource sharing in multi-tenant IaaS clouds. IEEE Trans. Parallel Distrib. Syst. **27**(9), 2589–2602 (2015)
12. Poullie, P., Mannhart, S., Stiller, B.: Defining and enforcing fairness among cloud users by adapting virtual machine priorities during runtime. Technical report, IFI-2016.04, Universität Zürich, Zurich, Switzerland, March 2016. https://files.ifi.uzh.ch/CSG/staff/poullie/extern/publications/IFI-2016.04.pdf
13. Poullie, P., Stiller, B.: Cloud flat rates enabled via fair multi-resource consumption. Technical report, IFI-2015.03, Universität Zürich, Zurich, Switzerland, October 2015. https://files.ifi.uzh.ch/CSG/staff/poullie/extern/publications/IFI-2015.03.pdf
14. Poullie, P., Stiller, B.: Cloud flat rates enabled via fair multi-resource consumption. In: Badonnel, R., Koch, R., Pras, A., Drašar, M., Stiller, B. (eds.) AIMS 2016. LNCS, vol. 9701, pp. 30–44. Springer, Cham (2016). doi:10.1007/978-3-319-39814-3_3
15. Zeldes, Y., Feitelson, D.G.: On-line fair allocations based on bottlenecks and global priorities. In: 4th ACM/SPEC International Conference on Performance Engineering, ICPE 2013, pp. 229–240, April 2013. http://doi.acm.org/10.1145/2479871.2479904

A History-Based Model for Provisioning EC2 Spot Instances with Cost Constraints

Javier Fabra[1(✉)], Sergio Hernández[1], Pedro Álvarez[1], Joaquín Ezpeleta[1], Álvaro Recuenco[2], and Ana Martínez[2]

[1] Department of Computer Science and Systems Engineering,
Aragón Institute of Engineering Research (I3A),
Universidad de Zaragoza, Zaragoza, Spain
{jfabra,shernandez,alvaper,ezpeleta}@unizar.es
[2] Health and Code Software Solutions, Zaragoza, Spain
{amartinez,arecuenco}@healthandcode.com

Abstract. The increasing demand of computing resources has boosted the use of cloud computing providers. This has raised a new dimension in which the connection between resource usage and costs has to be considered from an organizational perspective. As a part of its EC2 service, Amazon introduced spot instances (SIs) as a cheap public infrastructure, but at the price of not ensuring reliability of the service (hired SIs can be terminated by the service when necessary). The interface for managing SIs is based on a bidding strategy that depends on non-public Amazon pricing strategies, which makes complicated for users to apply any scheduling or resource provisioning strategy based on such (cheaper) resources. Although it is believed that the use of the EC2 SIs infrastructure can reduce costs for final users, a deep review of literature concludes that their characteristics and possibilities have not yet been deeply explored. In this work we present and evaluate a framework for the analysis of the EC2 SIs infrastructure that uses the price history of such resources in order to generate a provisioning plan by means of a simulation algorithm considering cost constraints.

Keywords: Cloud computing · Provisioning · Spot instances · Amazon EC2 · Cost constraints

1 Introduction

The cloud-computing paradigm has changed the traditional way in which software systems are built by means of the introduction of a new model in which infrastructures, platforms, applications and services are served on demand [1]. The consolidation of this new approach in the industry as well as in research and academic environments has arisen the need to reconsider the way technological resources are used in organizations, integrating cloud-computing along with these resources [2–5].

© Springer International Publishing AG 2017
J.Á. Bañares et al. (Eds.): GECON 2016, LNCS 10382, pp. 208–222, 2017.
DOI: 10.1007/978-3-319-61920-0_15

The cloud-computing approach promotes an on-demand model for the provisioning of resources: virtual servers, services or an application platform, for instance. This model is being adopted because of the features it offers, such as elasticity, flexibility or pay-per-use. At the same time, Infrastructure-as-a-Service (IaaS) providers have introduced some additional variables related to price, performance and reliability in the resources located on the cloud. These providers deploy cloud resource management systems in data centers distributed worldwide. Some of these providers also offer a special type of computing resource in order to take advantage of unused cycles on their datacenters looking at maximizing their benefits. The price of these resources varies over time, representing important savings with respect to the corresponding on-demand alternative. The most well known cases of this practice are Google Cloud Preemptible Virtual Machine (VM) Instances and Amazon EC2 Spot Instances (EC2 SI). In this work we will focus on the Amazon EC2 SI approach.

Amazon Spot instances are offered through an auction mechanism. The user must specify the maximum price that he is willing to pay (this is, the *bid price*) as well as other constraints such as the instance type and the deployment data center (the *availability zone* in AWS notation). In case the specified instance is available and the bid price is greater than the current spot price, the request is immediately fulfilled and the instance is launched. Otherwise, the request is postponed until both conditions are fulfilled.

The Spot instances created will run until either they are terminated by the user or there is a *Spot instance termination*, this is, Amazon EC2 must terminate them because of Spot Market fluctuations. AWS continuously evaluates how many Spot instances are available in each Spot instance pool, monitors the bids that have been made for each pool, and provisions the available Spot instances to the highest bidders. The Spot price for a pool is set to the lowest fulfilled bid for that pool. Therefore, the Spot price is the price above which you must bid to fulfill a Spot request for a single Spot instance immediately. Note that there is a maximum number of available Spot instances in a Spot instance pool. If the size of the pool drops to zero, then all the Spot instances from that pool would be interrupted.

There are three situations in which Amazon EC2 can perform a Spot instance termination: when the Spot price rises above the user's bid price, when the demand for Spot instances rises or, finally, when the supply of Spot instances decreases. Once a Spot instance has been marked for termination, a SI *termination notice* is sent. This is a two-minute warning window before it terminates. The user is responsible for programming a checkpointing mechanism that prevents processes and data been executed in the instance to be lost.

Although Spot instances do not provide users either reliable execution, a good analysis and offer strategy can drastically reduce the execution costs of systems when comparing to on-demand costs (between a 50% and a 90%) [6]. The capacity and performance of applications could be increased with the same budget, or even allow the use of new applications or configurations that were previously discarded because of economic reasons.

The use of spot instances perfectly fits on a vast variety of scientific computing experiments, from genomic sequence analysis to data distribution, physic simulations or bioinformatics, for instance. From an enterprise's point of view, there also exist some companies that take advantage of the use of spot instances. DNAnexus is an application case that bases their systems on the use of spot instances to carry out genomic analysis and clinical studies on a highly scalable environment [7]. Netflix is also a well-known case on the multimedia industry. They use spot instances in order to improve the broadcast of billion of data on their content network [8].

In this work we propose the analysis of Amazon EC2 Spot Instances mechanisms to provide a history-based model allowing final users to deploy a provisioning strategy for a given cost constraint. To this end, we have built a system that analyzes price variations on all regions and zones where SIs are offered. Given a deadline and cost constraints, the system provides the user with a complete overview of the suitability of using spot instances for the deployment of an experiment. We have used this system to construct and execute real provisioning plans in different regions and moments. We have also detected the existence of certain patterns in this variation that can be used to obtain a significant cost reduction. To the best of our knowledge, this is the first study to propose a user-oriented framework with such features.

The remainder of this paper is structured as follows. Section 2 presents related work on the analysis of EC2 Spot instances. The framework developed for the analysis of the EC2 SI infrastructure is introduced in Sect. 3. This framework is used to generate different provisioning plans with cost constraints by means of the experimentation depicted in Sect. 4. Finally, Sect. 5 enumerates some conclusions and future work.

2   Related Work

Some previous research has focused on the use of EC2 Spot instances to reduce computing costs when dealing with complex problems [9,10]. In [9], authors are especially sensitive with the reliability of spot instances, and manage checkpointing strategies to avoid data loss when instances are terminated because of overbidding. The economics of adding additional resources to dedicated clusters during peak periods was studied in [10]. Authors defined different provisioning policies based on the use of Amazon Spot instances and compared them to on-demand instances in terms of cost savings and total breach time of tasks in the queue.

Spot instances price variation over time has been deeply studied in [11,12], although authors have not given specific conclusions. [11] considers that price varies on real time and there is not a pattern for this variation. On the other hand, a reverse engineering technique is used in [12] in order to build a price model based on auto-regression techniques. The relation between Cloud Service Brokers and pricing is analised in [13], where authors discuss how performance variation in virtual machines of the same type and price raises specific issues for end users, which in the end affects to the final price for resource allocation.

There are few papers that achieve a statistical analysis as well as a modeling of price variations of Spot instances. A very interesting approach is presented in [14,15], where authors conducted an analysis of SI price and its variations limited to four specific regions of Amazon EC2. All different types of SIs in terms of spot price and the inter-price time (time between price changes) as well as the time dynamics for spot price in hour-in-day and day-of-week were studied. Authors proposed the characterization of this behavior through a statistical model and evaluated it by means of simulation techniques.

With respect to the generation of Spot instances provisioning, authors propose in [16] a decision-based model to improve performance, costs and reliability under the restrictions imposed by a SLA. In [17] the use of spot instances is also proposed to improve a map-reduce execution system, and a Markov chain model is proposed to predict the lifetime of a running spot instance. Authors focus on fail situations and propose provisioning policies for these cases, which is also the base for the work presented in [10]. Similarly, in [18] a Constrained Markov Decision Process (CMDP) is formulated in order to derive an optimal bidding strategy. Based on this model, authors obtain an optimal randomized bidding strategy through linear programming. Finally, in [19] Markov spot price evolution is also analyzed. A job is modeled as a fixed computation request with a deadline constraint in order to formulate the problem of designing a dynamic bidding policy that minimizes the average cost of job completion.

Finally, the analysis of the bidding system of Amazon Spot instances and the consequences of instance termination has been the focus of the research presented in [9,20–22].

Most research has focused on the impact of Spot instance termination and other aspects such as reliability. Other authors have concentrated their efforts to study general price variations in the Spot Market, considering specific Availability Regions and instance types. In this work, we aim at the analysis of SI prices considering costs and time constraints. As a result, our work focuses on the building of a provisioning plan for the final user, providing it with different options and results and allowing to decide the best option fitting his requirements/constraints.

Our framework considers all available data for every Availability Region and computing zones as well as every instance type and operating system. The developed framework is easy to use, ready to be integrated with other software components by means of its Web-service interface. Currently, this framework is integrated in the enterprise software infrastructure of Health and Code Software Solutions, allowing their system architects to generate provisioning plans using Spot instances and significantly reducing the costs of their computing infrastructure.

3   A Framework for the Analysis of the EC2 SI Infrastructure

Let us now briefly describe the developed framework. The architecture of the system is depicted in Fig. 1. The *EC2 SI Data Retrieval* component downloads price variations for all instance types of every EC2 region and zone. To do that, it uses the Amazon Elastic Compute Cloud API (API version 2015-10-01). This component is periodically executed (once per week), so only the data missing in the system is retrieved. Also, this allows us to keep the system updated with EC2 SI prices up to last week. The *Data Retrieval* component is connected to the *History Record* component, which keeps track of downloaded data and possible failures. In case the data retrieval fails (for a loss of connectivity, for instance), the history record marks a dataset as *failed* and then communicates this situation to the *Error Handler*. This component interacts with the *Data Retrieval* component in order to retry downloading the lost data. This process can be repeated up to three times before the data is marked as non-available. Non-available data are not used for further processing or simulation.

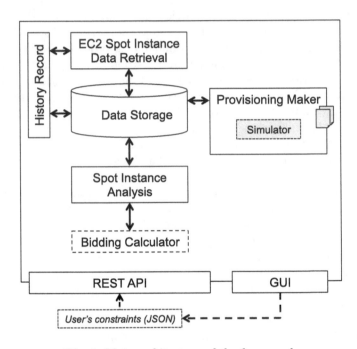

Fig. 1. Main architecture of the framework.

When data are successfully downloaded, they are stored in the *Database* component. This component implements a high input/output performance utility for data persistency, storing all the information related to a price entry: date and time, instance type, region, zone, price variation and absolute price. These price variations are then used by the *SI Analysis* component, which performs an analysis of price variations over time considering different variables. For the sake of simplicity, in this work we will focus on the analysis that this component does considering the maximum price the SI reached at each hour. This is done to ensure that the simulator is getting the highest price the instance got at each time period.

The *Spot Instances Analysis* component also allows us to perform a deep study of price variations in each region and zone for any specific instance type, as it provides us with some statistical information such as mean deviation, average price and peaks on variations, among others.

The *Provisioning Maker* component is responsible of proposing a provisioning plan that consists of a list of feasible time instants at which a specific instance type can be requested. Given a deadline, an EC2 region, an instance type, the number of execution hours and the maximum price per hour, the provisioning maker uses an internal simulator to generate all *feasible hours* at which a bid could be placed in the EC2 SI bidding interface with a price lower or equal to the maximum specified before the specified deadline expires. A *feasible hour* means that the simulation process estimates that the bid will succeed and, therefore, we would be able to create a SI of the requested type without it being preempted.

Obviously, the price specification is one of the key values on this process. The *Bidding Calculator* component is the one in charge of determining the best price at each moment for a specific instance type in a specific region. This component calculates a suitable bidding price by means of the use of weighted averages and hysteresis techniques.

Finally, all the functionalities of the framework are exposed using a *Web services interface* based on REST technology. This interface receives the user's constraints (described in JSON) and connects with the internal components in order to serve a Spot price analysis or a provisioning plan. The framework can be easily integrated with another applications or with a graphical user interface, as it is the case of the *GUI* component. For the experimentation conducted in this paper we used the REST API to generate an automated battery of experiments, but the framework is used everyday through its GUI.

The framework has been used to track Spot instances data since June 2015. Although Amazon provides a *Spot Bid Advisor* [23], the range of information that it offers is quite limited and it is restricted to a few weeks. We have collected more than 74 million price variations in 18 different zones that are categorized in the EC2 Availability Regions. Currently, we add 2.5 million new entries every week to the system.

4   Generation of a Provisioning Plan

Let us now depict how the presented framework works by means of a use case. We had to execute different processes that required running during one, three, six and, finally, ten hours. These processes were related to small tasks (one and three hours) and more complex ones – accounting tasks – (six and ten hours). The software to execute had to be deployed in an m3.xlarge EC2 instance requiring Linux as operating system. Due to customer's requirements, these processes had to be executed at least one time in the last week of January 2016. Our aim was to determine whether that processes could be executed by half the price of a regular on-demand instance and, if so, to proceed.

We used the framework to generate a provisioning plan considering these constraints. We also performed an analysis of the lowest SI price that we could pay with the previous requirements.

The framework requires specifying all our constraints as an input using the REST interface or the graphical interface (we used the last one). As we did not have any reason to execute the software in a specific region or zone, we first analyzed SI price variation in every Availability Zone. Figure 2 depicts how we used the Spot Instances Analysis component of the framework to get a detailed analysis for the previous months (December 2015 and January 2016). The parameters for the analysis are set on the top configuration area. Once they are have been set, the *Search* button launches the process and the evolution of SI price (Y-axis, in dollars) is displayed over time (X-axis).

Fig. 2. Spot Instances Analysis component.

As a result from the data obtained by the SI Analyzer, we selected two different regions to conduct the experimentation. On the one hand, the EU-West-1 region represented a stable region, which may prevent strong fluctuations in the Spot Market, but with higher prices as a counterpart. Figures 3 and 4 depict the price variation graph for the December 2015–January 2016 period. The analysis of the number of price variations during these months was low: 13,524 records. It was the region with less variance and standard deviation. Mean price was 0.041\$ for the three zones in EU region. Maximum price varied from 0.042\$ in EU-West-1c, 0.050\$ in EU-West-1b and 0.044\$ in EU-West-1a. Minimum prices were from 0.040\$ for zones EU-West-1c and EU-West-1b to 0.041\$ in EU-West-1a.

The standard deviation was quite small, being 0.001 in EU-West-1a and EU-West-1b zones.

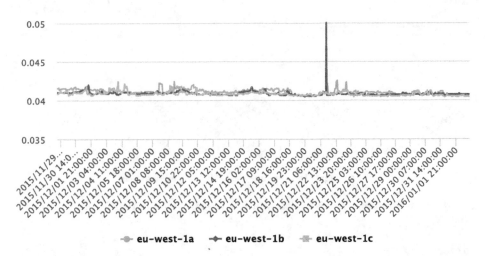

Fig. 3. Price variation (Y-axis, dollars) in EU-West-1 region during December 2015 (X-axis).

On the other hand, the US-East-1 region showed the highest price variation and standard deviation in both months. Prices were the lowest ones, but the risk of market fluctuations (and then the termination of SIs) was higher. For the region of US-East-1 153,178 records were stored from the analyzed months. In this case, the mean price ranged from 0.038\$ in US-East-1b and US-East-1c up to 0.039\$ in US-East-1a or the higher 0.066\$ in US-East-1e. Figures 5 and 6 depict price variation for zones US-East-1a to US-East-1c. Zone US-East-1e was excluded from Fig. 5 because prices were too high compared to the other zones. Mean deviation was 0.003 on a, b and c zones, whereas this value was 0.034 in zone US-East-1e. Also, standard deviation ranged from 0.005–0.007 in zones US-East-1a, 1b and 1c to 0.094 in US-East-1e.

We concluded that US-East-1 region seemed to be the cheapest one for the period of time analyzed. On the other hand, EU-West-1 region seemed to be the more stable one. We then used the framework to generate the provisioning plan for an m3.xlarge instance on these two regions, running a Linux operating system and for 1, 3, 6 and 10 consecutive hours of execution. As the processes had to be executed on a week as a deadline, we got a provisioning plan covering seven days.

Therefore, we had to execute the simulations considering the week starting on January 24th 2016 with some price variations. To do that, we used the Provisioning Maker Simulator.

We set up all the specified constraints: region and zone, instance type, operating system, maximum price to pay, number of hours and strategy to use in order

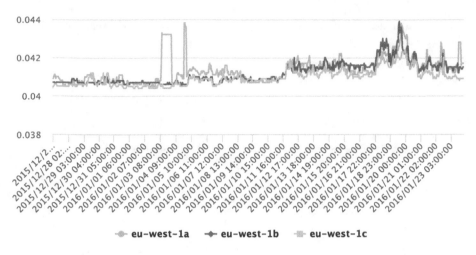

Fig. 4. Price variation (Y-axis, dollars) in EU-West-1 region during January 2016 (X-axis).

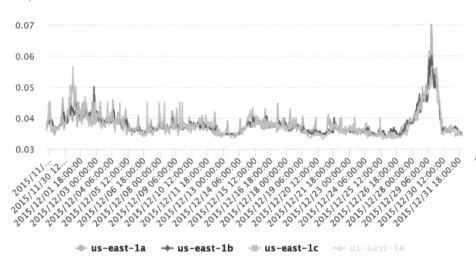

Fig. 5. Price variation (Y-axis, dollars) in US-East-1 region during December 2015 (X-axis).

to calculate the price in the simulator. Figure 7 depicts the graphical interface of the simulator, where all these constraints were set on the top. The simulation is then started by pressing the *Simulate* button. Once it has finished, results are shown. First, a table shows the number of slots with success ratios of 100% and 60–99% for every zone in every region simulated. After that, a graph shows the percentage of job success over time. Finally, the simulation process displays a table with the average price obtained in every slot for the constraints set.

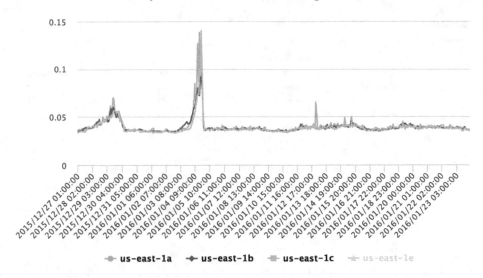

Fig. 6. Price variation (Y-axis, dollars) in US-East-1 region during January 2016 (X-axis).

The simulator provides with three strategies for price calculation: *maximum price*, *minimum price* and *mean price*. The Spot price can change several times within an hour. The maximum price strategy considers the highest one to set the Spot price in a specific hour during simulation. The minimum price strategy considers the lowest one. Finally, the mean price option calculates the average of all data within the hour. Selecting the maximum price we are ensuring that the highest prices are used, so the result of the simulation should avoid termination because of price overbidding.

The simulator proceeds to calculate if a Spot instance could be created considering that the bid cannot exceed (*maximum price/number of hours*)$. This is done for every hour in the period specified in the input to the simulator. For each hour, the simulator calculates the Spot price as a weighted average of the corresponding prices stored in the system in the last eight weeks (two months). The most recent week has a weight of 30%, and the consequent ones 20%, 15%, 10%, 8%, 6%, 4% and, finally, the oldest week is weighted with a 2%. The prices are obtained according to the selected strategy.

As a result of the simulation, we got a detailed overview of the success/fail of placing a bid of half the on-demand price for an m3.xlarge instance on each hour every day during the week. The result of the simulation considered that once the bid has been placed, in case it is accepted and the instance is launched, it will execute during one, three, six or ten consecutive hours (we carried out a simulation for each region and number of execution hours required). The results indicated that the best suitable day for execution using Spot instances was January the 24th.

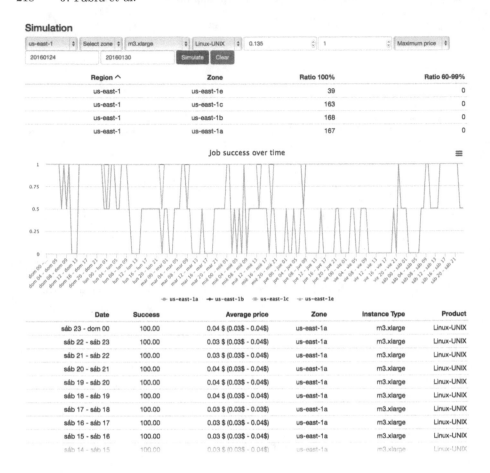

Fig. 7. Graphical interface of the simulator depicting the parameters configuration and the results of the process.

To analyze the correctness of the results from the simulation process, we decided to place several bids at various moments marked as success in both EU and US regions. We placed ten bids for each execution time at different times at Jan 24, so a total of 80 bids were used. We monitored the bidding process and the instance execution. All the bids were successful and we were able to perform the execution of each process four times without termination. From an economic perspective, the cost of each execution was less than half the price of on-demand instances, as the bidding price established by the Spot Market was below our bids.

4.1   Analysis of the Lowest SI Price

After the simulation analysis of the obtained results, we decided to carry out a post-simulation varying the bids in order to obtain the lowest cost we could have got.

We studied the success of the simulator results comparing them with the real Spot price at the time the bid would have been placed. We varied the price from the usual one (100% of the price) and progressively decreased it in ranges of a 5%. With this variation, we simulated the success of our input and got a provisioning plan that indicated that success on each possible slot of time.

Figure 8 depicts the results for region EU-West-1 along with the price variation considering the EC2 on demand price in January 24th 2016. Note that we *merged* successful moments from all zones inside the same region. Provisioning plans gave us a 100% of success (168 success/0 failures) in all possible times of the week until we bid under the 12% of the EC2 price (0.0348$). This behavior repeated for the different allocation options (from one to ten hours).

1 hour execution, m3.xlarge instance, EC2 price: 0.29$/h																			
100%	95%	90%	85%	80%	75%	70%	65%	60%	55%	50%	45%	40%	35%	30%	25%	20%	15%	10%	5%
168/0	168/0	168/0	168/0	168/0	168/0	168/0	168/0	168/0	168/0	168/0	168/0	168/0	168/0	168/0	168/0	168/0	168/0	0/168	0/168
3 hours execution, m3.xlarge instance, EC2 price: 0.29$/h																			
0%	95%	90%	85%	80%	75%	70%	65%	60%	55%	50%	45%	40%	35%	30%	25%	20%	15%	10%	5%
168/0	168/0	168/0	168/0	168/0	168/0	168/0	168/0	168/0	168/0	168/0	168/0	168/0	168/0	168/0	168/0	168/0	168/0	0/168	0/168
6 hours execution, m3.xlarge instance, EC2 price: 0.29$/h																			
100%	95%	90%	85%	80%	75%	70%	65%	60%	55%	50%	45%	40%	35%	30%	25%	20%	15%	10%	5%
168/0	168/0	168/0	168/0	168/0	168/0	168/0	168/0	168/0	168/0	168/0	168/0	168/0	168/0	168/0	168/0	168/0	168/0	0/168	0/168
10 hours execution, m3.xlarge instance, EC2 price: 0.29$/h																			
100%	95%	90%	85%	80%	75%	70%	65%	60%	55%	50%	45%	40%	35%	30%	25%	20%	15%	10%	5%
168/0	168/0	168/0	168/0	168/0	168/0	168/0	168/0	168/0	168/0	168/0	168/0	168/0	168/0	168/0	168/0	168/0	168/0	0/168	0/168

Fig. 8. Results for region EU-West-1 along with the price variation considering the EC2 on demand price on January 24th 2016.

For these experiments we bid a 15% (0.0435$/hour) for the different length configuration in all the possible time slots. After collecting the results, we found that the provisioning plan was correct and 100% of the bids were allowed to instantiate a machine in the EC2 infrastructure.

Figure 9 depicts the results for US East-1 region on January 24th 2016. Results were similar to the ones obtained for EU-West-1 region, although here the bid had to go above 20% (0.054$/hour) in order to guarantee a 100% success getting the required instance running for the specified number of hours.

1 hour execution, m3.xlarge instance, EC2 price: 0.27$/h																			
100%	95%	90%	85%	80%	75%	70%	65%	60%	55%	50%	45%	40%	35%	30%	25%	20%	15%	10%	5%
168/0	168/0	168/0	168/0	168/0	168/0	168/0	168/0	168/0	168/0	168/0	168/0	168/0	168/0	168/0	168/0	168/0	126/42	0/168	0/168
3 hours execution, m3.xlarge instance, EC2 price: 0.27$/h																			
0%	95%	90%	85%	80%	75%	70%	65%	60%	55%	50%	45%	40%	35%	30%	25%	20%	15%	10%	5%
168/0	168/0	168/0	168/0	168/0	168/0	168/0	168/0	168/0	168/0	168/0	168/0	168/0	168/0	168/0	168/0	168/0	125/43	0/168	0/168
6 hours execution, m3.xlarge instance, EC2 price: 0.27$/h																			
100%	95%	90%	85%	80%	75%	70%	65%	60%	55%	50%	45%	40%	35%	30%	25%	20%	15%	10%	5%
168/0	168/0	168/0	168/0	168/0	168/0	168/0	168/0	168/0	168/0	168/0	168/0	168/0	168/0	168/0	168/0	168/0	122/46	0/168	0/168
10 hours execution, m3.xlarge instance, EC2 price: 0.27$/h																			
100%	95%	90%	85%	80%	75%	70%	65%	60%	55%	50%	45%	40%	35%	30%	25%	20%	15%	10%	5%
168/0	168/0	168/0	168/0	168/0	168/0	168/0	168/0	168/0	168/0	168/0	168/0	168/0	168/0	168/0	168/0	168/0	124/44	0/168	0/168

Fig. 9. Results for region US-East-1 along with the price variation considering the EC2 on demand price on January 24th 2016.

This experimentation was performed considering alternative times achieving similar results. It is important to remark some conclusions. First, the use of SI allows reducing EC2 prices much more than the expected 50%. In our experimentations we found that normally a 15–25% of the EC2 price could be used to instantiate a SI machine. However, at certain moments there was a high variation trend on some regions. In these cases, bidding a 50% of the EC2 price guaranteed that the machine would be instantiated in most situations. Secondly, certain zones inside a region are much more prone to price variations. A good bidding strategy must consider merging all zones in order to place bids in those zones that have less variations at a specific moment. Thirdly, there is a common pattern that repeats among zones and regions: price variations are stronger in Sunday and Monday. It is common that most fails are obtained during these days. On the other hand, Friday and Saturday are the days in which fewer variations are concentrated (indeed, January 24th was Saturday). Finally, a detailed analysis of the price variation revealed that a cheaper region should not be considered the best candidate for the deployment and execution of an experiment when dealing with price constraints and Spot instances. In this work, we found that the final price for experimentation was cheaper on EU-West-1 region, which normally is more expensive than US-East-1 region for EC2 on demand instances.

5   Conclusions

The use of Spot instances can drastically reduce the deployment and execution costs of systems in a cloud-based infrastructure. However, the low reliability in the use of this approach suggests the need for a system that could assist the user when dealing with pricing analysis and termination possibilities. In the case of the Amazon Spot Instances, such system must be able to propose the best suitable moments in which a bid can be placed in terms of the maximum price the user wants to spend on it. In this work we have introduced a framework for the analysis of the Amazon EC2 Spot instance infrastructure. We have used it to generate a provisioning plan for the deployment of a specific instance in two different regions of the EC2 cloud (the one at which more price variations have been observed and the one with fewer ones). Results have shown than savings up to 88% can be obtained in some cases.

Currently, a very interesting and recent aspect we are studying is the new *Spot Block Model*, released on October 2015. This new SI model allows to bid for defined-duration workloads. Also, we are dealing with the automatic generation of bidding prices in base to history variations and specific times. To do that, we are working on the combination of SI prices at previous hours and the simulation using different analysis techniques such as hysteresis and step-variation. We are also considering the automation of the deployment process once the user has selected the most suitable time (or period) to launch the required instances.

Finally, we are studying the integration of Google Cloud Preemptible Virtual Machine (VM) Instances in our proposal. Preemptible VMs offer the same machine types and options as regular compute instances and last for up to 24 h.

They are up to 70% cheaper than regular instances, but differently to Amazon Spot instances, their pricing is fixed. This avoids variable market pricing and opens an interesting research line by means of the integration of both Spot instances and Preemptible VMs, which is being currently addressed.

Acknowledgements. This work has been supported by research projects TIN2014-56633-C3-2-R, granted by the Spanish Ministry of Science and Innovation, and JIUZ-2015-TEC-04, granted by the University of Zaragoza.

References

1. Buyya, R., Yeo, C.S., Venugopal, S., Broberg, J., Brandic, I.: Cloud computing and emerging it platforms: vision, hype, and reality for delivering it services as the 5th utility. Future Gener. Comput. Syst. **25**(6), 599–616 (2009)
2. Warneke, D., Kao, O.: Exploiting dynamic resource allocation for efficient parallel data processing in the cloud. In: TPDS, pp. 985–997 (2011)
3. de Assuncao, M.D., di Costanzo, A., Buyya, R.: Evaluating the cost-benefit of using cloud computing to extend the capacity of clusters. In: HPDC 2009, pp. 141–150 (2009)
4. Ben-Yehuda, O., Schuster, A., Sharov, A., Silberstein, M., Iosup, A.: Expert: pareto-efficient task replication on grids and a cloud. In: IPDPS, pp. 167–178 (2012)
5. Fölling, A., Hofmann, M.: Improving scheduling performance using a q-learning-based leasing policy for clouds. In: Kaklamanis, C., Papatheodorou, T., Spirakis, P.G. (eds.) Euro-Par 2012. LNCS, vol. 7484, pp. 337–349. Springer, Heidelberg (2012). doi:10.1007/978-3-642-32820-6_34
6. Amazon Spot Instances. https://aws.amazon.com/ec2/spot/. Accessed June 2016
7. CHARGE Project. https://www.dnancxus.com/usecases-charge. Accessed June 2016
8. AWS Case Study: Netflix. https://aws.amazon.com/es/solutions/case-studies/netflix/. Accessed June 2016
9. Yi, S., Kondo, D., Andrzejak, A.: Monetary cost-aware checkpointing and migration on amazon cloud spot instances. In: IEEE Transactions on Services Computing, pp. 236–243 (2011)
10. Mattess, M., Vecchiola, C., Buyya, R.: Managing peak loads by leasing cloud infrastructure services from a spot market. In: 12th IEEE International Conference on High Performance Computing and Communications, pp. 180–188 (2010)
11. Wee, S.: Debunking real-time pricing in cloud computing. In: 11th IEEE/ACM International Symposium on Cluster, Cloud and Grid Computing, CCGrid, pp. 585–590 (2011)
12. Ben-Yehuda, O.A., Ben-Yehuda, M., Schuster, A., Tsafrir, D.: Deconstructing Amazon EC2 spot instance pricing. In: 3rd IEEE International Conference on Cloud Computing Technology and Science, pp. 304–311 (2011)
13. O'Loughlin, J., Gillam, L.: Performance evaluation for cost-efficient public infrastructure cloud use. In: Altmann, J., Vanmechelen, K., Rana, O.F. (eds.) GECON 2014. LNCS, vol. 8914, pp. 133–145. Springer, Cham (2014). doi:10.1007/978-3-319-14609-6_9
14. Javadi, B., Thulasiram, R.K., Buyya, R.: Characterizing spot price dynamics in public cloud environments. J. Future Gener. Comput. Syst. **29**(4), 988–999 (2013)

15. Javadi, B., Thulasiramy, R.K., Buyya, R.: Statistical modeling of spot instance prices in public cloud environments. In: Fourth IEEE International Conference on Utility and Cloud Computing (UCC) (2011)
16. Andrzejak, A., Kondo, D., Yi, S.: Decision model for cloud computing under sla constraints. In: 18th IEEE/ACM International Symposium on Modelling, Analysis and Simulation of Computer and Telecommunication Systems, pp. 257–266 (2010)
17. Chohan, N., Castillo, C., Spreitzer, M., et al.: See spot run: using spot instances for mapreduce workflows. In: 2nd USENIX Conference on Hot Topics in Cloud Computing, HotCloud10, pp. 7–13 (2010)
18. Tang, S., Yuan, J., Li, X.Y.: Towards optimal bidding strategy for Amazon EC2 cloud spot instance. In: IEEE 5th International Conference on Cloud Computing (2012)
19. Zafer, M., Song, Y., Lee, K.-W.: Optimal bids for spot vms in a cloud for deadline constrained jobs. In: IEEE 5th International Conference on Cloud Computing (2012)
20. Chaisiri, S., Kaewpuang, R., Lee, B.S., Niyato, D.: Cost minimization for provisioning virtual servers in amazon elastic compute cloud. In: 19th IEEE International Symposium on Modeling, Analysis Simulation of Computer and Telecommunication Systems, MASCOTS, pp. 85–95 (2011)
21. Zhang, Q., Gurses, E., Boutaba, R., Xiao, J.: Dynamic resource allocation for spot markets in clouds. In: 11th USENIX Conference on Hot Topics in Management of Internet, Cloud, and Enterprise Networks and Services, Hot-ICE11, USENIX Association, Berkeley, CA, USA, pp. 1–6 (2011)
22. Rahman, M.R., Lu, Y., Gupta, I.: Risk aware resource allocation for clouds. Technical report 2011-07-11, University of Illinois at Urbana-Champaign, July 2011
23. Spot Bid Advisor. https://aws.amazon.com/ec2/spot/bid-advisor/. Accessed June 2016

Work in Progress on Resource Allocation

Enabling Business-Preference-Based Scheduling of Cloud Computing Resources

Azamat Uzbekov[✉] and Jörn Altmann

Technology Management, Economics, and Policy Program,
Department of Industrial Engineering, College of Engineering,
Seoul National University, Seoul, South Korea
batukasss@snu.ac.kr, jorn.altmann@acm.org

Abstract. Although cloud computing technology gets increasingly sophisticated, a resource allocation method still has to be proposed that allows providers to take into consideration the preferences of their customers. The existing engineering-based and economics-based resource allocation methods do not take into account jointly the different objectives that engineers and marketing employees of a cloud provider company follow. This article addresses this issue by presenting the system architecture and, in particular, the business-preference-based scheduling algorithm that integrates the engineering aspects of resource allocation with the economics aspects of resource allocation. To show the workings of the new business-preference-based scheduling algorithm, which integrates a yield management method and a priority-based scheduling method, a simulation has been performed. The results obtained are compared with results from the First-Come-First-Serve scheduling algorithm. The comparison shows that the proposed scheduling algorithm achieves higher revenue than the engineering-based scheduling algorithm.

Keywords: Cloud computing · Resource allocation · FCFS · Yield management · Scheduling · Pricing · Economics-based resource allocation · System architecture

1 Introduction

Cloud computing, which has become the infrastructure for ICT services, is even on its way to become a household utility, for which the processes of using cloud services and making payments are similar to other household utilities (e.g., water, electricity) [1, 14]. As for any household utilities, cost is most important. This fact makes an efficient resource allocation vital for cloud service providers (CSP).

Although many aspects of resource allocation have already been discussed in literature [2], resource allocation for cloud computing still allows new possibilities [1, 3–5], such as cloud service pricing strategies and scheduling algorithms [6, 7].

In detail, looking at existing research on resource allocation, a partition into two types of methods can be observed: (a) engineering-based resource allocation methods, which consider utilization, response time, and throughput for allocating CPU, memory, and storage [8–10]; and (b) economics-based resource allocation methods,

© Springer International Publishing AG 2017
J.Á. Bañares et al. (Eds.): GECON 2016, LNCS 10382, pp. 225–236, 2017.
DOI: 10.1007/978-3-319-61920-0_16

which consider profit, revenue, and cost for allocating resources [11–13]. Up to now, these two types of methods are not combined or integrated yet. This is the case despite the fact that CSPs aim at maximizing their profit, which can be achieved by considering the market demand and the cost of the engineering system used. Therefore, CSPs need to consider simultaneously the engineering aspects and the economics aspects of resource allocation [15].

Therefore, the objective of this article is to outline a system architecture that allows a CSP to integrate economics aspects of resource allocation with engineering aspects of resource allocation. The research questions, which can be derived from this objective, are: How does the system architecture look that can integrate economics aspects of resource allocation with engineering aspects of resource allocation? How does an integrating resource allocation method operate, combining an economics-based resource allocation method and an engineering-based resource allocation method? What is the performance of this integrated scheduling algorithm (i.e., business-preference-based scheduling algorithm)?

To answer these research questions, we conduct the following steps: First, based on a solid literature research on system architectures and resource allocation methods, we propose a cloud computing resource allocation architecture that integrates economics-based resource allocation and engineering-based resource allocation. Second, using this architecture, the integrating scheduling algorithm, which is called business-preference-based scheduling, is designed. Third, for showing the workings of the proposed architecture, one scenario with two demand-depending cases are simulated and analyzed. The first case represents normal demand for computing resources and the second case represents high demand for computing resources. The simulation results show that the performance of the business-preference-based scheduling algorithm is better than a FCFS scheduling algorithm with respect to the CSP revenue generated.

The contribution of this article is a new resource allocation architecture, which enables the integration of economics-based resource allocation and engineering-based resource allocation. This integration of these two types of resource allocation methods is missing in existing system architectures [16]. The core of the architecture is the business-preference-based scheduling algorithm, which allows expressing CSP business strategy parameters by adjusting the ready queue of the tasks. It combines yield management and priority-based scheduling.

The remainder of the paper is organized as follows: In the next section, an overview of related work on resource allocation is given. Section 3 introduces the proposed system architecture with a focus on the business-preference-based scheduling algorithm. The application of the architecture is evaluated through simulations in Sect. 4. Section 5 concludes the paper with a discussion.

2   Background

2.1   Cloud Computing Resource Allocation

Resource allocation methods can be divided into two types: economics-based methods and engineering-based methods [16]. To determine the intersection of both resource allocation methods (Fig. 1), relevant articles have been reviewed in the following paragraphs.

Engineering-based methods allocate resources based on task parameters (e.g., time of arrival, length of task, importance of task) and system objectives (e.g., maximization of throughput). The classical algorithms of this type are: First-Come-First-Serve (FCFS), Shortest-Job-First (SJF), Priority Scheduling (PS), and Round-Robin (RR) [17, 18]. In the last decade, each of these methods has been modified and enhanced. For example, RR was improved to use the optimal time quantum [8, 19, 20]. PS and SJF Scheduling have been adapted for cloud-based software systems [21]. CloudSim-based simulations of a generalized priority scheduler, which sets priorities not only for tasks but also VMs, showed good results with respect to execution times [22]. These algorithms, which focus only on engineering aspects, require technical skills but do not require an understanding of the interaction of the provider with the customer [23].

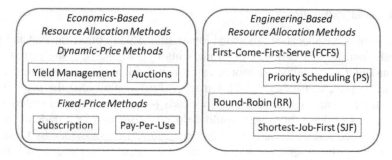

Fig. 1. Classification of resource allocation methods into engineering-based methods and economics-based methods.

Economics based resource allocation methods distribute cloud resources to users according to their preferences by using pricing [17–20, 28]. These methods can further be subdivided into fixed-price methods and dynamic-price methods. The fixed-price methods are implemented by major CSPs [29–31]. An example of the fixed-price method is the pay-per-use method, which assigns a fixed price to each resource. In [32], the authors consider the pay-per-use method, to propose a set of policies that allocate VMs according to the QoS purchased by the user. The article discusses cloud resources as a virtual pool of the physical infrastructure without giving detailed resource specifications. Another example of fixed-price methods is the subscription method, under which any number of cloud resources can be used for a fixed price for a certain period of time. With respect to the dynamic-price methods, Al-Roomi et al. used dynamic pricing to allow CSPs or users to change the price depending on pertinent factors [31]. Auctions and yield management are dynamic-price methods [33]. An example of a sealed-bid uniform price auction is Amazon EC2's spot instance. However, these economics-based methods do not consider any engineering aspects.

2.2   Yield Management

Yield management, as an example of a dynamic-price method, takes into account demand, prices, and resource availability [37]. It implements basic principles of supply and demand economics in a way to generate incremental revenues [16]. Yield management, which has been applied in the airline industry, helps selling resources to consumer at a specific time at the highest possible price [34]. The possibility of using yield management in computing grids has been studied in detail [34–36], outlining the requirements for applying yield management to computing grids and showed how the tools based on yield management could be executed. In our previous work [16], yield management has been applied as one of the resource allocation algorithms within a CSP business support framework. However, all yield management applications did not specify the engineering details for mapping yield management allocations efficiently onto ICT resources.

2.3   Demand Estimation

An issue in resource allocation is demand forecasting. Studies of the Internet and media workloads indicate that customer demand is highly variable (i.e., the peak-to-mean ratio is an order of magnitude or more), and it is not economical to overprovision the system using peak demands [38, 39]. Gmach, who has illustrated the peak-to-mean behavior for 139 enterprise application workloads [40], showed that an understanding of enterprise workloads burstiness could help choosing the right tradeoff between quality of service and the resource pool capacity requirements. The ability to plan and operate in the most cost-efficient way is a critical competitive advantage [40]. For this article, we consider historical data to estimate the demand.

3   Techno-Economic System Architecture

3.1   Proposed System Architecture

The system architecture (Fig. 2), which we propose for integrating an engineering-based resource allocation method and an economic-based resource allocation method (Fig. 1), comprises the following two stakeholders and three modules:

User: The user (customer), who is one of the two stakeholders, negotiates with the cloud service provider about the service level agreement (SLA) on cloud resources needed to execute an application.

Cloud Service Provider (CSP): This stakeholder interacts with the user (customer), in order to negotiate a service level agreement (SLA) that meets the users' needs and the provider's economic objective (e.g., profit maximization, revenue maximization, or social welfare maximization). The SLA determines the resources (e.g., VM) that the user can access and the pricing plan associated with the resources.

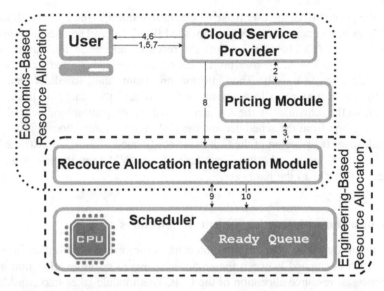

Fig. 2. Proposed techno-economic system architecture for integrating engineering-based and economics-based resource allocation methods.

Pricing Module: The pricing module allows specifying and applying different pricing plans that the CSP might want to offer in the market to attract customers. Yield-management-based pricing plan is an example of such a pricing plan.

Resource Allocation Integration Module: This module admits tasks and sets the order of tasks (i.e., VMs) in the ready queue, using information about VM prices paid by users and about the engineering-based resource allocation method used by the scheduler.

Scheduler: With the help of this module, tasks from the ready queue are allocated to the hardware (e.g., CPU). The scheduler can be implemented with any engineering-based resource allocation method. The ready queue is an ordered list of tasks (i.e., VMs) that are ready to be executed through the hardware.

3.2   Resource Allocation Process Between User and Cloud Service Provider

The resource allocation process from a user's first request about cloud resource availability to the execution of the VM on a hardware within the proposed system architecture can be described in ten steps (Fig. 2): (1) The user sends a request for VM prices to the CSP; (2) The CSP calculates the VM price with the pricing module, which also considers the status of the ready queue. The pricing module can run different economics-based resource allocation methods, depending on CSP's business strategy; (3) The ready queue status is obtained from the resource allocation integration module; (4) The CSP communicates the VM price (as part of a SLA) to the user; (5) If the user agrees to the price (SLA), the user makes a purchase request to the CSP; (6) If the CSP acknowledges the request, the SLA is established [26, 27]; (7) The user submits a task (VM) to the CSP; (8) The CSP informs the resource allocation integration module about the established SLA, the user profile information (e.g., customer status, demand history), and the task; (9) The information from the scheduler about the engineering-based resource allocation method used and the status of the queue is requested from the scheduler by the resource allocation integration module. (10) Based on the information from the scheduler and the CSP, the resource allocation integration module calculates the position of the task in the ready queue. Then, it enlists the VM in the ready queue. Continuously, the scheduler picks the VM from the top of the queue and allocates the VM to the hardware.

3.3   Comparison with Existing System Architectures

The novelty of the proposed system architecture is the resource allocation integration module, which is situated between the engineering-based resource allocation and the economics-based resource allocation of the CSP. This module takes into consideration business aspects of the CSP (e.g., pricing and user profile) as well as the engineering requirements (e.g., engineering-based resource allocation) coming from managing the cloud infrastructure. It also forwards information about the ready queue to the pricing module, such that the pricing module can calculate the optimal pricing plan.

To show the novelty of the proposed system architecture, it is compared with four existing system architectures that have been identified in the literature. All system architectures have been classified according to four criteria, namely type of system architecture, resource allocation method used, stakeholder interactions, and objective. The results of the classification are shown in Table 1.

Table 1 depicts that the resource allocation methods used and the objectives for the design of the system architectures vary widely.

With respect to the type of system architectures, however, two types can be distinguished. The first type designs marketplaces for users and CSPs, to negotiate the price of services [25, 33]. The second type provides middleware, in which the economics-engineering functions are integrated [13, 23].

With respect to stakeholder interactions, all system architectures address the interaction between users and provider businesses [13, 23, 25, 33], focusing on assisting CSPs in setting prices. One middleware architecture also focuses on information forwarding from engineering-based scheduling to provider business [23]. Only the proposed system architecture also considers stakeholder interaction to provider scheduling.

Based on this comparison between the existing architecture and the proposed system architecture, it can be stated that the proposed system architecture represents the first step towards the development of a system architecture for optimizing scheduling based on business preferences. It interconnects the business aspects with engineering aspects.

Table 1. Comparison of existing system architectures with the proposed system architecture.

Type of system architecture	Resource allocation method	Literature reference	Stakeholder interactions	Objective of system architecture
Marketplace	Different types of auctions	Wang et al. [33]	User to provider-business	Identification of auction implementation issues
Marketplace	Combinatorial double auction	Samimi et al. [25]	User to provider-business	Feasibility study
Middleware	Business analytics algorithms	Altmann et al. [23]	Provider-scheduling to provider-business	Price setting considering scheduling
Middleware	QoS negotiation platform	Buyya et al. [13]	User to provider-business	Combining market-based objectives and computing
Middleware	Business-preference-based scheduling	This article	User to provider-business to provider-scheduling	Scheduling that considers business preferences

4   Architecture Validation

4.1   Simulation Scenario

In order to demonstrate through simulations the workings of the proposed system architecture and, in particular, the business-preference-based scheduling, a scenario is assumed that considers two types of users with different preferences. Having different preferences makes the scenario applicable for economics-based resource allocation. In detail, the scenario considers a CSP, who offers two classes of services, namely, a premium service and a standard service. Users, who accept some delays in their task executions, can buy standard services (low-priced services), while users, who expect to experience no delay in any of their task executions, purchase premium services (high-priced services). If the aggregated demand of both types of users for resources is low (i.e., below the capacity of the executing hardware), both types of users get the same amount of resources for their tasks. If the aggregated demand for resources increases beyond the capacity, premium users get priority for obtaining resources, and standard users have to wait for tasks of premium users to finish. Therefore, standard users might experience delays or rejections of their task submissions.

To simplify the scenario, a few assumptions are made: Each task (i.e., VM) requires the same amount of resources; The hardware capacity handles up to 100 VMs/h without quality degradation (i.e., the ready queue length is limited to 100 VMs/h). If the number of VMs per hour exceeds 100 VM/h, quality degradation is experienced by users; The actual demand per hour is generated through two normal distributions.

To understand how the proposed system architecture operates at different levels of demand, two cases are distinguished: (a) the normal demand case, in which the number of VMs per hour is the sum of the draw from a normal distribution with a mean of 70 VM/h (premium users) and from a normal distribution with a mean of 30 VM/h (standard users); (b) the high demand case, in which the number of VMs per hour is the sum of the draw from a normal distribution with a mean of 80 VM/h (premium users) and the draw from a normal distribution with a mean of 40 VM/h (standard users). Figure 3 shows the VM demand in both cases for 60 time periods. For the normal demand case, the demand is above the hardware capacity (i.e., 100 VM/h) in 27 time periods only. For the high demand case, all time periods but one are above the hardware capacity.

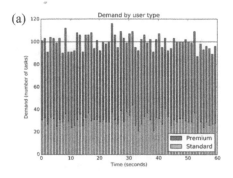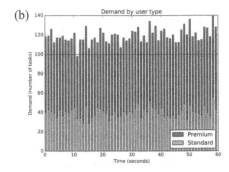

Fig. 3. Generated VM demand of premium users and standard users for the two cases: (a) the normal demand case; (b) the high demand case

The VM allocation integration technique, which is applied to the ready queue, is called expected marginal seat revenue (EMSR) and has been developed by Belobaba [24, 41]. The probability density function $f_i()$ for the number of service requests d_i in each service class i (i.e., $i = 1$ (premium service) or $i = 2$ (standard service)) is determined by using historical data. The EMSR takes the form of Eq. 1, where $F_i()$ is the cumulative distribution function for the total number of VM requests C_i in service class i. C_1 indicates the number of VM requests for service class 1 that will be accepted (i.e., C_1 ready queue slots are allocated to service class 1). The number of ready queue slots C_2 allocated to service class 2 is the maximum ready queue length C minus C_1.

$$F_i(C_i) = \int_0^{C_i} f_i(d_i)\partial d_i \tag{1}$$

Using Eq. 1, the aim is to determine the optimal number of ready queue slots that should be allocated to the two service classes, such that the total revenue is maximized. In other words, the protection level (PL) for the premium services must be determined, as the booking limit (BL) for the standard services is calculated as $BL = C - PL$. The protection level for the premium services is the maximum value of C_1 that satisfies the condition:

$$A * (1 - F_1(C_1)) \geq B \tag{2}$$

The variables A and B represent the full price and the discounted price, respectively. In this scenario, the CSP charges a full price of A = 0.05\$/h and a discounted price of B = 0.01\$/h. Based on these prices, the generated demand data (Fig. 3), and Eq. 2, PL and BL are calculated. For allocating the resources, the new business-preference-based scheduling algorithm is used:

```
Step1:   Based on price A,price B,and the cumulative
         probability functions for both VM classes, the
         protection levelPL and the booking limit BL
         are calculated;
Step2:   d₁(t) = 0; d₂(t) = 0; C(t) = 0;
Step3:   WAIT for VM service request from user;
Step4:   IF(C(t) ≤ d₁(t) + d₂(t))THEN {
             reject request /* ready queue is full;
             GOTO Step3}
Step5:   IF(VMrequest is from the standard service
         class&&d₂(t) < BL)THEN {
             addVM request to ready queue at time t;
             d₂(t) = d₂(t) + 1;
             GOTO Step3}
Step6:   If(VM requestis from the premium service
         class&&d₁(t) < PL)THEN {
             addVM request to ready queue at time t;
             d₁(t) = d₁(t) + 1}
Step7:   GOTO Step3;
```

4.2   Simulation Results

The total simulation time covers 5 days, which is split up into 60 time periods, representing one hour time slots. For demonstrating the effectiveness of the business-preference-based scheduling algorithm, the revenue generated through the algorithm during the 60 time periods was calculated and compared with the revenue of a FCFS scheduling algorithm (Fig. 4). Based on the results of the comparison, it can be stated that the proposed algorithm generates more revenue than the FCFS algorithm. With respect to the normal demand case, the proposed algorithm generates revenue equal to \$497, while the FCFS algorithm achieves revenue of \$494. The difference of \$3 in revenue represents only a 0.74% increase in revenue. With respect to the high demand case however, a more significant improvement in revenue is achieved. The proposed business-preference-based scheduling achieves revenue of \$534, compared to revenue of \$502 for the FCFS algorithm. This corresponds to an improvement of 6.4%.

Consequently, it can be stated that the proposed business-preference-based algorithm can optimize resource allocation based on the business strategy of a

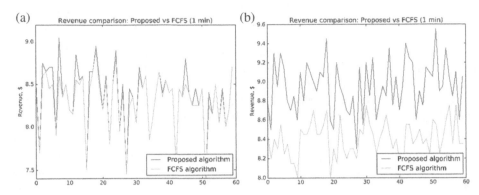

Fig. 4. Revenue of the business-preference-based scheduling algorithm compared with the revenue of the FCFS scheduling algorithm for (a) the normal demand case and (b) the high demand case.

CSP. Moreover, it can be stated that the idea of interconnecting engineering-based resource allocation with the economics-based resource allocation is viable.

5   Conclusion

Although cloud computing has established itself as a beneficial technology, economics-based resource allocation and engineering-based resource allocation are still separated. To address this source of inefficiency, this article proposes a system architecture for cloud computing that allows integrating economics aspects and engineering aspects in resource allocation. The integration of economics-based resource allocation and engineering-based resource allocation allows optimization at different levels.

The central module of the system architecture is the resource allocation integration module, which translates different pricing schemes (i.e., economics-based resource allocation method) into engineering-based scheduling by manipulating the ready queue. The module, which uses yield management as the economics-based resource allocation method, considers historical data to calculate the optimal protection level for deciding on the admittance of tasks to the ready queue. We name this scheduling algorithm as business-preference-based scheduling algorithm.

Our simulation results of the business-preference-based scheduling show that the proposed architecture generates higher revenue compared with a FCFS scheduling algorithm. This is very positive, as the current simulation considers only static pricing strategy with two price classes.

Our future work aims at extending this research, so that more complicated cases with a greater applicability in the real world can be modeled and assessed.

Acknowledgements. This research was conducted within the project BASMATI (Cloud Brokerage Across Borders for Mobile Users and Applications), which has received funding from the ICT R&D program of the Korean MSIP/IITP (R0115-16-0001) and from the European Union's Horizon 2020 research and innovation programme under grant agreement no. 723131.

References

1. Buyya, R., Yeo, C.S., Venugopal, S., Broberg, J., Brandic, I.: Cloud computing and emerging IT platforms: vision, hype, and reality for delivering computing as the 5th utility. Futur. Gener. Comput. Syst. **6**, 599–616 (2009)
2. Altmann, J., Kashef, M.M.: Cost model based service placement in federated hybrid clouds. Futur. Gener. Comput. Syst. **41**, 79–90 (2014)
3. Zhang, Q., Cheng, L., Boutaba, R.: Cloud computing: state-of-the-art and research challenges. J. Internet Serv. Appl. **1**, 7–18 (2010)
4. Rimal, B.P., Choi, E., Lumb, I.: A taxonomy and survey of cloud computing systems. In: IMS IDC, pp. 44–51 (2009)
5. Jeferry, K., Kousiouris, G., Kyriazis, D., Altmann, J., Ciuffoletti, A., Maglogiannis, I., Nesi, P., Suzic, B., Zhao, Z.: Challenges emerging from future cloud application scenarios. Procedia Comput. Sci. **68**, 227–237 (2015)
6. Risch, M., Altmann, J., Guo, L., Fleming, A., Courcoubetis, C.: The gridecon platform: a business scenario testbed for commercial cloud services. In: International Workshop on GECON, pp. 46–59 (2009)
7. Teng, F., Magoules, F.: Resource pricing and equilibrium allocation policy in cloud computing. In: International Conference on Computer and Information Technology, pp. 195–202 (2010)
8. Mishra, M.K., Rashid, F.: An improved round robin CPU scheduling algorithm with varying time quantum. Int. J. Comput. Sci. Eng. Appl. **4**, 1 (2014)
9. Buyya, R., Murshed, M.: Gridsim: a toolkit for the modeling and simulation of distributed resource management and scheduling for grid computing. Concurr. Comput. Pract. Exp. **14**, 1175–1220 (2002)
10. Dong, F., Akl, S.G.: Scheduling algorithms for grid computing: state of the art and open problems. Technical report (2006)
11. Foster, I., Zhao, Y., Raicu, I., Lu, S.: Cloud computing and grid computing 360-degree compared. In: Grid Computing Environments Workshop, pp. 1–10 (2008)
12. Osterwalder, A.: The business model ontology: a proposition in a design science approach (2004)
13. Buyya, R., Yeo, C.S., Venugopal, S.: Market-oriented cloud computing: vision, hype, and reality for delivering IT services as computing utilities. In: International Conference on High Performance Computing and Communications, pp. 5–13 (2008)
14. Mell, P., Grance, T.: The NIST definition of cloud computing (2011)
15. Haile, N., Altmann, J.: Value creation in software service platforms. Futur. Gener. Comput. Syst. **55**, 495–509 (2016)
16. Kashef, M.M., Uzbekov, A., Altmann, J., Hovestadt, M.: Comparison of two yield management strategies for cloud service providers. In: Park, James J.(Jong Hyuk), Arabnia, Hamid R., Kim, C., Shi, W., Gil, J.-M. (eds.) GPC 2013. LNCS, vol. 7861, pp. 170–180. Springer, Heidelberg (2013). doi:10.1007/978-3-642-38027-3_18
17. Khankasikam, K.: An adaptive round robin scheduling algorithm: a dynamic time quantum approach. Int. J. Adv. Comput. Technol (2013)
18. Srinivasan, S., Kettimuthu, R., Subramani, V., Sadayappan, P.: Characterization of backfilling strategies for parallel job scheduling. In: Workshops at International Conference on Parallel Processing, pp. 514–519 (2002)
19. Sirohi, A., Pratap, A., Aggarwal, M.: Improvised round robin (CPU) scheduling algorithm. Int. J. Comput. Appl. **99**, 40–43 (2014)
20. Alam, B.: Fuzzy round robin CPU scheduling algorithm. J. Comput. Sci. **9**, 1079–1085 (2013)

21. Ru, J., Keung, J.: An Empirical investigation on the simulation of priority and shortest-job-first scheduling for cloud-based software systems. In: Australian Software Engineering Conference, pp. 78–87 (2013)
22. Agarwal, D., Jain, S.: Efficient optimal algorithm of task scheduling in cloud computing environment. arXiv Prepr. arXiv:1404.2076 (2014)
23. Altmann, J., Hovestadt, M., Kao, O.: Business support service platform for providers in open cloud computing markets. In: International Conference on Networked Computing, INC, pp. 149–154 (2011)
24. Kjeldsen, A.H., Meyer, P.: Revenue Management - Theory and Practice. Master Thesis, Technical University of Denmark (2005)
25. Samimi, P., Teimouri, Y., Mukhtar, M.: A combinatorial double auction resource allocation model in cloud computing. Inf. Sci. (Ny) **357**, 201–216 (2014)
26. Breskovic, I., Maurer, M., Emeakaroha, V.C., Brandic, I., Altmann, J.: Towards autonomic market management in cloud computing infrastructures. In: CLOSER, pp. 24–34 (2011)
27. Breskovic, I., Altmann, J., Brandic, I.: Creating standardized products for electronic markets. Futur. Gener. Comput. Syst. **29**, 1000–1011 (2013)
28. Altmann, J., Courcoubetis, C., Risch, M.: A marketplace and its market mechanism for trading commoditized computing resources. Ann. des Télécommunications **65**, 653–667 (2010)
29. Weinhardt, C., Anandasivam, A., Blau, B., Borissov, N., Meinl, T., Michalk, W., Stößer, J.: Cloud computing - a classification, business models, and research directions. Bus. Inf. Syst. Eng. **1**, 391–399 (2009)
30. Armbrust, M., Fox, A., Griffith, R., Joseph, A.D., Katz, R., Konwinski, A., Lee, G., Patterson, D., Rabkin, A., Stoica, I., Zaharia, M.: A view of cloud computing. Commun. ACM **53**, 50–58 (2010)
31. Al-Roomi, M., Al-Ebrahim, S., Buqrais, S., Ahmad, I.: Cloud computing pricing models: a survey. Int. J. Grid Distrib. Comput. **6**, 93–106 (2013)
32. Hamsanandhini, S., Mohana, R.S.: Maximizing the revenue with client classification in Cloud Computing market. In: International Conference on Computer, Communication and Informatics, ICCCI, pp. 1–7 (2015)
33. Wang, H., Tianfield, H., Mair, Q.: Auction based resource allocation in cloud computing. Multiagent Grid Syst. **10**, 51–66 (2014)
34. Jallat, F., Ancarani, F.: Yield management, dynamic pricing and CRM in telecommunications. J. Serv. Mark. **22**, 465–478 (2008)
35. Kimes, S.E.: The basics of yield management. Cornell Hotel Restaur. Adm. Q. **30**, 14–19 (1989)
36. Anandasivam, A., Neumann, D.: Managing revenue in Grids. In: 42nd Hawaii International Conference on System Sciences, pp. 1–10 (2009)
37. Netessine, S., Shumsky, R.: Introduction to the theory and practice of yield management. INFORMS Trans. Educ. **3**, 34–44 (2002)
38. Cherkasova, L., Gupta, M.: Analysis of enterprise media server workloads: access patterns, locality, content evolution, and rates of change. ACM Trans. Netw. **12**, 781–794 (2004)
39. Arlitt, M.F., Williamson, C.L.: Web server workload characterization: the search for invariants. ACM SIGMETRICS Perform. Evalu. Rev. **24**, 126–137 (1996)
40. Gmach, D., Rolia, J., Cherkasova, L., Kemper, A.: Workload analysis and demand prediction of enterprise data center applications. In: 10th International Symposium on Workload Characterization, pp. 171–180 (2007)
41. Belobaba, P.P.: Survey paper-airline yield management an overview of seat inventory control. Transp. Sci. **21**, 63–73 (1987)

Bazaar-Score: A Key Figure Measuring Market Efficiency in IaaS-Markets

Benedikt Pittl$^{(\boxtimes)}$, Werner Mach, and Erich Schikuta

Faculty of Computer Science, University of Vienna, Vienna, Austria
{benedikt.pittl,werner.mach,erich.schikuta}@univie.ac.at

Abstract. Today's economy creates the need for dynamic, adaptive and autonomous building of enterprise value chains consisting of arbitrary virtualized computing resources, as hardware and software services. The current key technology for service provisioning is the cloud computing framework. In the course of this development digital service markets are becoming business reality.

Consumers in these digital markets apply typically the classical "take-it-or-leave-it" supermarket approach, which limits market performance. A solution to this problem is the so called Bazaar-based market, which extends the classical supermarket approach by enabling multi-round negotiation processes. Hereby business strategies of providers and consumers can be reflected in the negotiation processes to allow for smarter and more effective agreements in the market. In this paper we present a novel *genetic algorithm* based multi-round negotiation strategy between providers and consumers of services. This approach is realized within a Bazaar-Extension for CloudSim. To compare the market efficiency of resource allocations we introduce a novel key figure, the *Bazaar-Score* metric, which allows the evaluation of different business strategies.

Keywords: Service negotiation · Negotiation simulation · CloudSim

1 Introduction

A digital service market is the culmination point of stake-holders with integration of services along a value chain. Services are mainly traded directly for fixed prices from provider to consumer [1]. However, digital services are negotiated and contracted in a consumer-producer manner resulting in added value today. As for example Amazon's EC2 spot market shows that such service markets became business reality today. In the course of our research we introduced a generic multi-round negotiation framework for consumer provider contracting of web services [6], referenced in [2].

Cloud computing by its characteristic of metered services described by negotiable Service Level Agreements (SLAs) paves the way to the realization of these digital service markets [3,5]. In the following we consider IaaS (Infrastructure as a Service) as an example of a cloud service. Thus we use the terms IaaS provider

© Springer International Publishing AG 2017
J.Á. Bañares et al. (Eds.): GECON 2016, LNCS 10382, pp. 237–249, 2017.
DOI: 10.1007/978-3-319-61920-0_17

and cloud provider synonymously. Usually cloud providers run datacenters and sell their resources to other enterprises in the form of virtual machines (VMs). Consumers are represented by brokers on the market. We use the term resource for all possible resources of a provider which can be offered in form of virtual machines. A resource allocation mechanism defines the mechanism determining how providers and consumers sell and buy resources. Business strategies used by consumers and providers have significant influences on the resulting resource allocation of markets. The Bazaar-Score introduced in this paper is an economical key figure to compare efficiency of resource allocations. It represents the consumers surplus as well as the providers surplus of a resulting resource allocation. Virtual machines are goods characterised by the following descriptors: processing power, storage, RAM, and price. Specifically, processing power is provided by processing units and measured in million instructions per second (MIPS). Simulation frameworks like CloudSim use MIPS as measure for processing power which helps to calculate the exact utilization. RAM as well as storage are measured in Megabytes (MB). Thus, the remainder of the paper is organized as follows: The next Sect. 2 gives an overview over the used negotiation approach. Section 3 presents the negotiation mechanism based on genetic algorithms. The Bazaar-Score is introduced in Sect. 4. For a better readability of this section we created an appendix in [10]. A justifying negotiation scenario is implemented in Sect. 5. The paper is closed with the conclusion in Sect. 6.

2   Background and Assumptions

Figure 1 illustrates a simplified overview of the initial negotiation strategy which we use in this paper. In a typical bilateral negotiation scenario two negotiation partners such as provider and consumer exchange messages in an alternating way: each negotiation partner sends counteroffers, then it receives counteroffers to which it can respond again. This message sequence leads to a tree-based structure. The initial offer is called template and is usually published by the provider. We use the term offer for both, templates and counteroffers. An offer always contains a description of a VM and so we use them synonymously. Theoretically, a negotiation partner can create an arbitrary number of counteroffers in response to received offers. For more information about the negotiation sequence please see [9]. Consumer and provider usually receive several offers at the same time. Usually received offers are ranked by utility functions [9]. Based on this ranking it is decided how to respond to received offers. A high ranked offer will be accepted while a low ranked offer will be rejected. Further offers which are neither accepted nor rejected require the creation of counteroffers. The counteroffer mechanism introduced in this paper is based on genetic algorithms. Its purpose is to create Pareto efficient offers for negotiation scenarios where negotiation partners do not know the preferences of the other negotiation partners. The genetic algorithm is used for consumer as well as for providers. Negotiation between two negotiation partners is finished after an agreement was created or after all received counteroffers are rejected. After market participants have

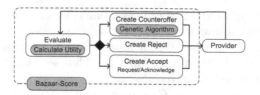

Fig. 1. Overview over negotiation strategy.

terminated negotiations the resulting resource allocation is evaluated using the Bazaar-Score to analyse market efficiency.

Each consumer and provider adheres to a business strategy. The created counteroffers should increase the utility of the consumer/provider according to the given strategy. As a strategy contains elements like risk assessment or considerations of partner relationships an analytical based optimization will be difficult and time intensive. Heuristic approaches can minimize the algorithmic complexity of calculating the utility of all possible counteroffers. Initially we considered the usage of different techniques from knowledge engineering for creating counteroffers like neural networks. However, genetic algorithms seem to be appropriate for our problem because their behaviour can be easily influenced by modifying the fitness function. So no training phase is required and counteroffers are created as byproduct as shown in the following. Our current implemented genetic algorithm does not consider history.

3   Genetic Algorithm Based Negotiation

Genetic algorithms were the focus of some research in the negotiation domain: The author of [8] uses a genetic algorithm for creating successful negotiation strategies for a specific and simplified domain. The population consists of a set of strategies whereby each strategy consists of a set of predefined rules. In [12] the approach of [8] was reworked. For the highly dynamic service markets dynamic strategies seem to be more successful than strategies with predefined rules.

In [4] a genetic algorithm was used for optimal assignments from sellers to buyer. The algorithm was described with an example of a product characterised with five attributes. Each attribute has a predefined value domain. Buyers and sellers assign a value to each attribute i. It is described that possible attributes may be the color of a product or the delivery date. An assignment of a buyer to a seller is optimal if they have the same valuation. The so called match value v_i for an attribute i forms the final fitness value and is calculated as follows $v_i = 1 - |b_i - s_i|$. b_i represents the value of attribute i for the buyer while s_i represents the value of the attribute for the seller. This equation shows the greater the difference of the valuation of buyer and seller the lower is the match value. We are not following this approach because of the following assumptions: (i) A consumer does not know the valuation of a provider and vice versa. (ii) Utility functions are eligible to present consumer and provider valuations.

Utility values resulting from different utility functions are not comparable. Thus the difference of the consumer and provider valuation can not be calculated.

Our implementation is based on the idea of [4] which considers the valuation of negotiation partners in the fitness function. Thus we map business strategies to simplified utility functions introduced in [9].

Population, Fitness Function, Crossover and Mutation form the anatomy of genetic algorithms. The *population* of the genetic algorithm consists of VMs representing the individuals. VMs are described using vectors of the form (a_1, a_2, a_3, a_4) where the first element represents the storage (GB), the second element the processing power (MIPS), the third element RAM (GB) and the last element the price (e.g. measured in $). An offer contains a description of a VM. We identified two basic strategies for creating the initial individual population. (I) The received offer is ignored and the initial population is created randomly. (II) The received offer is used as the basis for creating the initial population. An individual of the initial population is created by modifying one of the four characteristics of a VM. For example, an individual differs in processing power from received offer whereas another individual differs in RAM from the received offer. The required size of the initial population determines how many different modifications were executed. For example one individual will have 10% more RAM than the received offer while another one will have 5% less RAM. After some generations the individuals of the population have less similarity to the received offer. But the similarity is higher to the received offer than it would be by using a random initial population.

Offers received usually have a high utility for its sender. So we decided to create the population by using option (II) based on the received counteroffer. Individuals resulting from a random created initial population using option (I) may have no utility for the negotiation partner. An offer which may lead to an agreement has to have a high utility for consumer and provider. The used *fitness functions* represent this goal. Hence each fitness function has two components. The first component is the utility function used by the sender for evaluating offers. The second component is an estimation utility function representing the utility for the negotiation partner. An estimation of the utility function of the negotiation partner is necessary because we do not assume complete information. Thus individuals having a high fitness value usually have a high utility for both consumer and provider. Finding an estimated utility function is a complex task which may require heuristic approaches, like genetic programming. This is part of our further research. In this paper we use predefined utility functions. The estimated utility function which represents the utility of the negotiation partner may be imprecise. Thus an offer with a high fitness value does not imply that this offer has a high utility for the negotiation partner. The high fitness value may result from the imprecise estimated utility function representing the second component of the fitness function. By using strategy (II) for creating the initial population we keep the resulting counteroffer closer to the received offer. In other words, strategy (II) uses the received offer as guideline for creating counteroffers. This reduces the risk of creating offers which have a high fitness value but a low utility for the receiver. Equation (1) shows the basic structure of the fitness functions used by consumer and provider. The fitness function used by the consumer $F_{consumer}$ considers its utility function as well as an estimated utility function of the provider $\bar{U}_{provider}$. Similarly, the fitness function of the provider considers its utility function and an estimated utility function of the consumer $\bar{U}_{consumer}$. The weights w represent a impact factor of the negotiation partner. The higher w the stronger is the consideration of the negotiation partner:

$$F_{consumer} = U_{consumer} + \bar{U}_{provider} \cdot w, F_{provider} = U_{provider} + \bar{U}_{consumer} \cdot w \qquad (1)$$

Elitism is used for creating newly generations by taking over the best individuals regarding fitness of the old generation. The other individuals are generated by *crossover* and *mutation* operations. For the parent selection in the crossover operation we used the Roulette Wheel Selection. The selection probability is proportional to the fitness of an individual: $P_i = \frac{F_i}{\sum_{n=0}^{p} F_n}$. P_i is the selection probability of an individual i, F_i is the fitness of the individual i and p is the population size. The individual is created by taking randomly two characteristics of the first parent and the other characteristics of the other parent. The new generated individual may be mutated by modifying one of its characteristic. The best offers created by the algorithm are used as counteroffers.

For evaluation we executed some tests, where Table 1 shows the setup parameters. U is the utility function of the consumer, $\bar{U}$ is the estimated utility function of the provider. The utility function of the provider is based on the profit contribution so the numbers in $\bar{U}$ represent the prices. For example a MB RAM costs 0.001\$. Consumer fitness functions are created on concepts used in economical consumer theory. For example the used log function represents saturation. The utility functions were taken from [9] and are examples. A quick counteroffer generation is necessary during negotiation. Therefore we considered a small iteration and population size for the tests. For all tests it was assumed that the offer (200, 10000, 7, 30) is received. Eight parameter setups $S1 - S8$ were used for running the genetic algorithm (see Table 2). For four setups 50 generations (iterations) were generated while the other setups 100 generations (iterations) were generated. Each setup was evaluated using the average fitness value as suggested by [11]: each setup was executed 1000 times. After each execution the fitness of the best individual was stored. The average fitness value of best individuals is shown in the Table 2. Figure 2 visualizes the performance of setups. The first line represents the fitness value of the received offer. The initial offer has a fitness of 132338.8. The boxplots represent fitness values of the setups by executing each algorithm with each setup 1000 times. The median of the best fitness values of all experiments exceeds the fitness value of the received offer. Mutation as well as Elitism have obviously a positive impact. $S5$ seems to be the best setup. For the negotiation scenario presented in Sect. 5 we used the setup of $S5$ for counteroffer generation. The values in the offers have to be integers. By using the genetic algorithm we implicitly relaxed the problem to a non integer problem: As we measure storage in MB and processing power in MIPS we can round the numbers without loss of precision.

Table 1. Genetic algorithm setup summary (see [9] for utility functions).

Parameters	Values	Parameters	Values
Population size	96	Mutation probability	5%
Received VM	(200,10000,7,30)	Elitism	Best 5%
Fitness function			

$$U_x = \begin{cases} log(x) & x \geq Min_x \\ -\infty, & x < Min_x \end{cases} \qquad \text{x} \in \{RAM, Storage, Proc.Power\}$$

$$U_{Price} = \begin{cases} log(Max_{Price} - Price + 1) & Price \leq Max_{Price} \\ -\infty, & Price > Max_{Price} \end{cases}$$

$$U = 1 \cdot U_{Price} + 1 \cdot U_{RAM} + 1 \cdot U_{Storage} + 1 \cdot U_{Proc.Power} + 100000$$

$$\bar{U} = Price - RAM \cdot 0.001 - Storage \cdot 0.0005 - Proc.Power \cdot 0.001$$

$$w = 25$$

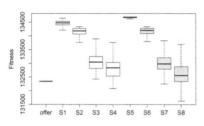

Fig. 2. Genetic algorithm scenarios.

Table 2. Genetic algorithm scenarios and results.

	Iterations	
	50	100
With Mutation/Elitism	S1-134453.7	S5-134669.3
Without Mutation with Elitism	S2-134134.7	S6-134142.9
With Mutation without Elitism	S3-133058.9	S7-133006.6
Without Mutation/Elitism	S4-132831.4	S8-132654.6

4   Bazaar-Score

For evaluation of our different negotiation strategies we have to find a key-figure which is able to answer the following questions: (i) How efficient is the resulting resource allocation? (ii) How big is the market surplus for consumers and providers in a given scenario? (iii) Is the market scenario with the used negotiation strategies beneficial for the consumers or for the providers?

Our first intention was to use utility values for comparing resource allocations. Consider a simplified example in which all consumers use the same utility function and all providers use the same utility function. Using utility values of the consumers allows to compare the happiness of consumers in different market scenarios. Using utility values of the providers allows to compare the happiness of providers in different market scenarios. However utility values are inappropriate to answer the first and the third question. Utility values resulting from different utility functions are not comparable because of their ordinal scale. Further, instead of using the same utility function for all consumers and for all providers, different market participants may use different utility functions. As utility values from different utility functions are incomparable, utility values are not appropriate for comparing the efficiency of resource allocations.

In appendix [10] a market efficiency figure introduced in [7] is presented. In the proposed market model only one good is traded for which all participants pay/charge a single price. The goods traded on IaaS-markets are VMs. VMs are no commodities as they have several characteristics such as RAM or storage. Therefore there is no single price for buying a VM. The price consumers are willing to pay depends on VM characteristics. Similarly, the cost of a provider depend on the resources delivered in form of a VM. Thus, the above described market model [7] cannot be directly applied to IaaS-markets. In summary, we can not apply the concept because we have no market price. The goal of the Bazaar-Score is to apply the concept introduced in [7] for IaaS-markets.

Thus, to make different resource allocations comparable, we define the *Bazaar-Score*. Similarly to the surplus described in [7], the Bazaar-Score measures the difference between the price paid and the maximum/minimum price at which the consumer/provider is willing to buy/sell. Hence, there is a consumer as well as a provider Bazaar-Score. The maximum price a consumer is willing to pay for a VM represents the consumers value of the VM. The minimum price at which a provider is willing to sell its VM represents the providers lower price range like cost or a profit contribution level. We used a profit contribution of 0 as lower price range in our simulation examples introduced in this paper.

Consumers and providers use utility functions as described in [9] for evaluating received offers (including the price). If an offer has a high utility for its receiver, then the receiver tries to form an agreement. The utility limit of a receiver trying to form an agreement is called utility acceptance threshold. If the utility value of an offer exceeds the utility acceptance threshold then the receiver tries to make an agreement. An agreement contains the characteristics of a VM including the price. Usually an increasing price reduces the consumers utility. So if the price for the VM described in the agreement is increased, the utility of the VM for the consumer is decreased. The price at which the utility of the agreement is equal to the utility acceptance threshold is called upper price limit, as shown in Fig. 3a. At this price limit the consumer will be undecided between buying and not buying the VM. The utility of the VM priced with the price limit is equal to the utility acceptance threshold.

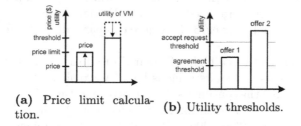

(a) Price limit calculation.

(b) Utility thresholds.

Fig. 3. Bazaar-Score calculation.

The difference between the price stated in the agreement and the upper price limit at which the utility of the VM equals the utility acceptance threshold is the consumer Bazaar-Score, as shown in the following equation:
Consumer Bazaar-Score = price limit − price. Our consumer strategy has two utility acceptance thresholds. (i) *Accept request threshold.* If an offer is received, which has a utility exceeding the accept request utility threshold, the receiver sends an accept request to the negotiation partner. However, the partner needs not to accept the request. (ii) *Agreement threshold.* If an accept request is received which exceeds the agreement utility threshold, an agreement is formed then. If an offer is received exceeding the agreement utility threshold, the consumer responds with usual counter offers. The agreement threshold is only considered if an accept request message arrives. It is always smaller or equal than the accept request threshold. If an accept request is received then the receiver can directly form an agreement. The risk of not finding an agreement can be avoided by accepting a lower utility.

An example is shown in Fig. 3b. The receiver of offer 2 responds with an accept request as the utility of the offer exceeds the accept request threshold; whereas the receiver of offer 1 responds with an usual offer. However, if offer 1 would be an accept request then it would be accepted by the receiver. Both thresholds may be modified during negotiation depending on the number of negotiation partners or negotiation duration. The Bazaar-Score uses the agreement threshold at the time of agreement for calculating the price limit. The agreement threshold is the lower utility limit at which a VM is accepted. Therefore it is comparable to the value of the offer for the consumer. Similarly to the consumer Bazaar-Score the provider Bazaar-Score is calculated. The provider evaluates offers with its utility function. Generally, the utility of the offer increases for a provider with increasing price. So, the provider Bazaar-Score is calculated by decreasing the price of the agreement until its utility is equal to the agreement threshold. The Bazaar-Score is calculated as follows, where the price limit is a lower price limit: Provider Bazaar-Score = price − price limit. The total surplus is calculated by summing up consumer and provider Bazaar-Score. Bazaar-Score = Consumer Bazaar-Score + Provider Bazaar-Score. The utility function measures the subjective happiness of a consumer/provider while the Bazaar-Score measures the *total surplus* which is the difference between value/cost and paid price/received price. The Bazaar-Score can be measured in monetary units e.g. dollar or euro. Therefore comparability of different scenarios is possible.

Usually a consumer has a higher Bazaar-Score if the characteristics of a VM meet its requirements and so its value is high. A provider's Bazaar-Score is not necessary decreased if the consumers Bazaar-Score increases. This is because consumer and provider have different preferences as shown by the following example: Consider that the offer $(300, 4000, 5, 10)$ was received by a consumer. The consumer wants more RAM. So it creates a counteroffer based on the proposed offer: $(300, 4000, 7, 11)$. The consumer increased the RAM and price. Nevertheless, the utility of the new offer is higher for the consumer: the consumer is willing to pay more than 1$ for 1 GB RAM. However, the consumer offers the provider 1$ for 2 GB RAM in the counteroffer. In case an agreement is formed its Bazaar-Score is increased by 1$. The provider evaluating the offer has lower cost than 1$ for the two additional GB RAM. So the new offer is better than the old one for both negotiation partners. Both have a larger Bazaar-Score.

5 Simulation Scenario

In this section a simulation scenario is introduced using the Bazaar-Extension we developed and using the Genetic-Algorithm as well as the Bazaar-Score described in this paper. In the scenario a consumer is represented by a broker. These terms are used synonymously.

During the development of the negotiation strategy we assumed a competitive market. Hence, we created a scenario consisting of 20 consumers and 30 datacenters. For the ease of simulation we assumed that a datacenter is able to host all consumers. All consumers respectively all datacenters use the same strategy. Setup parameters are shown in Table 4. The *minuspoints* shown in the table are used by the providers. If no acceptable offer is received from a consumer, the accept request threshold $U^{threshold}_{accept\ request}$ is decreased by the *minuspoints* for this negotiation. Thus the chance of receiving an acceptable offer is increased for further offers sent by the consumers and received by the provider. The utility functions described in Table 1 are used. So we assume that estimated utility function $\bar{U}$ in the Table 1 is the utility function used by the provider. However, instead of 0.001, 0.0005 and 0.001 the following cost are used: (i) price per MIPS: 0.0001 (ii) price per MB Ram: 0.0001 (iii) price per MB storage: 0.00004.

Table 3. Negotiation simulation scenarios.

Scenario	w for $\bar{U}_{consumer}$	w for $\bar{U}_{provider}$
Scenario 1	9.6	25
Scenario 2	8.8	23
Scenario 3	12.8	40

Table 4. Negotiation setup summary.

Parameters	Values
consumer $U^{threshold}_{accept\ request}$	utility of template+100
consumer $U^{threshold}_{agreement}$	$0.9 \cdot U^{threshold}_{accept\ request}$
consumer U^{reject}	0
provider $U^{threshold}_{accept\ request}$	58000
provider $U^{threshold}_{agreement}$	$0.9 \cdot U^{threshold}_{accept\ request}$
provider U^{reject}	26500
provider minus points	2000

The consumer has the weight 1 for each parameter and its maximal acceptable price is 100$. Consumers negotiate with all datacenters at the same time. However, an accept request is never sent to two or more datacenters at the same time to avoid winning the required VM several times. Both, consumer and provider, use the genetic algorithm described above. The setup of the most successful setup $S5$ described in Sect. 3 was used.

Negotiation scenarios use different fitness functions. As described above, each fitness function consists of the used utility function and an estimated utility function representing the negotiation partner. The consideration of the estimated utility function representing the negotiation partner with a certain weight should lead to offers which have utility for sender and receiver of the offer. In the negotiation scenarios the participants use the following fitness functions:

Consumer Fitness Function. The consumers fitness value is basically the consumer utility and estimated provider utility $\bar{U}_{provider}$ weighted with w. w is a factor for balancing the utility values resulting from different utility functions:

$$\text{Fitness Total} = U_{consumer} + \bar{U}_{provider} \cdot w \qquad (2)$$

For the scenario we assume the estimated function with

$$\bar{U}_{provider} = \text{Price} - \text{Ram} \cdot 0.001 - \text{Storage} \cdot 0.0005 - \text{Processing Power} \cdot 0.001 \qquad (3)$$

(i) price per MIPS processing Power: 0.001 (ii) price per MB Ram: 0.001 (iii) price per MB storage: 0.0005.

Provider Fitness Function. Similar to the consumer the providers fitness function uses a weighted estimated consumer utility.

$$\text{Fitness Total} = U_{provider} + \bar{U}_{consumer} \cdot w \qquad (4)$$

The estimated utility function used within the scenario is

$$\bar{U}_{consumer} = \text{Ram} \cdot 0.03 + \text{Storage} \cdot 0.005 + \text{Processing Power} \cdot 0.01 - \text{Price} \cdot 100 \qquad (5)$$

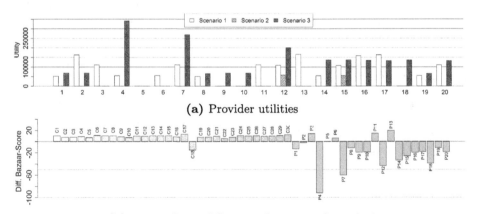

(a) Provider utilities

(b) Bazaar-Score difference: Scenario 1-Scenario 3

Fig. 4. Scenario results

The template offered by providers is (200,10000,7,30) in all scenarios. In the following we implement three negotiation scenarios (see Tabe 3). In each scenario the weights w used by provider and consumer (see Eqs. (2) and (4)) differ. The best four offers created by the genetic algorithm are used as counteroffers.

Scenario Setup. As shown in Table 3 negotiation partners are taken into account more strongly in Scenario 3 than in Scenario 2 and Scenario 1. The Bazaar-Scores are depicted in Fig. 5a. Scenario 2 has a Bazaar-Score of 83$, Scenario 1 has a Bazaar-Score of 1213$ which is a bit lower then the Bazaar-Score of Scenario 3 of 1328$.

Scenario 2 which has the lowest impact factor factors delivers the lowest Bazaar-Score. Only two brokers form an agreement in this scenario. Consequently the total Bazaar-Score is low. The consumers as well as the providers do not consider the negotiation partner strong enough due to the small impact factor. Consequently the generated offers have no value for the receiver leading to rejects. Only the two brokers 13 and 29 form an agreement in Scenario 2.

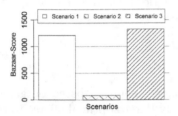

(a) Bazaar-Score of the three scenarios.   (b) Negotiation scenario- screenshot of Bazaar-Result View (Zoom).

Fig. 5. Plots created during the scenarios.

Scenario 3 seems to be the most efficient scenario. However, the used impact factor is unrealistic. This is because the consumer creates offers which have high utility for the provider but low utility for itself. All brokers form an agreement. Compared to Scenario 1 the consumer utilities of the agreements are smaller than in Scenario 3. However, the utilities of the providers shown in Fig. 4a are significant higher than in Scenario 1. One provider can serve several consumers. Thus some provider do not serve consumers. All providers and consumers use the identical strategy. So the random variables used in the genetic algorithm for counteroffer generation determines which provider forms agreements and hosts the VMs. In Scenario 3 the consumers and providers are very obliging. As the consumer creates generous offers for the provider it boosts the Bazaar-Score of the scenario. For the total Bazaar-Score it does not matter if the consumer renounces to improve the provider. The provider has also a big impact factor too. However, the consumer makes such good offers in response to the template so that they are never considered, as the provider tries to form an agreement based on the offers created by the consumers.

The impact factors used in Scenario 1 seem to be more realistic, as each negotiation partner tries to improve its utility. Figure 5b visualizes the negotiation between a consumer and a provider in Scenario 1. The red dot marked with *Template* is the template. Both consumer and provider create offers and counteroffers. All these offers and counteroffers have a better utility for both the consumer and the provider than the template. The big red dot marked with an *Agreement* is the agreement. All offers created within a negotiation iteration are represented as points with the same color. For example the yellow points represent offers created by the consumer in response to the template. In Fig. 5b the black points represent the approximate Pareto-border. By using the genetic algorithm for counteroffer generation the agreements are close to the Pareto-border. The thresholds and all the other parameters can be tuned to find a solution closer to the Pareto-border. Figure 4b shows the difference of the Bazaar-Scores of Scenario 1 and 3. For each participant the Bazaar-Score reached in Scenario 3 was subtracted from the Bazaar-Score reached in Scenario 1. C is an acronym for consumer and P is an acronym for Provider. Nearly all brokers have a higher Bazaar-Score in Scenario 1. However, Bazaar-Score for the providers is much higher in Scenario 3 than in Scenario 1. In Scenario 3 consumers give up their Bazaar-Score to increase the one of the providers.

6   Conclusion

In this paper we introduce a strategy using offer generation based on genetic algorithms enabling the creation of approximately Pareto-optimal offers. To this end we defined the Bazaar-Score, a key figure based on economical utility theory enabling comparison of different resource allocations. We simulated different multi-round negotiation strategies by a novel Bazaar-Extension for CloudSim.

References

1. Bonacquisto, P., Modica, G.D., Petralia, G., Tomarchio, O.: A strategy to optimize resource allocation in auction-based cloud markets. In: 2014 IEEE International Conference on Services Computing (SCC), pp. 339–346. IEEE (2014)
2. Hani, A.F.M., Paputungan, I.V., Hassan, M.F.: Renegotiation in service level agreement management for a cloud-based system. ACM Comput. Surv. (CSUR) **47**(3), 51 (2015)
3. Haq, I.U., Schikuta, E., Brandic, I., Paschke, A., Boley, H.: SLA validation of service value chains. In: International Conference on Grid and Cloud Computing, pp. 308–313. IEEE (2010)
4. Ludwig, S.A., Schoene, T.: Matchmaking in multi-attribute auctions using a genetic algorithm and a particle swarm approach. In: Ito, T., Zhang, M., Robu, V., Fatima, S., Matsuo, T. (eds.) New Trends in Agent-Based Complex Automated Negotiations. SCI, vol. 383, pp. 81–98. Springer, Heidelberg (2012). doi:10.1007/978-3-642-24696-8_5
5. Mach, W., Pittl, B., Schikuta, E.: A forecasting and decision model for successful service negotiation. In: 2014 IEEE International Conference on Services Computing (SCC), pp. 733–740. IEEE (2014)
6. Mach, W., Schikuta, E.: A generic negotiation and re-negotiation framework for consumer-provider contracting of web services. In: Proceedings of the 14th International Conference on Information Integration and Web-Based Applications & Services, pp. 348–351. ACM (2012)

7. Mankiw, N.: Principles of Economics. Cengage Learning, January 2014
8. Oliver, J.R.: On artificial agents for negotiation in electronic commerce. In: Proceedings of the Twenty-Ninth Hawaii International Conference on System Sciences, vol. 4, pp. 337–346. IEEE (1996)
9. Pittl, B., Mach, W., Schikuta, E.: A negotiation-based resource allocation model in iaas-markets. In: Utility and Cloud Computing (UCC) (2015)
10. Pittl, B., Mach, W., Schikuta, E.: Appendix for gecon paper (2016). http://homepage.univie.ac.at/a1347629/geconappendix.pdf
11. Sugihara, K.: Measures for performance evaluation of genetic algorithms (Extended Abstract). In: Proceedings of the 3rd Joint Conference on Information Sciences (JCIS 1997), pp. 172–175 (1997)
12. Tu, M.T., Wolff, E., Lamersdorf, W.: Genetic algorithms for automated negotiations: a fsm-based application approach. In: Proceedings of the 11th International Workshop on Database and Expert Systems Applications, pp. 1029–1033. IEEE (2000)

Understanding Resource Selection Requirements for Computationally Intensive Tasks on Heterogeneous Computing Infrastructure

Jeremy Cohen[1]([✉]), Thierry Rayna[2], and John Darlington[1]

[1] Department of Computing, Imperial College London, London, UK
{jeremy.cohen,j.darlington}@imperial.ac.uk
[2] Novancia Business School Paris, Paris, France
trayna@novancia.fr

Abstract. Scientists and researchers face challenges in efficiently configuring their scientific computing tasks so that they can be run in a timely and cost-effective manner. While the increasing availability of different types of computing platforms provides many opportunities to users, it can further complicate the job configuration process. In this paper we present work-in-progress to develop an approach to assist with identifying the most suitable computing platform and configuration for a computational task based on a user's financial and temporal constraints, using a decision support system. We use Nekkloud, a web-based tool for running computations via the Nektar++ spectral/hp element framework, as an exemplar and build a table that scores a range of properties for four example computing platforms to help select the most suitable platform for a job. We demonstrate our approach using three sample task scenarios.

Keywords: Resource selection · Decision support · Heterogenous platforms

1 Introduction

Computing platforms have evolved significantly over recent years with the emergence of multi-core processors containing increasingly large core counts and many-core architectures such as those used in GPUs. In addition, new models of accessing resources, such as the pay-per-use, on-demand access provided by Infrastructure-as-a-Service (IaaS) clouds, offer individuals additional opportunities for access to significant computational power.

While the capability to make use of new and different types of resources to undertake computations can offer scientists and researchers greater flexibility, it also presents a range of challenges. From a user perspective, these include selecting the most suitable resource(s) to use and correctly specifying the complex parameters and configuration files that are often required to run high performance scientific codes. Computing platforms have different costs, availability and

© Springer International Publishing AG 2017
J.Á. Bañares et al. (Eds.): GECON 2016, LNCS 10382, pp. 250–262, 2017.
DOI: 10.1007/978-3-319-61920-0_18

reliability and choosing the most suitable platform is a complex matter because it necessarily implies that trade-offs have to be made. Yet, it is not just an issue of 'time vs money' and there is most likely not a straightforward continuum of preferences that could be used to simply determine the most suitable platform considering the characteristics of the project at hand. The large number of parameters that are often involved in configuring High Performance Computing (HPC) codes mean that standard optimisation approaches can be impractical. This difficulty is compounded by the availability of multiple platforms and collaboration between different groups of individuals with different expertise when specifying task parameters. In this paper we describe work-in-progress to develop an alternative approach, relying on the expertise of those undertaking the job configuration and supporting this with a decision support framework that can assist in making the most appropriate decisions in a timely manner. We present the first stage of our research into approaches to help users in selecting a suitable target platform for running HPC jobs in environments where multiple resource types are available. Our use case is based on the Nekkloud [8] tool which, in combination with another tool, TemPSS [6], provides a web-based application for running spectral/hp element [12] computations via the Nektar++ [5] software. Using example scenarios, we demonstrate the challenges users can face in selecting a suitable target platform for their research computations. We then introduce the decision support framework, which will be implemented in the second stage of the research, and show, using the same scenarios, how it may be applied to help users in selecting suitable computational platforms for their tasks. As this work develops, we consider that the main contribution will be the ability to offer users of the Nekkloud tool, and others that adopt the decision support framework, recommendations of the most suitable computational platform to use to undertake their scientific HPC tasks. Ultimately we aim to enable automated selection of resources to support a user's required task configuration.

Related work is presented in Sect. 2 and we then introduce the HPC code and tools that provide our use case in Sect. 3. Section 4 presents and ranks four example computing platforms based on a set of properties. Section 5 presents the user scenarios and Sect. 6 discusses the properties of a decision support system to assist in efficient resource selection and looks at its application to the scenarios. We present our conclusions and details of future work in Sect. 7.

2 Related Work

Resource management and queuing systems such as TORQUE [1] and Grid Engine® [24] are widely used on HPC clusters to handle queuing and scheduling of jobs, and extensive work has been undertaken looking at approaches to job scheduling and resource management/selection. The emergence of computational grids raised additional challenges and [13] provides a survey of resource managers that support grid computing environments. Systems such as these handle a job when a platform has been chosen and the job submitted to it. As new models and hardware for undertaking computations have emerged, such as

Infrastructure-as-a-Service (IaaS) cloud platforms, GPUs and other accelerators, users have more opportunities to access computing power but also more challenges in understanding how best to select the most suitable platform(s) for their tasks. Our work focuses on the process of assisting users in selecting a suitable platform in an environment where multiple platforms are available.

Nekkloud users are currently required to select their chosen platform, resource type and related properties before running a job. However, it is often challenging for users to identify what they consider to be optimal and the level of risk they are willing to accept to achieve this. This is demonstrated in [4] which shows that where individuals have freedom of choice they take advantage of this even when its clear that the evaluation costs are high, possibly resulting in an inferior outcome compared to a case where choice is not available.

Describing platform capabilities and task requirements can be particularly challenging. Condor ClassAds [18], developed as part of the Condor workload management system [23], provide an approach to describing and matching requirements and capabilities. An extension of this mechanism, described in [15], provides a resource selection framework. In more complex heterogeneous environments, automating resource selection becomes especially challenging and [9] presents an algorithm that is designed to tackle this problem in a scalable manner. While it focuses on services, the SDL-NG framework [21] provides an alternative example of an approach, based on the use of domain specific languages, to provide formal descriptions of services. Our methodology defines a set of platform properties that are used to describe the capabilities of a platform, and could be represented using an approach such as ClassAds, and a decision support system that uses these properties to help address a user's requirements.

3   Software Environment

The spectral/hp element method [12], a type of high-order finite element method (FEM), can be used to solve systems of partial differential equations in order to carry out modelling of a range of physical mechanisms in a variety of scientific domains. Nektar++ provides an open source implementation of the spectral/hp element method and a set of solvers. It is well-documented but the complexity of such applications means it can still be challenging for end-users to work with.

Work to develop the libhpc framework [7,14], led to the development of a set of software tools and services to support and simplify running of scientific HPC codes on different computing resources. In this paper we base our investigations on two specific libhpc outputs, Nekkloud, and TemPSS (Templates and Profiles for Scientific Software). Nekkloud is a web-based user interface for running Nektar++ computations on different computing platforms and TemPSS is a service for managing sets of job configuration parameters for scientific applications. Figure 1 shows how the services are linked. TemPSS displays an application's configuration parameters as an interactive, visual tree. Users can build configurations by entering parameters into the tree nodes. The ability to store subsets

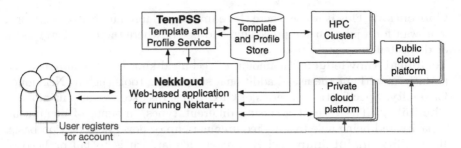

Fig. 1. The linking between Nekkloud, TemPSS, their users and computing platforms.

of parameters enables groups of individuals with different expertise to collaborate on building complete configurations. TemPSS can be used standalone or integrated into other applications and it has been built into Nekkloud.

The combination of Nekkloud and TemPSS offers an improved user experience and significantly simplified approach for running Nektar++ computations on remote platforms. It also helps to decouple the interactions between the different entities involved in running a computation. Nonetheless, in its current configuration, Nekkloud still requires that a user manually selects the computing platform on which they want to run a job, requiring some end-user knowledge about the pros and cons of running on different platforms and an understanding of the possible costs or issues of selecting one platform over another.

4   Computing Platforms

We introduce four example computing platforms and our methodology for comparing their capabilities. Table 1 shows the result of applying this methodology.

1. **Standalone server:** A multi-core x86_64 server with 2x16-core processors.
2. **HPC cluster using the PBS batch scheduler:** A large-scale HPC cluster consisting of several multi-core nodes interconnected with InfiniBand^{TM} low-latency networking and accessed via the PBS job scheduler.
3. **OpenStack private cloud:** An OpenStack private cloud IaaS system offering on-demand provisioning of virtual servers of different specifications.
4. **Amazon EC2 public cloud:** The Amazon EC2 [3] public cloud platform that offers on-demand, pay-per-use access to a variety of resources.

Our methodology for comparing the platforms involves the use of eight properties that are assigned values to rank platforms based on their pros and cons. The use of these properties to help select a platform under different requirements forms a type of multiple attribute analysis problem and an overview of various approaches to such problems is described in [16]. The properties are:

- **Cost (purchase and usage):** The cost to the end user or their institution of the initial platform purchase and the costs incurred at the point of use.

- **Contention:** This is worse where there may be a large number of users or a long wait for a job to begin processing and better where there are fewer users or dedicated access to a resource.
- **Technical knowledge:** The amount of technical knowledge required to use a platform without the use of additional supporting tools such as Nekkloud.
- **Capacity:** Specification in terms of CPU cores, disk storage and memory.
- **Flexibility:** The ease of accessing different types/amounts of computing capacity and being able to scale requirements up or down on a per-job basis.
- **Reliability/maintainability:** How likely a platform is to fail or become unavailable and the potential difficulty of maintaining it.
- **Communications:** The expected inter-node communication performance.

Assigning numeric values to these properties allows straightforward summation or application of weights to the parameter values, as used in the "additive weighting" approach described in [16]. We use a scale of values between 1 and 9 (inclusive) with 1 being the worst and 9 being the best. The size of the scale was selected to offer flexibility in the assigning of scores for parameters where there is considered to be similarity between two or more platforms. A smaller scale would reduce the scope for highlighting small differences between platforms while a larger scale provides an unnecessarily wide range of options. It is, nonetheless, accepted that there is an element of subjectiveness in the assigning of the values but it is still felt that they offer a good representation of platforms' capabilities and similarities. At the initial stage of this work we have opted to give all properties equal weights rather than applying a weighting factor to give values more or less significance. With the introduction of the decision support system in Sect. 6, there is the opportunity to introduce weights to the property values and to automate their selection in order to take user requirements into account.

Table 1. Summary of the pros and cons of different properties of the four example platforms described in this section. P1 = standalone server; P2 = HPC cluster; P3 = OpenStack cloud; P4 = Amazon EC2; '-' = Parameter not applicable.

	Cost		Contention	Tech knowledge	Capacity	Flexibility	Reliability	Comms	Total
	Purchase	Usage							
P1	7	7	7	6	1	2	5	-	35
P2	1	8	5	7	6	7	7	9	50
P3	5	7	7	3	5	6	4	2	39
P4	8	3	8	3	7	8	9	4	50

The values in Table 1 are based on example deployment scenarios for each platform. These scenarios are considered from the perspective of a researcher working in fluid dynamics wanting to use the platforms to undertake their processing jobs. Platform 1 is purchased and operated by the researcher's own team. The team needs the expertise to deploy and manage the resource but the researcher is then likely to have relatively uncontended access to it – it is likely to be shared only with other team members. The limited core count is an issue and maintenance is the responsibility of the researcher or their team. Platform 2, the HPC cluster, is designed for large-scale computations and is optimised for performance, providing high-speed, low-latency interconnects between nodes. Such a platform is very expensive to purchase but it may be supported through direct institutional funding and made available for researchers to use free of charge. Jobs are managed by the cluster's batch scheduling system and on a busy cluster, a job may be queued and take some time to begin running. The OpenStack private cloud platform offers much of the flexibility of a standalone server but with the potential to gain access to larger numbers of resources. A significant issue is that resources are interconnected using standard gigabit ethernet networking. This, combined with virtualised network interfaces on the cloud instances, can result in a significant performance penalty for parallel codes that undertake lots of inter-node communication. Reliability/maintainability may be an issue since this is, again, a locally operated platform. Platform 4, the Amazon EC2 public cloud, is accessed in a similar way to the OpenStack private cloud. However, EC2 offers a much wider choice of resource types and physical locations, which can be important if data is available in and must be processed in a specific geographic location. Access to Amazon EC2 resources is charged on a per-hour basis with a range of pricing options depending on the planned usage profile.

5   Usage Scenarios

We now look at three example usage scenarios, providing an initial platform recommendation for each based on the values in Table 1. The recommendations are revisited after the decision support system (DSS) is introduced in Sect. 6.

Scenario 1: A researcher is preparing a conference paper presenting analysis based on a 3-dimensional mesh that they have developed to support a fluid flow problem for a civil engineering project. The work is a collaboration between the researcher (a mathematician), and a group of civil engineering researchers. Around 3,000 CPU hours of computation are required for the analysis and the paper deadline is in two days. The lead researcher has limited funding for CPU time on their project which they would ideally like to retain for subsequent modelling tasks. Their institution operates an HPC cluster that is free at the point of use to researchers needing to undertake computationally intensive analysis.

Discussion: It is clear that the most important aspect here is the speed with which the job can be completed. From a pure computation perspective, the researcher would be best to undertake their job on the dedicated HPC cluster, requesting, say, 1024 or 2048 cores and having their computation completed in approximately 1.5–3 hours. However, this does not take into account job queuing time which, depending on the current cluster load, could be substantial. An alternative option would be to start a number of pay-per-use resources on the Amazon EC2 public cloud. The main issue with this approach will be the cost of purchasing around 3,000 CPU hours of compute time from the cloud service.

Platform recommendation: Local HPC cluster.

Scenario 2: An engineering team is developing a model of a gas pipe in a new structure. To test the correctness of their model and identify any issues with it, the team need to run a number of small-scale parallel tests. The number of time-steps to be run will need about 50 CPU hours per test and it will be necessary to undertake multiple runs with varying input parameters. The team are experts in their scientific domain but they need to collaborate with a software expert in order to select a suitable parallel computing environment and correctly configure their problem parameters to be used in the flow modelling solver.

Discussion: In this situation, the engineering team need the computation results as soon as possible in order to evaluate them and adjust the input parameters for the subsequent run. A platform where jobs are delayed by long queuing times is likely to be impractical, even if the ultimate computation performance is very quick. A better option could be to use a platform that may be slightly slower in terms of raw computation but where there is no contention for resource access. Such a scenario is likely to suit an in-house private cloud platform, or simply a multi-core standalone server. Software may need to be deployed and possibly built from source code to suit the target resources. The team are likely to require support from a computer scientist, if the software needs to be built from source code, and from the platform operator to identify the most appropriate parameters to suit the chosen platform when building and running the code.

Platform recommendation: Local, standalone, multi-core server

Scenario 3: A doctor wishes to model blood flow through an artery. They have collaborated with a CFD expert and a computer scientist and developed a one-dimensional model on which their computation will be undertaken using a Navier-Stokes solver. While the doctor understands the scientific problem they are tackling, their collaborators provide domain-specific knowledge to select or build a solver suited to the particular task. Computational requirements here are relatively low when compared to large three-dimensional models but funding is not available for computing time so low cost is the most important requirement.

Discussion: Time is not a significant constraint in this scenario. The lowest cost option depends on what resources are locally available to the doctor undertaking the modelling. We assume that a local server and institutional private cloud are available but not a cluster. For this computation, a local server offers the most straightforward option, despite the fact that computations may take some time to complete. However, a private cloud could offer the opportunity to scale computations and the developer working with the doctor should be equally capable of deploying their code to a local server or a remote cloud platform. The potential for complexity or delay that may result from having to work with a third-party platform is less of an issue with cloud infrastructure where a web based interface or API are normally available to start/stop and manage resources.

Platform recommendation: Institutionally-operated private IaaS cloud.

6   Decision Support System

6.1   System Model

As illustrated in the scenarios, constraints faced by users are heterogenous. While this means that access to different computing platforms is of critical importance, it also makes choosing the right platform quite complex, as all platforms have different properties. As a result, users are facing multi-dimensional trade-offs. There is obviously the matter of time and money (*cost* and *contention*). While this may, at first, look rather straightforward – there is a budget that cannot be exceeded and a deadline to be met – even such a trivial matter is actually not that simple. Indeed, what is the actual opportunity cost of a particular project? How much extra would a particular user or group of users be willing to pay to obtain their computation results a bit earlier? Conversely, how much money should they be offered to accept postponing completion of the computation for some period of time? In Table 1, property weights were considered to be equal. Yet, as with the property values assigned in Sect. 4, such weights are highly subjective and strongly depend on the project at hand. One task of the decision support system is to compute appropriate values for these weights given a particular scenario.

Previous literature [19] has emphasised the increasing complexity of choices in an environment when options are numerous and, as a result, the growing importance of decision support systems. In the case at hand, there is a clear need for a system that would enable identification of the most relevant option, based on the opportunity cost of each computational task. This question is particularly critical because the pricing of computing resources on certain types of computing platforms is often not stable (e.g. the 'spot' prices of computing units on Amazon EC2 [2] which evolve all the time). Being able to model the actual trade-off between time and money for a particular project provides the ability to identify opportunities as the project (and related computation) is being carried out. For instance, it may be possible to identify potential savings that can be achieved by delaying some of the computations. For some projects, this will be acceptable, but not for others. Hence the need to know the opportunity cost profile of the project. Determining this opportunity cost profile requires the following:

- knowing the 'super-boundaries': a maximum budget is sometimes not the actual maximum that can be spent on a project and even the strictest deadline might be extended by a small amount. Knowing what it would take for users to accept to 'go the extra mile' is critical to identify the best opportunities.
- knowing the 'boundary conditions': conversely, once a budget and time constraint have been assigned to a project, under which conditions is it acceptable to move away from these constraints?
- knowing the general opportunity cost of the project: considering the constraints of the project, what is the value of time (in money) for the users?

The first two points above can be determined through asking users a set of dedicated questions. The third point requires the use of an experimental methodology, such as the one used in [17] or described in [22]. When the project is carried out by a group of users instead of a single user and there are several stakeholders (meaning that the opinion of several users – including some that may not be interacting directly with the computing environment – has to be taken into account), it is possible to use methods such as Discrete Choice Experiments [20] to infer the trade-offs of the group (weighting can also be introduced in case different stakeholders have different weight in the final decisions).

Another critical aspect of the optimal choice of platform relates to users' attitude towards risk. Indeed, depending on the project at hand, a failure of the computing platform can have more or less dramatic consequences. Since one can reasonably expect reliability and price to be correlated, the attitude towards risk can have an important impact on expenditure. Evaluating risk aversion is, however, quite straightforward: users are asked to answer a series of questions related to lotteries and their answers are used to build their risk profile [10,11].

The methodologies used to evaluate the opportunity cost and the risk aversion can be extended to cover the other properties of platforms. For instance, a Discrete Choice Experiment (DCE) can be built to encompass the properties listed in Sect. 4. A shortcoming is that when more parameters are included, users need to answer more questions for an accurate trade-off profile to be built. When only one or a few users are involved, this can become quite tedious. A way to alleviate this issue is to make use of gamification to help make the data collection process entertaining for participants.

6.2   Application to Scenarios

We now revisit the three scenarios introduced in Sect. 5 and look at how the application of the decision support system can help to improve on the naive recommendations made based on the values from Table 1 in Sect. 4.

Scenario 1: Analysis of a fluid flow problem for a civil engineering project.

Initial platform recommendation: Local HPC cluster.

Impact of the Decision Support System: Time and money are clearly conflicting in this scenario. knowing the *super boundaries* (i.e. investigating additional funding, however limited, that could be used towards the project) would enable the DSS to offer alternatives to the use of the HPC cluster, in particular if the job queue is long, e.g. by monitoring spot prices on platforms such as Amazon EC2 that offer variable or demand-based pricing. Knowing the user's *boundary conditions* would enable the DSS to advise on substituting local HPC resources for external resources, as the former become available. In this case, it is essential to estimate the actual 'exchange rate' between time and money: how much money saved makes it worth delaying the obtention of the results? Finally, risk is, in this case, worth considering. Facing both a nearing deadline and funding shortage, the user might be willing to consider less reliable, alternative options. Assessing risk aversion of the user would enable a DSS to advise on such options.

Scenario 2: An engineering team modelling a gas pipe in a new structure.

Initial platform recommendation: Local, standalone, multi-core server.

Impact of the Decision Support System: In such a scenario, choosing the right platform is no longer just a matter of time versus money, other characteristics such as contention have to be considered. It is in cases such as this that a DSS becomes particularly important. Firstly, contention boundaries can be defined by the team. Then, both *super boundaries* and *boundary conditions* related to contention versus other factors (e.g. time, money) are assessed at the team level (with each team member undergoing the testing procedure to assess the various trade-offs). This enables evaluation of each computational option and identification of the most suitable one. A further interesting aspect is that it may be the case that not all team members have the same objectives. For instance, a more suitable option for the engineers may require a significant amount of additional work for the support team. This is why the decision is based on the combined trade-offs of each stakeholder in the project and strict boundaries and property weightings can be set to ensure selection of the most relevant platform.

Scenario 3: A doctor wishes to model blood flow through an artery.

Initial platform recommendation: Institutionally-operated private IaaS cloud.

Impact of the Decision Support System: In this scenario, the role of the DSS is essentially to identify cheap substitute alternative options to the local private cloud as they become available. The issue is, of course, that while local resources are often free at the point of use, external resources may not be (e.g. Amazon EC2). In such a case, an optimal solution would most likely make use of internal and external platforms. A DSS can help determine the right balance between the two platform types. Indeed, an accurate estimation of the time-money tradeoff enables a calculation of how much computation can be diverted towards paid-for external platforms. Furthermore, since time is not a significant constraint in this case, less reliable (and presumably cheaper) options may be considered. However, the involvement of a technical team in the project is likely to impact on the risk profile of the project. Indeed, while the doctor may not bear the consequences of unreliable sources (since the local server is always available as a back up), switching between options leads to additional deployment work for the technical team. Consequently, as time is not of the essence, the trade-offs made by the technical team are given a greater weight in the project profile.

7 Conclusions

Running complex HPC applications in modern computing environments with a variety of available hardware platforms presents a number of challenges in selecting the most suitable resources to address a user's requirements. We have observed that one of the key aspects in helping to ensure that users obtain the most appropriate resources is ensuring that they understand their own requirements and risk profile in sufficient detail to make the most suitable choice from the available options. However, it is clear that correctly identifying these requirements is key to obtaining the correct platform choice and to address this we introduce a decision support system. This system builds on approaches demonstrated in previous economics literature to help identify a user's risk aversion and the opportunity cost of different platform choices. The outputs of the decision support system can then be used to add weights to platform properties to help improve on the information provided by the platform feature matrix shown in Sect. 4 to obtain a platform choice.

In future work we aim to prepare an initial implementation of the decision support system and a framework for allowing straightforward addition of new platforms to the feature matrix. We intend to integrate this into the Nekkloud tool to provide a prototype platform recommendation feature for Nekkloud users.

Acknowledgements. The authors wish to acknowledge the Nektar++ team for their advice, particularly in relation to the scenarios and solvers. JC and JD acknowledge Imperial College London for funding the Pathways to Impact project "Simplifying High Performance Computing Access for the Nektar++ Framework" under Imperial's EPSRC Impact Acceleration Account. JC and JD also acknowledge EPSRC for their support of the completed libhpc (EP/I030239/1) and libhpc Stage II (EP/K038788/1) projects where Nekkloud and TemPSS were initially developed.

References

1. Adaptive Computing Inc.: TORQUE Resource Manager. http://www.adaptivecomputing.com/products/open-source/torque/. Accessed 19 July 2016
2. Amazon Web Services Inc.: Amazon EC2 Spot Instances Pricing. https://aws.amazon.com/ec2/spot/pricing/. Accessed 19 July 2016
3. Amazon Web Services Inc.: Elastic Compute Cloud (EC2) Cloud Server & Hosting - AWS. https://aws.amazon.com/ec2. Accessed 19 July 2016
4. Botti, S., Hsee, C.K.: Dazed and confused by choice: how the temporal costs of choice freedom lead to undesirable outcomes. Organ. Behav. Hum. Decis. Process. **112**(2), 161–171 (2010). http://dx.doi.org/10.1016/j.obhdp.2010.03.002
5. Cantwell, C.D., Moxey, D., Comerford, A., Bolis, A., Rocco, G., Mengaldo, G., de Grazia, D., Yakovlev, S., Lombard, J.E., Ekelschot, D., Jordi, B., Xu, H., Mohamied, Y., Eskilsson, C., Nelson, B., Vos, P., Biotto, C., Kirby, R.M., Sherwin, S.J.: Nektar++: an open-source spectral/hp element framework. Comput. Phys. Commun. **192**, 205–219 (2015). http://dx.doi.org/10.1016/j.cpc.2015.02.008
6. Cohen, J., Cantwell, C., Moxey, D., Nowell, J., Austing, P., Guo, X., Darlington, J., Sherwin, S.: TemPSS: a service providing software parameter templates and profiles for scientific HPC. In: 11th IEEE International Conference on e-Science (e-Science 2015), pp. 78–87, August 2015. http://dx.doi.org/10.1109/eScience.2015.43
7. Cohen, J., Darlington, J., Fuchs, B., Moxey, D., Cantwell, C., Burovskiy, P., Sherwin, S., Hong, N.C.: libHPC: software sustainability and reuse through metadata preservation. In: First Workshop on Maintainable Software Practices in e-Science, Chicago, IL, USA, position paper, October 2012

8. Cohen, J., Moxey, D., Cantwell, C., Burovskiy, P., Darlington, J., Sherwin, S.J.: Nekkloud: a software environment for high-order finite element analysis on clusters and clouds. In: 2013 IEEE International Conference on Cluster Computing (CLUSTER). IEEE, Poster paper, September 2013. http://dx.doi.org/http://dx.doi.org/10.1109/CLUSTER.2013.6702616

9. Costa, P., Napper, J., Pierre, G., van Steen, M.: Autonomous resource selection for decentralized utility computing. In: 29th IEEE International Conference on Distributed Computing Systems (ICDCS 2009), pp. 561–570, June 2009. http://dx.doi.org/10.1109/ICDCS.2009.70

10. Eckel, C.C., Grossman, P.J.: Men, women and risk aversion: experimental evidence. In: Handbook of Experimental Economics Results, vol. 1, pp. 1061–1073. Elsevier (2008). http://dx.doi.org/10.1016/S1574-0722(07)00113-8

11. Holt, C.A., Laury, S.K.: Risk aversion and incentive effects. Am. Econ. Rev. **92**(5), 1644–1655 (2002). http://dx.doi.org/10.1257/000282802762024700

12. Karniadakis, G., Sherwin, S.: Spectral/HP Element Methods for Computational Fluid Dynamics, 2nd edn. Oxford University Press, New York (2005)

13. Krauter, K., Buyya, R., Maheswaran, M.: A taxonomy and survey of grid resource management systems for distributed computing. Softw. Pract. Experience **32**(2), 135–164 (2002). http://dx.doi.org/10.1002/spe.432

14. libHPC. http://www.imperial.ac.uk/london-e-science/projects/libhpc. Accessed 19 July 2016

15. Liu, C., Yang, L., Foster, I., Angulo, D.: Design and evaluation of a resource selection framework for grid applications. In: Proceedings of the 11th IEEE International Symposium on High Performance Distributed Computing (HPDC 2002), pp. 63–72, HPDC 2002. IEEE (2002). http://dx.doi.org/10.1109/HPDC.2002.1029904

16. MacCrimmon, K.R.: Decisionmaking among multiple-attribute alternatives: A survey and consolidated approach. Technical report MEMORANDUM RM-4823-ARPA, The RAND Corporation, Santa Monica, CA, USA (1968). http://www.rand.org/pubs/research_memoranda/RM4823.html

17. Payne, J.W., Bettman, J.R., Luce, M.F.: When time is money: decision behavior under opportunity-cost time pressure. Organ. Behav. Hum. Decis. Process. **66**(2), 131–152 (1996). http://dx.doi.org/10.1006/obhd.1996.0044

18. Raman, R., Livny, M., Solomon, M.: Matchmaking: distributed resource management for high throughput computing. In: Proceedings of the Seventh IEEE International Symposium on High Performance Distributed Computing, p. 140, HPDC 1998. IEEE Computer Society, Washington, DC, July 1998. http://dl.acm.org/citation.cfm?id=822083.823222

19. Rayna, T., Darlington, J., Striukova, L.: Pricing music using personal data: mutually advantageous first-degree price discrimination. Electron. Mark. **25**(2), 139–154 (2015). http://dx.doi.org/10.1007/s12525-014-0165-7

20. Ryan, M., Gerard, K., Amaya-Amaya, M. (eds.): Using Discrete Choice Experiments to Value Health and Health Care, The Economics of Non-Market Goods and Resources, vol. 11. Springer, Netherlands (2008). http://dx.doi.org/10.1007/978-1-4020-5753-3

21. Slawik, M., Küpper, A.: A domain specific language and a pertinent business vocabulary for cloud service selection. In: Altmann, J., Vanmechelen, K., Rana, O.F. (eds.) GECON 2014. LNCS, vol. 8914, pp. 172–185. Springer, Cham (2014). http://dx.doi.org/10.1007/978-3-319-14609-6_12

22. Smith, V.L.: Theory, experiment and economics. J. Econ. Perspect. **3**(1), 151–169 (1989). http://dx.doi.org/10.1257/jep.3.1.151

23. Tannenbaum, T., Wright, D., Miller, K., Livny, M.: Condor: a distributed job scheduler. In: Sterling, T. (ed.) Beowulf Cluster Computing with Linux, pp. 307–350. MIT Press, Cambridge (2002). http://dl.acm.org/citation.cfm?id=509876.509893
24. Univa® Corporation: Products Suite (2016). http://www.univa.com/products/. Accessed 19 July 2016

Towards Usage-Based Dynamic Overbooking in IaaS Clouds

Athanasios Tsitsipas$^{(\boxtimes)}$, Christopher B. Hauser, Jörg Domaschka, and Stefan Wesner

Institute of Information Resource Management, Ulm University, Ulm, Germany
{athanasios.tsitsipas,christopher.hauser,joerg.domaschka,
stefan.wesner}@uni-ulm.de

Abstract. IaaS Cloud systems enable the Cloud provider to overbook his data centre by selling more virtual resources than physical resources available. This approach works if on average the resource utilisation of a virtual machine is lower than the virtual machine boundaries. If this assumption is violated only locally, Cloud users will experience performance degradation and poor quality of service. This paper proposes the introduction of dynamic overbooking in the sense that the overbooking factors are not equal for all physical resources, but vary dynamically depending on the resource demands of the virtual resources they host. It allows new pricing models that are dependent on the overbooking a Cloud customer is willing to accept. Additionally, we discuss prerequisites for supporting its realisation in an OpenStack private Cloud, including a monitoring system, dedicated metrics to be monitored, as well as performance models that predict the performance degradation depending on the overbooking.

Keywords: Cloud computing · Accounting · Dynamic overbooking · Monitoring

1 Introduction

Cloud systems have become popular in the last decade, not only for their technological and non-functional characteristics, but also because of the flexible accounting of used resources. Commercial cloud offerings (e.g. Amazon AWS, Google Cloud Platform) as well as private and public offerings based on non-commercial middleware (e.g. OpenStack), offer virtually unlimited amount of resources, which customers can acquire and use according to a *pay-as-you-go* model. A widely used approach is to access resources on the Infrastructure as a Service (IaaS) layer which offers access to entities such as virtual machines (VMs), storage capacity, and virtual networking.

While the customers use virtual resources, mainly VMs, these have to be mapped to physical resources, i.e. compute nodes (servers), operated by the cloud provider. When offering a cloud service, the benefit for the cloud provider lies in the chance to overbook the physical infrastructure to avail of a high amount

© Springer International Publishing AG 2017
J.Á. Bañares et al. (Eds.): GECON 2016, LNCS 10382, pp. 263–274, 2017.
DOI: 10.1007/978-3-319-61920-0_19

of customers—a technique also exercised by airline reservation systems [17]. In consequence, the total amount of offered and operated virtual resources is higher than the available physical resources. The *overbooking factor* denotes the ratio between virtual and physical resources. It is commonly enforced on the basis of individual physical machines (PMs).

Cloud data centre operators commonly use a static overbooking factor per physical resource. Hence, there are different factors for compute (CPU cores), amount of memory, and disks [7]. When a new VM was created by a user and shall be placed on a PM by the run-time system, the placement decision is a straight forward task: The cloud middleware places the VM in a best-effort manner on a PM such that no overbooking factor on that machine is violated [20].

The resource overbooking is only efficient, when on average VMs need less resources at run time than what they can access statically [10]. If this is not the case, overbooking exposes the cloud provider to the risk of resource congestion and thus to Service Level Agreement (SLA) violations, because application performance degrades [20]. Static overbooking strategies assume widely unchanged resource demands of each VM and do not consider the fact that workload and hence, resource demands may change over time due to several reasons such as periodic changes in use, load spikes, etc. A simultaneous increase in load for several VMs on the same physical node overloads this node and degrades performance and user experience. Thus, under these circumstances, the overbooking factor has to be lowered and VMs have to be re-distributed over the physical infrastructure. Optimising the distribution of virtual resources over physical ones is possible in all non-commercial middleware systems, but only in a manual way.

Hence, what is required is a dynamic overbooking factor per physical node: If VMs on that PM consume little resources, the overbooking factor can be increased until the node reaches the desired utilisation, e.g. 70%. When VMs use more resources, the overbooking factor shall be decreased down to 1 if required. The decision of the overbooking factor is not only dependent on the resources consumed by the VMs, but also by the performance degradation the data centre operator is willing to impose on his customers. Here, different customer types should be taken into account. While many authors have been working on finding optimisation algorithms for different scenarios, this paper focuses more on how to enact such optimisation algorithms in OpenStack and other cloud middleware and how to seamlessly collect the necessary information.

The remainder of the paper is structured as follows: The following section lists the requirements to realise our approach. In Sect. 3 our solution for dynamic overbooking is presented. Section 4 deals with the prototype integration of the solution in a real OpenStack setup. Section 5, discusses the related work. Finally, Sect. 6 concludes the paper with an outlook and future work plans.

2   Requirements

Towards an assured dynamic overbooking of a data centre, we distil core requirements from the area of monitoring, performance modelling and optimisation models are being described below.

In order to be able to take decision on how to reconfigure a data centre and the mapping of virtual to physical resources, it is necessary to monitor the system as a whole. Monitoring is a challenging task when *consistency* and *low latency* need to be met [1]. Systems with dynamic overbooking factors have to quickly adapt to changing workloads in order to ensure that targeted SLAs are not violated and hence, are depend on low latency. As data centres have grown large [22], the monitoring system has to be able *handle large scale systems*. The measurements required to obtain a comprehensive view on the status of such systems led to the generation of a large volumes of data. A scalable monitoring system should be able to efficiently record, transfer and analyse such volume of data *without impairing the normal operations of the cloud*. Monitoring data not only have to be recorded, but also be *accessible* through a common interface in a unified manner. Additionally, monitoring has to take place of both physical and the virtual level for a concise overview and in-depth data analysis.

A VM is not characterised only by its static properties (i.e. number of cores, size of memory), but also by its footprint in the system [16]. The footprint is a consequence of the physical resource utilisation. Monitoring a data centre, enables the performance modelling for individual resource dimensions. The performance models in combination with the system load affect the decision of an overbooking factor. Additionally, a dynamic overbooking factor allows more flexible pricing models. Different service groups can be exposed to different SLAs (e.g. Gold, Silver, Bronze) and each group may lead to different pricing.

Finally, performing dynamic overbooking in an infrastructure, implies topology aware optimisations. This entails the robust provisioning of information about the status of the data centre and the execution of corrective actions to avoid SLA violations. The optimisations performed in a infrastructure must be transparent to the customers and not impair the normal workload of their applications. The transparent nature of an optimisation in systems with dynamic overbooking enabled, is tightly coupled with the migration times of VMs. They have to be relatively low to enhance the experience of the customer and not violate the SLAs.

3   Proposed Solution

As highlighted in the previous section, dynamic overbooking in a cloud infrastructure has several strict requirements. In particular, it relies on robust monitoring mechanisms. In this section, we propose a solution to enact dynamic overbooking in cloud data centres. Section 3.1 sketches the features of a monitoring framework while Sect. 3.2 presents the information that needs to be collected by that framework. Performance modelling taking into account the VMs' CPU, memory and disk utilisation is subject to Sect. 3.3. There we also present how a cloud provider can introduce new SLA models to his customers on a *pay-for-what-you-actually-use* basis.

An amalgam of these individual solutions breaks the establishment of the billed per hour model, which deliver virtual resources of uncertain performance.

3.1 Monitoring Framework

Enabling in-depth monitoring mechanisms in a data centre unleashes the extraction of meaningful data to lay the ground for further analysis and correlation.

In a cloud infrastructure, monitoring tools have to cope with a varying number of VMs while maintaining high data collection throughput and respond in real-time [21]. Since, a plethora of monitoring frameworks exist, in our work we do not utilise just a framework. We give answers to open questions how such a framework can fulfil the requirements to enable dynamic overbooking in cloud.

Nowadays, data centres tend to be large. Hence the collection of data can not be done from a central point, but needs to be distributed. Also, in order to support dynamic overbooking factors, the data centres have to adapt to changing workloads no matter their size. Moving monitoring instances closer to the PMs, has the advantage of reducing latency. Thus, the monitoring system and the system being monitored are closely located. Despite of the distributed nature of the monitoring system, the data are accessed through a common interface while being fault-tolerant and highly available.

To retrieve the required information (cf. Sect. 3.2) a set of probes has to be installed on each PM with a per-probe runtime configurations (e.g., polling interval). Interestingly, probes in a VM are non-existent, as per se, they are not easily controllable. Obviously, only required probes shall be installed to keep the total amount of monitored data as low as possible.

Finally, the recording of data is not sufficient. Monitored data needs to be stored for further processing and historical matters. Aggregation mechanisms are a transparent step of pre-processing for dynamic data (e.g. CPU usage) which combine multiple metrics into a synthetic one that is inferred and not directly monitored [1]. Additionally, filtering the data reduces the volume of the collected data. Both of the aforementioned techniques, propagate the monitoring data at the storage backend providing meaningful insights(e.g. CPU usage the last hour).

3.2 Monitored Information

In this section, we discuss what kind of data has to be monitored to realise dynamic overbooking. A pre-dominant goal for our monitoring approach is to realise it non-invasive for the cloud customer. That is, no monitoring processes should be visible for the cloud customer and as many metrics as possible shall be collected from the hypervisor hosting the customer's VM.

When optimisations on application level shall be supported, monitoring application specific data, from inside, the VM can not be avoided. Yet, this feature is orthogonal to our work presented in this paper and is therefore not considered. Instead, we assume the VM as black-box and only examine the performance models on VM-level, without the networking dimension. Doing so, we completely disregard possible knowledge of what is running inside the VM. Incorporating this knowledge as well is subject to ongoing work.

VMs request CPU time, filesystem access and allocation of memory. A cloud provider depends on these dimensions to perform the overprovisioning. Hence, the monitoring framework must obtain data from both virtual and physical level. Table 1, presents the metrics that need to be collected for each dimension.

Table 1. Dimension metrics collected by the monitoring framework.

	Dimension	Metrics
Physical	CPU	cpu_cores, cpu_usr, cpu_sys, cpu_wio
	Memory	mem_size, mem_free, mem_cache, mem_buff, mem_swpd
	Disk	total, used, disk_readmax, disk_writemax, iops, disk_reads, disk_writes
Virtual	CPU	cpuCS, cpuIO, cpuVM, cpuPM, cpuST
	Memory	ram-total, ram-used
	Disk	disk-read, disk-write, disk-total, disk-used

As a methodology for the definition of the required metrics, a first layer of categorisation in physical and virtual level exists. Furthermore, a second layer of categorisation lies on the different dimensions - CPU, Memory and Disk.

On the *physical* level, we identify for the *CPU* dimension the need of knowledge about the number of cores in a PM (*cpu_cores*), to correlate what is the physical restriction in terms of cores and how can we translate them to virtual cores. Last, the CPU usage on the user mode (*cpu_usr*), on the system mode (*cpu_sys*) and when the CPU idles and waits for I/O completion(*cpu_wio*), are metrics needed to cover all the spectrum of CPU usage. With regard to the *Memory* dimension, the physical barriers as the memory size (*mem_size*) and the free memory(*mem_free*), are the simple way to define the allocation of memory. Additionally, the cached memory (*mem_cache*), the buffered memory (*mem_buff*), as also the swapped memory (*mem_swpd*), provide information of a possible over-provisioning on this dimension. Finally, the *Disk* dimension is described for the allocated with the used and the total disk capacity of the PM. Moreover, information about the operations per second (*iops*) facilitates if a PM is under a heavy operated mode. Additional information about the read/write rates and the read/write bandwidth are also recorded.

Moving to the *virtual* level, for the *CPU* dimension, the number of the provisioned virtual cores (*cpuCS*) is required. Moreover, *cpuIO* reports the utilisation needed for I/O operations in the VM. *cpuVM* reports the VM's CPU utilisation value as it is seen from inside the VM. *cpuPM* provides the VM's CPU utilisation value as it is seen from the physical level. *cpuST* accounts for the CPU time *stolen* from this VM. As far as the *Memory* dimension, the total memory and the used memory from the VM is sufficient to characterise the memory utilisation. Finally, the allocation of disk (*disk-total, disk-used*) for a VM is available and the reads and writes performed in the VM (*disk-read, disk-write*).

3.3 Performance Modelling

The monitored information introduced in the previous sections allows the calculation of performance models for each dimension of the VM from which, determine the overbooking factor per PM. The multi-level monitoring framework also eases the correlation and results in the overprovisioning identification.

Overbooking Identification. A customer's application will only receive a performance degradation, if the PM is overbooked and the application needs specific resources for it's execution while the other VMs on that PM leave fewer of these resources than required. Monitoring the resources with a multi-level flavour aids to quickly grasp the overutilisation of VM dimensions.

To identify overbooking on the CPU dimension, the request for processing time from virtual CPUs is more than can be served by the physical CPU. Since the physical CPU is loaded with max. 100%, the virtual CPUs get requested processing time "stolen", leading to an experience like reducing the processor's frequency. As soon as the steal value ($cpuST$) for any of the VMs hosted on a PM is >0%, the CPU got overbooked.

Overbooking the memory takes place when the actually requested resident amount of memory does not fit in the physically available memory. The main indicator of an overbooked memory on a PM is when the PM's operating system "swaps" out the memory to disk. The mem_swpd value should be as low as possible, since accessing memory from the disk is a costly and performance decreasing action.

The disk has two ways to be overbooked: (i) the disk allocation, and (ii) the disk I/O interaction to read and write data. Disk allocation can be safely overbooked with thin provisioned virtual disks, but should never be harmed to avoid unpredictable experiences inside the VMs. Additionally, it can be secured by watching the free disk space available on the PM. The disk I/O overbooking is a comparably fast changing metric. The bandwidth and the I/O operations ($iops$) have to be watched for all the VMs and the PM. Waiting times caused by disk interactions generally increase the cpu_wio and the $cpuIO$ values, yet not automatically due to overbooking. Instead, the maximum rates possible on the physical level have to be compared to the requests from the virtual level.

Workload Classification. Workloads that have spikes and bursty behaviour, are a good target for overbooking, since they only occasionally use all the system resources their VM provides. Furthermore, applications with period workloads can be co-located on the same PM with out performance degradation provided that the phases do not overlap. Moreover, the fact that VMs are multidimensional with respect to resources (CPU, memory, disk), it is also an option to co-locate applications that utilise resources in different locations [20]. A combination of different approaches is possible as well.

There is a need to have a wide range of different parameters because application types are different. For instance, the behaviour of a scientific application performing a computation differs from a gaming server. While the former requires resources in a bursty manner [11] and fluctuates between I/O and CPU bound phases and can tolerate short periods of under-provisioning, the latter is intolerant to violations of performance as this would harm the experience of the gamers connected to it.

Dynamic Overbooking. With dynamic overbooking enabled, a cloud provider can serve more customers, because the customers can buy some flexibility. Currently in the *state-of-the-art*, the only differentiation between the VMs are the number of virtual cores, the number of virtual memory and the allocated disk.

Our approach employs the resource utilisation to make optimisation decisions, while maintaining the maximum revenue for the provider and not harming the performance experienced for the customer. We define two types of optimisation actions: *(i)* use a customisable parameter depending on how risky the provider wants to be when performing optimisation actions and create SLAs based on that, and *(ii)* monitor the resources on physical and virtual level, correlate the values and perform optimisations or initial placement of VMs based on the overbooking factor that a customer agreed.

In particular, we propose to delegate the customisation of the overbooking factor to boundaries of the VM dimensions. These boundaries are defined as:

$$OVBFx_{threshold} = [OVBFx_{min}, OVBFx_{max}] \qquad (1)$$

Here, x denotes availability of CPU, memory, or disk. The definition can vary based on service groups that the provider offer to the customers.

Each of these service groups can then be associated with different SLAs with different privileges regarding the overbooking that will receive. When a new service is provisioned, the service group is associated with the appropriate SLA based on the customer's will. For example, a *Silver* and a *Bronze* customer will have more flexibility and will accept an overbooking factor of CPU for couple of hours during the day. On the other side a *Gold* customer will accept no overbooking on the PM or a minimal one. If the provisioned service was not what was intended to, the customer account can be reassigned to another service group that has a different QoS parameter defined in its SLA.

3.4 Summary

As a summary, we envision the enactment of dynamic overbooking in the cloud data centres by the following mechanisms: Enabling monitoring mechanisms to record the utilisation of the dimensions on both physical and virtual levels. The overbooking is extracted for the VMs of the customer and based on their utilisation and the service provider group of the customer, the decision for optimisations is taken.

4 Prototype Integration

In our prototype we set up an OpenStack driven private cloud with full root access to all PMs. The PMs run Centos 7 and use KVM [8]. In the following subsections we first explain the implemented monitoring system, the integration into the running OpenStack middleware with the *Data Centre Analysis (DCA)* toolkit, which controls the VM placement to enable the dynamic overbooking.

4.1 Monitoring

In our work, we introduce a customised version of Chukwa, an *open source* data collection system for monitoring and analysing *large distributed systems* [13]. Chukwa is built on top of Hadoop Distributed File System (HDFS) [15] and MapReduce framework [5]. Data is also accessible through HBase[1], a scalable, column-oriented database suitable to store the large amount of data [21].

Chukwa Overview. Chukwa has three main components: *(i)* The Agent, a service which run on every PM where data is collected. The agents feature a range of dynamically-controllable modules called *(ii)* adaptors. Adaptors act as source wrappers and enable the agent to collect data from a variety of sources, such as a file or Unix command line tools. Each Adaptor in an Agent reports the data that then forwarded to a group of *(iii)* Collectors. A Collector gathers the monitored data from several agents and stores them in HBase or sequence files in HDFS.

Monitoring Architecture. Figure 1 sketches the monitoring framework that consists of the cloud resources view and the monitoring software available, while illustrating the actions a user can execute upon the monitored data.

Since we chose KVM as a hypervisor for hosting VMs in our prototype, the Chukwa Adaptors for retrieving monitoring data have to be aligned accordingly. The monitoring takes place on the PM's operating system and hence outside of the VM, but collects as detailed information about the currently running physical-virtual setup and its load as possible. Monitoring a Linux based PM is a well established task, while the virtual level is a more complex one. In KVM, each virtual CPU core is represented as a process on the PM's operating system, and hence can be monitored as a usual application. To calculate the measurements for each VM, we rely on the Linux kernel's output and popular tools like virsh[2]. To measure the CPU utilisation of VMs with respect to overbooking, we introduced a new VM monitoring tool for KVM called kvmtop[3].

Implementation Details. For this work, Chukwa's mapping to HBase was enhanced by a further abstraction layer that allows to control more fine-grained how monitored data is mapped to HBase tables and rows. In addition, the enhancement unifies the representation of data and tenders its *consistency*.

This restructuring allowed to decreased the query time to the database by one order of magnitude compared to the default mapping of Chukwa mainly caused by a clear *data distinction* and *isolation*. Other dominant features of the Chukwa extension are: *(i)* support for storing data in multiple tables; *(ii)* easy and flexible specification of data mapping; *(iii)* definition of different row key strategies in tables; *(iv)* provision of an aggregation mechanisms.

---

[1] http://hbase.apache.org/.
[2] http://libvirt.org/.
[3] https://cha87de.github.io/kvmtop/.

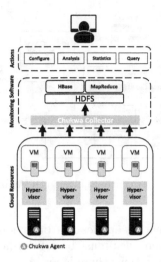

Fig. 1. Monitoring system framework.

Moreover, several additional Adaptors were developed that target the collection of vital health monitoring data of the infrastructure.

4.2 OpenStack Integration

The solution for dynamic overbooking presented in Sect. 3 is integrated as a prototype in an OpenStack based cloud system. OpenStack, as one of the most popular open source cloud middleware available, consists of a centralised management component and a local control unit in each PM, which can serve as VM hosts. OpenStack users may use a web dashboard, which uses a REST service, or may use the REST service directly to create or remove VMs. OpenStack schedules incoming VM requests to one of the PMs, if none is explicitly specified.

The work of the integration is part of a European project that aims to optimise a cloud data centre from infrastructure to application level for better performance, better utilisation and a higher energy efficiency [12]. To enable our approach in an OpenStack cloud, the monitoring framework needs to be enabled. To allow interactions from the OpenStack to the *Data Centre Analysis (DCA)* toolkit and back, a bidirectional communication needs to be established. Invocations to the OpenStack REST API are intercepted by a prototype-aware HTTP proxy. The proxy delegates calls for creating and deleting VMs synchronously to the prototype (cf. Fig. 2). Other calls are forwarded to OpenStack directly.

4.3 DCA Toolkit

The *DCA* toolkit starts with monitoring on each host of the data centre. The monitoring framework retrieves detailed information from physical and virtual level. The data is processed and stored in an HBase database. This amount

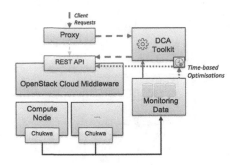

Fig. 2. Data centre analysis (DCA) toolkit.

of data is then used for creating application behaviour profiles. For periodical optimisations, access to OpenStack must be established in order to enable VM migrations. With these integrations there is an impeccable control of the workload placement for existing and new VMs.

5 Related Work

The popular public cloud providers like Google or Amazon charge customers of their IaaS offerings primarily based on time and various other aspects. The offerings are subject to SLAs that assist the mutual agreement.

Although respectful research works go towards a verifiable and sustainable resource accounting for cloud computing [3,4], they still lack a unified approach to optimise a data centre. [6] defines a resource-level SLA metric to offer QoS guarantees regarding the computing capacity of a cloud provider. However, the solution is single-sided and focuses only on the CPU dimension. In [14], the authors propose a technique based on capacity planning to support cloud providers to negotiate the cloud services offered to the customers. The downside of this approach is the requirement the customer's application workload as a precondition, whereas in our approach we do not consider any static preconditions as an input. [19] proposes a cloud computing management framework with admission control and scheduling mechanisms that are capable of resource overbooking. Yet, they assume that no SLA violations will occur if the used capacity is within the bounds of the PM. The dynamic overprovisioning of resources is synonym with the migration time of a VM during the reconfiguration of the system. The results of the research work in [2,9,18], will be used for further reference for the evaluation of our approach.

6 Outlook and Conclusions

IaaS cloud allows the provider to sell more virtual resources than physical resources available in his data centre. This overbooking works, if on average the resources required by a VM are less than the hardware specified for the VM.

On the down-side, VMs will suffer from performance degradation if the assumption is temporarily violated on the PM the VM is being executed.

In this paper, we propose dynamic overbooking to work around the risk of poor quality of service. We suggest to compute an overbooking factor per physical resource based on the resource demands of VMs running on. If VMs require little resources, the overbooking factor will be high; if VMs require many resources, the overbooking factor will be low.

As a main contribution, this paper investigates preconditions that have to be enabled in a data centre to support dynamic overbooking. These include the provisioning of a large-scale, low-latency monitoring and data aggregation system; the capability to capture distinguished metrics from the physical and virtual infrastructure; performance models that denote the behaviour and resource demands of particular VMs under dedicated workload patterns.

In addition to that, we present how to build and integrate such a system, into the open source cloud middleware OpenStack. The ground up monitoring mechanism we propose is pluggable to any data centre. Similar, the mechanism for automatic workload and overbooking adaptation is minimal invasive and can be ported to other cloud middleware with almost no effort.

Concluding, overbooking is equitable for cloud providers and their customers, economically but also trustworthy and can motivate further cloud adoption. Monitoring the resource utilisation may result in accounting profiles of applications running in the VMs and can lead to a fair billing for the customers.

We are currently working on evaluating our prototype system with different optimisation algorithms from literature. This will lead to valuable insight for different system parameters such as the time needed to execute an optimisation action based on the usage. Based on these evaluations, future work will derive suggestions for overbooking factors in different dimensions. Another extension to this work is to proceed with a further integration in our OpenStack prototype by developing a fair pricing and billing model based on the actual resources used.

Acknowledgments. The research leading to these results has received funding from the European Community's Seventh Framework Programme (FP7/2007–2013) under grant agreement no. 610711.

References

1. Aceto, G., Botta, A., De Donato, W., Pescapè, A.: Cloud monitoring: a survey. Comput. Netw. **57**(9), 2093–2115 (2013)
2. de Assuncao, M.D., Cardonha, C.H., Netto, M.A., Cunha, R.L.: Impact of user patience on auto-scaling resource capacity for cloud services. FGCS **55**, 41–50 (2016)
3. Berndt, P., Maier, A.: Towards sustainable IaaS pricing. In: Altmann, J., Vanmechelen, K., Rana, O.F. (eds.) GECON 2013. LNCS, vol. 8193, pp. 173–184. Springer, Cham (2013). doi:10.1007/978-3-319-02414-1_13
4. Chen, C., Maniatis, P., Perrig, A., Vasudevan, A., Sekar, V.: Towards verifiable resource accounting for outsourced computation. In: VEE 2013. ACM (2013)

5. Doulkeridis, C., Nørvåg, K.: A survey of large-scale analytical query processing in MapReduce. VLDB J. **23**(3), 355–380 (2014)
6. Goiri, Í., Julià, F., Fitó, J.O., Macías, M., Guitart, J.: Resource-level QoS metric for CPU-based guarantees in cloud providers. In: Altmann, J., Rana, O.F. (eds.) GECON 2010. LNCS, vol. 6296, pp. 34–47. Springer, Heidelberg (2010). doi:10. 1007/978-3-642-15681-6_3
7. Hoeflin, D., Reeser, P.: Quantifying the performance impact of overbooking virtualized resources. In: ICC 2012, pp. 5523–5527. IEEE (2012)
8. Kivity, A., Kamay, Y., Laor, D., Lublin, U., Liguori, A.: KVM: the linux virtual machine monitor. In: OLS 2007 (2007)
9. Lučanin, D., Jrad, F., Brandic, I., Streit, A.: Energy-aware cloud management through progressive SLA specification. In: Altmann, J., Vanmechelen, K., Rana, O.F. (eds.) GECON 2014. LNCS, vol. 8914, pp. 83–98. Springer, Cham (2014). doi:10.1007/978-3-319-14609-6_6
10. Matthews, J.N., Hu, W., Hapuarachchi, M., Deshane, T., Dimatos, D., Hamilton, G.: Quantifying the performance isolation properties of virtualization systems. In: Proceedings of the Workshop on Experimental Computer Science, USENIX Assoc. (2007)
11. Neuer, M., Mosch, C., Salk, J., Siegmund, K., Kushnarenko, V., Kombrink, S., Nau, T., Wesner, S.: Storage systems for I/O-intensive applications in computational chemistry. In: Resch, M.M., Bez, W., Focht, E., Kobayashi, H., Qi, J., Roller, S. (eds.) Sustained Simulation Performance 2015, pp. 51–60. Springer, Cham (2015). doi:10.1007/978-3-319-20340-9_5
12. Östberg, P.O., et al.: The CACTOS vision of context-aware cloud topology optimization and simulation. In: CloudCom 2014, pp. 26–31. IEEE (2014)
13. Rabkin, A.: Chukwa: a large-scale monitoring system. In: Cloud Computing and its Applications (2008)
14. Ranaldo, N., Zimeo, E.: Capacity-driven utility model for service level agreement negotiation of cloud services. FGCS **55**, 186–199 (2016)
15. Shvachko, K., Kuang, H., Radia, S., Chansler, R.: The hadoop distributed file system. In: MSST 2010, pp. 1–10 (2010)
16. Sonnek, J., Chandra, A.: Virtual putty. In: HotCloud 2009. USENIX Association, Berkeley (2009)
17. Subramanian, J., Stidham Jr., S., Lautenbacher, C.J.: Airline yield management with overbooking, cancellations, and no-shows. Trans. Sci. **33**(2), 147–167 (1999)
18. Sun, G., Liao, D., Anand, V., Zhao, D., Yu, H.: A new technique for efficient live migration of multiple virtual machines. FGCS **55**, 74–86 (2016)
19. Tomás, L., Tordsson, J.: Improving cloud infrastructure utilization through overbooking. In: CAC 2013, pp. 5:1–5:10. ACM (2013)
20. Urgaonkar, B., Shenoy, P., Roscoe, T.: Resource overbooking and application profiling in a shared internet hosting platform. TOIT **9**(1), 1:1–1:45 (2009)
21. Wlodarczyk, T.W.: Overview of time series storage and processing in a cloud environment. In: CloudCom 2012, pp. 625–628 (2012)
22. Yan, G., Ma, J., Han, Y., Li, X.: EcoUp: towards economical datacenter upgrading. TPDS **27**(7), 1968–1981 (2016)

Cloud Applications

A Privacy-Preserving Top-k Query Processing Algorithm in the Cloud Computing

Hyeong-Il Kim, Hyeong-Jin Kim, and Jae-Woo Chang[✉]

Department of Computer Engineering,
Chonbuk National University, Jeonju, Republic of Korea
{melipion, yeon_hui4, jwchang}@jbnu.ac.kr

Abstract. Cloud computing has emerged as a new platform for storing and managing databases. As a result, a database outsourcing paradigm has gained much interests. To prevent the contents of outsourced databases from being revealed to cloud computing, databases must be encrypted before being outsourced to the cloud. Therefore, various Top-k query processing techniques have been proposed for encrypted databases. However, there is no existing work that can not only hide data access patterns, but also preserve the privacy of user query. To solve the problems, in this paper, we propose a new privacy-preserving Top-k query processing algorithm. Our algorithm protects the user query from the cloud and conceals data access patterns during query processing. A performance analysis shows that the proposed scheme provide good scalability without any information leakage.

Keywords: Cloud computing · Database outsourcing · Database encryption · Privacy-preserving Top-k query processing · Hiding data access patterns

1 Introduction

Cloud computing has emerged as a new platform for storing and managing databases. As a result, a database outsourcing paradigm has gained much interests from researchers and entrepreneurs. In database outsourcing paradigm, a data owner outsources his/her databases to the cloud. Data owners can obtain significant economic benefits by outsourcing their data to the cloud. However, in this environment, the outsourced databases should be protected from the cloud and attackers because the data are private assets of the data owner and include sensitive information on individual users or organizations.

To tackle this, sensitive data should be encrypted before being outsourced to cloud servers. In addition, queries sent to the cloud server should be protected because they may disclose the sensitive information about users. For example, in case of location-based services, an attacker can obtain information concerning users' location or preferences from the queries of the users. Therefore, an important issue related to cloud computing is the maintenance of both data privacy and query privacy among data owner, users, and the cloud. By encrypting both data and queries, it is possible to prevent an attacker from being known about the actual contents of the data and the queries.

However, even if the data and the queries are encrypted, a cloud server can obtain sensitive information related to data items during query processing, typically by

© Springer International Publishing AG 2017
J.Á. Bañares et al. (Eds.): GECON 2016, LNCS 10382, pp. 277–292, 2017.
DOI: 10.1007/978-3-319-61920-0_20

recognizing data access patterns [1]. In addition, privacy-preserving query processing on the encrypted data without decrypting it is very challenging task. To do this, various techniques related to query processing over encrypted data have been proposed, including range queries [2, 3] and kNN queries [4, 5]. However, these techniques are not applicable or inefficient when used to solve Top-k query. A Top-k query finds the k number of data which has the highest scores for a score function being given by a user. The score function usually consists of coefficients each of which is related to how important the corresponding attribute (or dimension) is for the querying user. The Top-k query is very useful for various services because it retrieves data by reflecting the preference of each user. Thus, the Top-k query is widely used in various fields such as data mining, location-based services, and network monitoring. However, because a score function is closely related to a user's preference, Top-k queries should be more cautiously dealt to preserve the privacy of the users.

Over the past few years, various techniques have been proposed for the privacy-preserving Top-k query processing techniques (STopk) [6–9]. However, no existing work considers an encrypted score function that can preserve the privacy of a user query. Moreover, there is no existing work that can hide data access patterns during Top-k query processing. Because data access patterns are the good source to derive the actual data items and the private information of a querying issuer, they should be concealed. However, the data access patterns can be disclosed even though the encrypted data and the encrypted query are considered throughout the query processing [1].

To address the issues, we propose a new privacy-preserving Top-k query processing algorithm in this paper. Our algorithm basically guarantees the confidentiality of both the data and the user query by encrypting them. In addition, the algorithm hides data access patterns. To achieve this, we use an encrypted index search scheme which performs data filtering without revealing data access patterns [5].

Our contributions can be summarized as follows. First, we design secure protocols (e.g., SMAX and $SMAX_n$) to support secure Top-k query processing. Second we propose a new privacy-preserving Top-k query processing algorithm that guarantees the confidentiality of queries and conceals data access patterns. Finally, we also present an extensive experimental evaluation of our scheme with various parameter settings.

The rest of this paper is organized as follows. Section 2 introduces existing privacy-preserving Top-k query processing algorithms. Section 3 presents the system architecture of the proposed scheme and various secure protocols with their security proofs. Section 4 proposes the new privacy-preserving Top-k query processing algorithm. We also provide the formal security proof of the proposed Top-k query processing algorithm. Section 5 presents the results of a performance analysis of our privacy-preserving Top-k query processing algorithm. Finally, Sect. 6 concludes this paper with future research directions.

2   Related Work

In this section, we review existing privacy-preserving Top-k query processing algorithms in outsourced databases and describe the preliminary factors of our work.

2.1 Privacy-Preserving Top-k Query Processing Schemes

Most of privacy-preserving Top-k query processing schemes have been studied for distributed databases. The schemes assume that the databases are partitioned and distributed among a set of independent, non-colluding parties. In addition, the schemes usually depend on secure multiparty computation (SMC) techniques that enable multiple parties to process a protocol or a function using their private inputs without disclosing the input of one party to the others.

The typical Top-k query processing schemes for distributed databases are described below. First, L. Xiong et al. [6] proposed a Top-k algorithm for finding the k largest values among distributed databases. The scheme preserves data privacy in a probabilistic way by randomizing data values before distributing them among parties. However, this scheme has a limitation that it can deal with data with just one column.

Second, Vaidya et al. [7] studied privacy-preserving top-k queries using Gagin's AO algorithm [10] in which the data are vertically partitioned. The scheme uses the following property. If each party reports the scored data being ordered based on the local score until there are at least k common data in the output of all of the parties, the union of the reported data includes Top-k results. Then, the scheme determines the actual Top-k results by identifying an approximate cutoff score separating the k-th item from those below it. The scheme has an advantage that it does not reveal the score of individual datum by using a secure comparison technique. However, this scheme suffers from high computation cost and its query processing time linearly increases as the total number of data increases. Furthermore, if the number of common data reported from each party during the local score computation is less than k, the query processing performance drastically decreases because the scheme should process the query by considering all of the data. In addition, because the scheme guesses the cutoff score by using binary search over the range of values, the cutoff score can be estimated. This information should not be revealed since it can be used as a clue to guess the inclination of a user. In addition, data access patterns are not protected because the identification of the Top-k results are disclosed.

Finally, M. Burkhart et al. [8] proposed a Top-k algorithm which utilizes hash tables and secret sharing technique. The scheme finds the k key-value pairs with largest aggregate values on the distributed key-value data. To reduce the number of collisions, the scheme uses multiple hash tables. However, the scheme suffers from three drawbacks. First, it cannot guarantee the accurate result because the aggregated results are probabilistic. Second, since the scheme performs a binary search over the range of values, the intermediate threshold value separating the k-th item from the $(k + 1)$-th item can be estimated. Therefore, the approximate scores of Top-k results can be estimated. Finally, the scheme cannot conceal data access patterns because the index of hash table related to the Top-k results is revealed.

Meanwhile, a Top-k query processing algorithm for encrypted databases was proposed by M. Kim et al. [9]. To enhance data privacy, the scheme double-encrypts data and retrieves all of the data over the union of users' sets which appear more than a given threshold. Therefore, the goal of the scheme is different from our purpose that is to retrieve k number of data with highest scores for a given score function.

In conclusion, there is no existing work that hides data access patterns during Top-k query processing. Besides, the existing works have another common problem that they cannot preserve the privacy of a user query because they do not consider an encrypted form of a score function. Therefore, the user's preference over each attribute or dimension can be revealed to the server.

2.2   Preliminary Work

Paillier Cryptosystem

The Paillier cryptosystem [11] is an additive homomorphic and probabilistic asymmetric encryption scheme for public key cryptography. The public key pk for encryption is given by (N, g), where N is a product of two large prime numbers p and q, and g is in $Z_{N^2}^*$. The secret key sk for decryption is given by (p, q). Let $E()$ denote the encryption function and $D()$ denote the decryption function. The Paillier cryptosystem has the following properties. (i) Homomorphic addition: The product of two ciphertexts $E(m_1)$ and $E(m_2)$ results in the encryption of the sum of their plaintexts m_1 and m_2 (e.g., $E(m_1 + m_2) = E(m_1)*E(m_2) \bmod N^2$). (ii) Homomorphic multiplication: The bth power of ciphertext $E(m_1)$ results in the encryption of the product of b and m_1 (e.g., $E(m_1 \times b) = E(m_1)^b \bmod N^2$). (iii) Semantic security: Encrypting the same plaintexts with the same public key results in distinct ciphertexts. Therefore, an adversary cannot infer any information about the plaintexts.

Adversarial Models

There are two main types of adversaries, *semi-honest* and *malicious* [12]. In the *semi-honest* adversarial model, the clouds correctly follow the protocol specification but try to use the intermediate data to gain additional information. Meanwhile, in the *malicious* adversarial model, the cloud can arbitrarily deviate from the protocol specification. Protocols associated with *semi-honest* adversaries are efficient in practice while protocols against malicious adversaries are too inefficient. Therefore, according to earlier work [4, 5], we also consider the semi-honest adversarial model in this paper. A secure protocol under the semi-honest adversarial model can be defined as follows [13, 14].

Definition 1 (Secure protocol): Let $\prod_i(\pi)$ be an execution image of the protocol π at the C_i side and let a_i and b_i be the input and the output of the protocol π, respectively. Then, π is secure if $\prod_i(\pi)$ is computationally indistinguishable from the simulated image $\prod_i^s(\pi)$.

In Definition 1, an execution image generally includes not only the input and the output of π but also the intermediate results during the execution of π. To verify if a protocol is secure under the semi-honest adversarial model, it is essential to show that the execution image of the protocol does not leak any information regarding private inputs for the cloud [14].

3 System Architecture and Secure Protocols

The system consists of the data owner (DO), authorized user (AU), and two clouds (C_A and C_B). The DO has the original database (T) of n records. A record t_i ($1 \leq i \leq n$) consists of m attributes, and the jth attribute value of t_i is denoted as $t_{i,j}$. To provide indexing on T, the DO partitions T using a kd-tree. If we retrieve the tree structure in hierarchical manner, the access pattern can be disclosed. Consequently, we only consider the leaf nodes of the kd-tree, and all of the leaf nodes are retrieved once during the query processing step. Let h denote the level of the constructed kd-tree and F be the fan-out of each leaf node. The total number of leaf nodes is 2^{h-1}. Henceforth, a node refers to a leaf node. The region information of each node is represented as the lower bound $lb_{z,j}$ and the upper bound $ub_{z,j}$ ($1 \leq z \leq 2^{h-1}, 1 \leq j \leq m$). Each node stores the identifiers (id) of the data located inside the node region.

To preserve data privacy, the DO encrypts T attribute-wise using the public key (pk) of the Paillier cryptosystem [11] before outsourcing the database. Thus, the DO generates $E(t_{i,j})$ for $1 \leq i \leq n$ and $1 \leq j \leq m$. The DO also encrypts the region information of all kd-tree nodes to support efficient query processing. Specifically, lb and ub of each node are encrypted attribute-wise such that $E(lb_{z,j})$ and $E(ub_{z,j})$ are generated with $1 \leq z \leq 2^{h-1}$ and $1 \leq j \leq m$. In addition, the DO finds the maximum values for all the attributes and encrypts them as $E(max_j)$ for $1 \leq j \leq m$, respectively. These encrypted data are used when determining a node which includes the data with the highest score for a given score function. We assume that C_A and C_B are non-colluding and semi-honest (or honest-but-curious) clouds. Thus, they correctly perform the given protocols, but may try to obtain additional information from the intermediate data while executing their own protocols. This assumption, which was noted in earlier work [4, 5], has been used in related problem domains (e.g., [15]). Specifically, because most cloud services are provided by well-known IT companies, collusion between them that would damage their reputations is improbable [4].

To support Top-k query processing over an encrypted database, a secure multiparty computation (SMC) is required between C_A and C_B. To do this, the DO outsources the encrypted database and its encrypted index to C_A with pk and $E(max_j)$, but it sends sk to a different cloud, i.e., C_B, in this case. The encrypted index includes the region information of each node in cipher-text and the ids of data residing inside the node in plain-text. The DO also sends pk to AUs to enable them to encrypt a query. At query time, an AU initially encrypts the coefficients of a score function (i.e., $coeff_j$) attribute-wise. In addition, the AU generates $E(\psi_j)$ for $1 \leq j \leq m$ where $E(\psi_j) = E(1)$ if the corresponding coefficient is a positive number and $E(\psi_j) = E(0)$ otherwise. Then, the AU sends the $E(coeff_j)$ and $E(\psi_j)$ to C_A for $1 \leq j \leq m$. C_A processes the query with the help of C_B and returns the query result to the AU.

For example, assume that an AU has eight data instances in two-dimensional space (e.g., the x-axis and the y-axis) as depicted in Fig. 1. The data are partitioned into four nodes for a kd-tree; $node_1$, $node_2$, $node_3$, and $node_4$. To clarify the relationship between data and the nodes, in this example we assume that there is no data on the boundary of a node. To outsource the database, the DO encrypts each data instance and the region of each node attribute-wise. For example, t_1 is encrypted as $E(t_1) = \{E(2), E(1)\}$ while the

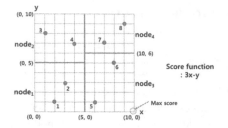

Fig. 1. An example in two-dimensional space.

Table 1. An example of an encrypted index.

Node id	lb (lower bound)		ub (upper bound)		Data id
	x	y	x	y	
$node_1$	E(0)	E(0)	E(5)	E(5)	1, 2
$node_2$	E(0)	E(5)	E(5)	E(10)	3, 4
$node_3$	E(5)	E(0)	E(10)	E(6)	5, 6
$node_4$	E(5)	E(6)	E(10)	E(10)	7, 8

encrypted index is shown in Table 1. If the AU considers a score function as $3x\text{-}y$, the AU sends E($coeff$) = {E(3), E(−1)} and E(ψ) = {E(1), E(0)} to C_A for Top-k query processing.

Our Top-k query processing algorithm is constructed using several secure protocols. All of the protocols apart from SBN protocol are performed with the SMC technique between C_A and C_B. The SBN protocol can be executed by C_A alone. Due to space limitations, first we briefly introduce six protocols found in the literature [4, 5, 16].

First, the SM (Secure Multiplication) protocol [4] computes the encryption of $a \times b$, i.e., $E(a \times b)$, when two encrypted data instances $E(a)$ and $E(b)$ are given as inputs. Second, the SBD (Secure Bit-Decomposition) protocol [16] computes the encryptions of the binary representation of the encrypted input $E(a)$. The output is $[a] = <E(a_1), ..., E(a_l)>$, where a_1 and a_l denote the most and least significant bits of a, respectively. We use the symbol $[a]$ to denote the binary representation. Third, the SBXOR (Secure Bit-XOR) protocol [4] undertakes a bit-xor operation when two encrypted bits $E(a)$ and $E(b)$ are given as input. Fourth, the SBN (Secure Bit-Not) protocol [5] undertakes a bit-not operation when an encrypted bit $E(a)$ is given as input. Fifth, the SCMP (Secure Compare) protocol [5] returns $E(1)$ if $u \leq v$, and $E(0)$ otherwise when $[u]$ and $[v]$ are given as inputs. Finally, the SPE (Secure Point Enclosure) protocol [5] returns E(1) when a point p is inside the region or on a boundary of the region, and E(0) otherwise. The SPE takes $[p]$ as well as $[lb]$ and $[ub]$ as inputs.

Next, we devise new secure protocols SMAX and $SMAX_n$ by modifying the existing protocols SMIN and $SMIN_n$ proposed in [4]. Thus, we briefly describe the SMAX and $SMAX_n$ protocols. First, SMAX (Secure Maximum) protocol returns the $[max]$ encryptions between two inputs $[u]$ and $[v]$.

The difference between the procedures of SMAX and SMIN is as follows. In step 2.c of the SMIN algorithm [4], the C_B sets α as 1 if data received from the C_A contain the value of 1. Otherwise, α is set as 0. In contrast, in SMAX, the C_B sets α as 0 if data received from the C_A contain the value of 1. Otherwise, α is set as 1. Apart from this, all of the steps of the SMAX are the same with that of the SMIN. Second, the $SMAX_n$ protocol returns $[max]$ among $[d_i]$ for $1 \leq i \leq n$. The $SMAX_n$ protocol finds the result by running the SMAX protocol $n-1$ times in an iterative manner.

To make our Top-k query processing algorithm secure under the semi-honest adversarial model, the secure protocols used in our scheme and algorithm should be secure under the semi-honest adversarial model. The security proofs of the existing secure protocols are given in [4, 5, 16]. Specifically, the detailed security proofs of SM and SBXOR are provided [4], while that of SBD is also described [16]. The detailed security proofs of SBN, SCMP and SPE are presented [5]. As mentioned earlier, we devise our proposed secure protocols, SMAX and $SMAX_n$, by modifying the existing protocols SMIN and $SMIN_n$. The execution images and the simulated images of both SMAX and $SMAX_n$ are identical to those of SMIN and $SMIN_n$, respectively. Therefore, the security proof of SMAX is same with that of SMIN while the security proof of $SMAX_n$ is same with that of $SMIN_n$. Because both SMIN and $SMIN_n$ are proven to be secure [4], our proposed SMAX and $SMAX_n$ are also secure under the semi-honest adversarial model. Consequently, all of the secure protocols used in our proposed Top-k query processing algorithm are secure under the semi-honest adversarial model.

4   Secure Top-k Query Processing Algorithm

In this section, we present our secure Top-k query processing algorithm with a secure index ($STopk_I$). Our $STopk_I$ consists of three steps: the encrypted kd-tree search step, the Top-k retrieval step, and the result verification step. We also provide the security proof of the proposed $STopk_I$ under the semi-honest adversarial model.

4.1   Step 1: Encrypted kd-Tree Search Step

To preserve a query confidentiality, we consider the encrypted coefficients of a score function as a query. In this step, the C_A securely extracts all of the data in a node that includes data with the highest score for a given score function. To find data with the highest score in the considered data domain, we use the following properties. If a coefficient of an attribute is a positive integer, a datum with the maximum value in the attribute domain has the highest score whereas if a coefficient of an attribute is a negative integer, a datum with the minimum value has the highest score. For example, in Fig. 1, the coefficient of x-attribute is a positive integer, i.e., 3, while the coefficient of y-attribute is negative integer, i.e., -1. Therefore, a datum with the maximum value in the domain of the x-attribute and the minimum value in the domain of the y-attribute has the highest score. Assuming that the maximum values for both attributes are 10, $(x, y) = (10, 0)$ has the highest score. Because all of the data outsourced to the C_A are cipher-text, we can find the data with the highest score by using Eq. (1).

$$E(q_j) = SM(E(max_j), E(\psi_j)) \ (1 \leq j \leq m) \tag{1}$$

Here, $E(max_j)$ is the maximum value in the jth-attribute outsourced by the DO and E (ψ_j) is a datum sent by the AU when a query is given. As we mentioned earlier, E $(\psi_j) = E(1)$ for an attribute whose coefficient is a positive integer, $E(\psi_j) = E(0)$ otherwise. Because the SM protocol multiplies two encrypted input data, the SM outputs $E(max_j)$ for attributes with positive coefficients and $E(0)$ for attributes with negative coefficients. In Fig. 1, for example, because $E(\psi) = (E(1), E(0))$, $E(q)$ is set as $(E(10), E(0))$ by using Eq. (1).

To extract all of the data stored in a node that contains the computed $E(q)$, we should retrieve the encrypted kd-tree. To do this, we perform the encrypted kd-tree search algorithm proposed in [5] by using $E(q)$ as an input. We briefly explain the overall procedure of this algorithm. First, C_A computes $[q_j]$, $[node_z.lb_j]$ and $[node_z.ub_j]$ for $1 \leq z \leq num_{node}$ and $1 \leq j \leq m$ by using SBD. Here, num_{node} means the total number of kd-tree leaf nodes. Then, C_A executes $E(\alpha_z) = SPE([q], [node_z])$ for $1 \leq z \leq num_{node}$ to securely find the node relevant to the query. Second, C_A generates $E(\alpha')$ by permuting $E(\alpha)$ using a random permutation function π and sends $E(\alpha')$ to C_B. Third, C_B obtains α' by decrypting the $E(\alpha')$ and counts the number of $\alpha' = 1$ and stores it into c. Here, c means the number of nodes that the query is related to. Fourth, C_B creates c number of node groups (e.g., NG). C_B assigns to each NG a node with $\alpha' = 1$ and $num_{node}/c-1$ nodes with $\alpha' = 0$. Then, C_B computes NG' by randomly shuffling the ids of nodes in each NG and sends NG' to C_A. Fifth, C_A obtains NG^* by permuting the ids of nodes using π^{-1} in each NG'. Sixth, C_A gets access to one datum in each node for each NG^* and performs $E\left(t'_{i,j}\right) = SM(E(node_z.t_{s,j}), E(\alpha_z))$ for $1 \leq s \leq F$ and $1 \leq j \leq m$ where $E(\alpha_z)$ is the result of SPE corresponding to $node_z$. If a node has the less number of data than F, it performs SM by using $E(0)$, instead of using $E(node_z.t_{s,j})$. When C_A accesses one datum from every node in a NG^*, C_A performs $E\left(cand_{cnt,j}\right) \leftarrow \prod_{i=1}^{num} E(t'_{i,j})$ where num means the total number of nodes in the selected NG^*. By doing so, a datum in the node related to the query is securely extracted without revealing the data access patterns. By repeating these steps, all the data in the nodes are safely stored into the $E(cand_{cnt,j})$ where cnt refers to the total number of data extracted during the index search. In Fig. 1, for example, $E(cand) = \{E(t_5), E(t_6)\}$ because $node_3$ includes E $(q) = \{E(10), E(0)\}$. The advantage of the algorithm is that it does not reveal the retrieved nodes for query processing while extracting data in the nodes relevant to the query. Therefore, we can hide the data access patterns during index search.

4.2   Step 2: Top-k Retrieval Step

In the Top-k retrieval step, we retrieve the k number of data which has the highest scores for the given score function. In this step, we only consider $E(cand_i)$ for $1 \leq i \leq cnt$ from step 1. Top-k retrieval step is conducted as follows. First, C_A calculates the scores $E(score_i)$ of $E(cand_i)$ for $1 \leq i \leq cnt$. To do this, C_A computes $SM(E(coeff_j), E(cand_{i,j}))$ for $1 \leq j \leq m$ and adds these scores together. Then, C_A obtains $[score_i]$ for $1 \leq i \leq cnt$ by computing $SBD(E(score_i))$. Second, C_A conducts

SMAX$_n$ to find the maximum value [$score_{max}$] among [$score_i$], where $1 \leq i \leq cnt$. Then, C_A converts [$score_{max}$] into E($score_{max}$) by computing E($score_{max}$) = $\prod_{\gamma=1}^{l}[score_{max,\gamma}]^{2^{l-\gamma}}$. Here, [$score_{max,\gamma}$] denotes each encrypted bit of [$score_{max}$] where [$score_{max,1}$] means the most significant bits of [$score_{max}$].

Third, C_A calculates differences between E($score_i$) and E($score_{max}$) by computing E (τ_i) = E($score_{max}$) $\times$ E($score_i$)$^{N-1}$ for $1 \leq i \leq cnt$. Note that only E(τ_i) corresponding to E($score_{max}$) has a value of E(0). For example, assuming that E($cand$) = {E(t_5), E (t_6)} are returned from the step 1, E($score$) = {E(17), E(19)} and E(τ_i) = {E(2), E(0)} because E($score_{max}$) = E(19). Next, C_A adds random numbers to E(τ_i) by computing E(τ_i') = E($\tau_i^{r_i}$)) and generates E(β) by shuffling E(τ') using a random permutation function π. Note that the only E(β_i) that corresponds to E(τ_i) = E(0) has a value of E(0). Then, C_A sends E(β) to C_B.

Fourth, C_B sets E(U_i) = E(1) by decrypting E(β) if D(E(β_i)) = 0 and it sets E (U_i) = E(0) otherwise. Then, C_B sends E(U) to C_A. For example, assuming that E(β) is permuted in reserve way from E(τ'), C_B sets E(U) as {E(1), E(0)} because of β = {0, r}.

Fifth, C_A obtains E(V) by permuting E(U) using π^{-1}. By computing $E\left(t_{s,j}'\right)$ = $\prod_{i=1}^{cnt} SM(E(V_i), E(cand_{i,j}))$ for $1 \leq j \leq m$, C_A can securely extract the datum corresponding to the E($score_{max}$). By performing SM using E(v_i) and E($cand_{i,j}$), the value of the only datum corresponding to E(U_i) = E(1) still remains the same. Otherwise, the value becomes E(0). Therefore, E(t_s') stores the datum corresponding to the E($score_{max}$). For example, assuming that E(V) = {E(0), E(1)}, C_A conducts both SM(E ($cand_1$), E(V_1)) = SM(E(6), E(0)) = E(0) and SM(E($cand_2$), E(V_2)) = SM(E(8), E (1)) = E(8) for x-attribute. By adding the two values based on the homomorphic property, the x-attribute value of E(t_6), i.e., E(8), is securely extracted. Similarly, by doing this for the y-attribute, we can extract E(5) which is the y-attribute value of E(t_6). By combining the values, we can store E(t_6) into E$\left(t_1'\right)$ without revealing data access patterns. To prevent the result from being selected in a later phase, C_A securely updates the score of the selected result as E(0). To do this, C_A conducts [$score_{i,\gamma}$] = SM(SBN(E (V_i)), [$score_{i,\gamma}$]) for $1 \leq i \leq cnt$ and $1 \leq \gamma \leq \ell$. Then, C_A performs E($score_i$) = $\prod_{\gamma=1}^{l}[score_{i,\gamma}]^{2^{l-\gamma}}$ for $1 \leq i \leq cnt$. As a result, the score corresponding to the result of the current round becomes E(0). C_A finally returns the k number of results, i.e., E(t'), by repeating this procedure for k rounds to find the Top-k result. For example, in the first round, E(t_6) with score E(19) is securely selected as the result among E($cand$) = {E(t_5), E(t_6)}. Since the score of E(t_6) is updated into E(0), E(t_5) with score E(17) is selected as the result in the second round.

4.3   Step 3: Result Verification Step

The result of step 2 is not accurate because the query is processed with partial data being extracted in step 1. Therefore, it is necessary to verify whether or not the current query result is correct. Assuming that the k-th highest score is $score_k$, the kd-tree nodes which contain data with higher score than $score_k$ need to be searched. To do this, we define the max-score point of a node as follows.

Definition 2(max-score point): The max-score point (*mp*) is a point in a given node whose score is highest for a given score function as compared with the other points in the node.

To find a *mp* in each node, we can utilize the method introduced in the encrypted kd-tree search step (step 1), which finds the datum with the highest score in the considered data domain. Specifically, if a coefficient of an attribute is a positive integer, a datum with the upper bound (*ub*) of a node has the highest score in the node. Meanwhile, if a coefficient of an attribute is a negative integer, a datum with the lower bound (*lb*) of a node has the highest score in the node. In Fig. 1, for example, the lower and upper bounds of $node_1$ are (0, 0) and (5, 5), respectively. Therefore, a datum with the highest score in $node_1$ is $mp_1 = (5, 0)$. Formally, a max-score point can be computed by using Eq. (3).

$$E(node_z.mp_j) = SM(E(\psi_j), \ E(node_z.ub_j)) \times SM(SBN(E(\psi_j)), \ E(node_z.lb_j)) \quad (3)$$

Here, $E(node_z.mp_j)$ is the *j*th-attribute value of the datum with the highest score in $node_z$. In addition, $E(node_z.ub_j)$ and $E(node_z.lb_j)$ mean the upper and lower bound of $node_z$ in j^{th} attribute, respectively. $E(\psi_j)$ is a datum sent by the *AU* at the query time.

The result verification is conducted as follows. First, among E(*cand*) from step 2, C_A computes the score of the $E(cand_k)$, which is the *k*-th highest score by using homomorphic properties, and stores it into $E(score_k)$. In addition, C_A computes [$score_k$] by executing SBD(E($score_k$)).

Second, by using Eq. (3), C_A computes the *mp* of each node for $1 \leq j \leq m$, i.e., E ($node_z.mp_j$). Then, C_A computes $E(mpscore_z)$ as the score of $E(node_z.mp)$ for $1 \leq z \leq num_{node}$ by using homomorphic properties. For example, E(*mp*) is computed as {(E(5), E(0)), (E(5), E(5)), (E(10), E(0)), (E(10), E(6))} for each node in Fig. 1. Thus, E(*mpscore*) are calculated as {E(15), E(10), E(30), E(24)}.

To prevent the searched node from being reconsidered during index search, C_A computes $E(mpscore_z) = SM(E(mpscore_z), \ SBN(E(\alpha_z)))$ for $1 \leq z \leq num_{node}$ where $E(\alpha_z)$ is the result of SPE in step 1. As a result, the $E(mpscore_z)$ of the searched node becomes E(0) because the value of $E(\alpha_z)$ of the node is E(1). Thus, we can safely prune out the searched node from further node expansions. Meanwhile, the $E(mpscore_z)$ of the other nodes are not affected by SM because $E(\alpha_z)$ of the nodes are E(0). Therefore, E(*mpscore*) becomes {E(15), E(10), E(0), E(24)} because the only $node_3$ is retrieved in the previous example in step 2.

Third, C_A computes [$mpscore_z$] by executing SBD($E(mpscore_z)$) for $1 \leq z \leq num_{node}$. In addition, C_A performs $E(\alpha_z) = SCMP([score_k], \ [mpscore_z])$ for $1 \leq z \leq num_{node}$. As a result, if a node contains data with higher score than $score_k$, its $E(\alpha_z)$ has E(1); otherwise $E(\alpha_z)$ has E(0). For example, because $E(mpscore_4) = E(24)$ which corresponds to $node_4$ is greater than $E(score_k) = E(17)$ in Fig. 1, E(α) is computed as {E(0), E(0), E(0), E(1)}.

Fourth, C_A securely extracts the data stored in the nodes with E(α) = E(1) through the lines 9–24 of Algorithm 3 in [5] and appends them to E(*t'*). Then, C_A executes step 2 based on E(*t'*) to obtain the final Top-k result E($result_i$) for $1 \leq i \leq k$. Therefore, the final result becomes {E(t_6), E(t_8)} because the score of E(t_8) is E(18).

Fifth, C_A returns the decrypted result to AU in cooperation with C_B to reduce the computation overhead at the AU side. However, when the result is decrypted, the data privacy is threatened. To tackle this problem, C_A computes $E(\gamma_{i,j}) = E(result_i) \times E(r_{i,j})$ for $1 \leq i \leq k$ and $1 \leq j \leq m$ by generating a random value $r_{i,j}$. Then, C_A sends E $(\gamma_{i,j})$ to C_B and $r_{i,j}$ to AU. Then, C_B decrypts $E(\gamma_{i,j})$ and sends the decrypted value to AU. Finally, AU computes the actual Top-k result by computing $\gamma_{i,j} - r_{i,j}$ in plaintext.

4.4   Security Proof of the Proposed Top-k Query Processing Algorithm

We prove the security of the proposed Top-k query processing algorithm based on the standard simulation paradigm [12] as mentioned in Sect. 2.2. We analyze the security of three steps of the proposed Top-k algorithm separately. Note that the input data of a step is the output data of a previous step, except the first step. Therefore, if the three steps are proven to be secure under the semi-honest adversarial model, the proposed Top-k query processing algorithm is secure under the semi-honest adversarial model, according to the Definition 1 and the composition theorem [14]. Due to the space limitations, we only show the security proof of both step 1 and step 3. However, the execution images of step 2 are similar to those of Algorithm 6 in [4]. For the detailed security proof of step 2, readers can refer to [4].

Security proof of the encrypted kd-tree search step. We undertake the security proof of the encrypted kd-tree search step (step 1) by analyzing the security of the execution images of the C_A side and the C_B side. First, the execution image of C_B is $\prod_B (step1) = \{ <E(\alpha'), \alpha' > \}$, where $E(\alpha')$ from C_A can be regarded as the input data for C_B and α' is derived by decrypting $E(\alpha')$. Without a loss of generality, we assume that the simulated image of C_B is $\prod_B^s (step1) = \{ <E(s_1'), s_1' > \}$. Here, $E(s_1')$ is randomly generated from Z_{N^2} and s_1' is a vector consisting of c number of value 1 and $num_{node}-c$ number of value 0. Because the resulting ciphertext size for the encryption scheme is less than N^2 and the encryption scheme provides semantic security, $E(\alpha')$ is computationally indistinguishable from $E(s_1')$. In addition, because a random permutation function π generated by C_A is oblivious to C_B, α' is computationally indistinguishable from s_1'. By counting the number of instances of $\alpha' = 1$, i.e., c, C_B can notice the number of kd-tree's leaf nodes related to a query. However, it is difficult to deduce meaningful information using c because most of the cases, c is one. By combining all of these results, we can conclude that $\prod_B (step1)$ is computationally indistinguishable from $\prod_B^s (step1)$ based on Definition 1.

Meanwhile, the execution image of C_A is $\prod_A (step1) = \{NG^*\}$ where each group of NG^* stores ids of nodes. Suppose that the simulated image of C_A is $\prod_A^s (step1) = \{s_2^*\}$, where each element of s_2^* indicates a distinct id of a node and is selected in $[1, num_{node}]$. For the stronger privacy proof, we assume that s_2^* is identical to NG^*. Even though NG^* is disclosed to C_A, it is impossible for C_A to know the actual node related to the query because the ids are randomly shuffled by C_B Furthermore, the number of nodes related to the query is one in most of the cases. Therefore, the probability that C_A finds out the actual node related to the query is $1/num_{node}$ where

num_{node} is the total number of nodes. In other words, the kd-tree search step (step1) satisfies the *k-anonymity* property. The *k-anonymity* is said to be satisfied if an object (e.g., data, query and user) cannot be distinguished from k-1 other objects [17]. The *k-anonymity* is widely used in various fields to preserve the privacy of data or users, such as the protection of data in databases [18] and the protection of a user issuing a query in location-based services [19]. The probability $1/num_{node}$ is very low as compared to the desirable *k-anonymity* level considered in the earlier works. Therefore, we can conclude that the kd-tree search step is secure based on the *k*-anonymity.

Considering all the above results, we can conclude that the step 1 is secure under the semi-honest adversarial model.

Security proof of the result verification step. During the result verification step, C_A cannot learn any information because all operations are executed on encrypted data. Therefore, we conduct the security proof of the result verification step (step 3) on the C_B side. The execution image of C_B is $\prod_B$ (step3) $= \{ <E(\gamma), \gamma> \}$, where $E(\gamma)$ is an input vector and γ is obtained by decrypting $E(\gamma)$. We assume that the simulated image of C_B is $\prod_B^s$ (step3) $= \{ <E(s_1), s_1> \}$, where $E(s_1)$ is randomly generated from Z_{N^2} and s_1 is randomly generated from Z_N. For the same reason described in step 1, $E(\gamma)$ and γ are computationally indistinguishable from $E(s_1)$ and s_1, respectively. Thus, we can conclude that $\prod_B$ (step3) is computationally indistinguishable from $\prod_B^s$ (step3) based on Definition 1. In addition, all of the protocols used in the result verification step are secure under the semi-honest adversarial model as described in Sect. 3. Meanwhile, the result verification step (step 3) uses both the encrypted kd-tree search step and the Top-k retrieval step. Because both steps are secure, the result verification step is secure under the semi-honest adversarial model, according to the composition theorem [14].

Considering all the above results, we can conclude that the proposed Top-k query processing algorithm is secure under the semi-honest adversarial model. Therefore, the proposed algorithm can guarantee the confidentiality of both the encrypted data and the user query while hiding data access patterns during the query processing.

5   Performance Analysis

5.1   Performance Environment

There is no existing Top-k query processing scheme that can hide the data access patterns. Therefore, in this section, we compare the proposed $STopk_I$ (secure Top-k query processing scheme with a secure index) with a baseline algorithm $STopk_B$ scheme. $STopk_B$ only performs the Top-k retrieval step (step 2) by considering all the data without using an index. Therefore, we can analyze the effect of using the index. We conduct a performance analysis of both schemes in terms of the query processing times with different parameters. We used the Paillier cryptosystem to encrypt a database for both schemes. We implemented both schemes using C++. Experiments were performed on a Linux machine with an Intel Xeon E3-1220v3 4-Core 3.10 GHz and 32 GB RAM running Ubuntu 14.04.2. We randomly generated synthetic datasets by

Table 2. Experimental parameters.

Parameters	Values	Default value
Total number of data (n)	2 k, 4 k, 6 k, 8 k, 10 k	6 k
Level of kd-tree (h)	6, 7, 8, 9, 10	9
Required k (k)	5, 10, 15, 20	10
# of attributes (m)	4	4
Domain size	12	12
Encryption key size (K)	512, 1024	512

considering parameter values. Parameters we used in the performance analysis are shown in Table 2.

In Fig. 2, we only measure the performance of the proposed $STopk_I$ when varying the level of the kd-tree because $STopk_B$ does not use an index. Figure 2(a) shows the performance of $STopk_I$ when varying h and n for $K = 512$. Regardless of n, as h increases, the query processing time is decreased until a certain point h and is again increased. This pattern is observed when h is 8 or 9. This result stems from the following properties. The total number of leaf nodes grows as h increases. Hence, as h increases, a higher computation cost is required for SPE to find a node related to the query. However, the number of data instances in a node decreases as h increases. Accordingly, as h increases, the lower computation cost is required when calculating the scores of the data instances. The trend is similar to that with $K = 1024$ as shown in Fig. 2(b). The query processing time increases by almost a factor of 2.8 with the same parameter settings when K is doubled from 512 to 1024. We found that this factor is almost the same regardless of the parameter settings. Therefore, we only show the performance with K = 512 below.

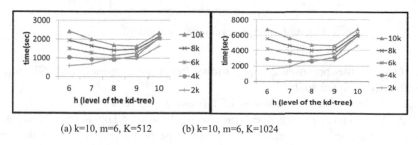

(a) k=10, m=6, K=512   (b) k=10, m=6, K=1024

Fig. 2. Query processing time when h and n varies.

When varying the level of h, the overall performance of $STopk_I$ depends on the kd-tree level. When $h = 9$, the best performance is achieved for many cases. For this reason, we use $h = 9$ for our performance analysis.

Figure 3 shows the performances of $STopk_I$ and $STopk_B$ when varying n for $K = 512$. As n becomes larger, the query processing time of both $STopk_I$ and $STopk_B$ linearly increases because secure protocols are required to use more data instances.

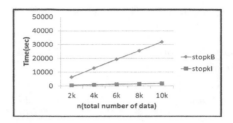

Fig. 3. Query processing time when n varies.

However, STopk$_I$ shows better performance than the STopk$_B$ by approximately nine fold and sixteen fold when $n = 2$ k and $n = 10$ k, respectively. This implies that we can achieve good performance for the large amount of data. Overall, the proposed STopk$_I$ shows better performance than STopk$_B$ by approximately fourteen fold.

Figure 4 shows the performances of STopk$_I$ and STopk$_B$ when varying k for $K = 512$. As k becomes larger, the query processing times of both schemes increase for all cases because the schemes must perform more iterations to find Top-k results. However, the query processing times of the STopk$_B$ is much rapidly increased because it considers all of the data while the proposed STopk$_I$ only considers data related to a

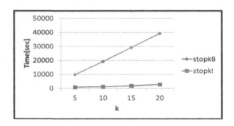

Fig. 4. Query processing time when k varies.

query. Overall, the proposed STopk$_I$ shows better performance than STopk$_B$ by approximately fourteen fold.

Figure 5 shows the performances of STopk$_I$ and STopk$_B$ when varying m for $K = 512$. As m increases, the query processing time of STopk$_B$ linearly increases because more number of computations needs to be performed. However the query processing time slightly increases compared to the performance with varying n. This is because most of the secure protocols are affected by n, rather than m. The query processing time of STopk$_I$ also increases as m increases. When $m = 6$, the query processing time of STopk$_I$ much increases compared to the other cases because it retrieves a number of kd-tree nodes during the result verification step. This result happens because the data distribution is sparse in the datasets with the larger number of attributes. Therefore the better indexing technique for the high dimensional data needs to be studied. We will leave this issue to future work. Nonetheless, the proposed

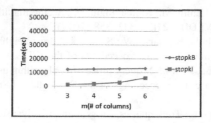

Fig. 5. Query processing time when m varies.

STopk$_I$ shows about six times better performance than STopk$_B$ on average because our STopk$_I$ processes the query by using the relevant data.

6   Conclusion

A database outsourcing paradigm has gained much interests with the growth of cloud computing. Due to privacy concerns, databases need to be encrypted before being outsourced to the cloud. Accordingly, various privacy-preserving Top-k query processing algorithms have been proposed. However, no existing work considers an encrypted score function that can preserve the privacy of a user query. Moreover, there is no existing work that can hide data access patterns during Top-k query processing. Therefore, we proposed a new privacy-preserving Top-k query processing algorithm which guarantees the confidentiality of both the data and a user query while hiding data access patterns. We showed from our performance analysis that the proposed algorithm provides good scalability without any information leakage.

As a future work, we plan to study other indexing techniques for the encrypted databases with the high dimensions. In addition, we will compare our work with the relevant works. We also plan to improve the efficiency of our method by processing queries in a parallel manner.

Acknowledgements. This work was partly supported by Institute for Information & communications Technology Promotion (IITP) grant funded by the Korea government (MSIP) (No. R0113-16-0005, Development of a Unified Data Engineering Technology for Large-scale Transaction Processing and Real-time Complex Analytics). This work was also supported by the Human Resource Training Program for Regional Innovation and Creativity through the Ministry of Education and National Research Foundation of Korea (NRF-2016H1C1A1065816).

References

1. Vimercati, S., Foresti, S., Samarati, P.: Managing and accessing data in the cloud: privacy risks and approaches. In: Proceedings of the CRiSIS, pp. 1–9 (2012)
2. Shi, E., Bethencourt, J., Chan, T.H., Song, D., Perrig, A.: Multidimensional range query over encrypted data. In: Symposium on Security and Privacy, pp. 350–364 (2007)

3. Hore, B., Mehrotra, S., Canim, M., Kantarcioglu, M.: Secure multidimensional range queries over outsourced data. VLDB J 21(3), 333–358 (2012)
4. Elmehdwi, Y., Samanthula, B., Jiang, W.: Secure k-nearest neighbor query over encrypted data in outsourced environments. In: Proceedings of the ICDE, pp. 664–675 (2014)
5. Kim, H., Kim, H., Chang, J.: A kNN query processing algorithm using a tree index structure on the encrypted database. In: Proceedings of the Big Data and Smart Computing, pp. 93–100 (2016)
6. Xiong, L., Chitti, S., Liu, L.: Topk queries across multiple private databases. In: Proceedings of the Distributed Computing Systems, pp. 145–154 (2005)
7. Vaidya, J., Christopher, W.: Privacy-preserving kth element score over vertically partitioned data. TKDE 21(2), 253–258 (2009)
8. Burkhart, M., Dimitropoulos, X.: Fast privacy-preserving top-k queries using secret sharing. In: Proceedings of the Computer Communications and Networks, pp. 1–7 (2010)
9. Kim, M., Mohaisen, A., Cheon, J., Kim, M.: Private over-threshold aggregation protocols. In: Proceedings of the Information Security and Cryptology, pp. 472–486 (2013)
10. Fagin, R.: Combining fuzzy information from multiple systems. In: Proceedings of the Principles of Database Systems, pp. 216–226 (1996)
11. Paillier, P.: Public-key cryptosystems based on composite degree residuosity classes. In: Proceedings of the EUROCRYPT, pp. 223–238 (1999)
12. Carmit, H., Lindell, Y.: Efficient secure two-party protocols: techniques and constructions (2010)
13. Liu, A., Zheng, K., Li, L., Liu, G., Zhao, L., Zhou, X.: Efficient secure similarity computation on encrypted trajectory data. In: Proceedings of the ICDE, pp. 66–77 (2015)
14. Goldreich, O.: The Foundations of Cryptography: Encryption Schemes, vol. 2, Cambridge, U.K., pp. 373–470 (2004). http://www.wisdom.weizmann.ac.il/~oded/PSBookFrag/enc.ps
15. Bugiel, S., Nürnberger, S., Sadeghi, A., Schneider, T.: Twin clouds: secure cloud computing with low latency. In: Proceedings of the CMS, pp. 32–44 (2011)
16. Samanthula, B., Chun, H., Jiang, W.: An efficient and probabilistic secure bit-decomposition. In: Proceedings of the ASIACCS, pp. 541–546 (2013)
17. Sweeney, L.: k-anonymity: A model for protecting privacy. Int. J. Uncertain. Fuzziness Knowl. Based Syst. 10(5), 557–570 (2002)
18. Al-Hussaeni, K., Fung, B., Cheung, W.: Privacy-preserving trajectory stream publishing. Data Knowl. Eng. 94, 89–109 (2014)
19. Kim, H., Kim, Y., Chang, J.: A grid-based cloaking area creation scheme for continuous LBS queries in distributed systems. J. Converg. 4(1), 23–30 (2013)

A Network Edge Monitoring Approach for Real-Time Data Streaming Applications

Salman Taherizadeh[1,4], Ian Taylor[2], Andrew Jones[2], Zhiming Zhao[3],
and Vlado Stankovski[4(✉)]

[1] Faculty of Computer and Information Science, University of Ljubljana,
Ljubljana, Slovenia
Salman.Taherizadeh@fgg.uni-lj.si
[2] School of Computer Science and Informatics,
Cardiff University, Cardiff, Wales
{TaylorIJ1,JonesAC}@cardiff.ac.uk
[3] Informatics Institute, University of Amsterdam, Amsterdam, The Netherlands
Z.Zhao@uva.nl
[4] Faculty of Civil and Geodetic Engineering,
University of Ljubljana, Ljubljana, Slovenia
Vlado.Stankovski@fgg.uni-lj.si

Abstract. Renting very high bandwidth or special connection links is neither affordable nor economical for service providers. As a consequence, ensuring data streaming systems to be able to guarantee desired service quality experienced by the users has been a challenging issue due to real-time changes in the network performance of the Internet communications. This paper presents a network monitoring approach that is broadly applicable in the adaptation of real-time services running on network edge computing platforms. The approach identifies runtime variations in the network quality of links between application servers and end-users. It is shown that by identifying critical conditions, it is possible to continuously adapt the deployed service for optimal performance. Adaptation possibilities include reconfiguration by dynamically changing paths between clients and servers, vertical scaling such as re-allocation of bandwidth to specific links, horizontal scaling of application servers, and even live-migration of application components from one edge server to another to improve the application performance.

Keywords: Edge computing · Network monitoring · Real-time data streaming

1 Introduction

Real-time applications such as online gaming, telemedicine services, environment monitoring systems, and video conferencing have highly on-demand needs to provide not only a high-quality result but also deliver the result as early as possible for the best real-time user experience—such as shorter response time via closer interaction with the application server or higher resolution via more stable connection. However, using cloud infrastructure to deploy such real-time applications provides some benefits, such as reduction of operation costs, on-demand resource allocation should be flexible

© Springer International Publishing AG 2017
J.Á. Bañares et al. (Eds.): GECON 2016, LNCS 10382, pp. 293–303, 2017.
DOI: 10.1007/978-3-319-61920-0_21

enough in order to dynamically assign infrastructure according to needs of such application and hence save the expense.

Since real-time applications may become sensitive to the network quality, such as latency between clients and running services, the requirements of such applications could potentially be addressed by emerging edge computing technologies, which allow computations to be performed at the edge of the network. The rationale of employing these technologies is that computing should happen at the proximity of data sources—e.g. cameras or sensors—and closer to where the results are needed [1].

Due to the federated nature of edge computing scenarios, real-time applications can be deployed on different edge nodes with diverse properties (for instance network performance, physical location, reliability, connectivity and so on). Hence, the performance of such real-time applications varies significantly depending on the runtime properties of their infrastructural resources as well as their clients' network conditions. To come up with these challenges, implementing effective, transparent and elastic methods to monitor the Quality of Service (QoS) at the network edge is difficult, yet also necessary. It is necessary because obtaining such network QoS parameters makes it possible to take appropriate adaptation decisions at strategic level (e.g. about the application topology and the selection of one or more physical machines on which it will be running at geographic locations) and dynamic level (e.g. about the application reconfiguration, vertical or horizontal scaling, re-location and so on). The edge servers should continue to monitor these parameters and determine if user experience needs to be improved. In this way, more dynamic adaptations to the user's conditions (e.g. network status) can be accomplished by utilising network edge-specific knowledge [2]. Therefore, particular attention has to be paid to monitoring network links between end-users' clients and edge servers.

The goal of the present paper is to implement a network edge monitoring approach that considers critical QoS metrics including delay, packet loss, throughput and jitter which are specific to the real-time applications we envisage. Therefore, it can be used for functionalities such as runtime service adaptations for streaming cases, for example automatically tuning the network quality by changing network paths to re-route via other edge servers or dynamically connecting the clients to the best servers based on their network edge conditions, location, etc. In this way, our proposed system is able to ensure the best possible Quality of Experience (QoE) for the users.

The rest of the paper is organized as follows. Section 2 presents the related work. Section 3 describes a real-time data streaming use case. Section 4 presents our network edge monitoring approach, followed by preliminary results in Sect. 5, and the discussion and conclusions appear in Sect. 6.

2 Related Work

There have been many research approaches, trying to provide network QoS guarantees for real-time data streaming services. A new paradigm, called edge computing, is emerging as an extension of cloud computing to support and meet the QoS requirements of real-time applications which are delay and jitter-sensitive [3]. Since edge computing is deployed at the edge of the network, it provides low latency, location awareness, and optimizes users' experience under QoS requirements for streaming and real-time applications [4].

Chen *et al.* [5] focused on the users' perspective in online gaming systems; from their point of view, the QoS metrics related to network conditions—namely delay, packet loss, bandwidth—have an important effect on gaming experience. Their results showed that packet loss and bandwidth limitations impose negative impact on the frame rates and the graphic quality in these systems. To provide more stable network performance for real-time services and optimizing the network path and resources, Jutila [6] presents adaptive edge computing solutions based on different traffic management methods that monitor and react to network QoS changes. To check the network quality in the context of such applications, the most important metrics to be analysed for adaptation are network throughput, latency, packet loss and jitter [7].

According to the cited literature, we can conclude that monitoring of these network-related metrics can help data streaming service providers guarantee QoE to end-users facing network resources limitations. Furthermore, an investigation of the recent related work supports the conclusion that a current challenge in this area is to continuously adjust the deployed environment according to the runtime changes in network conditions intrinsic to connections of both application servers and also users; this is the main focus of the research presented in the paper.

For dynamic adaptation of edge-based applications, emphasis should be put on the importance of scalability, robustness, non-intrusiveness, interoperability and possibilities to support live-migration of the service.

- Scalability: A scalable monitoring system is able to handle huge amounts of monitoring data across large numbers of resources and services [8].
- Robustness: A robust monitoring system is able to be highly tolerant of many failure scenarios and detect changes in environment, adapting to a new situation and continuing its operation [9].
- Non-intrusiveness: A non-intrusive monitoring system is capable of being lightweight to the normal flows of application and infrastructure [10]
- Interoperability: An interoperable monitoring system is not specific to a given infrastructure and is able to monitor an application that resides on other cloud providers' infrastructure [11].
- Live-migration support: In live-migration, applications migrate from a physical host to another one at any time without stopping operations [12].

Table 1 presents the analysis of the essential properties for the widely used multi-cloud monitoring tools. The goal of the comparison is to specify and trade-off the strengths, drawbacks and challenges which have been encountered in the context of self-adaptive edge-based applications.

Comparison in Table 1 is upon the reviewed literature and based on conducting experiments with the tools. These tools are investigated in order to find out an appropriate base-line technology for the needs of monitoring edge-based applications and the requirements of automatic adaptation to guarantee the QoS and the QoE performances which are subjective measure from the users' viewpoint on the overall value of the provided service.

Table 1. Requirement analysis for multi-cloud monitoring systems.

Tool	Scalability	Robustness	Non-intrusiveness	Interoperability	Live-migration support
Zenoss[a]	Yes	No	Yes	Yes	Limited
Ganglia[b]	Yes	Yes	Limited	Yes	Yes
Zabbix[c]	Yes	No	Yes	Yes	Limited
Nagios[d]	No	No	Limited	Yes	No
OpenNebula[e]	Yes	Yes	Yes	No	Limited
Lattice[f]	Yes	Yes	Yes	Yes	No
JCatascopia[g]	Yes	Yes	Yes	Yes	Yes

[a]Zenoss monitoring system, http://www.zenoss.org
[b]Ganglia monitoring system, http://ganglia.info/
[c]Zabbix monitoring system, http://www.zabbix.com/
[d]Nagios monitoring system, https://www.nagios.org/
[e]OpenNebula, http://www.opennebula.org/
[f]Lattice, http://reservoir-fp7.eu/
[g]JCatascopia monitoring system, http://linc.ucy.ac.cy/CELAR/jcatascopia/

3   Real-Time Data Streaming Use Case: WebRTC/MCU

Real-time communication plays an increasingly important role for many business applications, including cooperative working environments and video-conferencing for instance via WebRTC[1] (Web Real-Time-Communications) technology [13]. The WebRTC use case is explained here as an example of a large range of new potential real-time applications which need to have very high QoS in regard to their communication service, detect and respond to network-based urgent events very rapidly and also operate reliably and robustly throughout their lifetime.

The WebRTC open project enables real-time communications directly in the browser, and its performance may be influenced by highly fluctuating quality of the Internet connections. To this end, intermediate devices called Multipoint Control Unit (MCU) servers, which can be running on different data centers all around the world, are being used to manage the communication between the clients. The function of these MCU servers deployed at the edge of the network is to coordinate the distribution of audio, video, and data streams amongst the multiple participants in a multimedia session. These data centers allow interconnecting MCU servers in different regions. Therefore, for every user, there is an opportunity to have more than one MCU server to provide the service and hence it would be possible to connect a user to the best possible MCU. Figure 1 shows an example of how to interconnect all MCU servers to each other.

There are plenty of other applications, similar to MCU servers in a WebRTC video-conference, in which communication between users is required to pass through

---

[1] WebRTC, https://webrtc.org/.

Fig. 1. A deployment of MCU servers' interconnection globally running all over the world.

intermediate servers. Examples include the Openfire[2] server in instant messaging (IM) group chat, and CipSoft[3] servers in online gaming.

4 Design and Implementation of the Monitoring Approach

In our work, we focus on performance indicators from the user perspective; since they can be used to evaluate the network quality delivered to an end-user, then it is possible to improve the overall acceptability of the service, as perceived subjectively by each user. Figure 2 provides the schema of a user's communication via an MCU server as intermediary, which has to be monitored and compared with the other alternatives as potential MCU servers deployed in highly distributed, edge computing infrastructures. Supported by edge computing platforms such as Docker, the intermediary service can be deployed on-the-fly or on several running instances in different edge computing nodes.

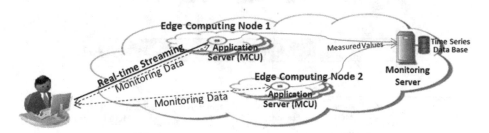

Fig. 2. Use and monitoring of MCUs to support real-time streaming.

---

[2] Openfire, http://www.igniterealtime.org/projects/openfire/.
[3] CipSoft, http://www.cipsoft.com/.

An overview of the proposed monitoring architecture is shown in Fig. 3.

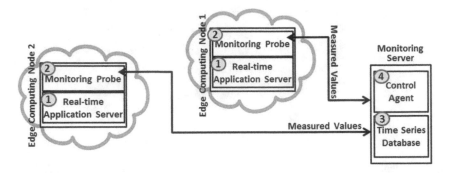

Fig. 3. Overview of the proposed model for user-centric network monitoring.

This monitoring system employs a number of distinct components. The light-weight, scalable, custom-made monitoring system implemented in JCatascopia framework [14] is responsible for monitoring QoS parameters of connections between the real-time application edge server and clients at the network layer. The implemented monitoring system is not limited to operating on specific cloud providers and can be utilized to monitor federated cloud environments where applications are residing on multiple infrastructures. As shown in Fig. 4, the network-level monitoring probe could separately represent a standalone application that runs amongst other running applications.

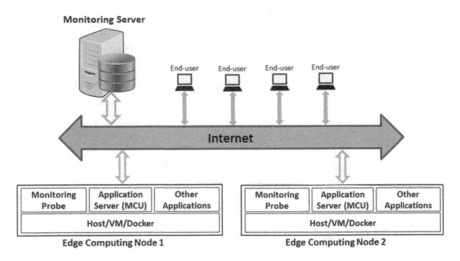

Fig. 4. Network-level monitoring probe running amongst other applications.

Different network-level QoS metrics—including throughput, delay, jitter and packet loss, which have been considered as important parameters for various video/audio streaming applications—are measured by monitoring probes on top of each edge node. The pseudocode of the developed algorithm for the monitoring probe is depicted in Fig. 5.

A monitoring server is responsible for orchestrating and collecting QoS data from each monitoring probe. The monitoring server consists of two parts: a Time Series

```
1:/* Monitoring probe running on a Host/VM/Docker which resides in Edge Computing Node i (ECNᵢ)*/
2:/* PL: Packet Loss */
3:/* NT: Network Throughput */
4:/* AD: Average Delay */
5:/* AJ: Average Jitter */
6:while(true){
7:   TS ← TimeStamp()
8:   for each current Userₓ do {
9:     PL ← Calculate_PL(ECNᵢ, Userₓ) //Calculate PL of link between ECNᵢ and Userₓ
10:    NT ← Calculate_NT(ECNᵢ, Userₓ) //Calculate NT of link between ECNᵢ and Userₓ
11:    AD ← Calculate_AD(ECNᵢ, Userₓ) //Calculate AD of link between ECNᵢ and Userₓ
12:    AJ ← Calculate_AJ(ECNᵢ, Userₓ) //Calculate AJ of link between ECNᵢ and Userₓ
13:    Message ← Make_Message(ECNᵢ, Userₓ, TS, PL, NT, AD, AJ)
14:    Send_To_Monitoring_Server(Message)
15:   } // end of for
16:   wait(interval)
17:} // end of while
```

Fig. 5. Pseudocode for the implemented monitoring probe.

Database (TSDB) and a control agent. The TSDB, implemented by Apache Cassandra server, is used to store the measured values, while the control agent, implemented in Java, is responsible for network-based QoS analysis, evaluating relevant policies and returning decisions consistent with these policies. It analyses the running servers' status and provides adaptation plans, for instance, changing network paths to re-route via other edge servers, or vertical scaling by resizing the resources e.g. to offer more bandwidth, or application server check-pointing/live-migration, and so forth. The pseudocode of the developed algorithm for the control agent is depicted in Fig. 6 where the coefficients C_1, C_2, C_3 and C_4 are the weights assigned to each network-level QoS metric. These weights could be dependent on the use case. For example, for VoIP applications, jitter is more important than delay. Consequently, jitter should have bigger weight in this case as it has more influence on user experience.

Considering Fig. 3, when our monitoring solution executes, it proceeds as follows: (1) A real-time application server (e.g. MCU server implemented by Medooze[4] as an open source conference application in our experiment) typically serves a large number of users and can be deployed and run on a selected edge computing node. (2) All relevant QoS metrics are measured at regular intervals by a monitoring probe and then all measured values will be reported to the monitoring server. (3) The monitoring server

---

[4] Medooze, http://www.medooze.com/.

```
 1: /* Control agent running as a part of monitoring server*/
 2: /* NQ_{i,x}: Network Quality of link between Edge Computing Node i (ECN_i) and User_x */
 3: /* BECN_x: The Best Edge Computing Node to provide the service for User_x: */
 4: while(true){
 5:   for each current User_x do {
 6:     for each ECN_i do { //Calculate Network Quality for each Edge Computing Node
 7:         NQ_{i,x} ← C_1*PL + C_2*NT + C_3*AD + C_4*AJ
 8:     } // end of for
 9:     BECN_x ← Choose_The_Best_Node_With_Maximum_Network_Quality(NQ_{i,x})
10:     if BECN_x has better network quality compared to the current Edge Computing Node
11:     during the last α intervals do{ // α can be defined according to the use case
12:         Adaptation plan is launched
13:     } // end of if
14:   } // end of for
15:   wait(interval)
16: } // end of while
```

Fig. 6. Pseudocode for the implemented control agent.

stores the collected metrics in a TSDB. The collected data can be analysed and used for capacity planning and strategic analysis like longer-term usage trends. (4) The control agent checks possible degradation of the required network quality for each edge computing node, and relates any such information to the current demand. When the current condition does not satisfy the expected requirements, an adaptation plan to achieve the desired performance can be launched. Using Docker's container-based virtualization, the control agent includes Kubernetes[5] technology for dynamically automating deployment, scaling, and management of containerized applications.

5   Measurements

In order to demonstrate the presented monitoring approach, network QoS is evaluated through four metrics, namely delay, packet loss, throughput and jitter. Deployed monitoring probes can measure these network QoS metrics which particularly affect the application performance. In case of any deterioration of system health, for example due to the presence of excessive jitter, control agent may trigger an adaptation mechanism to fix the QoS-related problem. The possible adaptation mechanism could be, for instance, re-connecting users to a set of the best reliable servers offering fully-qualified network performance.

For experimentation, we used a WebRTC client with a low-throughput connection and two MCU servers (A and B) running on infrastructures in different geographical locations with one Gbps bandwidth and the same processing power and memory— 2397.222 MHz and 2 GB RAM respectively. The monitoring probes use *ping* results to periodically measure the QoS metrics via the ICMP (Internet Control Message Protocol) protocol. The monitoring probes deployed on the two MCU servers send 10

---

[5] Kubernetes, http://kubernetes.io/.

ICMP packets at an interval of 200 ms to the WebRTC client and then they calculate the QoS metrics on an average basis. Each ICMP packet includes 500 bytes of data. The set of measurements are repeated continuously at a frequency of 15 times per minute which means every 4 seconds.

The implemented network edge monitoring technique takes into account two types of conditions, shown in Fig. 7: when ICMP packet filtering is (a) disabled or (b) enabled, inside a private network which is depicted by a rectangle. It is not unusual that ICMP traffic is filtered in private administrative domains due to various security concerns. In such case, the ping command returns no response and the packet loss is 100%; hence, the monitoring probe changes its mode of operation and uses traceroute to identify the path to the edge router. With this information available, the monitoring probe measures the QoS metrics between the edge server and the edge router (instead of the client). This measurement is an appropriate approximation of network-based QoS between the server and the client; since our main target is to compare the QoS of different routes from the MCU servers to the edge router.

The measurements presented in Fig. 8 show how this tradeoff helps the system monitor the network-level QoS metrics related to two different connections with the

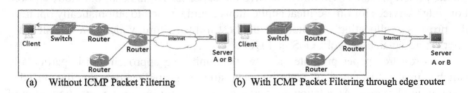

   (a)   Without ICMP Packet Filtering   (b) With ICMP Packet Filtering through edge router

Fig. 7. Path between an edge server and a client with different administrative domains.

same destination, the first connection between edge server A and a client, the second one between edge server B and the same client.

Figure 8(a) shows that according to the delay, the performance of edge server A is better than that of edge server B for a certain period of time. Since jitter is calculated as the magnitude of the delay variation, it will always be a positive number with zero indicating that no jitter is present. The standard deviation of delay was computed to measure jitter. Server A, as depicted in Fig. 8(b), provides better QoS in terms of jitter

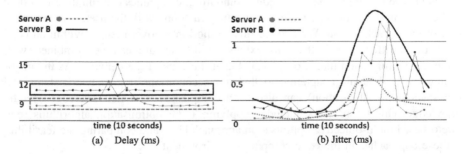

Fig. 8. Experimental results related to two different connections with the same destination.

on the average than the server B. Besides, throughput belonging to the both MCU servers was almost steady in the conducted experiment, whereas in real-time systems, continuous fluctuation is significant to be considered as an issue. Also, the system showed that packet loss ratio is zero, which indicates efficient packet transmission in both connections related to server A and server B.

A running monitoring probe does not provoke a meaningful network overhead for one user as we investigated the output of *nethogs* tool to compute its bandwidth overhead. We discovered that the implemented monitoring probe transmits ~ 1714 and receives ~ 1397 bytes per second for every user in average. Furthermore, in our experiment, it consumes only 0.7% of the whole CPU time and 2.28% of the whole memory usage in average.

6 Discussion and Conclusions

Cost issues and other associated network-related parameters such as bandwidth capacity and data transfer are outstanding issues for multi-cloud service providers [15]. Therefore, effective usage of network resources plays a significant role in the distributed interoperable environment to save the expense. To this end, our study showed how edge services for time-critical applications could be used to automatically optimize the process of allocating and choosing the best infrastructure, which is responsible for offering acceptable network QoS and QoE.

This research paper presented a network monitoring approach that is particularly suitable in the adaptation of real-time data streaming applications running on edge computing platforms. Adaptation approaches could be, for instance, re-configuration of connections among running application servers and users, or vertical scaling by resizing the network resources e.g. to offer more bandwidth, or even live-service migration by moving running application servers from the current infrastructure to another one. One of the goals of this paper was also to investigate those network-level metrics that are particularly important for the development and adaptation of time-critical applications. Because these network-based measures can vary greatly and have significant effects on the system's performance and users' satisfaction. One important aspect is the design of adaptation mechanisms that can help the real-time services to react to environmental conditions and events, such as sudden increase in workload or in the number of users.

Due to the distributed nature of edge computing, companies can run their real-time applications in different edge nodes, connecting each one with the users that are using the service in each region. We applied this method in a novel manner within an edge computing platform, such that this extensible architecture can be combined with monitoring information that is only available at the edge of the network. As the major finding, more dynamic adaptation to the user's conditions (e.g. network status and user's geographical location) can also be accomplished with network edge specific knowledge. Our future work includes applying more optimisation algorithms (e.g. Pareto-based multi-objective optimisation approach [16]) and comparing the feasibility of these approaches in the edge computing environment.

Acknowledgements. This project has received funding from the European Union's Horizon 2020 Research and Innovation Programme under grant agreement No. 643963 (SWITCH project: Software Workbench for Interactive, Time Critical and Highly self-adaptive cloud applications).

References

1. Shi, W., Cao, J., Zhang, Q., Li, Y., Xu, L.: Edge computing - vision and challenges. Technical report MIST-TR, Wayne State University (2016)
2. Zhu, J., Chan, D., Prabhu, M., Natarajan, P., Hu, H., Bonomi, F.: Improving web sites performance using edge servers in fog computing architecture. In: IEEE 7th International Symposium on Service Oriented System Engineering (SOSE), pp. 320–323 (2013)
3. Shojafar, M., Cordeschi, N., Baccarelli, E.: Energy-efficient adaptive resource management for real-time vehicular cloud services. IEEE Trans. Cloud Comput. **PP**(99), 1–14 (2016)
4. Stojmenovic, I., Wen, S.: The fog computing paradigm - scenarios and security issues. In: Conference on Computer Science and Information Systems (FedCSIS) (2014)
5. Chen, K.T., Chang, Y.C., Hsu, H.J., Chen, D.Y., Huang, C.Y., Hsu, C.H.: On the quality of service of cloud gaming systems. IEEE Trans. Multimedia **16**(2), 480–495 (2014)
6. Jutila, M.: An adaptive edge router enabling internet of things. IEEE Internet Things J. **3**(6), 1061–1069 (2016)
7. Cervino, A.J.: Contribution to multiuser videoconferencing systems based on cloud computing. Doctoral thesis, Technical University of Madrid (2012)
8. Clayman, S., Galis, A., Mamatas, L.: Monitoring virtual networks with lattice. In: Proceedings of 2010 IEEE/IFIP Network Operations and Management Symposium Workshops (NOMS Wksps), Osaka, pp. 239–246. IEEE (2010)
9. Fatema, K., Emeakaroha, V.C., Healy, P.D., Morrison, J.P., Lynn, T.: A survey of cloud monitoring tools: taxonomy, capabilities and objectives. J. Parallel Distrib. Comput. **74**(10), 2918–2933 (2014)
10. Taherizadeh, S., Jones, A.C., Taylor, I., Zhao, Z., Martin, P., Stankovski, V.: Runtime network-level monitoring framework in the adaptation of distributed time-critical cloud applications. In: Proceedings of the 22nd International Conference on Parallel and Distributed Processing Techniques and Applications (PDPTA 2016), Las Vegas, 6 pp. ACM (2016)
11. Alhamazani, K., Ranjan, R., Mitra, K., Rabhi, F., Jayaraman, P.P., Ullah-Khan, S., Guabtni, A., Bhatnagar, V.: An overview of the commercial cloud monitoring tools: research dimensions, design issues, and state-of-the-art. Computing **97**(4), 357–377 (2015)
12. Nadjaran-Toosi, A., Calheiros, R.N., Buyya, R.: Interconnected cloud computing environments: challenges, taxonomy, and survey. ACM Comput. Surv. (CSUR) **47**(1), 1–47 (2014)
13. Perkins, C., Westerlund, M., Ott, J.: Web Real-Time Communication (WebRTC) media transport and use of RTP. IETF active internet draft (2012)
14. Trihinas, D., Pallis, G., Dikaiakos, M.D.: JCatascopia - monitoring elastically adaptive applications in the cloud. In: 14th IEEE/ACM International Symposium on Cluster, Cloud and Grid Computing (2014)
15. Sookhak, M., Gani, A., Talebian, H., Akhunzada, A., Khan, S.U., Buyya, R., Zomaya, A.Y.: Remote data auditing in cloud computing environments: a survey, taxonomy, and open issues. ACM Comput. Surv. (CSUR) **47**(4), 1–34 (2015)
16. Al-Jubouri, B., Gabrys, B.: Multicriteria approaches for predictive model generation: a comparative experimental study. In: 2014 IEEE Symposium on Computational Intelligence in Multi-Criteria Decision-Making (MCDM), pp. 64–71. IEEE (2014)

Distributed Simulation of Complex and Scalable Systems: From Models to the Cloud

Victor Medel[✉], Unai Arronategui, José Ángel Bañares,
and José-Manuel Colom

Aragon Institute of Engineering Research, Universiy of Zaragoza, Zaragoza, Spain
{vmedel,unai,banares,jm}@unizar.es

Abstract. Simulation is a standard technique to understand or to analyze complex Discrete Event Systems (DES). Distributed simulation techniques try to improve the elapsed time of sequential simulations for large DES models by dividing a monolithic simulation application into communicating concurrent Logical Processes. The performance of the simulator is usually evaluated on the basis of the time needed and the involved resources to complete a simulation run. Additionally, cloud computing, under a pay-per-use model, introduces the costs of the resources that must be allocated to run the simulation. In this paper, a Petri Net based modeling methodology for complex systems is presented producing hierarchical and modular models. From this model, an elaboration process produces a heterarchical model for efficient execution of the simulation over cloud platforms using well known techniques. The required partitioning of the model may be subject to different criteria such as cost, elapsed time, and synchronization constraints, where the structural properties of the Petri Nets can aid in this task.

Keywords: Distributed simulation · Cloud · Petri nets

1   Introduction

The Internet of Things (IoT) and cyber-physical systems (CPS) allow tightly interconnected and coordinated physical and computational processes to work together effectively. As environments become more complex, it is not anymore viable to engineer individual self-contained systems but rather integrate large-scale Systems of Systems (SoS) involving several domains, e.g. Smart Factories, Smart Cities, Smart Power Grid, Intelligent Transportation Systems, etc. [2].

A fundamental challenge arisen by the IoT and CPS, and resulting large-scale SoS, is the need of models to cope with the complexity of todays techno-socio-economic systems, describing physical and computational interactions, integrating human behaviour into the processes and with sustainability and economical requirements. Separation of concepts and lifting the level of abstraction have proven to be effective software engineering strategies to afford complexity. However, the interrelationship of these separate models is part of the essential

© Springer International Publishing AG 2017
J.Á. Bañares et al. (Eds.): GECON 2016, LNCS 10382, pp. 304–318, 2017.
DOI: 10.1007/978-3-319-61920-0_22

complexity of the problem domain, and an early separation between different facets of the system design makes difficult to assess the impacts and tradeoffs of alternatives that affects all involved processes in complex domains [11].

In addition to the modeling of different facets and the interplay between them, a rigorous model-based approach is required to use them in a formal verification of design, coding and testing phases for detecting defects in the requirements compliance. However, formal-model based analysis tools are only useful under certain assumptions or are insufficient to afford the study of even simple software systems. On the other hand, simulation may be useful to discover some (un)desirable behaviours, but in general it does not allow to proof the (in)existence of some properties. Therefore, the synergic combination of simulation and formal models for functional, performance, and economical analysis are necessary for efficient an reliable design and/or optimization. We give a central role in our approach to Petri Net models describing the behaviour of the system including timing and cost information. The goal is to use these models in an intensive way for analysis and simulation purposes.

Independently of the formal model, as systems become increasingly sophisticated, the state space of the system becomes larger and the use of analysis and simulation techniques becomes impossible by a single-processor machine. Distributed simulation and cloud computing to scale to a huge amount of resources that can be rented (and disposed) in every moment seems the natural way to afford this scalability problem [5]. The intention of a *cloud-based simulation* service is to migrate the simulation software into the cloud, providing users with appropriate tools to hide the modeler low level details of this migration process considering cost and performance requirements.

The main challenges of translating a simulation to the cloud come from the nature of the models of SoS. Each model view can represent a facet/subsystems describing, in a precise way, some behaviour. However, models resulting from the composition of different subsystems and facets trend to become an spaghetti-like specification. This model characteristic is a serious handicap because parallel abstractions are based on exploiting some regular structures and declarative specifications that may be materialized on distributed systems [14]. Additionally to this difficulty for finding the maximum concurrency to scale the model, the partitioning of the model must preserve its original semantic taking into account low level details (e.g. synchronisation and state-management) [7], and must be a trade-off between performance and cost of resources.

The paper is structured as follows. Section 2 presents basic notions of distributed simulation of timed Petri nets. Section 3 describes the adopted approach for modeling complex systems. Then, the elaboration process to obtain a simulation model in the cloud is illustrated in Sect. 4. Finally, concluding remarks are discussed in Sect. 5.

2 Distributed Event Simulation of Complex Systems

Complex and scalable Discrete Event Systems (DES) require simulation and verification techniques during the design process, to prevent bad behaviors, to ensure that certain good properties hold, and to evaluate performance. Petri Nets (PNs) have been pointed out as a good modeling tool, since many properties may be easily analyzed in a great number of cases. Moreover, when formal analysis becomes impracticable, the model may be simulated. As simulation tool, PNs allow the formulation of models with realistic features (as the competition for resources) absent in other paradigms (as nude queueing networks).

Given a PN model of a DES, we *simulate* the system by *playing the token game* on that PN, i.e. by firing transitions as a result of the available tokens. This is also referred as *implementing* the PN. If a deterministic or stochastic time interpretation is associated to transitions – Timed PNs (TPNs) or Stochastic PNs (SPNs) –, the implementation of the TPN or SPN yields, actually, a Discrete Event Simulation system. In fact, SPNs have been proposed as the minimal discrete event notation, and both TPNs and SPNs are in the scope of works on DESs and Parallel and Distributed DES (PDES) simulation [3,10]. Observe that tokens in places represent the state, transition firings represent events, and timed transitions represent the duration of activities.

The construction of an application to simulate PNs requires: (1) a representation of the net structure plus the marking (state of the system that will be updated during the simulation); and (2) the *simulation engine* (Simulation Machine). The simulation engine follows a repetitive cycle that involves three stages: a) to test the enabling of transitions; b) to fire some enabled transitions (simulating, maybe, some associated activity), and c) to update the marking (the state) of the PN (taking tokens out of the input places and putting new tokens in the output places of each fired transition). The first stage –the enabling test of transitions– may be a rather time-consuming operation that it is worth being lightweighted. To reduce the costs of the enabling test there exist two main approaches: (1) **Place-driven approaches.** Only the output transitions of some representative marked places are tested for firability. This gives a characterization of the partial enabling of transitions; (2) **Transition-driven approaches.** A characterization of the enabling of transitions is supplied, and only enabled transitions are considered. The firing of a given transition modifies the enabling conditions of the transitions connected to its input and output places. In general, it is not necessary an explicit representation of the marking.

Distributed simulations of general DES requires the decomposition of a sequential simulation into a set of *logical processes* (LPs) that interact exchanging time-stamped messages. Each LP ensures that all its internal events are processed in time stamp order. It is easy for each LP to process internal events in time stamp order; however, due to the mapping of LPs to different processes or machines, errors resulting from out-of-order event processing are referred to as *causality errors*, and this problem is called the synchronsation problem [7]. An overview of the extensive literature about the synchronization problem can be found in [6]. Two classical approach have been proposed to guarantee *causal safety*: *conservative* and *optimistic* approaches.

Distributed simulation of Petri Nets will be based on many identical simulation engines (Simulation Machines) distributed over the execution platform, and each one devoted to the simulation of a subnet of the original one. Each subnet is represented in the corresponding simulation engine as a data structure and a set of variables for the local state. Therefore, each simulation engine play the role of a LP in the context of Discrete Event Simulation, and the time stamped messages will be the tokens generated by the firing of a transition that must update its output places belonging to other simulation engines. This means that the previous considerations about conservative/optimistic approaches must be taken into account in the context of simulation of PNs.

The efficiency of the distributed simulation of a PN is strongly dependent on the partition of the original model into subnets, each of which is assigned to identical simulation engines composing the distributed application. Partitioning requires to proceed, a priori, identifying the *good* subnets in which the original one is divided. In this sense strategies based into the identification of sequential state machines (computing for example p-semiflows in an incremental way), or minimizing the number of tokens to be interchanged between subnets is necessary to obtain efficient applications to simulate the PN. Nevertheless, during execution is possible to observe congestion in the flow of messages between simulation engines, or mutual exclusions in the execution of several simulation engines, or other kind of phenomena against the efficiency because the interchange of messages. In this cases, thanks to a simulation based on identical simulation engines working on data structures and variables representing PNs, it is possible to realize a dynamic reconfiguration of the initial partition: (1) by fusion of the data structures of two simulation engines in only one; or (2) by splitting the data structure of a simulation engine into two separated data structures over two distinct simulation engines. This dynamic reconfiguration is not possible in simulation contexts where the system to be simulated is not a data structure (e.g. the system is a program that must be compiled).

Furthemore, the use of ordinary Timed PN in the modeling of large complex DESs can lead to models of unmanageable size. This drawback has been reduced by using Object PNs which provide more compact and manageable descriptions. Nevertheless, this high level models introduce two additional characteristics to the simulation of Place/Transition nets that are: modularity and hierarchy. In order to obtain an efficient simulation, instead of the direct emulation of the high level model, we propose transform the original model to be simulated into a flat model composed by sequential state machines, each one simulated into a simulation engine, and interchanging tokens. This transformation process is called *elaboration* of the simulation model. It will be illustrated with the elaboration of an Object PN to the flat model of sequential state machines, but it can be developed from languages as that presented in [9,12] with a semantics based on Object PNs.

3   A PN Modeling Methodology for Complex Systems

We propose an example in order to illustrate the kind of applications that can be modeled with the methodology presented in [9,12]. The presentation will be focussed in the construction of an Object PN, but for the lack of space, this methodology for the modeling of large and complex systems, is not illustrated by using the modeling language designed to support modularity and hierarchy in a component oriented methodology [9].

Let us consider an *Electric Vehicle* (EV) hiring service to travel in the city without air and noise pollution (like London, Paris or Madrid). Users of the service take a vehicle in a so called *EV station*, and they travel in the city until they leave the vehicle in other EV station. This basic scheme can lead to an unbalanced number of available vehicles in the EV stations which can reduce the quality of service to customers of EVs in certain service stations or, worse, refusing to supply EVs in some station causing a denial of service. The parking of the EV station has a limited capacity that cannot change. A control strategy which distributes the vehicles among the parkings is needed to solve the unbalance problem.

The aim is to analyze the behaviour of this system of EV service and the control policies to guarantee the quality of service for a given interval time (for example, a day). To do that, it is necessary to known *a priori* what is the program of scheduled activities of the customer that rent an EV for that interval. For instance, when and which places the user wants to visit. This abstraction will be called *agenda*. The nature of this program of activities is strictly *sequential* because there is only one user following a sequence of activities, but the agenda can contain flexible adaptations in the sense that the user can program alternative behaviors that are taken depending on the availability of resources, or simply, depending on internal decisions of the driver that are taken with a certain probability.

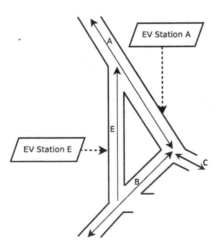

Fig. 1. Topology of the city represented as a set of streets and the sense of traffic.

The considered example throughout the paper first requires the definition of the topology of the city that is presented in Fig. 1. This definition is composed by a set of connected streets represented in the figure where the arrows represent the sense of the traffic. For traffic in each direction there is only one lane. If the street is one way, then the traffic lane is designated by the letter shown in the drawing. If the road is two-way, the traffic in one direction will be designated with the letter that appears in the drawing and the oncoming traffic with the same letter with the prime notation. There are *EV stations* in the streets A and E that are identified with the name of the street. These two parkings have a limited capacity, where customers can find parked EVs that can be rented for their displacement, or leave the EV at the end of its travel whenever there is space in the parking station for it. The number of available EVs depends on the behaviour of the users over the time and on the balance strategy between stations.

Observe that the model to be constructed is hierarchical in the sense that we have a first level where we have a set of EVs, each one represented by means of its agenda of activities, and a second level corresponding to the urban space where the EVs move, interact, realize activities and so on. Therefore, a good choice for the construction of the model is the formalism of Object PNs [13]. In this model, the *Object Nets* (the nets that are tokens inside a global Petri Net, of a higher level, named *System Net*) are the agendas corresponding to the EVs moving in the urban space of streets and EVs stations. The *System Net* will represent the set of connected streets and EV stations throughout the EVs can move. The Object Nets corresponding to agendas can be modeled directly by means of a state machine (in essence an automata representing the sequential program of activities to be realized for a user renting the EV). The System Net will be constructed in a modular way from elementary modules representing the streets of the urban space and modules representing the EVs stations.

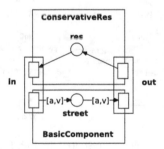

Fig. 2. Module corresponding to a model of a street.

The module representing the street model is depicted in Fig. 2. We begin modeling a conservative resource (with a *get* and a *release* transition) and we use it to build the street. The place *street* represents the state of a user (conceptually an agenda a) going through the street by the EV v. In other words, this place will contain a token corresponding to the object net representing the agenda of the user of the EV v when this vehicle is traversing the street. The model of a street could be refined including the parking space in each street or additional parkings, but for legibility and illustrative issues we present the unrefined model.

Instantiation of this basic module for each one of the streets of the urban topology, and a further connection of the instances according to the topology, allows to build the entire topology net where the nets representing the agendas of the EVs move. Figure 3 shows, for example, the composition of modules for the street A. The $getA'fromA$ transition represents to entering in street A' from street A. Each transition is synchronised with the agenda through an interaction, in this case $getA'A$. The number of nodes of the connectivity graph is the number of resources in the topology net; and the number of edges is the number of transitions between streets. For illustrative purpose, we have not shown the interaction with the EV; however, with the proposed metodology it is straight forward. We would have to include the battery consumption in each transition, and to synchronize them with the EV model.

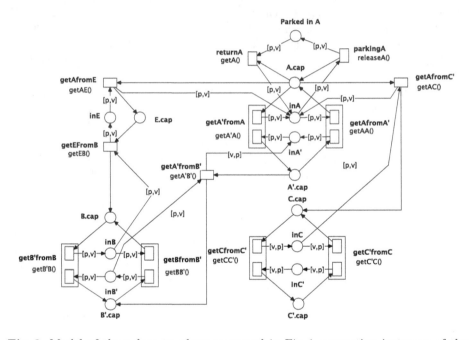

Fig. 3. Model of the urban topology presented in Fig. 1 connecting instances of the module of Fig. 2.

Figure 4 depicts the module corresponding to the model of the EV stations, with the corresponding resources (parking space and available EVs) and the output street. When a user takes an EV, the user releases a parking space and he/she takes an EV resource. The fusion between transitions is shown in Fig. 4. For simplicity, the figure only shows the station A. The $enterA$ transition represents entering in the EV station and the $leaveA$ transition represents leaving the station. The enter and leave transitions are synchronized with the user's agenda through inscriptions in the transitions.

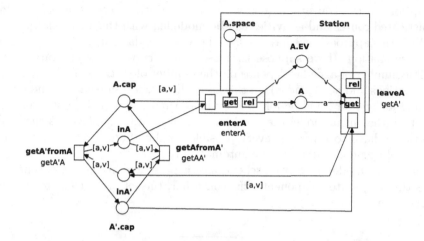

Fig. 4. Module corresponding to the model of the EV station in street A.

The previous rules allow to construct the System Net of the full model of the system. The last part of the modeling task corresponds to the construction of the PNs representing the agendas. These PNs will be the Object Nets that will act as tokens inside the System Net previously described in a succinct way. A user, throughout its agenda, appears in the system in the station place and its aim is to travel from that place to other station. However, during its route, the user may do some activities. A user's agenda represents sequential program of activities that a user of the service has planned to do and the route that he/she follows. When a user begins his agenda, he/she takes an EV in a certain station and, when the agenda is finished, he leaves the EV in the same or in another station. The correspondence between the agenda and the EV is the token that is moving through the net (the $<a, v>$ token in Figs. 2 and 4).

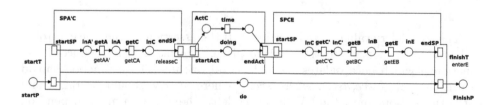

Fig. 5. A user's agenda with two routes and one activity.

In Fig. 5, we illustrate a user's agenda. In the example, the user starts in EV station A and he travels to street C to do an activity; then, he travels to EV station E and he leaves the EV. As he leaves the EV, we are not interested in the activity that the user does in that place or what he does next. The agenda nets are syncronized with the topology that we have presented before, through the inscriptions in the transitions (e.g. with the inscription *enterD* or *getA*). More sophisticated routes and activities can be modelled with this methodology.

With this approach, we have to model every agenda that is going to happen in the simulation. If we suppose that users only travel between stations, the possible number of agendas depends on the number of stations (in our example, three stations and six agendas). In this case, the token inside each agenda is the EV, and an agenda could be followed by more than one user. In any case, when we deploy the entire model the total number of agendas deployed is the same, because we have to represent every possible combination. The composition of routes and agendas could be done automatically.

Finally, we model the control scheme as it is presented in Fig. 6. Conceptually, it has three separate components: the controller, the set of control agendas and the resources.

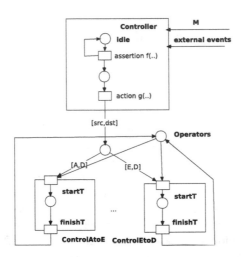

Fig. 6. Model of the controller to balance the EVs in stations.

The controller evaluates an assertion f. If the assertion is true, the controller will produce a message to the *outMsg* place. The message is produced by a function g which encapsulates the balance algorithm. The g function should return the pair $<src, dst>$, where src is where an EV should be taken and dst is the station where the EV should be left. The assertion might depend on external events or on the current state of the simulation, among others. The way this information is obtained is implementation dependant; for example, the state of the simulation could be in a shared memory or the communication could be made through a dedicated point-to-point channel. The controller is continuously iterating the previous steps. The set of control agendas represents the activity to travel from an EV station to another. They are used to move vehicles among the stations. Additionally, in our example, the resources in the control algorithm are the operators which move the vehicles.

The communication between the controller and agendas is made by message passing. The controller puts in a place the pair $<src, dst>$ and, if there is enough resources, the place in the agenda which is waiting that pair will take the message and the agenda starts. The scheme presented is very simple and general. Other complex solutions can be implemented; for example, there could be some operators reserved to some plans to establish a priority policy.

4   Elaboration Process of Modular and Hierarchical Petri Net Models for Simulation in the Cloud

The result of the modeling process is an Object Petri Net as in the example of the previous section. The obtaining of this PN can be done directly (as in this article) or may be the result of the deployment of a component-based model that has been described in a textual language as presented in [9]. The simulation of this model will consist in *playing the token game* on that Object Petri Net. Proceeding in this way give rise to several drawbacks that are related to the particular semantics of this kind of PNs. This is because the necessary simulation engine is a very particular algorithm that requires to be carefully analyzed in order to be distributed in, for example, a cloud platform. This task is not trivial because the simulation engine must cope to modularity and hierarchy properties of the model that are not very well-adapted for distributed programming.

Instead of the direct emulation of the high level model, a transformation of the original model is proposed trying to obtain a model well-adapted for distributed execution, by only using primitive concepts that can be easily adapted to changes in the execution platform. We consider as primitive concepts those of sequential processes that communicate/synchronize by message passing. This transformation process will be called *elaboration* of the simulation model, and the transformed model will be called *elaborated model*, composed by sequential state machines and interchanging tokens by message passing mechanisms. Therefore, the elaboration process will be realized by: (1) Transformation of each synchronization transition between a token net and its system net into a subnet implementing a protocol for this synchronization but based on message passing mechanisms; (2) Algorithms that identify and extract sequential state machines from the original Object Petri Net covering all transitions of this net, i.e. every transition of a token net or system net must belong to one and only one sequential state machine; (3) algorithms for the identification of places such that its set of connected transitions belong to more than one sequential state machine previously identified, because the flow of tokens throughout these places will be implemented by the message passing mechanism (the messages will be the tokens) in the distributed platform of execution.

In the sequel, the elaboration process is briefly illustrated throughout the example presented in the previous section. The first step is the elaboration of

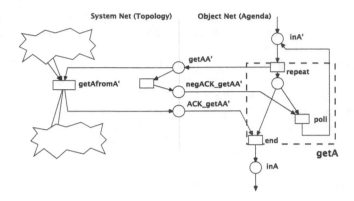

Fig. 7. Elaboration of the synchronization of transition **getA** of the agenda in Fig. 5 and transition **getAfromA'** of the system net in Fig. 2, through the label *getAA'*.

the synchronization transitions between the token nets and the system net. Each synchronization transition in a token net has a label used to identify the transitions to be synchronized (i.e. a transition of the system net and a transition of the object net sharing the same label). For example, let us consider the transition **getA** of the agenda (token net) depicted in Fig. 5. This transition is synchronized with transitions of the system net sharing the label *getAA'*, for example, the transition **getAfromA'** of the system net depicted in Fig. 3. The elaboration of this synchronization give rise to the transformations shown in Fig. 7. In the elaborated model appears three new places associated to the label for the synchronization: (1) Place **getAA'**: A token in this place represents a request from the transition **getA** of the agenda to synchronize with a transition in the system net with the label *getAA'*. Initially, it is empty, and it has as output transitions all transitions of the system net sharing the same label and an special transition representing the denial of synchronization; (2) Places **negACK_getAA'** and **ACK_getAA'** represents the answer of some transition of the system net for denial or approval the synchronization over the label. The next transformation (see Fig. 7) is based on the substitution of the transition **getA** in the token net by a *polling algorithm* that sends requests of synchronization with some transition of the system net while receives denials of synchronization. The timing of this new transitions is implementation dependent but the value must be much lower than the time of the original transitions.

After the elaboration of the synchronization transitions, the next step will be the identification of state machines in the Object PN. The goal is to identify a set of state machines covering all transitions of the token nets and system net, in such a way that a transition belongs to one and only one of the identified state machines. In the example of the previous section, the reader can observe that the token nets are agendas of the users and therefore they are state machines as the example depicted in Fig. 5 shows. Therefore, the first set of state machines is composed for the nets corresponding to the token nets, and so all transitions in the token nets are covered by this set. State machines of this first set are not connected to each other by message passing. However, there may be communication between these state machines and the system net because of the transitions synchronized by label as in the example of Fig. 7.

The same process of state machine identification must be applied to the system net. In this case, observing the net in Fig. 3, it is easy to see that this net is not a state machine and then general methods for state machine decomposition must be applied. For example, in [8] an algorithm based on OBDDs is used to decompose a general place transition net into a set of state machines. It is also possible to use algorithms based on linear algebra [4] that compute minimal marking linear invariants that in many cases are associated to state machines. There exist many other methods to realize this identification operation, and all exploit the structure of the net using different strategies.

The last step, to obtain the elaborated model, is the identification of the messages that must be interchanged by the different state machines distributed in the execution platform. Messages are the tokens generated by the occurrence of a transition, that must be added to a place that does not belong to the state machine of the fired transition. This place will be called communicating place. If the input and output transitions of a communicating place belong to the same state machine the messages will be internal, but if this place is connected to at least two state machines then two things happen: (1) All state machines containing at least one output transition of the communicating place will be grouped in the same simulation engine in order to avoid the distribution of a conflict between the output transitions of the communicating place; (2) The firing of an input transition of a communicating place leads to send the produced tokens from the state machine containing this transition, to all the state machines where this communicating place has an output transition throughout the message passing mechanism of the platform. The tokens to be sent as a message can be of two types: (1) Black tokens, that only requires to include in the message the name of the destination place of the token and the identification of the state machine where the place must be present; (2) Colored tokens, that require to include in the message, in addition to the information included for tokens black, the identifier of the token net to which refers the transmitted token (because the colored tokens only appear in the system net and they are references to token nets that have been deployed somewhere in the distributed platform).

The heterarchy of processes resulting from the elaboration of our specification is the starting point providing a raw description for a cloudificable model. Partition schemes over the flattened model pursue a trade off between performance and cost of resources for the distributed execution of simulations in cloud environments. The TPN formalism impose some partitioning constrains. Arbitrary arc cutting can decrease performance due to the overhead of involved messages in the required protocols between LP with distributed conflict resolutions, e.i, transitions sharing input places. This overhead of messages can ruin the potential advantages of a distributed simulation. In the following, we will assume that a Virtual Machine is assigned to each LP. A LP consists of a TPN region, an interpreter engine that simulates the token game of the region and preserve causality with events simulated in other LPs, and an interface. Some solutions of petri net partitions [3,10] have improved the arbitrary strategy of cutting of arcs, with methods and rules for minimum region extraction, aggregation of suitable regions and automated mapping of regions to nodes.

The LP interface is defined by the arcs from LP_k to LP_i. Therefore, the input interface is defined by means of places and the output interface by means of transitions of adjacent LPs. The first idea to develop the partitioning is to minimize the number of tokens (messages) to be interchanged between subnets. In this way, all tokens transferred from LP_k to LP_i are sent over the same channel, and communication complexity is reduced considerably. Additionally, we will use the idea of *coupled conflict*, which can be inferred from structure of the TPN for defining the minimal region assigned to a LP. Two transitions t_i, t_j are in *coupled conflict*, $t_i CC t_j \Leftrightarrow {}^\bullet t \cap t^\bullet \neq \emptyset$ or $\exists t_R$ such that $t_i CC t_R \wedge t_R CC t_j$. The CC relationship is an equivalence relation that defines a partitioning in a set of distinct equivalence class called CCC (coupled conflict class). The set of distinct CCC defines a partition with the minimal possible regions.

Depending on the communications overhead, this partition on minimal regions may be too fine grained. The size and elements included in regions shape execution and communication results. Too small regions entail too many nodes, with high communication and short execution of LPs, that can hurt overall performance and economic cost. Big regions need few nodes that can help to curve cost, but also reduce performance. The computation/communication threshold gives the upper bound for the maximum number of compute nodes to maximises the speed up. The second idea to afford this trade-off is to cover with sequential state machines the partition defined by transitions in conflict. Therefore, the problem is a graph partition problem, where the set of logical processes ($LP = \cup_i LP_i$) together with the directed communications channels ($CH = U_{i,j}(LP_i, LP_j)$) constitutes the graph of logical processes $GLP = (LP, CH)$. The coverture that defines the partition is produced taking into account the objective function to minimise, which is the cost given a simulation time t_s.

Formally, if $\mathscr{P}$ is a partition of GLP with N logical processes (LP_i), and $R(LP_i)$ is the set of sequential processes included in LP_i, we can estimate the economical cost associated to the partition $\mathscr{P}$: $\hat{C}(\mathscr{P}) = N * \hat{T}_{wc}$ where $\hat{T}_{wc}$ represents the estimated wallclock time. $\hat{T}_{wc}$ is defined by the maximum bottleneck estimated wallclock time of all LP_i ($\hat{T}_{wci}$):

$$max_{1 \leq k \leq N} \left\{ \hat{T}_{wci} \left(\sum_{j \in R(LP_i)} (e_j), \sum_{j \in R(LP_i), k \notin R(LP_i)} w_{jk}, \gamma, t_s \right) \right\}$$

We need to associate an execution weight e_i to each LP_i (by the addition of all ej corresponding to the sequential processes included in LP_i), which represents the amount of computation time per simulation time unit, and a communication weight w_{ij} between every pair of LPs. In [3] it is proposed to define e_i as the number of places and transitions in LP_i; and equal w_{ij} to the number of arcs crossing between LPs i and j. In our case, we propose to estimate $\hat{T}_{wci}$ in a similar way as a function of e_i, w_{ik}, the execution and communication relation in the cloud γ, and the simulated time.

Initially, $\hat{T}_{wci}$ values can be approximated by simulations to get computing and communication values. These values can be grossly approximated with a partition requiring the minimum number of VMs to store the biggest admissible regions in memory of each VM, or the maximum number of VMs allowed with an initial budget for estimating these values. The objective function is to minimise the cost considering initial constraints, budget and quality of simulation,

Graph partitioning is a fundamental problem in many domains in computer science. Important applications of graph partitioning include scientific computing, partitioning various stages of a VLSI design circuit and task scheduling in multi-processor system. There is a vast literature about graph partition (see for a recent review [1]). The most promising partitions divide the graph in equal sets while minimising edges between the sets. In the case of TPN partitions, structural information and time labels can also be exploited to define balanced lookahead values in all logical processes. More information about the cloud infrastructure, such as the coefficient of variation of execution time and communication, can also be included in the objective function to improve the estimated cost of a partition ($\hat{C}(\mathscr{P})$).

5 Conclusions and Future Work

Distributed simulation allows to understand and analyse complex and scalable systems. In this paper we have proposed a PN based modeling methodology for complex DESs and a way to automatically translate the high level specification to an executable model suited to be partitioned on the cloud. The high level model provides an specification language suited for the designer of the system that allows a formal description of different facets of the system, and a hierarchical and component decomposition. On the other hand, we use the TPN formalism, as a low level model, to simulate the system. This low level model for simulation can be automatically generated, distributed and executed in an efficient and cost effective way. An elaboration process translates the high level specification in a flat TPN model. Finally, a partitioning step is proposed to deal with the decomposition of the flat low level model in regions to be distributed in cloud nodes. The regions obtained are evaluated in respect of the economic cost of their execution to decide the effective distributed deployment on the cloud.

Future work will enhance this proposal with the development of a platform as a service to support the modeling and distributed simulation of large complex systems. Involved tasks are to implement the elaboration process, the adaptation of current PN structural analysis tools for large TPNs, the refinement of objective functions to define balanced partitions attending to different criteria (size, lookahead values, etc.) and the use of graph processing frameworks.

Acknowledgments. This work was co-financed by the Industry and Innovation department of the Aragonese Government and European Social Funds (COSMOS research group, ref. T93); and by the Spanish Ministry of Economy under the program "Programa de I+D+i Estatal de Investigación, Desarrollo e innovación Orientada a los Retos de la Sociedad", project id TIN2013-40809-R. V. Medel was the recipient of a fellowship from the Spanish Ministry of Economy.

References

1. Buluç, A., Meyerhenke, H., Safro, I., Sanders, P., Schulz, C.: Recent advances in graph partitioning. CoRR abs/1311.3144 (2013). http://arxiv.org/abs/1311.3144
2. Carbone, A., Ajmone-Marsan, M., Axhausen, K.W., Batty, M., Masera, M., Rome, E.: Complexity aided design. Eur. Phys. J. Spec. Top. **214**(1), 435–459 (2012)
3. Chiola, G., Ferscha, A.: Distributed simulation of petri nets. IEEE Concurrency **3**, 33–50 (1993)
4. Colom, J.-M., Silva, M., Villarroel, J.: On software implementation of petri nets and colored petri nets using high-level concurrent languages. In: 7th International Workshop on Application and Theory of Petri Nets, pp. 207–222 (1986)
5. D'Angelo, G., Marzolla, M.: New trends in parallel and distributed simulation: from many-cores to cloud computing. Simul. Model. Pract. Theory **49**, 320–335 (2014)
6. Fujimoto, R.: Parallel and distributed simulation. In: Proceedings of the 2015 Winter Simulation Conference, pp. 45–59 (2015)
7. Fujimoto, R.M.: Parallel and Distributed Simulation Systems, vol. 300. Wiley, New York (2000)
8. García-Vallés, F., Colom J.-M.: A Boolean approach to the state machine decomposition of Petri nets with OBDD's. In: Intelligent Systems for the 21st Century, IEEE International Conference on Systems, Man and Cybernetics, 1995, vol. 4, pp. 3451–3456, October 1995
9. Merino, A., Tolosana-Calasanz, R., Bañares, J.Á., Colom, J.-M.: A specification language for performance and economical analysis of short term data intensive energy management services. In: Altmann, J., Silaghi, G.C., Rana, O.F. (eds.) GECON 2015. LNCS, vol. 9512, pp. 147–163. Springer, Cham (2016). doi:10.1007/978-3-319-43177-2_10
10. Nicol, D.M., Mao, W.: Automated parallelization of timed petri-net simulations. J. Parallel Distrib. Comput. **29**(1), 60–74 (1995)
11. Rajhans, A., Cheng, S.W., Schmerl, B., Garlan, D., Krogh, B.H., Agbi, C., Bhave, A.: An architectural approach to the design and analysis of cyber-physical systems. Electron. Commun. EASST **21**, 10 (2009)
12. Tolosana-Calasanz, R., Bañares, J.Á., Colom, J.-M.: Towards petri net-based economical analysis for streaming applications executed over cloud infrastructures. In: Altmann, J., Vanmechelen, K., Rana, O.F. (eds.) GECON 2014. LNCS, vol. 8914, pp. 189–205. Springer, Cham (2014). doi:10.1007/978-3-319-14609-6_13
13. Valk, R.: Object petri nets. In: Desel, J., Reisig, W., Rozenberg, G. (eds.) ACPN 2003. LNCS, vol. 3098, pp. 819–848. Springer, Heidelberg (2004). doi:10.1007/978-3-540-27755-2_23
14. Yu, L., Moretti, C., Thrasher, A., Emrich, S.J., Judd, K., Thain, D.: Harnessing parallelism in multicore clusters with the All-Pairs, Wavefront, and Makeflow abstractions. Cluster Comput. **13**(3), 243–256 (2010)

Author Index

Printed in the United States
By Bookmasters